THE LEAVEN OF THE ANCIENTS

SUNY series in Islam
Seyyed Hossein Nasr, editor

THE LEAVEN OF THE ANCIENTS

Suhrawardī and the Heritage of the Greeks

JOHN WALBRIDGE

State University
of New York
Press

Published by
State University of New York Press, Albany

Production by Susan Geraghty
Marketing by Dana Yanulavich

Printed in the United States of America

Library of Congress Cataloging-in-Publication Data

Walbridge, John.
The leaven of the ancients : Suhrawardī and the heritage of the Greeks / John Walbridge.
p. cm. — (SUNY series in Islam)
Includes bibliographical references and index.
ISBN 0-7914-4359-0 (alk. paper). — ISBN 0-7914-4360-4 (pbk. : alk. paper)
1. Suhrawardī, Yaḥyá ibn Ḥabash, 1152 or 3-1191. 2. Philosophy, Islamic—Greek influences. I. Title. II. Series.
B753.S84W35 1999
181′.5—dc21 98-54756
CIP

10 9 8 7 6 5 4 3 2 1

To Linda,
with love

CONTENTS

ABBREVIATIONS

AA	Aetius [Pseudo-Plutarch], *Aetius Arabus*
APPA	Fārābī, *Alfarabi's Philosophy of Plato and Aristotle*
DPA	*Dictionnaire des philosophes antiques*
DPsA	Pseudo-Ammonius, *Die Doxographie des Pseudo-Ammonios*
EIr	*Encyclopædia Iranica*
Fihrist	Ibn al-Nadīm, *al-Fihrist*, ed. Khalīfa and al-ʻAwza
GAL	*Geschichte der arabischen Literatur*
GAS	Sezgin, *Geschichte des arabischen Schriftums*
HGP	Guthrie, *A History of Greek Philosophy*
HI	Suhrawardī, *Ḥikmat al-Ishrāq*
HP	Long and Sedley, *The Hellenistic Philosophers*
ITP	Ibn al-Ṭayyib, *Proclus' Commentary*
JAOS	*Journal of the American Oriental Society*
JRH	Fārābī, *Kitāb al-Jamʻ bayna Ra'yay al-Ḥakīmayn*
KAA	al-ʻĀmirī, *Kitāb al-Amad ʻalā 'l-Abad*
KAP	Kingsley, *Ancient Philosophy, Mystery, and Magic*
MVT	Suhrawardī, *Mystical and Visionary Treatises*
OPR	O'Meara, *Pythagoras Revived*
PSL	Guthrie, *The Pythagorean Sourcebook and Library*
QDS	Quṭb al-Dīn, *Sharḥ Ḥikmat al-Ishrāq*
RIS	Ikhwān al-Ṣafā', *Rasā'il*
RMP	Rowson, *A Muslim Philosopher*
SAe	Suhrawardī, *L'Archange empourpré*
ShNA	Shahrazūrī, *Nuzhat al-Arwāḥ*, ed. Aḥmed
ShNR	Shahrazūrī, *Nuzhat al-Arwāḥ*, ed. Abū Rayyān
ShS	Shahrazūrī, *Sharḥ Ḥikmat al-Ishrāq*
SMj	Suhrawardī, *Majmūʻa*
SML	Walbridge, *The Science of Mystic Lights*
SMM	Suhrawardī, *al-Mashāriʻ wa'l-Muṭāraḥāt*
SMN	Shahrastānī, *al-Milal wa'l-Niḥal*
SPI	Suhrawardī, *The Philosophy of Illumination*
SVF	*Stoicorum Veterum Fragmenta*
ZKI	Ziai, *Knowledge and Illumination*

PREFACE

This book is a study of the appropriation of non-Aristotelian Greek thought in Islamic philosophy as illustrated through the system of the most influential and colorful anti-Aristotelian Islamic philosopher, Shihāb al-Dīn al-Suhrawardī. In this book I continue the study of his "Illuminationist" philosophy that I began in *The Science of Mystic Lights: Qutb al-Din Shirazi and the Illuminationist Tradition in Islamic Philosophy.*[1] In this earlier book I worked out the interpretation of Suhrawardī's philosophical system summarized in chapter 3 and presumed throughout the present book. It is also reflected in the translation of Suhrawardī's chief work, *The Philosophy of Illumination (Ḥikmat al-Ishrāq)*, done by Hossein Ziai and myself.[2]

I hope to clarify the philosophical context within which Suhrawardī should be understood. I will argue that Suhrawardī was a Pythagoreanizing Neoplatonist in the tradition of Porphyry, Iamblichus, and Proclus. This focus on philosophical-historical context does not simply represent my own taste in research topics but arises from the nature of Suhrawardī's philosophy. He stressed that his philosophy was a revival of the "wisdom of the Ancients" and that it was to be so understood. In situating Suhrawardī in the context of the non-Peripatetic philosophical tradition, I spend a good deal of time discussing the texts and positions of these traditions. For the most part I discuss them as they appear from the Islamic sources, but I also use Greek and other texts when it seems useful.

I have tried to avoid having my discussions of Greek philosophy become fragments of a potted history of ancient philosophy—after all, I am not plowing virgin soil here—but I would ask a degree of patience from those readers for whom Plato and Pythagoras are familiar figures: not all of my readers can be expected to have the argument of the *Timaeus* at their fingertips, or even remember the difference between Pythagoras and Empedocles. In particular, I would remind my classicist friends that I am generally not discussing the "real" Pythagoras or Plato but rather these figures as seen from the vantage point of twelfth-century Aleppo. I hope too that I have explained enough about Islamic philosophy to make the book useful to those interested in the general history of philosophy and particularly of Neoplatonism.

I start the book with some introductory material dealing with

Suhrawardī's general philosophical position, his view of the problem of philosophy, and his life and works. After that I proceed roughly chronologically through the Greeks in an attempt to follow the history of philosophy as it appeared from his perspective. Inevitably, this procedure requires the reader to keep in mind features of Suhrawardī's philosophy that have not yet been discussed in detail. For this reason chapter 3 is a systematic presentation of Suhrawardī's major philosophical positions as I understand them. The reader unfamiliar with Suhrawardī and his *Philosophy of Illumination* will want to read this chapter with some care as a guide to his thought. The more experienced reader may find it useful as a guide to my interpretation of Suhrawardī. The place of Suhrawardī in the *Islamic* philosophical tradition is worthy of a book, but for the most part I have not written it. Nor have I written a systematic study of Suhrawardī's thought as a whole.

This book should thus be understood as a study of the history of philosophy, not a philological study of the transmission of particular texts and ideas. Nonetheless, I express my gratitude to those for whom problems of transmission are a major concern, for a project such as this would have been impossible without their exacting labors. In the study of the history of ideas, theories and interpretations come and go like the waves of the sea, but the rocks and beaches against which they beat and break are provided by the philologists, the editors, the translators, and the compilers of reference books who labor to provide the solid foundations for progress in scholarship.

I have also tried to draw some larger lessons about the place of Suhrawardī in Islamic thought—why his philosophical tradition survived in the east when the Peripatetic tradition died out in the west, and what effect this had on the development of Islamic thought as a whole. In particular, I draw some conclusions about why modern natural science arose in Europe and not in Islam and why in its place the Muslims came to cultivate a subtle epistemology of mystical experience.

I had originally intended to deal with the other major aspect of Suhrawardī's view of the history of philosophy, the "oriental" wisdom of Egypt and Hermes Trismegistus, Persia and its sages, and India, along with the more general question of Platonic orientalism. Unfortunately, the book outgrew the forebearance of the publisher, so these sections had to be omitted. It will be published in the same series as *The Wisdom of the Mystic East: Suhrawardī and Platonic Orientalism.* Finally, there is no chapter devoted to the Platonic Forms, a central theme of Suhrawardī's Platonism. To have done them justice would have taken disproportionate space, and on reflection I concluded that it was best to approach the question of Suhrawardī's interpretation of the Forms in the larger context of the interpretation of the Forms in Islamic philosophy as a whole, which must be a different book.

NOTE ON TERMINOLOGY

I use terms like 'Islamic philosophers', 'Muslims', and the like to refer to the practitioners of the tradition of philosophy carried on mainly by Muslims who mostly wrote in Arabic. I have generally tried to avoid 'Arab' and 'Arabic'—the 'Arabian philosophy' that one finds mentioned in older books on medieval European philosophy. Many of the people involved were not Arabs—including, of course, Suhrawardī himself, whose native language and ethnic background were Iranian—and some were Christians, Jews, and even Zoroastrians. The proper adjective would be Marshall Hodgson's 'Islamicate', but it is not especially elegant and has not caught on. The point is not central for my particular project.[3]

I have consistently rendered *ḥakīm* as 'sage' and *ḥikma* as 'wisdom'. These two native Arabic terms are often used as synonyms for the Greek loan words *faylasūf* and *falsafa*, which I render as 'philosopher' and 'philosophy'. Arabic, with its rigid morphology of triliteral roots, is not hospitable to foreign words, particularly if they cannot be fit naturally into Arabic word forms. The earliest Arabic translations of Greek philosophical and scientific texts were littered with transliterated terms, but these largely disappeared from the later translations and from all but the earliest independent Islamic philosophical texts. As early as the tenth century Fārābī and 'Āmirī used *ḥakīm* and *ḥikma* for 'philosopher' and 'philosophy'. I have maintained the distinction because there is a difference in connotation in Arabic. *Faylasūf* and *falsafa* soon acquired a disagreeable connotation of foreignness and irreligion, which even the philosophers themselves preferred to avoid. Moreover, *ḥakīm* and *ḥikma* can also be used in contexts that are not philosophical—to refer to traditional gnomic wisdom, for example. Thus, in a famous text, the early Islamic philosopher Abu'l-Ḥasan al-'Āmirī lumps together the legendary Arabian sage Luqmān with five major Greek philosophers under the rubric of those "to whom wisdom was attributed."[4]

The terms 'orient' and 'oriental' have gone out of scholarly fashion in the face of blistering criticism. Marshall Hodgson, the deepest thinker among modern historians of Islam, complained that these terms imply that all those who lived on the southern and eastern shores of the Mediterranean and and in all the lands east to Japan shared some common "oriental" essence, typically one conceived to be inferior to that of the West.[5] Edward Said's madcap but influential book *Orientalism* criticized not only the concept but also the orientalists themselves, a group into which he lumped both philologically oriented Western academic scholars studying the Islamic world and a variety of imperialist adventurers, writers, artists, and cranks who romanticized the East.[6] I am inclined to agree with Hodgson's critique but to reject Said's on the grounds that it is based on imprecise categories. Certainly, 'oriental' is a perfectly useless category for most serious historical study. However, Said has served me well by leaving the terms 'orient', 'oriental', and 'orientalist' free to carry the sense of "the East as romantically conceived." Thus, whenever 'orient' or its derivatives appear in this book, they are used in the romantic sense of the unchanging, fuzzily conceived exotic ancient lands of wisdom, spices, etc., etc.

I have used 'mysticism' and 'mystical' to render *dhawq*, *ta'alluh*, and other such terms referring to direct experience of the spiritual or the intelligible. (I also use 'intuition' in certain contexts.) I am aware that the term 'mysticism' has been criticized as a universal religious category and, in particular, that questions have been raised about whether it refers to a single kind of experience.[7] My friend and collaborator Hossein Ziai has questioned the appropriateness of its use in connection with Suhrawardī's ideas concerning intellectual intuition and knowledge by presence. I have used the term, first, because in its ordinary English usage it corresponds reasonably well with the range of phenomena that Suhrawardī believes are characteristic of the Illuminationist philosopher or sage. Second, Suhrawardī himself is firmly of the opinion that mystical experience is universal and that only its symbolic expression varies. Finally, Suhrawardī's attempt to bring mysticism into systematic relationship with philosophy parallels my task of explaining what Suhrawardī meant by "mysticism." The reader should keep in mind that mysticism is a category that Suhrawardī sought to clarify and that is being explored in the present book.

The transliteration is more or less that of the Library of Congress. I tend to omit the 'al-' from names, a habit to which Persian has accustomed me and which usually seems more natural in English.

REFERENCES AND TRANSLATIONS

Whenever possible, reference is given by some standard system rather than the pagination of particular editions, although I normally indicate the edition or translation that I am using. Classical references are given in the usual form and should pose no difficulties. References to Suhrawardī's works are given according to the paragraph numbers of the standard editions, usually Corbin's. In the case of *Ḥikmat al-Ishrāq (The Philosophy of Illumination)*, the most important of his works for this book, I have used the text and translation prepared by Hossein Ziai and myself. The text differs slightly from that of Corbin's edition, although rarely enough to affect the present work, while the translation is our own. In practice either edition can be used with the present book.

All translations are mine unless stated. Nonetheless, for the convenience of readers I cite translations of Arabic texts when they are available, even when I am giving my own translations. When this is the case, I will cite the Arabic text, followed by a citation of the published translation. When I do cite someone else's translation, I cite the translation first and give the reference to the original text second.

Unless otherwise noted, quotations from Aristotle are from Jonathan Barnes, ed., *The Complete Works of Aristotle* (2 vols.; Bollingen Series 71; Princeton: Princeton University Press, 1984), but I often translate from the Arabic translations of Aristotle, either because there is some relevant feature of the Arabic or just to keep closer to Aristotle as known to Suhrawardī and his fellow Islamic philosophers.

Greek quotations from Plato are from the Loeb edition unless otherwise noted. Translations of Plato are identified.

ACKNOWLEDGEMENTS

I would like to express my gratitude to the University of Toronto Press for permission to quote several extracts from Brad Inwood, *The Poem of Empedocles: A Text and Translation with an Introduction* (Phoenix Presocratics 3; Toronto: University of Toronto Press, 1992). Chapter 11 is a revised version of my article "Suhrawardī, a Twelfth-Century Muslim Neo-Stoic?" *Journal of the History of Philosophy* 34.4 (October 1996): 515–33. I gratefully acknowledge the permission of the editors to reproduce it here.

Production of this book was assisted by several grants from Indiana University, particularly a Summer Faculty Fellowship in 1996 under which much of this book was written. At an earlier stage of the process an Indiana University Undergraduate Research Partnership grant with matching funds from the Department of Near Eastern Languages and the Middle East Studies Program allowed me to work with a very bright undergraduate, Daniel Davison, on the transmission of Stoicism through the works of Galen. The final revisions were done while I was a Fulbright scholar in Pakistan, with additional assistance from the College of Arts and Sciences and the Graduate School of Indiana University.

I am also grateful to a number of colleagues for their encouragement and assistance. First among them are Hossein Ziai of UCLA and Paul Vincent Spade of the Philosophy Department of Indiana University, Bloomington. Hossein has been my partner and advisor in Suhrawardī studies for many years. Paul has been my mentor at Indiana, has read this manuscript, has given much useful advice, and has taught me a great deal of logic and philosophy. Above all, in the best traditions of the Middle Ages, he stood by me loyally and without counting cost through a very difficult period.

I would like to thank Seyyed Hossein Nasr for agreeing to include this book in his series even though, as he says, he completely disagrees with me about the interpretation of Suhrawardī.

I am also grateful to the collegues who have read or heard parts of this work and who have advised, cautioned, assisted, or inspired me in various ways. I think especially of Parviz Morewedge, Juan Ricardo Cole, James Russell, Edward Grant, and the encouraging but punctillious Reader B, John Bussanich. On another front, I would like to thank my attorney, Julie Knost, who insisted that I persevere and ensured that I would be employed after I finished this book.

Above all, I must acknowledge the patience and forebearance of my family, especially Linda, my wife of a quarter century.

PART 1

Suhrawardī as a Non-Peripatetic

Among the Greeks, the last to speak of [the obliterating light] was the great sage Plato. Among those to have experienced it and whose names are preserved in the histories is Hermes. Among the Pahlavis was the lord of the earth Gayomarth and those of his dynasty, Feridun and Kaykhusrow. As for the lights of mysticism in these recent centuries, the leaven of the Pythagoreans passed to the brother of Ikhmīm [Dhu'l-Nūn al-Miṣrī]. From him it descended to the wayfarer of Tustar [Sahl al-Tustarī] and his followers. The leaven of the Khusrawānīs in mysticism descended to [Bāyazīd], the wayfarer of Basṭām, then to the youth of Bayḍā', and then to the wayfarer of Āmul and Kharraqān [Abu'l-Ḥasan al-Kharraqānī]. A portion of the leaven of the Khusrawānīs came down and mixed with a path formed from the leaven of the followers of Pythagoras, Empedocles, and Asclepius upon the tongues of those who remember the word from the western and eastern sides. From there it came down to a people who speak by the shekina.

—Suhrawardī, *al-Mashāri' wa'l-Muṭāraḥāt*, para. 223

The steady decline of intuitive philosophy continued until our age when one man arose prepared for intuitive philosophy and dissatisfied with pure speculation.

—Shahrazūrī, *Commentary on The Philosophy of Illumination*

CHAPTER 1

The Problem of Suhrawardī and Illuminationism

When the Renaissance humanists of Europe turned back to the classics and began reading Plato and other non-Aristotelian ancient philosophers, they did not simply adopt a new form of an ancient philosophy; rather their contact with the non-Aristotelian philosophy of the ancient world freed them from the Peripatetic elf hill in which the philosophers of Europe had been bound for so long. The Europeans rediscovered the past and in the process made themselves into something very new with immense consequences for science, philosophy, and thought and culture in general. When the twelfth-century philosopher Suhrawardī returned to the ancient materials of non-Aristotelian philosophy, he claimed—and certainly sincerely thought—that he was reviving and purifying an ancient tradition. In fact, he was transforming Islamic philosophy. Having found warrant in Pythagoras and Plato for making mysticism central to philosophy, having found in the notion of symbolic philosophical language justification for rejecting the differences among the ancient philosophers who claimed mystical experience and for dismissing those who did not, he set himself on the path of rejecting the foundations on which the great systems of the Ancients had been founded: mathematics in the case of Pythagoras and Plato, and natural philosophy in the case of Aristotle. The visible world is the imperfect expression of the intelligible world, he said with Plato, and so it ought to be investigated through the intelligible world. Yet having firmly anchored the whole of the universe in the One of mystical experience and the highest knowledge in the direct apprehension of the intelligible realm, Suhrawardī was driven to a strange kind of Platonic nominalism in which the Forms acquire individuality, but at the cost of their link with reason and the independent existence of the mathematicals and the prestige of mathematics. Philosophy, for Suhrawardī, collapsed into logic and metaphysics.

Yet logic too was unable to resist the corrosive force of mysticism. By having placed mysticism at the center of philosophical investigation, Suhrawardī handed later Islamic philosophers a powerful tool to explore the depths of the universe as it reveals itself to the sensitive human soul and mind. The Greek and Islamic philosophers had argued for sixteen centuries or more about the nature of reality, and now Suhrawardī announced the rediscovery of a tool to resolve those issues. It was a gift all the more tempting since it also promised to resolve the newer issue of the relation between philosophy and revelation. Ghazālī had proposed this solution eighty years earlier, and now Suhrawardī gave it rigorous and intellectually satisfactory expression. Yet the acceptance of this gift, as Ghazālī also had seen, allowed the abandonment of logic, except in its most trivial form. For Avicenna, as for Plato and Aristotle, logic dealt with accurate formal reasoning but was inextricably linked with ontological and metaphysical concerns. Avicenna could clarify the concepts of reasoning and thereby learn something about the nature of being. But the mystic is not bound by logic, for he sees very clearly the delusory quality of human ratiocinations. Suhrawardī condemned Avicenna for building his ontology on the fallacy that the structure of being must be like our conceptual structures. After Suhrawardī those philosophers who wished to rescue some aspect of Avicenna's thought—Mullā Ṣadrā, who wished to assert the reality of pure existence, for example—had to justify themselves in other ways, usually on the basis of mystical experience. The structure of reality is to be discovered by analyzing our supersensory experience of reality, not by analyzing our conceptions.

The damage to logic is deeper than at first appears. We might think that the distinction of the metaphysical and the formal aspects of logic would open the way to clearer and more fruitful logical analysis. Yet because logic has been dethroned in the name of mysticism, such would not happen. Logic is a ladder that the mystic leaves behind as he nears his goal, and the ladder need not be the same for every seeker. For thinkers like Ibn 'Arabī and those influenced by him, the ladder is different for every soul. God is not bound by the laws of logic, for from the point of view of the world, each creature looks towards a different God. Suhrawardī predates Ibn 'Arabī and does not go so far in marginalizing logic, yet the seeds are there. Suhrawardī recognizes that logic is no longer important, for in his *Philosophy of Illumination* logic is reduced to a few simple rules, "sufficient for one with sound understanding." This logic serves the purpose not of establishing the truth of Suhrawardī's own system but of challenging the claims of the Peripatetics. The real tool for discovering truth is *dhawq*, mystical intuition. Suhrawardī remained a philosopher and was prepared to put his conclusions into rigorous logical system, but he could express himself equally well in other ways—through allegory and poetry, for example. Nonetheless, he set Islamic philosophy on a path very different from that followed by European philosophy in the Middle Ages and beyond. Medieval European philosophy led to modern science, modern scholarship, and the protean philosophy of Renaissance and modern Europe. Islamic philosophy in the meantime carried on the tradition of scholasticism, developing a subtle metaphysics and epistemology of mystical experience beyond anything that the Europeans ever achieved. What Suhrawardī found in the surviving fragments of the ancient philosophers and how he transformed that material into a system that was the foundation for later Iranian Islamic philosophy is the subject of this book.

Suhrawardī (d. 1194) was the most important philosopher in the eastern Islamic world in the period between Avicenna and Mullā Ṣadrā. His importance in that period is rivalled only by his contemporaries Averroes (Ibn Rushd) and Ibn 'Arabī. Suhrawardī's influence was greater than that of Averroes, for while the latter was largely forgotten in the Islamic world, Suhrawardī has continually attracted Islamic readers, followers, and opponents up to our own day.

In the view of Islamic philosophers Suhrawardī was the founder of the Illuminationist school within Islamic philosophy, a school that is distinguished by specific views on epistemology, logic, metaphysics, and ontology. A chart of the history of Islamic philosophy that would be acceptable both to modern scholars and the Islamic tradition itself would portray the situation as in figure 1.1. Such a portrayal of the place of Suhrawardī in the Islamic philosophical tradition is uncontroversial only insofar as it refers to the situation *within* Islamic philosophy. When we consider his relation to schools outside of Islam, the matter becomes difficult.

Suhrawardī claimed to be reviving the tradition of the 'Ancients' *(aqdamīn, awwalīn)* in philosophy and claimed an intellectual affiliation including, in one sense or another, Hermes Trismegistus, Pythagoras, Empedocles, Socrates, Plato, Aristotle, the oriental sages of ancient Persia and India, and certain Sufis. Since Suhrawardī certainly did disagree with Avicenna and the Peripatetics on various basic philosophical points and since he unquestionably did agree, against Aristotle, with certain of the Ancients on well-known philosophical doctrines, there has been general agreement that he does represent, in one sense or another, a revival of a pre-Islamic philosophical tradition.

But what tradition is it? The name that Suhrawardī gave to his school—Ishrāqī, "Illuminationist"—is not the name of an ancient school. Several answers have been given. Suhrawardī himself said that the Ancients were in agreement on certain views—on the existence of a Creator, four levels of being, and the Platonic Forms, for example—but that many of the sages had spoken in symbols that were not to be understood literally. Most consistently, he identifies himself as a non-Peripatetic.

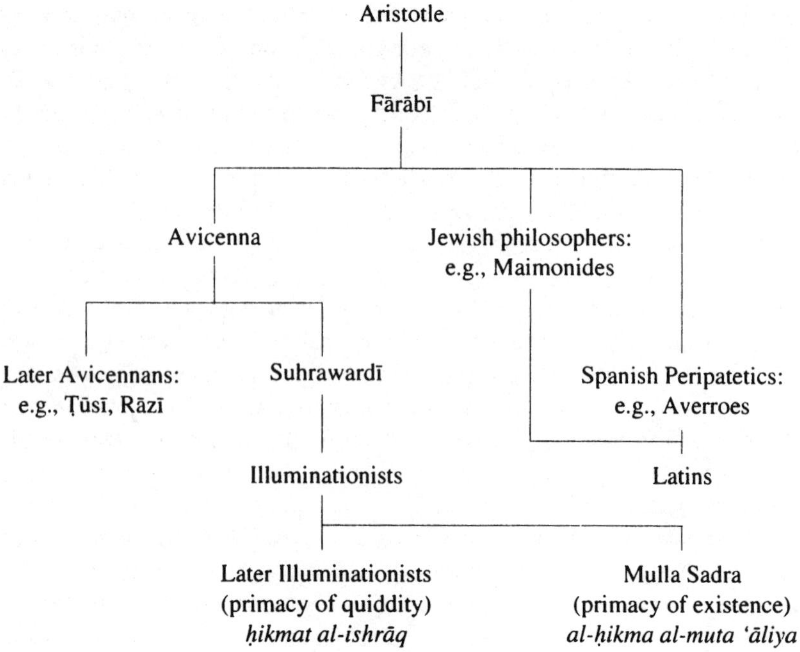

FIGURE 1.1
The History of Islamic Philosophy

Suhrawardī's followers tended to describe themselves as Platonists, but their rivals often called them Stoics. In a passage in his *Words of Sufism* Suhrawardī says that in *The Philosophy of Illumination* he "revived the noble wisdom of light" of the ancient Persians "to which the intuition of Plato and the sages before him had testified."[1] On the basis of this passage and other scattered references to Iranian themes and symbols, many modern interpreters have further confused the issue by portraying him as the reviver of a pre-Islamic tradition of Iranian wisdom.

It is not sufficient simply to analyze Suhrawardī's statements about his school affiliation. He was a systematic and careful philosopher who clearly identified his disagreements with the prevailing Avicennan, neo-Aristotelian tradition. These disagreements do not necessarily correspond clearly to what we know of the ancient philosophical schools. If we are to take Suhrawardī seriously as a philosopher, we must answer our question in a way that explains why he said what he did about his philosophical affiliations and why he took the particular philosophical positions that he did, basing our explanation on the difficulties that Suhrawardī detected in the Avicennan synthesis and what he knew, might have known, or might have thought he knew about the ancient philosophers. A combination of philosophical and philological analysis is called for if we are to avoid falling into the sort of romantic interpretations that have muddied the waters so far in Suhrawardī studies.

In general, modern Western scholarship on Suhrawardī, particularly that done by or under the influence of the late Henry Corbin, has stressed this philosophical-historical aspect of his thought. Corbin, though, was convinced that Suhrawardī's project was the revival of the thought of the ancient Persians. I believe this to be wrong; Suhrawardī's interest in ancient Iran was derivative and of the same nature as the exoticism of such philosophers as Porphyry and Iamblichus. For Suhrawardī the central point of the philosophical tradition was Plato, not Zoroaster. Corbin's stress on the supposedly Iranian character of Suhrawardī's thought led him and his followers, I believe, to lay too much stress on the symbolic elements of his thought and too little on Suhrawardī's "Peripatetic" texts—that is, those written in conventional philosophical language. As a result, the philosophical relationships of Suhrawardī to his predecessors were minimized, misunderstood, or ignored. The prime example of a key but neglected text is the chapter containing *sophismata* in Suhrawardī's most important work, *The Philosophy of Illumination.* These sections analyze the philosophical differences between Suhrawardī and the Peripatetics and in many cases are the clearest statements of Suhrawardī's key philosophical positions. These are not included in Corbin's French translation of *The Philosophy of Illumination.*[2]

A second approach to Suhrawardī concentrates on his philosophical criticism of Avicenna. This has been the approach of Mullā Ṣadrā and the Iranian tradition of philosophy up to the present and of orientalists such as Izutsu, Ziai, and myself. Its key problems are ontology, epistemology, and logic. For such analysis the main points of reference are Avicenna and the later Iranian philosophers such as Mīr Dāmād, Mullā Ṣadrā, and Sabziwārī.[3] Analysis of this sort is generally more satisfactory from a philosophical point of view, but it does not solve the historical question—as opposed to the philosophical question—of why Suhrawardī adopted the views he did and why he attributed them to the Ancients. If there are insights to be gained by considering the alternatives opened to Suhrawardī by the works of the Ancients, this method will not find them.

The present work is an attempt to create a comprehensive explanation of the origin of Suhrawardī's philosophical system insofar as it is grounded in Greek philosophy. The problems which I hope to solve, to my own satisfaction at least, are the following:

1. Why did Suhrawardī choose to reject the prevailing neo-Aristotelian synthesis in Islamic philosophy?
2. What was his knowledge and understanding of non-Aristotelian Greek philosophy?
3. Which ancient philosophers was he attempting to follow?
4. How are his specific philosophical teachings on such matters as logic, ontology, physics, and metaphysics related to his understanding of non-Aristotelian ancient philosophy?
5. How did his system relate the major Greek philosophers, schools, and traditions of learning which he mentions in his books, in particular the Presocratics, Plato, and the Stoics?

Such an explanation must consider the problem of what non-Peripatetic Greek philosophical materials were available to Suhrawardī in the light of what Suhrawardī has to say about Greek philosophy. It must also take account of what the distinctive features of Suhrawardī's system actually are, as opposed to what is taken as part of the common heritage of Aristotle and Avicenna. It must then determine how these doctrines are grounded in the philosophical materials available to him. This is not just an exercise in source-tracing, as we might do when trying to determine the origins of a doxography. Suhrawardī is clearly responding to what he sees as flaws in the dominant philosophical tradition of his time by making creative use of non-Peripatetic materials known to him. That he actually did this is shown by the simplest example: his use of Plato's doctrine of Forms. My assumption will be that Suhrawardī was making intelligent use of the philosophical resources available to him to create a coherent system and that he believed that system to be in essential respects identical with that of the Ancients. The task of the present work is to determine precisely what that claim might mean, both historically and philosophically, and thus to deliver Suhrawardī from the hands of the myth-makers.

Suhrawardī probably had considerably more access to translations of Greek material than we might at first think. Just before the year 1000, Avicenna was able to find virtually the whole of the Greek philosophical and scientific literature that had been translated into Arabic on the shelves of the royal library of Bukhara. Averroes seems to have had access to nearly as much in Cordova, five thousand kilometers to the west and almost two centuries later. What exactly Suhrawardī may have found in his studies in Iran, Anatolia, and Syria, we do not know, but it was surely more than now survives in Arabic. Moreover, we are dealing, on both sides of the Greek/Islamic line, with competent, insightful philosophers upholding coherent positions. Suhrawardī lived in an age that believed in reading important texts carefully. He could and, I think, did take scattered hints and use them to infer the essential features of the philosophical systems he was interested in. Unlike his follower Shahrazūrī, he was no antiquarian; he was purely a philosopher and primarily interested in philosophical issues. Much as a paleontologist infers the skeleton of a dinosaur from a few bones, Suhrawardī was quite capable of understanding the philosophical implications of various Greek systems from the fragmentary information available to him. In other words, I do not think we are justified in presuming medieval Islamic philosophers to be ignorant of Greek views unless proven otherwise through unambiguous philological evidence. It is not always true—I will argue, for example, that his view of Stoicism was distorted by misleading sources—but Suhrawardī reconstructs—or perhaps reinvents—large portions of the Pythagorean system on the basis of very fragmentary evidence. Such a method is also forced upon us by the fact that Suhrawardī almost never cites his sources directly, requiring us to infer the nature of the debate of which he was a part from the structure of the arguments themselves.

To make an analogy: Suhrawardī looked at the tapestry of Greek philosophy through a very dirty window; we, with our direct access to the texts, have a much cleaner window to look through, and so we see more clearly. Suhrawardī's window—the Arabic textual tradition—is still there, though dirtier than when Suhrawardī last looked through it, and so I have recorded the view from that window whenever it seemed useful, but I have also peeked through our cleaner modern window to make sense of what I have seen through Suhrawardī's window and to try to figure out what he might have still been able to see in his day. But Suhrawardī was not really interested in the tapestry; he was interested in what the tapestry portrayed, for he wished to weave his own. To do that, he would have to turn and look at the real world. His understanding of the world was shaped by the faded glories he saw through that old and dirty window, but he could also see for himself and seeing, weave once more the tapestry woven by the Ancients.

Now, I do not wish to be misunderstood or to have my method exaggerated. I will, in fact, pay constant attention to problems of transmission and to the sources known to have been available to Suhrawardī. The Pythagoras and the Plato that I constrast to Suhrawardī are the Plato and Pythagoras of Islamic sources, not those of Zeller, Diels, Burkert, and Guthrie. I simply wish to give Suhrawardī the benefit of the doubt, assuming that he understood the materials available to him unless the case is clearly the contrary. For example, Suhrawardī's Plato is the Pythagoreanizing Plato of the *Timaeus*, not the political Plato of the

Republic. The Arabic evidence explains why this is so, but, on the other hand, I assume that Suhrawardī correctly understood the philosophical underpinnings of this aspect of Platonism. It is a tradition that runs from the Academy of Plato's old age through the Pythagoreanizing Neoplatonists like Iamblichus and Proclus into the Islamic world and that has its defenders still. One could, as others have, try to document the exact extent and channels through which this particular tradition reached Islam. Generally, I am content simply to assume that it did. It may have been in a fragmentary form, but its quantity and detail were sufficient that medieval Islamic philosophers were able to understand the position and modify or build on it—the 'leaven' to which Suhrawardī alludes and which supplies me with my title. Where quirks of transmission are relevant, as they are for the Stoics, I will discuss them, but they are not my main interest.

I can best elucidate Suhrawardī's philosophical views through comparison with philosophers of his tradition. I start with the allusions in Suhrawardī's own works. He nowhere discusses his predecessors in detail, but I assume that his commentators had an accurate understanding of the context of his work. I also assume—cautiously—that relevant Arabic texts available to me were, in one way or another, available to Suhrawardī. Sometimes I can do this with confidence, as in the case of standard bits of lore found in all the biographical dictionaries, but sometimes I just have to assume that Suhrawardī and the authors whose texts I am examining had access to the same sources, as with Averroes' *Great Commentary on the Metaphysics*. At the end of the project, I have no reason to doubt the soundness of this procedure.

The larger context is provided by the non-Aristotelian philosophical tradition as a whole, particularly the Pythagoreanizing Neoplatonists. Occasionally I can show that the relevant Greek texts were in circulation among Muslims: Porphyry's biography of Pythagoras from his *History of the Philosophers* is a prime example. More often, no direct textual connection can be established. However, whether the relationship is due to an unknown textual connection or simply due to the fact that Suhrawardī and his late antique predecessors were working on similar material, the parallels are fruitful, reflecting the internal dynamic of their common tradition. It is no accident that these philosophers should all be interested in both Pythagoras and Plato, that they considered mysticism central to philosophical inquiry, and that they were interested in the views of "oriental" sages. These are positions that grow naturally from their common underlying commitments. The Greek texts, relatively well understood, thus clarify the nature and logic of Suhrawardī's position.

THE COMMENTATORS

I have made the assumption that Suhrawardī's works and their intellectual context were correctly understood by two of his early commentators, Shams al-Dīn Shahrazūrī and Quṭb al-Dīn Shīrāzī. There is a certain risk in this proceeding. There was no chain of teachers and students connecting Suhrawardī with the thirteenth-century philosophers whom I assume to speak for him, and they themselves admit that their attempt to revive the Illuminationist tradition was a purely literary enterprise.[4] Nonetheless, based on a good deal of time spent with these commentators, I have no reason to doubt the accuracy of their understanding of the master. I have mainly used three works of the early commentators, two by Shahrazūrī and one by Quṭb al-Dīn.

Shahrazūrī seems to have been responsible for the revival of serious interest in Suhrawardī's thought. His reputation is based on his three major works. The first, *Sharḥ Ḥikmat al-Ishrāq* (The Commentary on *The Philosophy of Illumination*), established the tradition of Suhrawardī interpretation and has recently been published for the first time. The second, *Nuzhat al-Arwāḥ wa-Rawḍat al-Afrāḥ fī Tārīkh al-Ḥukamā'* (The Delight of the Spirits and the Garden of Delights, on the History of the Sages) is a well-known biographical dictionary of philosophers written from an Illuminationist viewpoint.[5] There is little doubt that this work is in its way a commentary on Suhrawardī. I will assume that in the absence of information to the contrary the *Delight* represents what Suhrawardī knew about the history of philosophy. The history of philosophy from an Illuminationist viewpoint that follows is thus largely based on the *Delight*. The third, *al-Shajara al-Ilāhīya* (The Divine Tree) is a survey of philosophical doctrines, organized topically. It has never been published but is extensively cited by later writers such as Mullā Ṣadrā.[6] I have not used it in this study.

Shahrazūrī's commentary was superceded in general use by the commentary of Quṭb al-Dīn al-Shīrāzī, which is based on it but is easier to use. I will also sometimes cite his *Durrat al-Tāj* (The Pearly Crown), a Persian philosophical encyclopedia reflecting Illuminationist principles.

CHAPTER 2

Suhrawardī's Life and Works

FROM MARĀGHA TO ALEPPO

Suhrawardī belongs to that select company of philosophers who paid for their philosophical teachings with their lives: Socrates, Bruno, Pythagoras by some accounts, and not many others. Suhrawardī also has the distinction of having been put to death by a worthy foe, the fabulous Saladin. Though the story as we have it is fragmentary, it is worth the retelling, for Suhrawardī's philosophy, his life, and his death are bound together in much the same way as for Pythagoras and Socrates.[1]

Suhraward is a village in the province of Zanjān, three hundred kilometers northwest of modern Tehran. If that is where he was born, he did not stay there, for the first information the biographers give about him is that he went to Marāgha, a town in northwestern Iran, to study philosophy with Majd al-Dīn al-Jīlī. This man "was prominent in his time, wrote excellent books," and also taught philosophy to the famous theologian Fakhr al-Dīn al-Rāzī.[2] In Mārdīn, a town in Anatolia, Suhrawardī studied with Fakhr al-Dīn al-Mārdīnī (d. 594/1198), a prominent teacher of medicine and the rational sciences in his day, an exponent of the works of Avicenna and seemingly a Sufi.[3] In Isfahan he studied the *Baṣā'ir* of Ibn Sahlān al-Sāwī with Ẓahīr al-Qārī (or al-Fārisī). Ẓahīr is completely lost to history, but the *Baṣā'ir* is an innovative work of logic whose organization foreshadows certain aspects of Suhrawardī's works, as Shahrazūrī remarks.[4] After this he seems to have wandered, mainly in central Anatolia, which at that time was largely Iranized. He is said to have lived in Diyārbakr and in Syria. Anecdotes also place him in Tabrīz and Mayāfāriqīn. The earlier stages of this wandering were certainly in search of knowledge, the later stages in search of patronage and, if we are to believe Suhrawardī himself, of an intellectual equal.[5] He was to find the first, though he was to pay for it with his life, but not the second.

Suhrawardī also became a Sufi. Shahrazūrī tells of his extreme austerities and his spiritual powers, yet he is not recognized by most Sufi writers and biographers as one of them. Perhaps this was because of his philosophical interests, his reputation as a magician, and his ultimate fate.

Shahrazūrī says, "He travelled to many other places, associating with the Sufis and learning something from them. He acquired the habit of independence in mystical exercises and thought, attaining the highest stations of sages and saints" and adds that he sometimes but not always wore Sufi dress. The sources do not tell us the names of his Sufi masters or identify his *silsila*, his spiritual affiliation, so perhaps the explanation is simply that he learned from the Sufis but never fully joined them, as Shahrazūrī seems to imply. Shahrazūrī writes of "his austerities unprecedented among the sages," adding that he ate but once a week, cared nothing for the world, had no awe of rank and power, wore ragged dress, prayed constantly, kept silence, and loved *samā'*, the Sufi music and dance.[6] Our sources, friendly and unfriendly, are eager to tell us about the wonders he performed. Shahrazūrī rejects the slander that these powers were based on natural magic or prestidigitation *(sīmīyā, muḥīl);* in actuality, the mystics have "the power to bring forms into being at will, as Basṭāmī, Ḥallāj, and others could do. God gave me certainty of the existence of this station, but some things should not be mentioned."[7]

There is no doubt that he was seen as someone special during his lifetime. 'Abd al-Laṭīf al-Baghdādī (557–629/1162–1231), who was studying in Mosul in the 1180s with Kamāl al-Dīn b. Yūnus, tells of the excitement about Suhrawardī and his works, though he himself was disappointed when he gained access to them.[8]

In 579/1183 he came to Aleppo where he immediately drew the attention of both the learned elite of the town and the prince-governor, al-Malik al-Ẓāhir, the son of Saladin. He impressed and alarmed the 'ulamā' by his boldly argued and unorthodox opinions, and won access to the prince by a fabulous gem that he had produced by magic—or perhaps alchemy, if we are to take the story seriously.[9] The 'ulamā' were soon jealous of his ascendancy and agitated against him to Saladin in Damascus. Saladin, alarmed by the threat to his son's orthodoxy, ordered him to put Suhrawardī to death, and the prince in the end was forced to comply. Shahrazūrī tells us that the stories about Suhrawardī's death differed. Some said he refused or was denied food, while others said that he was strangled or killed with a sword or thrown from the walls of the citadel. Ibn Shaddād, Saladin's *qāḍī* who was involved in the death sentence, says that he was crucified.[10] Perhaps al-Malik al-Ẓāhir reported the grisly death by crucifiction to Saladin and the more dignified death by starvation to Suhrawardī's grieving teacher, al-Mārdīnī. The date is variously given as 586/1190, 587/1191, 5 Rajab 587/28 July 1191, late Dhu'l-Ḥijja 587/early January 1192, and 588/1192. Ibn Khallikān claims to have reliable information supporting the 5 Rajab 587 date.[11] There being no date recorded for his birth, various estimates are given for his age at the time of his death: thirty-six, thirty-eight, nearly forty, and fifty.

A number of aspects of his life and death are relevant to his philosophy and its interpretation, so they will be discussed in detail in their proper places.

SUHRAWARDĪ'S WORKS

In the beginning of *The Philosophy of Illumination*, the book that everybody agrees is the key to his philosophy, Suhrawardī writes:

> Know, my brethren, that your frequent demands that I record the philosophy of illumination have finally overcome my reluctance. Were it not for an incumbent obligation, a prior word, and a command given from a place disobedience to which would lead to straying from the path, I would not have felt obliged to step forward and openly reveal it, for the difficulty therein is known to you. But you went on, my friends—may God direct you towards what He loves and approves of—begging me to write you a book in which I would tell what I have obtained through my intuition during my retreats and visions. . . .
>
> Before I wrote this book and during the times when interruptions prevented me from working on it, I wrote other books in which I have summarized for you the principles of the Peripatetics according to their method. Among these books is the short work known as the *Intimations of the Tablet and the Throne*. Many principles are summarized in it despite its brevity. Then there is my book, *The Flashes of Light*. I also have composed other works, some in my youth. But the present work has another method and a shorter path to knowledge than their method. It is more orderly and precise, less painful to study. I did not first arrive at it through cogitation, but rather it was acquired through something else. Subsequently I sought proof for it so that should I cease contemplating the proof, nothing would make me fall into doubt.[12]

The books he refers to are all extant, and it is clear from what he says that they should not all be given equal weight. But how exactly are we to understand their interrelationships? The books written in his "youth" are probably to be understood as juvenalia. The books that "summarize the principles of the Peripatetics according to their method" would seem at first glance to be irrelevant to the understanding of Suhrawardī's distinctive philosophy as found in *The Philosophy of Illumination* with its "other method" and "shorter path to knowledge." But if that is the case, why was he writing works on the Peripatetic system at the same time as he was writing *The Philosophy of Illumination*? Such questions can only be answered by closer examination of Suhrawardī's works and methods.

Suhrawardī wrote voluminously, and while no one has done a systematic bibliographic study of his works, it seems that we have most of his writings and all the major works.[13] For our purposes, these works may be divided into four classes:

1. *The Philosophy of Illumination*, identified by Suhrawardī as his masterwork. His metaphysics based on the concepts of light and darkness occupies only about half of the book. The remainder is devoted to logic and a critique, in Peripatetic terminology, of various Peripatetic doctrines.
2. Three major "Peripatetic" works, *al-Talwīḥāt*, *al-Muqāwamāt*, and *al-Mashāri' wa'l-Muṭāraḥāt*.[14] The sense in which these works are 'Peripatetic' is a matter of controversy, though so far they have not been studied in enough detail to settle the question. At the least, they are written in Peripatetic language, which is to say they use the conventional philosophical terminology of Avicenna and others of his school rather than the 'Illuminationist' terminology of the second part of *The Philosophy of Illumination*. Their arrangement also generally conforms to the usual format of the Islamic Peripatetics. On the other hand, it is not difficult to identify parallels with the doctrines of *The Philosophy of Illumination*.
3. The juvenalia.
4. A collection of allegories, mostly in excellent Persian prose.

There are also a variety of other works, such as prayers, most not used in this study.

Suhrawardī himself mentions two decisive events in his philosophical development: a dream of Aristotle that led him to his doctrine of knowledge by presence and mystical experiences that convinced him of the reality of the Platonic Forms. These experiences—it is the dream of Aristotle that he retells in detail—led him to abandon his youthful allegiance to the Islamic Peripatetic philosophy of Avicenna and his school and to adopt the philosophy of the "Ancients." Thus, we can assume that there is a discontinuity between the juvenalia and at least *The Philosophy of Illumination*. That cannot be said of the major Peripatetic works, which are more or less contemporaneous with *The Philosophy of Illumination*. They seem far too substantial to be mere academic exercises in the explication of somebody else's philosophical system. At the same time, Suhrawardī makes it clear that *The Philosophy of Illumination* is the fullest and truest exposition of philosophy that he has written. The situation would probably be clearer were it not for the argument that Suhrawardī's system is a revival of some sort of ancient Persian wisdom or "theosophy." The most Persian-looking part of Suhrawardī's system is, of course, the metaphysics of light and darkness, whereas the 'Peripatetic' works seem to have nothing whatever to do with Iranian thought. In the absence of this "Iranian" interpretation of Suhrawardī, the situation would appear much simpler; like other Neo-platonists he is using Aristotle to explain the things of this world and Plato to explain higher things. I think that these books represent Suhrawardī's view of philosophical truth as it can be known by unaided reason and that they thus represent an integral part of his philosophical system.

The allegories are a different problem. At one extreme it has been argued that they represent the pinnacle of Suhrawardī's thought.[15] I will argue for the other extreme, that they are intended for beginners and for students, that they are points of entry into philosophical and mystical thought. I will further argue that they contain none of the most distinctive doctrines of Suhrawardī's mature philosophy, thus placing them either among his early works or among works that are deliberately shorn of higher and abstruse doctrines.

Suhrawardī's life and Suhrawardī's thought were intimately connected, just at they were for Pythagoras and many later philosophers who believed that philosophy required a philosophical life. Philosophy for him was the love of wisdom and implied the obligation to live his philosophy; it was not simply the love of talking about wisdom.[16] To pursue the Illuminationist philosophy, it is necessary to seek enlightenment from the divine lights.[17] Likewise, the nature of the philosophy he pursued—the philosophy of Plato and the Divine Ancients—determined the kind of books he would write. For the Peripatetics writing philosophy was a matter of recording arguments and conclusions in proper syllogistic form, but Pythagoras had shown the unwisdom, and Plato the impossibility, of recording the deepest philosophical teachings in writing. The writing of philosophy was a dialectical endeavor, requiring both knowledge and a subtle sense of how to guide the student through the various levels of knowledge. The books were never intended to be used alone to teach the full Illuminationist philosophy.

After his death, one of Suhrawardī's teachers sadly remarked, "His knowledge was greater than his prudence." Yet considered from within his system, the events of the last years of his life and the fact, and even the manner, of his death were determined by his Platonic convictions. Platonism implies a philosopher-king, and Suhrawardī, like Plato, was driven by the logic of his thought to attempt to create one when the opportunity offered. For Suhrawardī, as for Plato fifteen centuries earlier, the attempt proved to be a failure paid for in blood.

CHAPTER 3

A Summary of the Illuminationist Philosophy

THE STYLE OF SUHRAWARDĪ'S PHILOSOPHIZING

This summary of Suhrawardī's philosophical system is intended as a point of reference in what follows. It is mainly based on *The Philosophy of Illumination.*[1]

Suhrawardī was both a philosopher and a mystic. He was a philosopher first, in that his mysticism was shaped and interpreted within a clearly articulated philosophical system. His philosophical tradition was that of Avicenna and hence of Aristotle. The arrangement of his philosophical works reflects the arrangment of Aristotle's works, as modified in the fifteen centuries that separated them, but this arrangement has been further modified, especially in *The Philosophy of Illumination*, to reflect the peculiarities of his own system.

Certain general approaches are characteristic of Suhrawardī's thought. He is suspicious of metaphysical constructs, preferring to take individual entities, the objects of direct experience, as the fundamental units of his system. He thus treats both ordinary worldly things—individual animals, for example—and supernatural entities like God and the Platonic Forms in a similar way, treating both classes of entities as objects of possible direct experience. This general metaphysical principle came to be known as the 'primacy of quiddity' *(aṣālat al-māhīya)*, a term that Suhrawardī himself did not use. On the other hand, he rejects such philosophical constructs as existence and prime matter as illegitimate reifications of concepts. Accordingly, subjective experience is the critical ingredient of all kinds of knowledge.

LOGIC

Traditionally, Islamic philosophers divided logic into nine parts, reflecting the arrangment of the nine books of the Arabic version of the *Organon*: predicables, categories, propositions, syllogisms, demonstration, dialectic, rhetoric, fallacies, poetics. In *The Philosophy of Illumination* Suhrawardī adopted a simpler and more intuitive three-part logic: semantics, proofs, and fallacies.

The characteristic Illuminationist doctrine in semantics is the rejection of the Aristotelian theory of essential definition. The Peripatetics held that science dealt with the essential attributes of natural kinds. Thus, the foundations of a science are the knowledge of the essences of the subject being studied and first principles known with certainty prior to the investigations in that science. A geometer, for example, must know the essences of the objects of his science—points, lines, solids, and so on—and must also know principles that cannot be proven in geometry—that the whole is greater than the part, for example. Naturally, there can be arbitrary linguistic definitions and definitions that identify by accidentals without revealing the essence of the thing. An example of the latter is 'man is a biped that can laugh.' Thus, to be scientifically useful, a definition must capture the essence of a natural kind. What is needed for a science is essential definition (Ar. *ḥadd*; Gk. ὅρος), definitions compiled from the proximate genus and all the differentiae of the natural kind. The stock example is 'man is a rational animal', where 'animal' is the proximate genus and 'rational' is the differentia.

Suhrawardī objects strongly to this notion. He sees two major difficulties. First, the enterprise of constructing such definitions is circular. If we know the essential properties of a natural kind, we already know it and the definition teaches us nothing. Second, how can we know that the definition contains a complete enumeration of the differentiae? Such a criterion of knowledge would make all scientific knowledge impossible. He points out that the Peripatetics had great difficulty constructing such definitions even for the simplest concepts. 'Black is the color that gathers vision', another stock definition in Islamic Peripatetic logic, is a good example. Anyone who can see knows what black is, but 'gathers vision' is incomprehensible.

His own theory is that concepts are known by apprehension of their instances. We know black by seeing black. For Suhrawardī the most that a definition can do is identify the thing defined by elimination. 'Laughing biped' and 'rational animal' serve equally well to distinguish man from all other things.

Proof

Suhrawardī's theory of proof is distinguished by the reduction of all forms of the syllogism to the first figure by the conversion of all propositions to necessary universal affirmative propositions. In the Aristotelian logic of terms, the main object of interest is predication. Propositions vary by being universal or particular, affirmative or negative, and necessary or contingent. This allows many combinations, exhaustively cataloged by Avicenna, among others. The propositions most useful in science are those that are affirmative, necessary, and universal, such as the first two. In syllogisms the others tend to yield results that are contingent or partial and create immensely complicated sets of forms, requiring complicated rules.

In part because he saw the concern with such details as obscuring the basic foundation principles of ancient philosophy, Suhrawardī set out to reduce the complication of logic by simplifying the forms. First, he proposed a set of procedures for converting all propositions to the simplest form, the universal necessary affirmative. Thus, we get

> It is necessary that all men are contingently literate.
> It is necessary that all horses are nonrational.

This procedure serves two purposes. First, it allows him to dismiss the most complex achievements of Peripatetic logic as unnecessary complications. Second, the reduction of syllogism to necessary affirmative forms parallels the causal structure of his cosmos in which each ontological level of being is completely determined by the higher levels.

The sophistics of Suhrawardī's logic really are part of his polemic against the Peripatetics. While he does discuss various formal fallacies, these do not comprise a distinctive system and are introduced for the purpose of allowing him to criticize various Peripatetic doctrines. Thus, the chapter on sophistry in *The Philosophy of Illumination* is very important for understanding his criticisms of the Peripatetics but has little importance for logic.[2]

FIRST PHILOSOPHY: BEINGS OF REASON

It is convenient here to divide metaphysics according to the distinction used by some Islamic philosophers, including some in Suhrawardī's school, between first philosophy *(al-falsafa al-ūlā)* and theology *(al-'ilm al-ilāhī)*, the former dealing with being and related fundamental concepts and the latter dealing with God and the supersensible.[3] In *The Philosophy of Illumination* first philosophy is treated under sophistics, since it is not part of the distinctive Illuminationist doctrine but rather belongs to the critique of the Islamic Peripateticism.

Suhrawardī held that Avicenna had fallen prey to the fallacy of assuming that there must be real distinctions corresponding to mental distinctions—that he had reified beings of reason. Certain concepts, though essential to the functioning of our minds, do not correspond to any separate external reality. These are concepts such as existence, unity, necessity, and contingency. A concept such as horse comes about in the mind by the contemplation of horses. Concepts such as existence and contingency come about through our contemplation of our concepts of horses, cows, rocks, and so on. Horses exist, so one can talk about the existence of horses, and likewise the existence of cows and rocks. In our minds we can think of existence in general—abstracted from particular horses, cows, and rocks, but it does not follow that there is something that all existing horses, cows, rocks, and so on, share by which they are existent. Suhrawardī calls these conceptions *i'tibārāt 'aqlīya*. The term is not easy to translate. Such conceptions are more commonly called *ma'qūlāt thānīya*, "secondary intelligibles," indicating that they are abstracted from conceptions, not from external things. Suhrawardī's term indicates that they are posited by the mind. The term might thus be translated as "intellectual fictions,"[4] a term made on the analogy of 'legal fictions', to indicate that these are artificial but not arbitrary constructions. In the present work it will be translated as 'beings of reason',[5] rendering the medieval European term *entia rationis*, though the Latin term tends to apply specifically to logical concepts.

Suhrawardī uses this distinction to make various fundamental criticisms of Avicenna's metaphysical thought. Avicenna does his metaphysical reasoning on the basis of these concepts, but if Suhrawardī's criticism holds, such arguments reveal only the structure of the innate prejudices of the human mind, not the structure of external reality.

PHYSICS: THE CONSTITUENTS OF BODY

Peripatetic philosophy constructs the world from dualistic compounds: existence and essence, matter and form, substance and accident, genus and differentia. Each level of being is conceived as somehow compounded of substrate and structure. In each case the two components are never found in isolation but are only known through reasoning. It is a general characteristic of Suhrawardī's system to reject such compounds in favor of a unitary concrete entity, directly known. Thus, he condemns Aristotle's hylomorphism as incoherent. There is no such thing as prime matter, he insists, only magnitude. Body is simply magnitude with its accidents, nothing more.

The commentator Quṭb al-Dīn remarks that the science of lights treats of the First Principle, the (celestial) intellects, and souls. That which is based upon it includes most of physics, and some of metaphysics.[6] Nonetheless, although most of physics may be "based" on the science of lights, Suhrawardī has little interest in the minutiae of physical science. It is the first principles of physics, not its details, that are dealt with in the Illuminationist system.

KNOWLEDGE BY PRESENCE

Suhrawardī has rejected pure reason as a device for knowing the world, insisting that our most general concepts do not reveal the fundamental structure of being but only tell us how we ourselves think. He is saved from a descent into Kantian empiricism by his doctrine of knowledge by presence. He makes two general arguments in favor of his view. In the first and narrower argument, he points out that the characteristic of all forms of knowledge and perception is subjective experience of "I know"—not the transfer of a form of some sort. We cannot explain perception simply by some sort of intermediary mechanism; ultimately, there must be a knowing subject that perceives, knows, imagines, or dreams. Thus, a characteristic of all knowledge is that the knower must be in the unveiled presence of the known. The second, broader argument deals with the intermediary machinery of perception and knowledge. When we see a mountain, it is certainly the case that the mechanism of the eye, optical nerve, and brain are essential conditions for our seeing the mountain (though Suhrawardī is singularly uninterested in these details). However, what we see is not an image in the brain; it is the mountain itself. We see the mountain as larger than the brain cavity that is the physical seat of vision, for example. Thus, what we see cannot be an image in the brain; it must be the mountain itself. The functioning of the eye and brain are a condition for our perception, but they are not the perception.

He makes a similar argument about mysticial intuition. With proper preparation we can remove, at least temporarily, the veils that keep us from apprehending the supersensible entities like God and the celestial lights/intellects. Mystical intuition *(dhawq)* does not supercede reason but supplies it with knowledge of fact on which rational knowledge can be built. One who has beheld the Platonic Forms mystically cannot doubt their existence. The comprehension of this experience, however, is a matter for rational thought.

For Suhrawardī knowledge by presence is what enables us to have real knowledge of the external world, both sensible and supersensible. Having rejected Avicenna's reliance on self-evident concepts as the basis of our true knowledge, he thinks that only direct intuition of the world can provide a sure basis for philosophical and scientific knowledge.

METAPHYSICS AND RATIONAL THEOLOGY

Suhrawardī is best known for the metaphysics of light and darkness expounded in *The Philosophy of Illumination.* Light is not identical with existence since both light and darkness exist, nor is it substance, since there are also dark substance and accidental light. Suhrawardī makes three fundamental distinctions in order to derive the basic classes of beings: light and darkness, substance and state, and independent and dependent. The first two distinctions define the kinds of beings in the universe:

	Light	*Darkness*
Substance	Immaterial, substantial light: immaterial intellects (angels), human and animal souls	Dusky substances: bodies
State	Luminous accidents: luminous accidents in immaterial lights, physical lights, rays	Dark accidents, whether in immaterial lights or in bodies

The third distinction relates to the chain of causation. In its purest sense only God, the Light of Lights, is independent and all other existing entitities are dependent. Immaterial light is nearly identical with intellect in the Peripatetic tradition but differs from it in admitting of differences in intensity. Immaterial light differs from physical light in that it does not require a physical body and is sentient. For Suhrawardī light is not a stream of energy moving from a luminous body in all directions. Rather, light is the ability to make something else manifest. Thus, anything in the presence of a light becomes manifest, but nothing moves from the light to the illumined thing. A ray, therefore, is the luminous accident in the thing illumined, not a line of energy moving from the light to the thing illuminated.

Suhrawardī has general principles that he uses to deduce his metaphysics. The most important is a form of the principle of sufficient reason, "the principle of the most noble contingency" *(qā'idat al-imkān al-ashraf)*, which asserts that nothing can exist without a cause of higher ontological level, and if two aspects exist in something, there must be two aspects in its cause to explain it. This is a straightforward application of the principle, "Ex nihilo nihil fit." A second principle, which limits the first and ultimately comes from Aristotle, is the impossibility of an ordered, actual infinity: there can be no countable infinity existent simultaneously. Thus, real numbers can be infinite because they are potential, and a chain of physical causes can be infinite, because they are not existent simultaneously. Combined, these principles show that there cannot be an infinite number of levels of being and that there must be one being whose essence is necessary in itself—Avicenna's 'Necessary of Existence' *(wājib al-wujūd).*

Suhrawardī's light cosmology is a straightforward application of these categories and principles. There must be a first cause, necessary by its own essence, itself uncaused, utterly simple, whose power is unending and potentially infinite. This is the Light of Lights, which we can identify with Aristotle's Unmoved Mover, Avicenna's Necessary of Existence, and the monotheistic God. A second light is generated from the Light of Lights, and a third from the second. Because it is utterly simple the Light of Lights as such can generate only one thing, but already in the second light there are two aspects: its luminosity based on its relation to its Creator and a dark accident reflecting the distinction of the second light from the Light of Lights. This dark accident means that it is conceivable for two distinct beings to be generated from the second light, one of which might be a body. As the chain of generation continues downward, the lights become weaker and more complex: weaker because of the greater distance from the Light of Lights and more complex because the lower lights are a product of the higher lights. The line of lights generated solely with respect to the luminosity of the light above form the chain of ten (or more) lights corresponding to Avicenna's ten planetary intellects. These differ only in luminosity. There are also other lights of equal intensity that differ with respect to accidents based on their various relations with the higher lights. These lights serve two purposes in Suhrawardī's system. First, they are the cause of the complexity of the lower world. Second, they are the Platonic Forms that are the cause of the stable natural kinds in the lower world. Suhrawardī refers to them as the horizontal order of lights, since they can differ in kind without differing in intensity or rank.

There is likewise a hierarchy of celestial bodies and souls caused by the dark aspects of the celestial lights. Their motions are complex because they are attempting to express serially the intricate relations among the celestial lights. (The incomprehensible order of the fixed stars is another expression of this complexity.) The movements of the spheres are the cause of generation and corruption in the sublunar world. Thus, the formal cause of sublunar beings is the Platonic Forms/horizontal order of lights, and their efficient cause the movements of the spheres.

Many features of Suhrawardī's philosophical theology are parallel to or identical with doctrines of Avicenna: the simplicity of God, for example. The most conspicuous difference is the presence of the Platonic Forms.

THE MYSTICAL: IMAGINAL WORLD, AFTERLIFE, CYCLES, REINCARNATION

There remain several topics that might be grouped under the heading *al-Ma'ād*, "the Return," having to do with the reconciliation with philosophy of religious notions about the fate of the soul. The central theme is the World of Image *('ālam al-mithāl)*. It is not clear to me where exactly this concept arises, nor do I know of a case in which Suhrawardī uses exactly this term, but the concept is clearly present in his writings and is identified as one of the characteristic doctrines of the Ancients. The World of Image is an intermediary world between the physical world and the immaterial world of mind. It is the plane of being in which images are found not embedded in matter. It is the plane of ghosts, of the forms in mirrors, dreams, and worlds of wonder beyond our own. It is obviously useful as a way of accommodating the miraculous and the eschatological, as well as odds and ends not conveniently fitting into the Aristotelian scheme of forms-in-matter. Suhrawardī does not systematically develop the concept, but his followers did. (It has nothing to do with the Platonic Forms, which are entirely different in function and ontological level.)

Related to this are the questions of afterlife and reincarnation. Plato had written myths of reincarnation, thus establishing the concept firmly in the philosophical tradition. Suhrawardī suggests a theory in which the souls of the imperfect are reincarnated in the bodies of animals corresponding to their ethical flaws and are thereby purified. The problems, both philosophical and political, with such a theory are obvious, and he offers it as a suggestion, not a demonstrated fact. It might, he says, occur in the World of Image, not in our world, or in both.

His position on universal cycles—the Great Year—is implicit but clear. There cannot be an infinity of distinct events in history. Temporal events are caused by the motions of the spheres, and those motions in turn are caused by the exceedingly complex interrelations among the celestial lights. Since these interrelations, though very numerous, are necessarily finite in number, eventually the spheres must return to their original positions and begin again. When that happens, all events great and small in our world will be repeated exactly. The same individual will not return, though an exact duplicate of that individual will come into being. This is also the explanation of providence. Things cannot be other than they are since the existing universe reflects the rational order existing among the celestial lights.

CHAPTER 4

Suhrawardī on the History of the Ancient Philosophy

THE "ISHRĀQĪ" SCHOOL

The question of what is to be understood by the term *Ishrāqī*, "Illuminationist," as used by Suhrawardī has led to much confusion and disagreement. On the simplest level 'Illuminationist' is the name that Suhrawardī gave to his own philosophical school, particularly in his best-known work, *The Philosophy of Illumination*. In a discussion of the attributes of God in the largest of his "Peripatetic" works, the *Paths and Havens*, Suhrawardī writes:

> This is the most that can be determined using the methods of the Peripatetics. The real heart of the matter is contained in the symbols of our book *The Philosophy of Illumination*, but we do not discuss it except with our Illuminationist companions.[1]

Thus, 'Ishrāqī' was the name born by a series of philosophers of Iran or the Iranian world from the twelfth to the twentieth century. Their systems were characterized by a number of views advocated by Suhrawardī, notably the doctrine of the primacy of quiddity. In this sense 'Ishrāqī' applies to the philosophers primarily influenced by Suhrawardī—just as 'Peripatetic' applies to those primarily under the influence of Aristotle. Closely related to this usage is his practice of referring to his significant non-Peripatetic doctrines as 'Illuminationist principles'.[2]

The difficulty is that this is not the only sense in which Suhrawardī himself uses the term. The distinction he claims is not that he has devised a new philosophical system but that he has revived an extremely ancient one. Now, in addition to naming his "Illuminationist" philosophy, Suhrawardī has identified its distinctive features: the use of certain non-Peripatetic elements, the use of intuition as a philosophical tool, and the use of symbolic forms of expression. These are also traits of the "intuitive" philosophy of the "Ancients"—that is, philosophers like Empedocles, Pythagoras, Socrates, and Plato. The commentator Shahrazūrī explains:

> Very few of the philosophers attain this intuitive philosophy, for it is acquired only by some virtuous individual divine philosophers. Among them were the Ancients who came in the time before Aristotle—Agathadaemon, Hermes, Empedocles, Pythagoras, Socrates, Plato, and other learned Ancients whose learning and precedence are attested by the different nations.[3]

Suhrawardī himself explains the characteristics of the philosophy of the Ancients:

> In all that I have said about the science of lights and that which is and is not based upon it, I have been assisted by those who have traveled the path of God. This science is the very intuition of the inspired and illumined Plato, the guide and master of philosophy, and of those who came before him from the time of Hermes, "the father of philosophers," up to Plato's time, including such mighty pillars of philosophy as Empedocles, Pythagoras, and others. The words of the Ancients are symbolic and not open to refutation.[4]

Thus, although Suhrawardī does not say so explicitly in *The Philosophy of Illumination*, his interpreters understood him to be saying that the Ancients were Illuminationists and that his Illuminationist philosophy was their intuitive wisdom. Since in *The Philosophy of Illumination*, *ishrāq*, "illumination," is a technical term for mysical intuition, it is quite appropriate to interpret *ishrāqī* as a synonym for *dhawqī*, "intuitive."

Later Islamic philosophers attempted to reconcile Suhrawardī's references to the Illuminationists with other information on the ancient philosophers, sometimes identifying them as "Stoics" or as one of the schools arising among Plato's students.[5] At any rate, late Islamic philosophers usually understood that the ancient Illuminationists were the Greek Pythagoreans and Platonists, or some group of them.

There is a second interpretation of the term 'Illuminationist' that associates it more specifically with Iran. In *The Words of Sufism* Suhrawardī comments that *The Philosophy of Illumination* revives the luminous wisdom of the ancient Persian sages.[6] It was well known that the ancient Persians venerated light and divided the universe between light and darkness, and *The Philosophy of Illumination* used a number of Persian terms and concepts. It was thus natural to speculate that *ishrāqī* meant "eastern." The commentator Quṭb al-Dīn writes:

> Philosophy of illumination, i.e., the philosophy based on illumination, which is visionary experience *(kashf)*; or the philosophy of the Easterners, i.e., the Persians. This amounts to the same thing since their philosophy is based on revelation and intuition. It is thus limited to the revelation of the lights of the intellects, their rays, and the outpouring upon the soul during its abstraction from the body. In philosophy, the Persians

> relied on intuition and revelation, as did the ancient Greeks with the exception of Aristotle and his school, who relied only on study and demonstration.[7]

Conversely, one major commentary and most later manuscripts read *ishrāq* for *sharq*, "east," in a passage discussing the Persians.[8] This interpretation has been particularly important in the history of the interpretation of Suhrawardī. Thus the foremost modern intepreter of Suhrawardī, Henry Corbin, refers to the Ishrāqīs as "the Platonists of Persia" and portrays Suhrawardī as the reviver of the wisdom of pre-Islamic Persia. This interpretation may be traced back to Shahrazūrī, the first commentator on *The Philosophy of Illumination* and was further popularized by Zoroastrian Illuminationists in Moghul India.

To a considerable extent, this is all a matter of emphasis, since no one denies that both Greek and Iranian themes play a role in Suhrawardī's thought. The question of what exactly is meant by *ishrāqī* must eventually be answered by a closer examination of Suhrawardī's statements about his intellectual affiliation and of the doctrines that he himself identifies as "Illuminationist."

Suhrawardī, "the master of illumination" as his followers call him, is conscious of his place in the history of philosophy, in the way that Aristotle and Hegel are and Avicenna is not. The history of philosophy is thus part of the intellectual background required to understand him. He also had unusual respect for the views of certain earlier philosophers. Thus, to understand why he held certain views it is relevant to understand what information about past philosophers might have been available to him and how he might have understood it. Suhrawardī was certainly not a slavish follower of the Ancients, for he was a philosopher, not a sectarian nor an antiquarian. However, the views of philosophers like Plato, Hermes, and Pythagoras carried great authority with him since he believed that they too had based their philosophy in part on mystical experience.

Suhrawardī himself did not systematically write on the history of philosophy, although there are many allusions to various ancient philosophers and their views scattered through his books. These allusions are sufficient to tell us where to look but do not tell us what we must know. It is from the expansions in the commentaries and from such works as Shahrazūrī's *Delight* that the full story can be reconstructed.

THE PHILOSOPHICAL GENEALOGY

There is a pronounced tendency in the Islamic world to see the transmission of knowledge genealogically, as a matter not of books but of oral transmission from teacher to student. The model for this way of thinking about learning is the hadith literature, in which stories of the Prophet are transmitted orally, and the authority of the stories is judged on the basis of the probity of the transmitters. The genealogical model of knowledge was easily transferred to mysticism, where it was the mystical practices and training that were transmitted from master to student. It was not so natural a way of thinking about philosophy and the rational sciences where knowledge is accessible to the clever mind and the teacher is not—in principle, at least—necessary. Suhrawardī falls somewhere in the middle. He was a Sufi of sorts, and so for him mystical attainment generally required the guidance of a spiritual master. Intuitive philosophy, in contrast to speculative philosophy, was partly revelation, and the ancient sages expressed its truths symbolically, so that the significance of their symbols could be passed on from master to student. For the most part, however, the ancient masters of the Illuminationist philosophy were exemplars, encouraging the seeker by showing him that others had preceded him on the Path. In the history of intuitive philosophy there had been several traditions, varying somewhat in their methods and symbols, but they converged in Suhrawardī himself.

Suhrawardī gives several versions of his philosophical genealogy. The names he mentions fall into six families:

1. Egyptian: Hermes, Agathadaemon, Asclepius
2. Greek: Empedocles, Pythagoras, Socrates, Plato, Aristotle
3. Persian or Pahlavi: Kayomarth, Jāmāsaf, Farshāwastar, Buzurjmihr, Zoroaster, Kaykhursaw, and others
4. Orientals: Indians, including Buddha and the Chinese
5. Islamic Pythagoreans: Dhu'l-Nūn al-Miṣrī, Sahl al-Tustarī
6. Khusrawānī: Abū Yazīd Basṭāmī, Ḥallāj, al-Kharaqānī

Thus his view of his intellectual ancestry would seem to be as in figure 4.1. Several points must be noted and will be explored later in detail.

1. Suhrawardī identified himself with the Pythagorean line in Greek philosophy, at least if we place Socrates and Plato in that line.
2. The Ionian physicists are ignored, as are all Greek philosophers after Aristotle.
3. The Persians are not the historical Zoroastrian priests but the mythical kings and viziers, understood as sages.
4. The Sufis mentioned are divided into separate traditions and do not include many of the best-known figures who usually appear in Sufi spiritual genealogies.

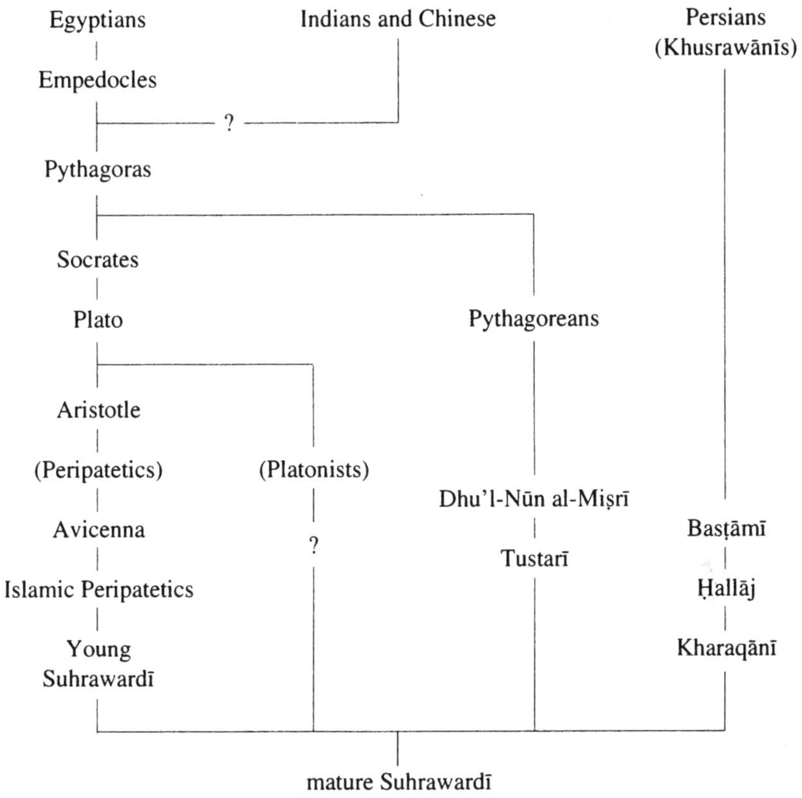

FIGURE 4.1
Suhrawardī's Philosophical Genealogy

5. There are no Christians.
6. This is no Islamic (except Sufi) side to the intellectual genealogy—that is, no connection to Muḥammad, 'Alī, al-Ḥasan al-Baṣrī, or some other major, distinctively Islamic, figure.
7. The connections to the Persians and Orientals are much vaguer than those to the Greeks.

THE GREEK LINE IN SUHRAWARDĪ'S PHILOSOPHICAL ISNĀD

Diogenes Laertius's *Lives and Opinions of Eminent Philosophers* is the one general history of philosophy—or, more properly, of philosophers—to come down to us from ancient times. Diogenes classifies the philosophers in various ways: as dogmatists and sceptics (δογματικοί, ἐφεκτικοί), by whether they left writings and or not, by the sources of the names of their schools, by their schools in particular disciplines such as ethics, and so on. The organizing principle of his own work is genealogical: successions of masters and students. He first mentions, and dismisses, the claims to philosophy of the barbarian sages (1.1–11) and asserts the primacy of the Greeks in philosophy, whose "very name refuses to be translated into foreign speech" (1.4). He begins his history with "the men who were commonly regarded as sages (σοφοί δε ἐνομίζοντο)"—Thales, Solon, Pherecydes, and others. Apparently they occupied an intermediate position between nonphilosophical wisdom and philosophy proper (1.13, 23–122). He divides the philosophical tradition into two lines, each beginning with a philosopher taught by one of the sages. The Ionian school began with Anaximander, the pupil of Thales, passed through Socrates and Plato, and included the Academy, the Peripatetics, the Cynics, and the Stoics. The Italian school began with Pythagoras, the student of Pherecydes, and included Empedocles, Parmenides, Zeno of Elea, Heracleitus, Democritus, Protagoras, Pyrrho, and Epicurus, among others (1.13–15). A certain artificiality attends these proceedings, but such classifications seem to have been popular in later classical times.

Several factors kept Islamic philosophers and historians from acquiring a clear picture of the history of philosophy in the classical world. First, since the Arabs were interested in the science and philosophy of the Greeks, not their history, no comprehensive history of philosophy or philosophers was translated into Arabic,[9] nor was there a general history of the Greeks and Romans within which the philosophers might be placed or even a common era to date the various figures. Second, while a good deal of Greek philosophical literature was translated into Arabic, almost all of it soon passed out of common circulation, to be replaced by Islamic syntheses of the same material. Thus, Avicenna's works, written in a much more accessible style, supplanted the Arabic translations of Aristotle. Third, the practical problems of interpreting the translated texts with their strange and often corrupt names posed a serious obstacle to correctly understanding the history of Greek philosophy. While the names of Plato and Aristotle were almost always recognizable, the names of lesser figures were soon scrambled beyond recognition. Other confusions occurred, such as conflating the two Zenoes. Fourth, misattributions and pseudepigrapha abounded, including works like *The Theology of Aristotle*, actually excerpts from the *Enneads* of Plotinus. There were also pseudo-Empedoclean and Neopythagorean texts, occult Hermetica, and other such works, originating on both sides of the line of translation, often attributed to famous philosophers. Finally, there was the historical accident that no scholar in the early period, when accurate information, extensive texts, and Greek-speaking Syriac scholars were available, produced a full history of Greek philosophy in Arabic—a work analogous to Bīrūnī's works on India and calendars or Ibn al-Nadīm's catalog of early Arabic literature—that might have served as a reliable guide to later scholars.

As a result, Islamic scholars of philosophy had to depend on fragmentary information. This information tended to be atomistic—set pieces transmitted whole whose interrelationships were not very clear. First, there were biographies of physicians and sages, usually accompanied by collections of wise sayings. Second, there were nuggets of information transmitted in particular contexts: the report that a Greek philosopher had held a certain view on a topic. An important example was the report that Plato had held that there were more than ten intellects and that these were known as 'Platonic Forms'. Finally, there were various accounts, not all compatible, placing the individual Greek philosophers in some larger context—successions of philosophers of the sort found in Diogenes Laertius—copied from source to source. One common example is a text going back to a work of Ḥuanyn b. Isḥāq, in which he explains that there were seven schools of Greek philosophy, each of which received its name in a different way—the Stoics, for example, being named for the place in which instruction was given, and the Peripatetics for what the teacher and students were doing while the instruction was given.[10] Another is a text taken from the *De Placitis* 1.3 of Pseudo-Plutarch discussing the views of the Greek philosophers on the first principles of being. At another extreme are the accounts of Hermes and the city of wisdom in Iraq and their role in the origin of philosophy in the various nations.

Suhrawardī's account of Greek philosophy was mostly likely based on a text portraying a succession of philosophers: the legendary Arabian sage Luqmān, Empedocles (who was a student of Luqmān and/or David), Pythagoras (who was a student of Empedocles and Solomon or Solomon's students in Egypt), Socrates (a student of Pythagoras), and Plato. This account appears for the first time, so far as I know, in *Kitāb al-Amad 'alā 'l-Abad* (The Book of Hope for Eternity) by Abu 'l-Ḥasan al-'Āmirī (d. 992). 'Āmirī was young when Fārābī was old, old when Avicenna was young, and overshadowed by both. He was a student of Abū Zayd al-Balkhī, a student of Kindī. A native of Khorasan, he visited Rayy and Baghdad, where he was snubbed by the local philosophers. He was interested in reconciling Islam and philosophy, a project to which the work being cited was a contribution. He died in 381/992. A number of his works survive.[11] This work, as its title suggests, is a philosophical account of the soul and its survival after death, evidently based on some commentary on the *Phaedo*. The passage we are interested in begins:

The first to whom wisdom [*ḥikma*, which could also be rendered 'philosophy'] was attributed was Luqmān the sage, as God says, "We gave Luqmān wisdom."[12] He was in the time of David, and the homeland of both was the land of Syria.

According to what is related, Empedocles the Greek had associated with him and learned from his wisdom. However, when he returned to the land of Greece, he spoke about the nature of the world according to his own wishes, in such a way that if literally understood, his view of the afterlife is unacceptable. The Greeks attributed wisdom to him due to his association with Luqmān the Sage. A sect of the Bāṭinīya adhere to his wisdom and honor him. They claim that his symbols are rarely unravelled.

Another to whom they [the Greeks] attribute wisdom is Pythagoras. He had associated in Egypt with the disciples of Solomon, son of David, when they had gone there from the land of Syria. Previously he had learned geometry from the Egyptians, and so he then also learned natural and divine sciences from the disciples of Solomon. He brought those three sciences—geometry, physics, and theology—back to Greece. By his own intelligence he deduced the science of melodies, reducing them to ratios and numbers. He claimed to have acquired these sciences from the niche of prophecy.[13]

He continues, mentioning Socrates, Plato, and Aristotle as each being "one of those to whom they attribute wisdom." Socrates is said to have confined himself to the divine objects of knowledge. He was killed for having offended the polytheists. Plato was influenced by both Socrates and Pythagoras and wrote using symbols. The importance of mathematics is shown by the story in which Plato delivers Athens from a plague by knowing how to double the size of the Delian altar. Aristotle, the last of the five, is described as Plato's brilliant student, the founder of logic, and the teacher of Alexander the Great.

These are the five to whom they attributed wisdom. No one other than them received the title 'sage'; rather each was associated with a single art or way of life. For example, there is Hippocrates 'the Physician', Homer 'the Poet', Archimedes 'the Geometer', Diogenes 'the Cynic', and Democritus 'the Physicist'. When Galen in his time had written many books, he sought to take the title 'Sage' in place of the title 'Physician', but the people made fun of him.[14]

Something very similar occurs in Nicomachus of Gerasa's *Introduction to Arithmetic:*

The earliest of the Ancients, those who followed the path of the knowledge of certain truth, began in the time of Pythagoras to define philosophy as the quest for wisdom, as is indicated by the meaning of the word

> 'philosophy' in the Greek language. As for the philosophers prior to Pythagoras, the people would use the term 'wisdom' to refer indiscriminately to a variety of things. For example, carpenters, shoemakers, and butchers were called 'wise' in their crafts, in general applying the word to whomever was skilled, adept, and experienced in one of the crafts or arts. Pythagoras restricted this name to designate only knowledge with certitude of an existent thing in accordance with its true existence, confining the name 'wisdom' to knowledge of the reality of all the aspects of this existent thing. Thus, it is necessary to use 'philosophy' to refer only to the desire for, choice of, and striving after this knowledge. Therefore, philosophy is the love of wisdom.[15]

It is possible that this text is part of the reason philosophy came to be known as 'wisdom', *ḥikma*, in Islam.

'Āmirī's account of the chief Greek philosophers is quoted by almost all the Islamic writers on the history of philosophy, included Shahrazūrī. Its origin is obviously heterogeneous. These five philosophers are linked in the Greek tradition, and the phrase "those to whom they attributed wisdom" must have some connection with the σοφοί δὲ ἐνομίζοντο of Diogenes Laertius 1.4. The concern with grounding the origins of philosophy in Judaism is Jewish and Christian.[16] Its present form, with Luqmān at the head of the list and two references to the Qur'ān, is clearly Islamic.

For Suhrawardī these five represent the tradition of 'divine philosophy'. He cites virtually no other Greek philosophers. His only modification to this list is to cite Hermes in place of Luqmān. Since Suhrawardī himself does not quote this account, we cannot know for certain that it is the source of his views on the history of Greek philosophy. In fact, his knowledge of Greek philosophy was considerably more detailed and sophisticated than 'Āmirī's account. Nonetheless, this text does represent his general view of the history of Greek philosophy, and it makes a convenient outline and starting point for discussing Suhrawardī's use of the major Greek philosophers.

PART 2

The Divine Philosophers

The great sages of the time when wisdom was rhetorical—like the father of sages, the father of fathers, Hermes, Agathadaemon before him, and like Pythagoras and Empedocles and that great sage Plato—all were greater in worth than the Islamic ones.

—Suhrawardī, *al-Talwīḥāt*

It is necessary for the student in his studies and the sage in his teaching to know the lives of the ancient sages and divine philosophers, both Greeks and Egyptians. Student and sage must understand their words of wisdom, their ethical counsels, and the examples they set by their virtuous and praiseworthy ways of life. He who would seek eternal happiness must know all this that he may be guided by them and imitate their words and deeds.

—Shahrazūrī, *Delight of Spirits*

Then the wisdom of Hermes circulated on the tongues of his pupils until it reached these mighty pillars, who are the people of Greece, for the pillar is that by which the building stands and the roof is supported.

—Shahrazūrī, *Commentary on* The Philosophy of Illumination

CHAPTER 5

Empedocles: The Philosopher as Mystic and Magus

According to 'Āmirī, the first of the Greeks to whom the Greeks attributed wisdom—philosophy—was Empedocles. Empedocles, he further explained, was the first to correctly understand the problem of the attributes of God.

The modern philosopher is a professional pedant, paid to instruct the young in philosophical doctrines and to write books and articles. He is a professor of philosophy, not so very different from a professor of biology or of marketing. He need not reshape his inner being to the model of the doctrines he discusses in his classes. If pressed, he will perhaps claim that he is useful because he teaches the young to think more clearly and, less plausibly, that he forces his fellow professors in other departments to clarify their concepts. The proud cities of metaphysics were long ago abandoned as indefensible and have fallen into ruin. The philosophers have for the most part retreated to the safer territory of language and logic, creating for themselves a sort of analytical Formosa.

Such an approach to the practice of philosophy is not new—Socrates knew them as Sophists, and Suhrawardī condemned the Avicennan Peripatetics as their representatives in his age—but it was not the usual ideal of ancient philosophers, nor of all medieval philosophers. Philosophy was a special life, a life of wisdom, holiness, and perhaps supernatural powers. Socrates is the most familiar example of the type: called to a life of questioning by the oracle at Delphi, pestering the complacent in his search for wisdom, protected by his private spirit (δαίμων) from wrong actions. He was the model for ethically oriented philosophers throughout antiquity, particularly for groups like the Cynics and Stoics.

Socrates claimed only that his δαίμων warned him when he was about to do wrong, but other philosophers sought greater supernatural powers. Sages like Pythagoras and Empedocles were philosophers and shamans, mystics and magicians. Plotinus might spurn magic, but he did not question its efficacy, and mystical knowledge is at the core of his thought. His successors delved into the occult, creating the art known as theurgy and interesting themselves in astrology, divination, and alchemy.[1] Parallel to them were gnostic sects like the Hermetists, in which philosophical ideas were taught as revelation and mixed freely with occult arts and exotic and ancient oriental wisdom. The literature and thought of both philosophical and gnostic occultists passed into the Arabic-speaking world through much the same channels as the more austere sciences of Aristotle, Ptolemy, and Galen.

Suhrawardī could draw on other traditions linking wisdom and supernatural powers. The Persians, by now largely Islamized, still remembered the supernatural light of divine glory, the *xvarenah* that descended on the man chosen by God for kingship. If the king practiced wisdom and justice, this light remained with him, and through its influence the kingdom prospered. When the king deviated from justice, this light would desert him, catastrophes would befall the kingdom, and his throne would be lost. The Sufis, the mystics of Islam, also linked supernatural powers with holiness and wisdom. Among them, unrecognized by the generality of men, were the saints who were the true rulers of the world and whose protection kept it from ruin.

Suhrawardī partook of all these traditions, claiming as his predecessors the line of philosopher-mystics of Greece, the divinely aided kings and sages of Iran, and the ecstatic Sufis of Islam. It is the principal thesis of this book that Suhrawardī is to be understood first and foremost as a philosopher and that his thought must be understood primarily from a philosophical point of view. But he was not a philosopher like modern philosophers, and Empedocles makes a convenient starting-point for our discussion of those aspects of his life and thought that are not like our notion of the philosopher. Empedocles, more than any of the other Greeks whom Suhrawardī venerated, embodied the unification of philosophy, mysticism, and magic that is characteristic of Illuminationism. For Suhrawardī true philosophy must begin with mystical exercises and end in mystical intuition and occult powers. Also, there are certain points of contact between the doctrines of Empedocles, real and pseudepigraphic, and those of Suhrawardī.

THE EMPEDOCLES OF HISTORY

The Greeks no longer seem so rational to us as once they did; Freud, anthropology, and the madnesses of our own age have taught us to recognize and respect the irrational when we encounter it. Modern scholarship has also taught us that the Presocratics cannot be understood if seen only through Aristotle's eyes—as rational thinkers attempting, more or less unsuccessfully, to become Aristotles. The works of the Presocratics, Empedocles included, survive only in quotations in later authors, of whom Aristotle is usually the earliest. Since Aristotle had direct knowledge of their works and discusses them at length, modern students of the Presocratics, despite some misgivings, long assumed that Aristotle was the rock on which they could build their church. Unfortunately, it has now become painfully clear that Aristotle was quite willing to misrepresent the views and purposes of the Presocratics to make his own philosophical points. A prime example is his "history" of the development of the theory of the four causes in *Metaphysics* A.[2] Empedocles was particularly ill-suited to be understood by Aristotle, as witness the opening lines of one of his two poems, *The Purifications:*

> O friends, who dwell in the great city of the yellow Acragas,
> up in the high parts of the city, concerned with good deeds,
> <respectful harbours for strangers, untried by evil,>
> hail! I, in your eyes a deathless god, no longer mortal,
> go among all, honoured, just as I seem:
> wreathed with ribbons and festive garlands.
> As soon as I arrive in flourishing cities I am revered
> by all, men and women. And they follow at once,
> in their ten thousands, asking where is the path to gain,
> some in need of divinations, others in all sorts of diseases
> sought to hear a healing oracle.[3]

There is no doubt that Empedocles was considered a philosopher by the Greeks, but he was certainly not a philosopher of the sort usually found in modern philosophy departments, in Aristotle's Lyceum, or even in Plato's Academy.

Empedocles was a Sicilian, a native of Acragas, the modern Agrigento. He lived, modern scholars deduce, from about 492 to 432 B.C.E., making him a generation older than Socrates. He belonged to a wealthy family that had played a conspicuous role in the restoration of democracy in the city. His democratic politics seem to have led to his exile. He visited Thurii, the panhellenic colony founded on the site of old Sybaris, a town close to the centers of Pythagoreanism and Orphism in southern Italy. He had a practical side as well. The verses just quoted indicate his medical interests, which are amply attested from other sources. When the city of Selinus suffered an epidemic due to polluted water, Empedocles diverted two other rivers to clear out the poisoned waters. He is said to have brought winds that were damaging crops under control, though whether this was done by catching the wind in bags, as Aeolus had done in the *Odyssey*, or whether he had simply erected a windbreak of some sort depends on the credulity of the scholar and the source. Other achievements claimed for him are frankly magical: divination, keeping a woman alive without breath or pulse for thirty days, and reviving the dead.[4] His death is variously reported as occurring by natural causes while in exile in the Peloponnese or by suicide performed by leaping into Mount Etna, leaving behind as evidence a single bronze slipper. Modern scholars, not surprisingly, have favored a natural death, but a vigorous defense of the plausibility—or at least the meaningfulness—of the leap into Etna is given by Peter Kingsley.[5]

Empedocles recorded his system in two poems, *On Nature* and *The Purifications*. Both are lost except for fragments, and they have been reconstructed in various ways, usually on the assumption that the former dealt with scientific and the latter with religious subjects.[6] Their interpretation is not easy either, so our understanding of Empedocles' views as a whole rests on the three very wobbly legs of imperfectly understood fragments of poetry, Aristotle's summaries, and the literal-minded reports of doxographers, often on such peripheral matters as the sterility of mules. The details of Empedocles' system—which are not easily determined anyway—will not detain us. Except for the doctrines of love and strife and of the fall of the soul and reincarnation, they have almost nothing directly to do with Suhrawardī's thought. What is relevant here is Empedocles as the type of a certain kind of philosopher.

It is primarily the "religious" side of Empedocles that explains why Suhrawardī and his school should have found him such an appealing figure. Whatever he may have had to say about scientific topics, his real interest was the quest for divinity and potent knowledge. We have already heard him claim godhood. To his disciple he promises:

> All the potions which there are as a defence against evils and old age,
> you shall learn, since for you alone will I accomplish all these things.
> You shall put a stop to the strength of tireless winds,
> which rush against the land and wither the fields with their blasts;
> and again, if you wish, you shall bring the winds back again;
> and you shall make, after dark rain, a drought timely
> for men, and after summer drought you shall make
> tree-nourishing streams which dwell in the air;
> and you shall bring from Hades the strength of a man who has died.[7]

In this fragment Empedocles claims the power to heal, to defeat old age, to control the wind and the rains, and to raise the dead. Despite the rationalizing explanations found even in the ancient sources (the windbreaks, for example), these are the powers of a shaman and a magus, not a philosopher in the modern, or even the Athenian, sense. This knowledge is obtained, at least in part, by mystical contemplation

For if, thrusting them deep down in your crowded thinking organs,
you gaze on them in kindly fashion, with pure meditations,
absolutely all these things will be with you throughout your life,
and from these you will acquire many others; for these things themselves
will expand to form each character, according to the growth [lit., nature]
of each.
But if *you* reach out for different things, such as
the ten thousand wretched things which are among men and blunt
their meditations,
truly they will abandon you quickly, as time circles round,
desiring to arrive at their own dear kind [lit., birth or generation]
For know that all have thought and a share of understanding.[8]

Because thought and explanation have a place in his system beside magic and mysticism, the ancients always considered Empedocles a philosopher, as did, in spite of all temptations, the rationalizing classicists of the nineteenth and twentieth centuries. Empedocles the mystic and magician has proven easier to ignore or dismiss.

Yet Aristotle and the historians cannot be excused on the grounds that Empedocles belonged to another time and place, the Sicily of the early fifth century,[9] for Empedocles' blend of philosophy, mysticism, magic, and poetry never became entirely obsolete in the Greek world or its successor civilizations. The Platonists, with their claim to belong to the traditions of the Orphics and Pythagoreans, understood this perfectly well. The irrational was intertwined with philosophy in the classical world. This fact is obscured for us because our best source for the views of the Presocratics, Aristotle, is of all the ancient philosophers the one least sympathetic by temperament to this kind of esotericsm. The history of Greek philosophy is usually pictured as a process of increasing rationalization as the mythical elements are purged and replaced by rational explanation with the process culminating in Aristotle—as Aristotle himself tells us. We are told that all the trends that had been developing earlier came together in Plato and Aristotle and then diverged to form the schools of the Hellenistic and Roman periods—a schematization enshrined in the organization of almost every modern history of ancient philosophy. But such is not really the case, nor was it thought to be so by the ancients. The Platonists always gave recognition to Orpheus, Pythagoras, and Empedocles that they would not concede to Aristotle, recognizing their claims to mystical knowledge and powers. The occult heritage of Empedocles lived on among the Neoplatonists until the end of antiquity and long after, even unto our own time.

It was not only through Plato and antiquarian Neoplatonists that the Empedoclean intellectual and spiritual heritage survived. There is reason to believe that it was brought to Egypt and thus to the realms of Egyptian magic and gnosticism by paths independent of Athens and its rationalizing philosophers. Connections between Sicily and southern Italy on the one hand and Alexandria on the other were always close, and known historical links can be matched to parallels between the magical traditions of Egypt and Sicily.[10] And Egypt, we should remember, was the home of the magician Hermes Trismegistus and the alchemist Sufi Dhu'l-Nūn al-Miṣrī, who also figure in Suhrawardī's intellectual *isnād*.

SHAHRAZŪRĪ'S ACCOUNT OF EMPEDOCLES

The biographical accounts of Empedocles in Islamic literature are remarkably stereotyped and nowhere near as detailed as those of Pythagoras, Socrates, Plato, and Aristotle, the other Greek philosophers normally ranked with him. Almost all the biographical sources go back to 'Āmirī's account of the five "properly called wise" in his *Book of Hope for Eternity*.[11] Shahrazūrī's version is a typical expansion of 'Āmirī.

> The great and lordly sage Empedocles, son of Bādar, of Agrigentum, was one of the greatest of the company of sages. . . . When he had learned wisdom from David and Luqmān in Syria, he returned to Greece and spoke of wisdom [in specific, the unity of the Creator's attributes with His essence].[12] . . . He lived in the time of David and learned wisdom from Luqmān in Syria—or, it is also said, from Solomon. Then he traveled to the lands of the Greeks and spoke of the creation of the world from something. Some of them exiled him. A group of the Bāṭinīya depend on his wisdom and claim that his symbols are understood by few. Muḥammad b. 'Abd-Allāh b. Masarra al-Jabalī al-Bāṭinī of Cordoba was devoted to the study of his philosophy.
>
> In general, he was of high station, great worth, devoted to mystical exercise, divinity *(ta'alluh)*, indifferent to comfort, detached from the world, and attentive to the afterlife. He was particularly master of knowledge of the soul and the incorporeal entities and their states and combinations. I have seen a book of his on philosophy showing his mystical intuition *(dhawq, kashf)*, his strength on the mystic path, and his excellence in theology and its wisdom. [Aḥmed's edition reads here, "His wisdom is prophecy mixed with philosophy."]
>
> He was the first to combine the attributes of God and show that they

> all applied to one entity and that there were no distinct meanings corresponding to these things, there being no multiplicity unlike the case for other existent things. He held that the exalted unities *(waḥdānīyāt)* could not have multiplicity either by parts, by meanings, or by similars *(naẓā'ir)* and that the creator was above all these. 'Alī b. Abī Ṭālib, al-Ḥasan al-Baṣrī, some of the Mu'tazila, and all the philosophers held this view.[13]

Several points are worthy of note. First, 'Āmirī's account has the peculiarity that Empedocles is put before Pythagoras rather than after. This error in chronology is characteristic of all the accounts derived from 'Āmirī and consequently of most Islamic accounts of Empedocles. This curious ordering could be linked to *The Theology of Aristotle* 1.30 ff., which discusses Empedocles' view of the descent of the soul and then adds, "With this philosopher Pythagoras agreed in his summons to mankind. . . . The sublime and divine Plato has described the soul"—implying an order of Empedocles-Pythagoras-Plato. *Metaphysics* A.4–5 also discusses Empedocles before Pythagoras, though Aristotle at 985b24 does specifically remark that the Pythagoreans were contemporary to or earlier than the philosophers he had just discussed. Second, Empedocles is linked with Luqmān and David, thus making him dependent on both the Jewish and Qur'ānic traditions of prophecy. Third, Shahrazūrī adds a reference to Empedocles' mystical attainments, something not mentioned by 'Āmirī. Finally, there is the assertion that certain of the Isma'ilis ('Bāṭinīya, adherents of the inner meaning) and Ibn Masarra of Cordoba were followers of Empedocles.[14]

The other accounts in the biographical dictionaries are more or less the same, but there are some other scraps of biographical information about Empedocles available in Arabic, although they did not circulate so widely. The commentary on the *Golden Verses* attributed to Proclus reports that Empedocles was one of the 250 students of Pythagoras and that he composed the *Golden Verses* as a compilation of Pythagoras' ethical teachings. While that piece of information is not repeated by Shahrazūrī, the text comments on Empedocles' mystical views in a form that could be an indirect source of some of Shahrazūrī's additions to 'Āmirī's account.[15]

THE EMPEDOCLEAN TRADITION IN ISLAM

S. M. Stern writes, "The authentic Empedocles, however, plays no role in Islamic philosophy."[16] This is an overstatement, for there were authentic reports of Empedocles' doctrines available in Arabic. The best known was from the often quoted section on the first principles of being *(al-mabādi')* in Pseudo-Plutarch's *De Placitis Philosophorum* 1.3. The full text is several pages in length and is otherwise notable for its distinction between the Ionian and Italian schools of philosophy. It is one of Shahrazūrī's direct or indirect sources. On Empedocles Pseudo-Plutarch writes:

> Empedocles of Agrigentum, son of Meton, held that there were four elements—fire, air, water, and earth—and two principles—love and strife *(al-maḥabba wa'l-ghalaba)*. One of them created unity and the other division. He said the following: "The roots of all things are four. They are Zeus, the aether; Hera, who gives life; Aidoneus; and Nestis, who fill the streams with their tears. By 'Zeus' he means fire, boiling, and sky *(jaww)*; by 'Hera, giver of life', earth; by 'Aidoneus', air; and by 'Nestis' and 'human flowing' *(al-saylān al-basharī)*, the human spirit and water.[17]

Pseudo-Plutarch contains dozens of other specific citations of Empedoclean teachings, but none of them are widely cited in Arabic sources. Most are on physical matters such as astronomy, biology, and medicine. Some other works from which we derive many of the Empedoclean fragments and testimonia were also available in Arabic—commentaries on Aristotle and the works of Galen, for example. Medieval Muslims also had access to Aristotle's "discussions and refutations" of Empedocles.[18] There is an example in Suhrawardī's *Paths and Havens* in a chapter arguing that God's actions have no final cause: "The views attributed to Empedocles—that he believed in chance and luck *(al-ittifāq wa'l-bakht)* and that he did not recognize final causes *(ghāyāt)*—are for the most part spurious and contradictory."[19] He is alluding to two passages in Aristotle. In a discussion of the inadequacies of the Presocratic accounts of chance in *Physics* 2.4 (196a18–22), Aristotle criticizes Empedocles for employing the notion of chance without properly introducing it. In *Metaphysics* A.4 (985a1–985b4) he says that Empedocles, like other Presocratics, failed to give an adequate explanation of the role of the final cause. Suhrawardī's judgment that the evidence is "contradictory" may be explained by the fact that the passage introducing this discussion (1.3, 984b9–21) implies that Empedocles and the others discussed in this passage denied the existence of luck and chance. Suhrawardī explicitly states that he has read a text attributed to Empedocles, but it is not certain whether his argument here is an inference based on one of the texts that we have or a more exact citation of a text that we do not have. It does indicate that Suhrawardī knew Aristotle's *Metaphysics*, for which there is other evidence.

However, the bulk of the material commonly attributed to Empedocles in Arabic falls into a category known to scholarship as the "Pseudo-Empedoclean literature." This particular philological swamp is a backwater of Neoplatonism. Happily, only a few of its bayous need concern us. The most important book of this literature is said to have been the "Book of Five Substances." It is evidently lost, although quotations survive here and there, mainly in Hebrew.[20] We do not know whether this was the "book of his on philosophy showing his mystical intuition, his strength on the mystic path, and his excellence in theology" that Shahrazūrī mentions seeing.[21] The other important pieces of Pseudo-Empedocleana are in Pseudo-Ammonius and Shahrastānī.[22]

Whether or not the Pseudo-Empedoclean writings originated in Greek or in Arabic, their roots are certainly Greek. Empedocles was one of the Presocratics adopted by the Neoplatonists; like Pythagoras, Socrates, and Plato he was a member of the "Italian school." The result was that the Neoplatonists interpreted Empedocles in Neoplatonic terms. Syrianus, for example, the early-fifth-century philosopher who was Proclus' teacher, wrote in his commentary on Aristotle's *Metaphysics:*

> It seems to me that Empedocles supposes 'Friendship' to be nothing other than the One, not the One that is not co-ordinate with anything [i.e., the ultimate One], but that which is co-ordinate with the unlimited dyad, which he refers to as 'Strife', from [both of] which what primarily is and all the intelligibles and the sensible world come to be.[23]

It should not surprise us then to find that the Empedocles of Shahrastānī, the fullest surviving account of him in Arabic, should sound like a popularization of some late Greek Neoplatonist, made respectable by a slight editing and the occasional quote from the Qur'ān.[24] Nonetheless, not all contact with the "authentic" Empedocles is lost, for Shahrastānī gives us a perfectly accurate summary of his theory of the four elements, love, and strife.[25]

Finally, as Kingsley argues, there is a hidden current of Empedocleanism coming into the Islamic world through occult channels. The practitioners of the magical tradition preserved in Egypt never forgot the ancient association of Empedocles with their arts. The Arabic alchemical work, *Turba Philosophorum*, which now survives only in Latin, gives an account of the alchemical views of a number of the Presocratics, Empedocles included. Kingsley is suspicious of the notion of an Arabic "Pseudo-Empedocles," arguing that while the materials attributed to Empedocles in Islam are mixed with a generous amount of material from other sources, they nonetheless contain a core of material coming from Empedocles and much more that arose in his tradition.[26]

EMPEDOCLES IN SUHRAWARDĪ'S WORKS

Suhrawardī's Empedocles is above all a mystic. He appears most commonly in lists of the ancient philosophers who were masters of the intuitive philosophy—that is, the philosophy based on mystical intuition.

> In all that I have said about the science of lights and that which is and is not based upon it, I have been assisted by those who have traveled the path of God. This science is the very intuition of the inspired and illumined Plato, the guide and master of philosophy, and of those who came before him from the time of Hermes, "the father of philosophers," up to Plato's time, including such mighty pillars of philosophy as Empedocles, Pythagoras, and others.[27]

In the *Paths and Havens* Suhrawardī says:

> I have studied the words of this man [Empedocles]. The worth that I found in them indicates the power of his wayfaring and intuition and the lofty and holy visions that he had. Most of what they say about him is slander.[28]

Empedocles, like Pythagoras and Plato, like the ancient Persian sages and kings and the ecstatic Sufis, was one of those who attained the supreme mystical state of the "lesser death" *(al-mawt al-aṣghar).*[29] In the *Philosophy of Illumination* Suhrawardī describes this state:

> The mightiest state is the state of death, by which the managing light sheds the darknesses. If it has no remnant of attachment to the body, it will emerge into the world of light and be attached to the dominating lights. There will it behold all the veils of light as though transparent in relation to the glory of the eternal, the all-encompassing Light, the Light of Lights. It will become, as it were, placed within the all-encompassing Light. This is a station mighty indeed! Plato spoke from his own experience of this station, as did Hermes and the great sages. The Author of this Law [Muḥammad] spoke of this station, as did many of those who divested themselves of the rank of humanity. Such people are always found throughout the ages.[30]

In particular, his mystical intuitions are cited as evidence for the doctrine of Platonic Forms.[31] Empedocles thus was one of those mystical observers, the records of whose observations provide the basis for intuitive philosophy, just as the observations of long dead astronomers provide the basis for astronomical theories.[32] Suhrawardī must also have known of Empedocles' teachings on the fall of the soul and reincarnation and knew too that they were linked to mysticism.[33] Finally, Empedocles was one of those ancient philosophers who couched his works in symbols.[34]

LOVE AND STRIFE

In one case there seems to be a direct use of a distinctively Empedoclean doctine by Suhrawardī: his view that the divine lights are characterized by relations of love and dominance *(maḥabba, qahr)*. "At the root of the deficient light is passion for the higher light. At the root of the higher light is dominance over the lower light. . . . Thus, all existence is ordered on the basis of love and dominance."[35] He goes on to discuss the "aspects of love and dominance" in the immaterial lights as bases of their differentiation and the differentiation of their effects in the sublunar world.[36]

The most distinctive teaching of Empedocles is probably the doctrine of Love and Strife as organizing principles of the universe. Empedocles, as has been noted, was the inventor of the theory of the four elements. Unlike Aristotle, he did not believe that these elements could be transmuted, only mixed in various combinations. Love (φιλία) brings the elements together; Strife (νεῖκος) separates them. This doctrine was perfectly familiar to medieval Muslims. Shahrastānī wrote:

> It is reported that Empedocles said, "The world is composed of four elements, and nothing is simpler than they. Things are concealed within each other." He denied generation, transmutation, and growth, saying, "Air does not become fire, nor water air. Such things happen through compression and rarefaction, concealment and manifestion, and composition and division. Composition in composites is through Love *(maḥabba)*, and division in things divided is through Strife *(ghalaba)*.[37]

The exact source of this passage is not clear, but it could have been derived from various passages in Pseudo-Plutarch, Pseudo-Ammonius, or, of course, Aristotle.[38]

Shahrastānī's account of Empedocles has other references to Love and Strife, most with a Neoplatonic twist of the sort seen in the passage from Syrianus quoted above.

> Empedocles said: "The first element *('unṣur)* is simple with respect to the essence of the intellect that is other than it and is not simple absolutely—i.e., purely one with respect to the essence of the cause—for every effect is compound, either intellectually or sensibly. The element in its essence is composed of Love and Strife *(al-maḥabba wa'l-ghalaba)*, and from them are created the spiritual simple substances and the bodily composite substances, so Love and Strife are two attributes or forms of the element, two principles for all existents. The spirituals *(rūḥānīyāt)* are disposed by nature for pure Love, the bodily for Strife, and the compounds of both for the two natures of Love and Strife and duality and opposition, and by the magnitude of the two in composites is known the magnitudes of the spiritual [substances] in the bodily [substances]." He said, "By this means the dual [substances] are united with each other, species by species and kind by kind, and the contrary [substances] avoid each other, species by species and kind by kind.
>
> "The unity *(i'tilāf)* and love that is in them are from the spiritual

[substances], and the difference *(ikhtilāf)* and strife are from the bodily [substances], and they may be united in a single soul by two differing relations."

Love is often linked to Jupiter and Venus, and strife to Saturn and Mars, so that they are individualized as auspicious and inauspicious.[39]

Another passage associates Love with the universal soul and Strife with universal nature.

> Love is the property *(khāṣṣīya)* of the Universal Soul, because when it looks to the intellect and its glory and beauty, it loves its beloved passionately and seeks to unite with it and move towards it. Dominance is the property of the universal nature. Because it is alone, it cannot see the soul and intellect to love them, but from them contrary powers flow to it.[40]

Apart from the fact that Suhrawardī nowhere explicitly associates Empedocles with this particular doctrine, there are three objections to identifying Suhrawardī's 'love and dominance' with Empedocles' and Pseudo-Empedocles' 'Love and Strife'.

First, the terms used do not exactly match. The passages on Empedocles in Arabic consistently use *maḥabba* and *ghalaba*, whereas Suhrawardī uses *maḥabba* and *qahr*. The use of *maḥabba*—"love" or "friendship" in a general and not necessarily passionate sense—in place of the *'ishq*—"passionate love"—that we would expect from a Sufi-oriented thinker like Suhrawardī certainly could be a reference to Empedocles' *maḥabba*/φιλία. *Ghalaba* and *qahr* are a closer match that at first appears. *Ghalaba* as a rendering of νεῖκος/'strife' is not very accurate. *Ghalaba* means "victory" or "conquest," not "strife," so perhaps the translation was contaminated by associations with νίκη, "victory." Be that as it may, *qahr* is a synonym of *ghalaba* and is used in association with it in one passage in Shahrastānī's account of Empedocles and at one point in *The Philosophy of Illumination*.[41]

Second, Suhrawardī uses love and dominance in a completely different way from Empedocles. Empedocles had used the concepts to explain the interactions of the physical elements, and Suhrawardī uses them to explain the relations among the immaterial lights/intellects. This difference is also not as great as might at first appear, especially from Suhrawardī's point of view. He holds that Empedocles' writings were symbolic—which, of course, they were; Aristotle grumbles about it:

> Avoid ambiguities; unless, indeed, you definitely desire to be ambiguous, as those do who have nothing to say but are pretending to mean something. Such people are apt to put that sort of thing into verse. Empedocles, for instance, by his long circumlocutions imposes on his hearers;

> these are affected in the same way as most people are when they listen to diviners, whose ambiguous utterances are received with nods of acquiescence.[42]

The contrast between the Platonic and Aristotelian styles of philosophizing could scarcely be put more clearly. Suhrawardī would argue that he had no obligation to interpret Empedocles' doctrines literally. Moreover, it is exactly these differing relations among the immaterial lights that are the causes of differences and interrelations among the natural kinds of the sublunar world.

Third, the Neoplatonists use love and strife in an opposite way from their use by Suhrawardī: love is characteristic of the higher for Pseudo-Empedocles and strife/dominance of the lower. Yet once more the difference is not so great as it appears. First, these are relations and can thus be considered from either pole of the relation. One might legitimately associate love with either the lover or the beloved, and dominance with either the ruler or the ruled. Moreover, in the second passage from Shahrastānī, the love of the Universal Soul for the Universal Intellect is described exactly as Suhrawardī would have done: when "the Universal Soul . . . looks to the intellect with its glory and beauty, it loves its beloved passionately."

Given the prominence of Empedocles in his philosophical pantheon and the familiarity of love and strife as an Empedoclean doctrine, I think it is highly probable that Suhrawardī's love/dominance distinction is an explicit allusion to Empedocles.

SUHRAWARDĪ AS MYSTIC AND MAGUS

While there are more intellectual lines to be traced between Empedocles and Suhrawardī than we have examined, the chief importance of Empedocles for our story is as a paradigm and a warning not to misunderstand the philosophical enterprise that we are examining. Empedocles was not a philosophy professor, nor was Suhrawardī. For each, philosophy was not simply theory, though the theory was there and underlaid the rest; it was also mysticism and magic. Guthrie, writing of Empedocles, could equally well be describing Suhrawardi:

> When all allowance has been made for legend, he appears at once as philosopher, mystic, poet, political reformer and physician, with something of the magician about him and a corresponding touch of arrogance and showmanship, although sometimes, in relating the sins which involved him in the miseries of earthly life, he may seem to show an anguished humility.[43]

Guthrie saw the Presocratics, Empedocles included, as part of a teleological process in which various aspects of the rational emerged from the mythical.[44] Yet such an idea of scientific and philosophical progress and the whole notion that there is some distinction to be made among philosopher, mystic, and magician is as alien to Suhrawardī as it was to Empedocles and the Neoplatonists of late antiquity. The Neoplatonic tradition generally rejected the notion of progress in philosophy. The foundations of philosophy are mystical, and the Neoplatonists found the greatest exponents of such thought in the ancient past. Aristotle and his followers might seek scientific progress, but Suhrawardī and his predecessors saw them as doing no more than elaborating the surface features of knowledge. It was the ancient sages who had gone deep. Philosophy is something to be revived by those able to repeat the experiences of its founders, not something in which steady progress can be made.

Suhrawardī's spiritual kinship to Empedocles can best be seen by considering his life and claims. When Suhrawardī came to Aleppo, he did three things. He debated the 'ulamā' and thus demonstrated his intellectual ascendancy, he asserted his intention to live a life of extreme asceticism in order to gain access to mystical knowledge, and he demonstrated his spiritual powers by producing a wonderful gem.

> Shaykh Shihāb al-Dīn 'Umar [sic] al-Suhrawardī came to Aleppo and took lodgings in the Madrasat al-Ḥalāwīya. At that time its *mudarris* was the Sharīf, the head of the Hanafites, the late Iftikhār al-Dīn. When Shihāb al-Dīn attended the class and argued with the jurists, he was dressed as a dervish and had only a ewer and a wooden staff, so no one knew him. But when he entered the discussion and stood out among the jurists, Iftikhār al-Dīn realized that he was learned, so the latter got out a robe of watered taffeta, a gown, a coat, and a large turban and said to his son, "Go to this dervish and say to him, 'My father sends his regards to you and says that you are a jurist and that you attended the class with the jurists. He has sent you something to wear when you come.'" When his son came to Shaykh Shihāb al-Dīn and said to him what he had been bidden to say, the latter was silent for a long time and said, "My boy, leave these rags and do something for me." He took out a Badakhshan ruby that looked like a pomegranate the size of a chicken egg. No one had one like it, either in size or color. He said, "Go to the market and advertise this stone. Whatever you are offered, do not undertake to sell it until you have told me." So when he arrived in the market, he sat by the *'arīf* [assistant market supervisor] and advertised the gem. The offers finally reached 25,000 dirhams, so the *'arīf* took it to al-Malik al-Ẓāhir Ghāzī, the son of Ṣalāḥ al-Dīn, who was at that time governor of Aleppo. The *'arīf* said to him, "That price was bid for it." Al-Malik al-Ẓāhir was astonished at its shape, color, and beauty, so he raised the bid to 30,000 dirhams. The *'arīf* said, "I will go down to the son

> of Iftikhār al-Dīn and tell him." He took the gem and went down to the market and gave him the price. He said, "Go and consult your father about this price," for the *'arīf* believed that the gem belonged to Iftikhār al-Dīn. When he came to Shihāb al-Dīn al-Suhrawardī and told him what had been bid for the gem, the latter was embarrassed. He took the gem, placed it on a rock, and struck it with another stone until he shattered it. He said to the son of Iftikhār al-Dīn, "Take these clothes and go to your father. Kiss his hand on my behalf and say to him, 'If I had wanted clothing, I would not have been prevented from getting it.'"[45]

Whatever the truth of this particular story, all three aspects of Suhrawardī's supposed actions reflect claims in his writings.

Suhrawardī lived after Aristotle and in an age when untutored mystics were common, so he understood that discursive and mystical knowledge need not come together. Nonetheless, it is knowledge that is the greatest human perfection. In a famous passage he asserts that intuitive—that is, mystical—knowledge is superior to discursive knowledge, but the person who combines both is superior to all others and is the rightful sovereign.[46] The Illuminationist philosophy combines both kinds of knowledge. Still, discursive knowledge must come first if one is to be a philosopher. The Illuminationist, like Empedocles, seeks to understand and thus falls within the ranks of philosophers. Practical wisdom is a branch of theoretical philosophy, as Shahrazūrī observes, and "human perfection consists in the theoretical sciences. The science of practical wisdom is also theoretical, and improvement of character is acquired by turning the soul away from distractions and by purifying it from hindrances to becoming perfected. Therefore, human happiness is conditioned on acquiring sciences."[47]

Yet deep understanding requires access to realms not reached by normal sensation or thought. It is mystical knowledge—intuition—that gives the Illuminationist philosophy its depth. The Illuminationist philosopher must also seek to transform his inner being, an enterprise that must then rule every aspect of his life. The acquisition of mystical knowledge is not like doing research in the Lyceum; it demands a special way of life. "The reader of this book must have reached at least the stage in which the divine light has descended upon him, not just once but regularly. No one else will find any profit in it."[48] The biographical sources attest to Suhrawardī's extreme asceticism and devotion, and he frequently refers to his visions and mystical experiences.

The hardships of the Illuminationist philosophical path are not without their rewards, thus the production of the fabulous gemstone. "The brethren of incorporeality have a special station in which they are able to bring into existence self-subsistent images in whatever form they desire."[49] Shahrazūrī explains:

> I heard from one of the ordinary scholars who had no share in true sciences that [Suhrawardī] knew the science of natural magic *(sīmīyā)*. Others claimed that he was a prestidigitator *(muḥīl)*. These are slanders, for they do not know the power of the mystics *(ikhwān al-tajrīd)* to bring forms into being at will, as Basṭāmī, Ḥallāj, and others could do. God gave me certainty of the existence of this station, but some things should not be mentioned.[50]

The Illuminationist philosopher, like other great mystics, has magical, or rather, spiritual powers by virtue of his spiritual attainments.

With these intellectual and magical powers comes asendancy over men. Suhrawardī enjoyed the patronage of the prince, and there is every reason to believe that he sought to subject the state to the rule of philosophy. "The godly leader may indeed rule openly, or he may be hidden—the one whom the multitude call 'the Pole'. He will have authority even if he is in the deepest obscurity. When the government is in his hands, the age will be enlightened."[51] Suhrawardī tried to put this teaching into practice, but his arrogance or his good fortune aroused envy and led to his death.

This type of philosopher is no longer familiar to us and must be grasped, if at all, through an effort of the imagination. Yet the philosopher/mystic/magus is found from the very beginnings of philosophy up to fairly recent times: Empedocles, Pythagoras, Iamblichus and the other Neoplatonic theurgists, Suhrawardī and many of those who followed his tradition, Bruno, even Newton. They can be misunderstood in different ways—by reducing them to philosophers or mystics or magicians and dismissing the other aspects of their thought. They are to be distinguished from mystics and magicians by virtue of an underlying desire to understand that brings them finally within the company of philosophers. Nonetheless, they have always seen the effort to pursue philosophy as a purely intellectual discipline as a trivial and probably futile enterprise. The groaning shelves of the "New Age" sections of modern bookstores, where books of serious philosophy mix with books of mysticism, magic, and the occult sciences indicate that their ideal is not yet dead.

CHAPTER 6

Pythagoras: The Brotherhood of the Lovers of Wisdom

The second of those to whom the Greeks attributed wisdom was Pythagoras. The historical Pythagoras predated Empedocles, but the influence of al-'Āmirī's account of the five sages is such that in Islamic sources, Pythagoras is usually placed after Empedocles.

THE PYTHAGORAS OF HISTORY AND LEGEND

Pythagoreanism flows like a river through the great plain of thought that owes its allegiance to Greece. We see it first in the distant time of Pythagoras himself as it precipitates itself from the hills at the beginning of Greek philosophy, a vigorous stream flashing in the sun, bordered by green meadows but too far away for us to see into the pool it forms or to descry its exact course as it flows into the plain. Names next mark its further course—Philolaus, Archytus, Timaeus, and others—but where they might be on that plain, we cannot precisely tell. We can first stand upon its banks in the groves of the Academy and watch its waters sweet but deep and green. Already it is mixed with other streams—Meander, that flows through Miletus, and the ever-changing river contemplated by Heracleitus. Pythagoras' stream is now forever mixed in the broad river of Platonism, but in its long course this river sometimes enters a rocky gorge, flowing fast and deep, as when Iamblichus sought to restore the Pythagorean Plato, or a branch breaks off the main channel for a time, and we again see the bright stream of Pythagoras, the water leaping down the rocks as among the occult philosophers of Renaissance Europe. The stream of Pythagoreanism flows through the East as well—fittingly, for the Ancients said its origin was there, in the Nile and the Tigris—and once a branch reached Aleppo and flowed from there through underground channels to Isfahan.

Pythagoreanism is not an easy problem for the historian of philosophy. The difficulty is not lack of material. A popular collection of ancient Pythagorean philosophical sources contains four biographies of Pythagoras in a hundred pages, and another one hundred and fifty pages of philosophical fragments attributed to later Pythagoreans.[1] The addition of other ancient material on Pythagoreanism—biographies of other Pythagoreans, the surviving books and fragments of Iamblichus' *Pythagorean Philosophy*, texts on mathematics, science, and music, and stray fragments preserved in the works of philosophers of other schools would no doubt double or triple the amount of material available. Works of Pythagoreans of the Middle Ages, Renaissance, and modern periods, would again—in good Pythagorean fashion—multiply this many more times.

But still Pythagoras remains a mysterious figure, and the doctrines of his school remain obscure. There are several reasons for this. First, Pythagoras lived a long time ago, about 150 years before Plato, and our knowledge of the views of all of the Presocratic philosophers is fragmentary at best and surely distorted in his case. Our sources are often far later, antiquarians like Diogenes Laertius and Neopythagorean Platonists like Iamblichus. The latter, who wrote the most influential classical treatment of Pythagoreanism, was as far removed in time from Pythagoras as Aquinas is from us, and his views are inevitably distorted by the rich philosophical tradition that separated them. Second, although Pythagoras formed a school that lasted for at least a century, its doctrines were secret. When Suhrawardī tells us that the Ancients wrote their philosophical works in symbols, this is preeminently true of Pythagoras and his greatest pupils, Empedocles and Plato. Much was doubtless lost when the school died out, and the Pythagoreans did not mean us to understand what survives. Finally, it is no longer possible to distinguish true Pythagoreanism from the views of later philosophers. No one who reads Plato and the accounts and fragments of the early Pythagoreans side by side can doubt that there was a connection between them. Does this mean that the bulk of Pythagorean fragments are to be dismissed as post-Platonic pseudepigrapha, as most modern critics would hold? Or is Plato to be seen as a true disciple of Pythagoras? Shahrazūrī thought so, as did Iamblichus and the modern Pythagorean Kenneth Sylvan Guthrie: both point to the *Timaeus* as the connecting link. Certainly, Suhrawardī would see Plato as the culminating figure of the Pythagorean tradition, and his position remains tenable. Those who hold to this interpretation of Plato see the *Timaeus*, not the *Republic*, as the high point of Plato's philosophy.

But our problem is simpler, just to understand how Suhrawardī understood and used the Pythagorean tradition.

If something is to be reconstructed of the historical Pythagoras and the early Pythagoreans, it can only be by patiently piecing together fragments from early sources in order to determine how far the later sources can be trusted.[2] The bulk of the information on Pythagoras comes from much later Neoplatonists, particularly Iamblichus and his partially extant *On*

Pythagoreanism. Many of the Neoplatonists saw Pythagoras and Plato as two ends of a single tradition, with Pythagoras as the original fount of Plato's wisdom—and even Aristotle's. As evidence they could point to the pseudo-Pythagorean works then in circulation, works attributed to Timaeus, Archytus, and other Pythagorean luminaries. The Pseudo-Archytus' work on the categories demonstrated the dependence of Aristotle's *Categories* on Pythagoras. Other such works showed the close links of Plato to Pythagoras. Neoplatonist interpretation of the master in any case stressed those elements of his thought most closely related to Pythagoras—the *Timaeus* rather than the *Republic.*

Porphyry's biography of Pythagoras from his otherwise lost *History of Philosophy* is one of the three major biographies of Pythagoras surviving from ancient times, the others being by Diogenes Laertius and Iamblichus. Iamblichus' biography is longer and more credulous than the others, but their portraits of Pythagoras are not that different. As it happens, Porphyry's biography was translated into Arabic and exists almost intact in all the major biographical dictionaries of philosophers. Since this is the Pythagoras known to both the Neoplatonists of the Roman Empire and to Muslim scholars, it is worth summarizing, for the story it tells, despite the many obscure Greek names, would have been perfectly familiar to Suhrawardī.[3] How closely this story corresponds to the historical Pythagoras is a question I leave to the classicists.

According to Porphyry, Pythagoras of Samos was born in Sidon, the son of a Samian merchant who had gone there to trade. He was said to have been of good birth, and later tradition made him a descendent of Apollo. He studied under Pherecydes the Syrian and then Hermodamas. Pherecydes was sometimes added to the list of the "Seven Sages" and has a biography in Diogenes Laertius 1.116–22, but he was little known in Arabic. The Arabic text calls him "Siryānī," Syrian, and says that he was from the city of "Dīlūn" in Syria. Actually, he was from the island of Syros in the Aegean and died in Delos. The error probably also has something to do with the fact that the Arabic rendering of "Tyre" is "Ṣūr." Nothing is known about Hermodamas except that he was Pythagoras' teacher and was supposed to have been descended from one Creophylus, the host of Homer.[4] Pythagoras' father eventually brought him back to Samos, and as a young man he came to the attention of Polycrates, the tyrant of Samos. Finding the atmosphere of the tyranny inauspicious for study, he escaped to the mainland of Ionia, where he came to know Anaximander and Thales. The latter recommended that he go to Egypt to study with the priests. He sailed to his home city of Sidon and learned the religious mysteries to be found in the various Phoenician towns, including perhaps those of the Israelites—the "descendents of Moschus." He lived for twenty-two years in Egypt, being intiated into the mysteries of the priests and learning the sciences of the Egyptians. When Cambyses conquered Egypt, Pythagoras was taken prisoner to Babylon, where he learned the sciences of the Babylonians and of the Magi. In his fifty-sixth year, he returned to Samos. There he established a school, but he found the Samians not particularly eager to learn the mathematical sciences, and he was distracted by the political obligations placed upon him as a prominent citizen of the place. Realizing that all the philosophers had made their greatest achievements in foreign places, he sailed for Italy.

He was welcomed in the Greek town of Croton, in southern Italy. There he gathered several hundred disciples, and together they governed the place according to the dictates of philosophy. They liberated and gave laws to a number of the Greek towns of Italy and Sicily and created for a time a philosophical republic. The Pythagoreans followed a strict discipline, a sort of monastic order whose best-known precept was a refusal to eat beans. His disciples were organized into several degrees, separated by initiations, with the doctrines of each kept secret from the lower degrees. The power of the Pythagoreans led to jealousy. Cylon, a prominent citizen of Croton, was rejected when he tried to join the Pythagorean brotherhood. A revolution resulted, and many of the Pythagoreans were killed when the house they had taken refuge in was burned over them. Pythagoras himself fled to the temple of the Muses in Metapontum, another town in southern Italy, where he soon died—some say of grief, others of starvation.

Critics argue as to how much credence ought to be given to this biography. There are clearly elements of the legendary and the miraculous in the Pythagoras biographies, but certainly by Roman times, philosophers were in broad agreement about the life of Pythagoras—the childhood connections with the Middle East, the extended stay in Egypt, the teaching in Samos and Croton, and the death at the hands of those tired of rule by the wise.[5] Likewise, there was general agreement about the important features of his system: the fascination with number and its properties; the mixture of mysticism, magic, science, and ethics in a hierarchical cult; and the attempt to produce a rational and all-encompassing account of the cosmos based on number.[6] In fact, the question of the authenticity of the traditional life of Pythagoras is not relevant to our concerns since it was known to and believed by both the Illuminationists and the late antique philosophers who were their intellectual predecessors.

Pythagoreanism reached the Muslims through several channels, giving them a balanced picture of Pythagoreanism as it was known to the scholars of late antiquity.[7] A briefer and more mythical account is found in the commentary on the *Golden Verses* attributed to Proclus:

> The birth of Pythagoras of Samos, it is said, was announced by an oracle *(kahāna)*—i.e., celestial information from the god *(al-ilāh)*—and he was born of a virgin. He associated with Thales, one the seven sages . He journeyed to Egypt and the Nile, associated with the sages, and learned geometry and the methods of soothsaying. He went on to Babylon and confered with the astrologers and the Magi. (Plato says that Magianism means "worship of God.") It is further said that his wisdom reached such a degree that the sages came to him from various countries. His wisdom was of such a rank that he rejected wealth and worked miracles *('amala 'l-i'jāz)*. He instructed students to keep silence for five years, after which he would teach them some philosophy and mathematics. During this period they would mortify their desires, reform their souls, and be trained in moral qualities. These philosophers kept silence in order to bring their intellects back to the essences of their intellects *(dhawātihā)*. Thus their conversation would be with their intellects and not with strangers. If they happened to speak with a stranger, they were required to purify themselves in the same way that was required of someone whose intellect was attracted to something external. Pythagoras had about 250 followers.[8]

This account differs from Porphyry's by its added stress on the oriental sources of Pythagoras' thought and by its clear exposition of Pythagoreanism as a mystical order whose founder had supernatural powers.

It is the more formulaic 'Āmirī who gives us the clearest account of the relevance of Pythagoras to Islamic philosophers.

> Another of those to whom wisdom was attributed was Pythagoras. In Egypt he associated with the disciples of Solomon, son of David, after they moved there from Syria. Before meeting them he learned geometry from the Egyptians. He also learned natural and divine sciences from the disciples of Solomon. He brought the three sciences—that is, the science of geometry, the science of natures and the science of religion—back to Greece. By his own wit he deduced the science of melodies, reducing them to ratios and numbers. He claimed that he acquired these sciences from the niche of prophecy.[9]

Shahrazūrī quotes this passage twice, adding that Pythagoras had organized his system of cosmology on the basis of numbers. He then mentions various Pythagorean ethical commandments: the prohibition against touching a corpse or a killer, the purification of the senses, the obligation to investigate the nature of all things, fasting, sitting on chairs, and the like. He adds that Pythagoras was the first to say that the property of friends is in common and that he had concealed his philosophy by the use of symbolism. Shahrazūrī cites as an example one of the ethical commandments and its symbolic interpretation.[10]

Shahrazūrī's account highlights several features of Pythagoreanism of particular interest to the Illuminationist thinkers. First, the bases of Pythagoras' system are identified as prophetic and mystical. His predecessor Empedocles had been the student of Luqmān, a pre-Islamic prophet who was himself a pupil of David. Pythagoras studied with the students of Solomon, who had by then migrated to Egypt. His contacts with the Egyptian priests link him with Hermes/Idrīs, the "Father of Philosophers," to use the title repeatedly given him in Illuminationist texts. Music, the science held to be a Pythagorean invention, was acquired from "the niche of prophecy." Shahrazūrī does not endorse or criticize this claim, but he does point out that Pythagoras, like Empedocles, believed that there was an intelligible realm accessible to purified spirits. Second, the account identifies the Pythagoreans as a mystical community, following special rules and pursuing both the truth and spiritual purification. Third, the Pythagorean teaching was presented in the form of symbols, both of speech and practice. Finally, the mystical and metaphysical aspects of Pythagoreanism are stressed, rather than its scientific and mathematical aspects. These features, as we will see, are very close to a description of the ways in which the Illuminationist school differed from the main tradition of Avicennan philosophy in Islam.

Shahrazūrī's account in the *Delight*, in accordance with the design of the book as a whole, does not deal much with the teachings of Pythagoras but rather confines itself to biography and gnomic sayings.

THE COMMENTARIES ON THE *GOLDEN VERSES* AND THE *AKOUSMATA*

For medieval Muslims, as for their ancient predecessors, Pythagoras was associated with a particular kind of ethical wisdom expressed in pithy, often cryptic proverbs and commandments. The mystical and religious aspects of Pythagoreanism were easy for a Muslim philosopher to understand; Pythagoreanism was a Sufi *ṭarīqa*, a mystical band of brothers and sisters, united in obedience to a single master and his way, and pursuing both knowledge and salvation. The notion that mystical experience played an important role in philosophical investigation was a familiar one, well known from Greek sources and increasingly central in Islamic philosophy. The teachings connected with this aspect of Pythagoreanism were specific rules and maxims—difficult to interpret, perhaps, but posing no special intellectual problems.

There are in Arabic two commentaries on the *Golden Verses*, a didactic poem containing a collection of ethical maxims attributed to Pyathagoras. These commentaries were attributed to Proclus and to Iamblichus. The

Golden Verses also circulated independently and can be found in the Arabic gnomic literature.[11] The identity of the work attributed to Proclus is something of a puzzle. There is no reason to doubt that the commentary in its present form comes from Ibn al-Ṭayyib (d. Oct. 1043), a contemporary of Avicenna, but it does not seem right to refer to it as "Ibn al-Ṭayyib's commentary," as the editor does. The title in the manuscript is "Ibn al-Ṭayyib's *istithmār* of the *Golden Verses* in the commentary of Proclus," and the content is thoroughly pagan, refering to "the gods" *(al-āliha)* from time to time. Given that Ibn al-Ṭayyib was, among other things, a Christian theologian, this little book can hardly be his work in the strict sense. Probably, *istithmār* means "notes" or "epitome," and the text as we have it is an abridgement of some lost Greek original. It certainly often reads like a scholar's notes on a text read.[12] Since there is no record of such a commentary by Proclus, Walzer suggested that the work was actually taken from the commentary by Hierocles; in undotted Arabic script Proclus *(brqls)* and Hierocles *(yrqls)* could easily be confused. Linley, the editor, was unable to confirm this. A more recent study has show that this work has nothing to do with Hierocles and suggests that the original might not have been by Proclus but by another man of the same name, Proclus Procleius of Laodicea, a Neoplatonist who lived around 400.[13] Whoever the author of the underlying text actually was, he certainly wrote in Greek and was a pagan, probably some late Pythagoreanizing Neoplatonist. For convenience I will refer to the text as Ibn al-Ṭayyib's, for he does not otherwise enter into our story.

Ibn al-Ṭayyib's text, despite its not very promising raw material, contains much that is interesting to us. The short biography with which it begins has already been discussed. It is followed by a brief account of Empedocles and his philosophical views, since in this text the *Golden Verses* are supposed to be an epitome of Pythagoras' ethical teachings composed by Empedocles. The purpose of the *Golden Verses*, says the commentator, is religious: "One group says that the Golden Words are a guide to the divine life *(al-ḥayāt al-ilāhīya)*, the imitation of God, and purification from matter."[14] The author goes on to explain that good and pious deeds vary in accordance with the nation. The Athenians and the Egyptians differed in their rites *(sunan)*, and Hermes had established the principle that men were to follow the customs of their own ancestors.[15] The intermediate spirits are demons and heroes, the heroes being those who have become divine *(ta'alluh)* through a blameless life, Pythagoras being a conspicuous example.[16] The numbers are explained as Forms and symbols *(muthul wa-rumūz)*.[17]

We do not know if Suhrawardī was familiar with this text, but it is in harmony with his views, interests, practices, and vocabulary at several points: the primacy of Hermes as the founder of philosophical religion, the acceptance of national religious diversity combined with a demand for rigorous observances of the rites of one's own nation, the reference to Egypt as a key ancient nation linked with the Greeks, and the repeated use of the term *ta'alluh*. The latter perhaps explains the curious use of this term in *The Philosophy of Illumination* to mean something like mysticism, despite the fact that the word "has a bad sound in the ears of Muslims."[18] Pythagoreanism, as understood by this "Proclus," was something that Suhrawardī would have been able to accept.

The commentary attributed to Iamblichus is of less interest for our purposes and can be dealt with quickly.[19] It is a straightforward commentary, citing the text and then paraphrasing it at slightly greater length. It does not have any of Proclus' interesting digressions, and the commentary is Islamicized—referring, for example, to Allāh, the angels, and the divine men *(ilāhīyūn)*, rather than Zeus, *daimons*, and heroes.[20]

OTHER INFORMATION ON PYTHAGOREANISM: LORE, NUMBERS, AND SYMBOLS

Other Pythagoean materials came to the Arabs. There was seemingly some version of Pseudo-Artchytas' works on the categories, for Suhrawardī had read it.[21] Translated Greek texts on mathematics and mathematical sciences contained frequent references to Pythagoras. Aristotle often mentioned the views of the Pythagoreans. There were also pseudo-Pythagorean texts in circulation—on alchemy, for example.[22]

There were also various bits of specific Pythagorean scientific lore, especially in Pseudo-Plutarch. From this book an attentive Islamic reader might have collected several dozen Pythagorean doctrines on questions of physics, meteorology, biology, and the like: the shape of the universe, the nature of sperm, the roles of the heart and brain, and the like.[23] It would have been hard to know what to do with such information.

Suhrawardī seems to have ignored the various specific doctrines about mathematics and mathematical science, transmitted through scientific channels. Unlike most of his predecessors in Islamic philosophy, he was neither a physician nor a scientist. He displayed little interest in scientific problems in his works, apart from elementary astronomy in the allegories he wrote for novices. He devised his theory of vision, for example, without concern for the problems of mathematical optics. His "sciences" were logic and mysticism, and it was the problems and teachings of logic and of Sufism that inform his system.

Most important was the metaphysics of number. This posed larger problems. First, Pythagorean ideas about number were peculiar, nearly as peculiar to a medieval thinker as to us, and as early as the fourth century B.C.E. Aristotle had complained of the naivité of Pythagorean number metaphysics.[24] In the introduction to his *Delight* Shahrazūrī summarizes a chapter from Pseudo-Plutarch on the various views concerning the nature of the first principles of being. Between the accounts of the Ionian philosophers and Pythagoras he interjects:

> It seems obvious that these views attributed to them here and the views attributed to others of the Ancients are symbols for their mystical and secret teachings *(ramzan 'an umūr wa-aḥwāl wa-asrār lahum)*, for otherwise no one possessing discrimination—let alone learned sages—would say those things that are attributed to them.[25]

The justice of Shahrazūrī's ejaculation may be seen from the following account of the Pythagorean metaphysics in the widely read Arabic Pseudo-Ammonius:

> For Pythagoras held that the first of the numbers was one, which is male. The second number is female, for it is the second of the first, so the number two is female. This cycle goes on through many numbers, for the number three is male and four, the end of number, is female. Pythagoras mentions that the first one is fire and is male; the second is air, which is female; the third, water, which is male; and the fourth, earth, which is female.[26]

Such arbitrary speculations were no longer acceptable to sophisticated philosophers of the twelfth and thirteenth centuries, just as they had been unacceptable to Proclus. Neither was Suhrawardī attracted by the Pythagorean deification of numbers; he was no mathematician and thus was not bewitched by the eerie ability of numbers to capture and predict the behavior of tangible things. Nor, despite his interest in the occult, was he interested in numerology.

In fact, a metaphysics of number, whether Pythagorean or neo-Pythagorean, was incompatible with Suhrawardī's nominalist Platonism. Like existence, necessity, and contingency, both unity and numbers were beings of reason *(i'tibārāt 'aqlīya)*, products of the operation of the human mind. Suhrawardī points out that counting is an exercise in attention, and that considering four things to be four does not mean that they participate in some higher four-ness. In what way does their essence change when one mentally adds a fifth to the group?

On the other hand, Suhrawardī could not ignore Pythagoras as he had ignored the Ionian physicists, with their equally odd speculations about material first principles of being. Apart from the respect that Pythagoras had received from the ancient philosophers, Pythagoras had had, by all accounts, extensive and authentic mystical experiences. Suhrawardī was committed to the view that such experiences yield data on which philosophical systems can be built and truth found. To dismiss Pythagoras' views as false would put his own method into doubt. Since Pythagoras had true mystical experiences, his system must be "true" in some real sense. The key was provided by Pythagoreanism itself.

Pythagoreanism was a secret school, whose higher doctrines were kept from those unworthy of them. It was also a real institution, not simply an intellectual tradition. Among the elements of Pythagoreanism best known to outsiders was a collection of maxims of behavior, often rather specific injunctions and taboos. The best known of them—whose true meaning was never known for certain outside the school—was the bean taboo.[27] While some were practical injunctions, others were primarily symbolic: "Do not stir the ashes with a sword" and "Do not wear the image of a god on your ring." Both ancient and Islamic sources give these maxims, sometimes with explanations. Iamblichus explains these last two as meaning that one should not further inflame the quarrelsome and that one should not profane the name of a god. More generally, the ancients understood that the Pythagoreans presented their abstract philosophical doctrines in symbolic form. Iamblichus wrote:

> The preparation for philosophy through symbols and secret conveying of beliefs, handed down as education only to those who know, in accordance with the practice of the Egyptians and the most ancient Greek theologians.
>
> But the most necessary form of teaching, for Pythagoras, was by symbols. Almost all Greeks were enthusiastic about this kind of teaching, because it is of very great antiquity; the Egyptians gave it its most subtle form and highest status.
>
> In the same way Pythagoras also valued it greatly, as may be seen by those who can perceive the meaning and unspoken content of the Pythagorean symbols, and can realize how much rightness and truth is in them once they are freed from the concealment of their riddling form, and how well their simple and straightforward transmission suits the greatness, indeed the closeness to god which surpasses human understanding, of these philosophers. . . . [The Pythagoreans] in their conversations and discussions, their notes and records . . . did not use common, vulgar, ordinary language, which could be superficially understood by anyone who heard it, in an attempt to make what they said easy to follow. Instead, they kept Pythagoras' rule of "holding your peace" about the divine mysteries, using secret devices to exclude the uninitiated and protecting their exchanges of speech and writing by the use of symbols. Unless one can interpret the symbols, and understand them by careful

> exposition, what they say would strike the chance observer as absurd—old wives' tales, full of nonsense and idle talk. But once they are deciphered as symbols should be, and become clear and transparent instead of obscure to outsiders, they impress us like utterances of the gods or Delphic oracles, revealing an astounding intellect and having a supernatural influence on those lovers of learning who have understood them.[28]

Suhrawardī adopted such a method of writing in his own works, expressing his own peculiar doctrines in the symbolic language of *The Philosophy of Illumination* and, it seems, keeping certain doctrines and explanations for oral transmission. As a key for understanding Pythagoras and the ancient philosophers, the doctrine of symbolic language was invaluable. It meant that their doctrines need not be read literally but could be unpacked in the light of the Illuminationist system. Such interpretation was not wholly arbitrary, to be sure, but it allowed for a diversity of approaches while still maintaining respect for the integrity of the views in question.

THE PYTHAGOREANIZING NEOPLATONISTS AND THE ILLUMINATIONISTS

Of course, the Pythagoreanism closest in time to Suhrawardī was not the doctrine the "real" Pythagoras, the Pythagoras painfully reconstructed from early fragments by modern scholars. It was the eclectic pythagoreanizing Neoplatonism of late antiquity, a tradition that reaches almost to Suhrawardī's time in the person of Michael Psellus, an eleventh-century student of Proclus and the other ancient philosophers.[29] The writings of these Neopythagorean Neoplatonists—Porphyry, Iamblichus, Syrianus, Proclus, and others—contain a great deal that seems familiar to a reader of Suhrawardī and the other Illuminationists and thus raise tantalizing questions of transmission. There are many problems in reconstructing the exact attitudes of these late antique philosophers toward Pythagoreanism. Lost texts are a problem. In every case except Proclus, and to a lesser extent, Iamblichus, the evidence for their views is fragmentary; Porphyry's views on Pythagoras, for example, must in considerable part be reconstructed from his treatise on vegetarianism. Even in Iamblichus' *On Pythagoreanism* the later books on physics and metaphysics are lost. Thus, the nuances of such questions as the exact metaphysical nature and role of mathematicals are often obscure. For our purposes, however, the situation is clearer; what is at issue is not precise metaphysical doctrines but a particular view of the history of philosophy and of the relation of philosophy to other kinds of thought. Its main features are as follows:

1. Pythagoras as the key pre-Socratic. For these philosophers Pythagoras assumed a prominent and distinguished role as the founder of philosophy and the master of Socrates and Plato. Iamblichus wrote an account of Pythagorean philosophy in ten books. The pseudo-Pythagorean fragments attributed to such early figures as Pythagoras himself, Archytas, Timaeus, and others were accepted as authentic. Interpretations of Plato were heavily Pythagoreanized. Parallel to doctrinal writings, hagiographical accounts of Pythagoras' life assumed importance.

2. Plato as the central figure of the history of philosophy. Though we now call them 'Neoplatonists', all of these philosophers considered themselves simply Platonists. Whether or not Plato's thought was considered different in degree, more complete in presentation, or quite different in kind than that of other philosophers, in practice Plato was the supreme philosopher. Proclus, for example, distinguished Plato from the Orphics and Pythagoras as being uniquely scientific in his method, developing a theory of dialectic to explain Plato's achievement.[30]

> The scientific [mode of exposition] is peculiar to Plato's philosophy. For he alone, as I believe, among those known to us, undertook to distinguish and order appropriately the ordered progression of the divine kinds, the differences between them, the common characteristics of all levels and those proper to each.[31]

3. Aristotle to be corrected by reference to Plato and the Pythagoreans. Aristotle, though hardly to be ignored, carries little authority and is to be corrected when he contradicts the greater authority of Plato and Pythagoras. Thus, the Neoplatonic commentators on the *Categories* cited the logical works of Pseudo-Archytas as Aristotle's (plagiarized) source and corrected Aristotle in terms of them. Syrianus' commentary on the *Metaphysics* dealt with books M and N, correcting those sections where Aristotle criticized Pythagoras and Plato.[32]

4. Philosophy as an eclectic revelation. The Pythagoras biographies contain much that is marvelous and/or mystical, and they assert as well that Pythagoras' source was not primarily discursive thought but rather revelation, either directly or through the medium of barbarian sages. 'Āmirī has Pythagoras claiming that he derived the science of music from "the niche of prophecy."[33] Though the term is Islamic, the sentiment could as well be that of Iamblichus or Porphyry. Pythagoras himself, we are told, learned not just from his own mystical experiences but also from his studies with the sages of Egypt, Syria, Chaldaea, and Persia. Parallel to this, the Pythagoreanizing Neoplatonists saw Platonic philosophy revealed in the wisdom of the sages of other nations: in the Orphic writings, Homer, and the Chaldaean oracles, in the writings and traditions of the priests of Egypt, and among the Magi, the Indians, and even the Druids.[34] There was a brisk traffic in spurious books attributed to such barbarian sages. Thus, Porphyry and Iamblichus each made diligent studies of what they thought to be foreign wisdom, hoping to find support for their views and further wisdom. So it was that Porphyry put the following incongruous questions to an Egyptian priest:

> What do the Egyptians think the first cause is? Is it Intellect or above Intellect? Is it alone, or with another or others? Is it incorporeal or corporeal? Is it identical with the demiurge, or prior to the demiurge? Are all things derived from one or from many? Do they know of matter or primary qualitative bodies, and is matter ungenerated or generated?[35]

These were hardly questions to be answered from the mythology of the Egyptian temples.

The similarity of this overall view of the history of Greek philosophy to that of Suhrawardī is plain. It is not difficult to identify channels of transmission sufficient to account for these parallels, but such an account of the history of philosophy was sufficiently widespread in late antique thought as to make the identification of specific textual channels academic. The ʻĀmirī text contains the essential elements: the "Italian" succession stressing Pythagoras and Plato, the oriental connections of Pythagoras, and the stress on religion and revelation as sources of Greek philosophy. The question of *why* Suhrawardī should have chosen to have become a Pythagoreanizing Platonist will be addressed later.

WHAT THE ILLUMINATIONISTS LEARNED FROM PYTHAGORAS

Suhrawardī's relation to Pythagoras involved not just a general respect for him as the founder of true philosophy but also the acceptance of various specific Pythagorean and Neopythagorean doctrines, which Suhrawardī and his followers identify as the doctrine of four worlds, the role of mystical intuition in philosophy, numbers and Platonic Forms, the music of the spheres, and reincarnation, in addition to the more general ideas about the nature of philosophy and the community of philosophers already discussed above. These teachings play varying roles in Suhrawardī's system as fundamental philosophical doctrines, symbols to be explained, and curiosities to be explained away.

The Intelligible Worlds

Quṭb al-Dīn Shīrāzī, the thirteenth-century commentator on *The Philosophy of Illumination*, writes:

> There are four worlds: the world of the intellects that have absolutely no connection with bodies; the world of the souls that are attached to celestial and human bodies; the world of the bodies, comprising the spheres, the elements, and what is in them; and the World of Image and imagination.[36]

He goes on to attribute the doctrine of the World of Image *('ālam al-mithāl)* to "the Ancients," by whom he means Plato and his predecessors, including Pythagoras. In the context of Pythagoras it suffices to mention that Suhrawardī and the Illuminationists held that Pythagoras had believed in the existence of higher levels of being accessible only through the mind and through mystical experience, that this lower world of ours was in some way a shadow of the higher worlds, and that it was possible and desirable for philosophers to behold that higher world. Thus, Pseudo-Ammonius writes, "He mentions that these worlds are innumerable and differ in degree of beauty, splendor, and delight."[37] This is a decidedly Neoplatonic understanding of Pythagoras.

Mystical Intuition as a Basis of Philosophy

In the stock lists of philosophers given by the Illuminationists, Pythagoras is always listed among the masters of intuitive philosophy. This view of Pythagoras can easily be traced to earlier sources. The Pseudo-Ammonius writes, "The words of the sage Pythagoras of Samos are not from mere opinion but are from a spiritual awareness of the worlds and their contents."[38] The Greek sources tend to express this concept less clearly, stressing his dependence on revelation through the intermediary of the Egyptian and Chaldean sages with whom he had studied and stressing also his pious and ascetic lifestyle.[39]

The Music of the Spheres

The charming notion that the motions of the planets produce sounds and harmonies is among the best-known teachings attributed to Pythagoras. Plato writes in the *Republic*: "'It is probable,' I said, 'that as the eyes are fixed on astronomy, so the ears are fixed on harmonic movement, and these two kinds of knowledge are in a way akin, as the Pythagoreans say and we, Glaucon, agree.'"[40] The topic is discussed in more detail by Aristotle in *De Caelo* 2.9, 290b14–30:

> Some thinkers suppose that the motion of bodies of that size must produce a noise, since on our earth the motion of bodies far inferior in size and in speed of movement has that effect. Also, when the sun and the moon, they say, and all the stars, so great in number and in size, are mov-

> ing with so rapid a motion, how should they not produce a sound immensely great? Starting from this argument and from the observation that their speeds, as measured by their distances, are in the same ratios as musical concordances, they assert that the sound given forth by the circular movement of the stars is a harmony. Since, however, it appears unaccountable that we should not hear this music, they explain this by saying that the sound is in our ears from the very moment of birth and is thus indistinguishable from its contrary silence, since sound and silence are discriminated by mutual contrast. What happens to men, then, is just what happens to coppersmiths, who are so accustomed to the noise of the smithy that it makes no difference to them.

Pythagoras, in accordance with his semi-divine state, was able to hear the harmonies of the spheres.

It would seem that in its simplest form the Pythagorean doctrine was concerned only with the orbits of the sun, moon, and stars, with the other planets thought to be at the same height as the fixed stars.[41] There are many difficulties in making such a doctrine work in detail, particularly once the harmonies came to be conceived of as analogous to a seven-string lyre rather than the simple monochord that was the basis of Pythagorean harmonic theory. The obvious difficulty would be that however the relative distances of the planets were arranged, the result would be cacophany. However, the most influential counterargument was that of Aristotle, who objected that there was no physical evidence of such sounds, which would surely be of such a volume as to be destructive. He offers a counteranalogy to a ship drifting on a river, which, though certainly in rapid motion, produces no sound because the ship and river move as a single unit.[42]

The doctrine of the harmony of the spheres was tolerably well known to Islamic scholars. *De Caelo* was available in Arabic, as was Alexander of Aphrodisius' commentary on the *Metaphyics*, which contained a detailed account on the theory.[43] Pseudo-Ammonius wrote: "The speech of this world is like the speech of the higher worlds, for Pythagoras mentioned that the speech of the higher worlds is by simple spiritual tones, so thereby their bliss becomes unending and uninterrupted."[44]

Suhrawardī too is aware of the doctrine of the harmony of the spheres and discusses it in both his Peripatetic and his Illuminationist works. His Illuminationist explanation is the following:

> The spheres have sounds not caused by the same causes as our sounds. We have explained that sound is not the vibration of the air; the most that one can say is that sound here is conditioned on it. However, it does not follow that if something is conditioned on a thing in one place, its like is necessarily so conditioned. A universal thing may have different causes in different instances, and so too it may have different conditions in different

> instances. Just as the colors of the planets are not conditioned on that on which colors with us are conditioned, so too is the case with their sounds. The awful sounds heard by the mystics cannot be said to be the vibration of air in the brain, for it is inconceivable that the vibration of air by that power is due to a ringing in the brain. Instead it is an image of sound—which is a sound. Thus there may be sounds and music in the spheres not conditioned on air or ringing. There is no conceivable music more pleasurable than their music, just as no desire is conceivable like unto their desire. Peace be upon a folk gone dazed and drunk in desire for the world of light and in passion for the glory of the Light of Lights, whose existents are become like unto the Mighty Seven! Therein is "a lesson for those possessed of hearts."[45] The heavens possess hearing not conditioned on ears, sight not conditioned on eyes, olfaction not conditioned on nostrils. This is the most noble contingency and is necessary therein.[46]

Though the music of the spheres is not a central teaching for Suhrawardī and not a doctrine that he builds on, it merits explanation as enjoying the venerable authority of Hermes, Pythagoras, and Plato.[47] Also, Suhrawardī has as evidence the experience of the mystics, perhaps including himself, who had often heard such sounds. Shahrazūrī offers an explanation that is evidently a somewhat pedantic expansion of Suhrawardī's discussion in the *Mashāri'*: "However, the Pythagoreans held that there is air between the spheres and that [the air] comes out from them. They say that we do not hear their sounds because our hearing is filled with them."[48] Though Shahrazūrī is not sure exactly what this argument means, to us it is an easily recognizable as a version of the coppersmith analogy cited by Aristotle. Shahrazūrī mentions two Peripatetic objections to this view: (1) that there is no air or other medium among the spheres to transmit sound, and (2) that the planets are of such a size that sounds caused by them would be extremely loud and destructive. The latter is Aristotle's objection from *De Caelo*. Shahrazūrī accepts that there is no air or other sort of medium between the spheres that might transmit sound vibrations, and so he is puzzled as to whether this teaching is meant literally or symbolically. He leans towards the view that the "air" is a symbol, though Quṭb al-Dīn admits that it certainly seems to be meant literally.

Happily, the dilemma can be resolved through Illuminationist principles well established elsewhere in Suhrawardī's system. First, Suhrawardī points out that a single kind of effect can have causes of different kinds—Aristotle and the Peripatetics are guilty of a "defective induction," to use Shahrazūrī's term. Just because we in our world normally find sound associated with vibrations in air, such vibrations are not part of the reality of the sound. The argument is exactly analogous to that of visual forms, which are usually but not always conditioned on viewing a material object with a material organ. If sounds need not be associated with vibration, then Aristotle's objection concerning the destructiveness of such sounds also falls since there is no reason to suppose that the music of the spheres involves vibrations. Second, Aristotle had taught that the spheres have souls and thus must have the senses of hearing and vision, though not necessarily with material organs of our sort.[49] There is, indeed, positive evidence for the existence of such sounds in the experience of the mystics, who hear sounds that others do not. Such sounds are obviously not caused by vibrations in the air or in the brain but are the "image" *(mithāl)* of sounds in the World of Image. Among those mystics was Pythagoras himself, who "says that he ascended to the higher world and heard with the pure substance of his soul the melodies of the spheres and the sounds of the movements of the planets. He . . . returned to his body and composed scales *(alḥān)* according to what he had heard and completed the art of music."[50] Among Muslims, Shahrazūrī cites the Isma'ili Brethren of Purity as asserting the doctrine of the music of the spheres and gives various other bits of mystical lore related to this teaching—the choir of the angels and the hidden realm of Hūrqalyā, for example.

Shahrazūrī's explanation, an unpacking of Suhrawardī's argument, is an excellent example of Suhrawardī's Illuminationist method at work:

1. The authority of the Ancients makes it necessary to consider the doctrine.
2. The possibility that the doctrine was intended symbolically must be considered and must be decided by philosophical critique rather than by analysis of Pythagoras' teachings in isolation.
3. Objections to the doctrine must be considered from within the conceptual framework of Peripatetic philosophy.
4. The truth of the doctrine can be decided by reference to the testimony of the mystics—the assertoric demonstration.
5. The truth of the doctrine must be understood by reference to Illuminationist philosophical principles—the causal demonstration.[51]

The result is that an archaic and colorful doctrine has been brought into firm, systematic connection with the Illuminationist system. That said, it must also be admitted that the doctrine has come adrift from its moorings in the process. Pythagoras was led to the doctrine by what would seem to be a mystical sense of the mathematical order of the cosmos. Having successfully reduced music to mathematics, Pythagoras saw the mathematics of music as being the basis of the orderliness of the heavenly motions. Shahrazūrī quotes the explanation of the Brethern of Purity:

> The author of *[The Epistles of] the Brethren of Purity* and the Ancients who agree with him hold that the bodies of the spheres were created with the best possible firmness, hardness, smoothness, and unending movement. They rub together when they move, resulting in ineffable melodies.[52]

In either case the argument is essentially physical. For Suhrawardī it is not. The spheres sing to each other, sounds that can only be heard by the purified. His account of the music of the spheres is closer to that of Plato, who tells of a siren sitting on each sphere, singing a single note.[53] There is no longer an argument showing that there must be music of the spheres; there is only an empirical argument that there is such music—the mystics hear it—and an explanation of how such music can be. There is nothing in Suhrawardī's non-mathematical universe that physically requires there to be such music. It is a phenomenon that can be explained in the Illuminationist system but that is not central to it and does not advance it in the sense that other teachings depend on it. Since Suhrawardī has devised a system in which mathematics plays no central role, the music of the spheres can be no more than a curiosity.

Numbers as Platonic Forms

For Suhrawardī the greatest difficulty with Pythagoras is the centrality of mathematics: "There are ratios of number among the intellects and their luminous divine states, for as the divine Pythagoras said, 'The bases of existents are number.'"[54] Suhrawardī and his followers were not the first philosophers to be puzzled by the Pythagorean notion of numbers as principles of being, and in solving the problems it posed Suhrawardī faced a well-worn set of choices. The problem of number is a more complex problem than the music of the spheres, for it touches the bases of metaphysics. It is also is a doctrine that scarcely any philosopher writing after the fourth century B.C.E. could accept in its literal form, however much he might venerate Pythagoras as a philosophical saint.

As usual with Pythagoras, the question of authenticity haunts the feast. At one extreme is Jonathan Barnes, who observes with barely concealed satisfaction, "Scholarly huffing and puffing has blown this chaff from the heap of history; and it has left few grains on the floor."[55] The "grains," in his view, primarily consist of doctrines about the soul. Muttering about "mysticism," "intellectual folly," and "mumbo-jumbo," Barnes discusses Pythagorean number metaphysics under Philolaus, a fifth-century B.C.E. Pythagorean whose fragments receive some credibility from allusions in Aristotle.[56] Guthrie is more charitable to the evidence, allowing that

> the religious doctrines of immortality and transmigration are assigned to Pythagoras on incontrovertible positive evidence. His character as one of

> the most original thinkers in history, a founder of mathematical science and philosophical cosmology, although not directly attested by such early and impregnable sources, must be assumed as the only reasonable explanation of the unique impression made by his name on subsequent thought.[57]

Such puzzlement is nothing new. As early as Aristotle the true doctrines of Pythagoras were in doubt, for he writes cautiously of "Pythagoreans," not of Pythagoras, and the secrecy of the Pythagorean order was already notorious.[58]

Happily, we can leave the details of the authenticity of Pythagorean number metaphysics to the philologists, for Suhrawardī did not share Barnes' scepticism. Since the fourth century B.C.E. philosophers have faced two kinds of evidence about it: (1) texts, typically in doxographies, testifying to a naive metaphysics in which things are in some sense made of numbers, and (2) a series of more-or-less philosophically sophisticated attempts to make sense of this doctrine in the light of mature forms of Greek philosophy. Suhrawardī and his commentators were familiar with the first group, and they themselves are contributors to the second. I will first look at the texts of class (1) that were available to Muslim scholars, in particular texts attested in Illuminationist works. I will then consider the philosophical tradition represented by class (2), looking at the main philosophical alternatives represented in this series of texts and the intellectual dynamics driving this particular tradition of interpretation. Finally, I will discuss Suhrawardī's own solution to the old problem of making these ancient doctrines intellectually respectable.

Three texts of the "naive" doxographical tradition of Pythagorean number metaphysics are of special note: Pseudo-Plutarch (Aetius) on the first principles of being; Aristotle, *Metaphysics* A.5; and Pseudo-Ammonius, part of which has been quoted above.[59]

In a passage much quoted by Islamic doxographers, including Shahrazūrī, Pseudo-Plutarch writes:

> Pythagoras . . . believed that the first principles *(mabādi')* were the numbers and the ratios between them, which he called 'harmonies'. The things compounded from all of them were the elements, or, as he also called them, the 'geometricals'. He also placed the unlimited First and Second among the first principles. He held that one of these principles was the specific efficient cause, which is God and the intellect, and the other was the element that admitted of being influenced by them.[60]

Shahrazūrī, quoting a shortened version of this text, interrupts in exasperation with the comment, "He did not mean that numbers were self-subsistent"—but the comment is necessary because it sounds as though that is exactly what Pythagoras did mean. The passage goes on to explain how ten—the so-called *tetraktys*—comes into being from the monad and the dyad and why ten thus occupies such a high position among the Pythagoreans.

Less familiar to most medieval Islamic readers was Aristotle's famous account of Pythagoreanism in *Metaphysics* A.5:

> Contemporaneously with these philosophers and before them, the Pythagoreans, as they are called, devoted themselves to mathematics; they were the first to advance this study, and having been brought up in it they thought its principles were the principles of all things. Since of these principles numbers are by nature the first, and in numbers they seemed to see many resemblances to the things that exist and come into being . . . they supposed the elements of numbers to be the elements of all things.[61]

The text of the *Metaphysics* used by Averroes was defective in the beginning and starts shortly after these lines. Averroes quotes a passage a few pages later:

> [B]ut [the Pythagoreans] were distinctive in speaking of finitude, the one, and infinity. They were not wont to call fire, earth, or something else 'nature'. Rather, infinity itself and the one itself were substance *(jawhar)*. From these they make them and number them.[62]

Averroes responds to this with the same patronizing sophistication as Aristotle, translating the Pythagorean doctrines into Aristotelian categories. The Pythagoreans, like the Ionian physicists, believed in two of Aristotle's four causes—in their case, the material and formal causes, which they called 'finitude' and 'infinity'. In this they differed from the physicists, whose causes were the material and the efficient.[63] Averroes is simply fitting a superceded school into Aristotle's schematic history of philosophy. In this the faithful Averroes interprets Pythagorean number doctrine in terms of Aristotle's system. This interpretation is too far from the Pythagorean spirit to be considered a philosophical reinterpretation. Rather, it is the attempt of Aristotle, ever the biologist, to pin the Pythagoreans into the proper box with the other exotic specimens he has collected.

The real interpreters of Pythagoras were the Platonists, for they considered themselves, with some justification, to be the heirs of the Pythagorean tradition. The problem faced by the Neopythagorean Platonist in interpreting the Pythagorean number metaphysics is not unlike that faced by a religious philosopher trying to make philosophical sense out of a holy book produced in a simpler time. The inspired word must be both preserved and transcended. The process began in the Pythagorean school itself, but its first triumph was Plato's *Timaeus*. This work will be discussed in detail in later chapters;[64] here we need only say that the title character, Timaeus of Locri, a Pythagorean, is made to present a complete scientific system in which the properties of material things are explained in terms of the microscopic triangles composing them. It is an atypical work in the Neopythagorean tradition, for its use of mathematics is wholly rational and physical, having little trace of the numerological mysticism otherwise characteristic of Pythagorean and Neopythagorean thought. There is also no evidence apart from this dialogue for the historical existence of Timaeus of Locri.[65] Nonetheless, it served to convince ancient philosophers that Plato's thought was firmly rooted in Pythagoreanism.

More typical were the Pythagoreanizing Neoplatonists of the Roman period, philosophers like Porphyry and especially Iamblichus. For such as these Pythagorean number metaphysics was neither a crude foreshadowing of Aristotle nor a system of the physical world as in the *Timaeus*, where physical reality is composed of geometrical objects in a way not so different from that of the atomists. It was an esoteric system of great profundity.

Iamblichus can be taken as typical of this approach to reconciling Pythagoras and Plato. As has been mentioned, he wrote the ten-book *On Pythagoreanism*. Its first book was the biography of Pythagoras, from which I have already quoted. The second book was the *Protreptic to Philosophy*, an introduction to philosophy integrating Platonic materials into a Pythagorean framework. The remaining volumes dealt with mathematics, beginning with an introduction to mathematics (book 3), arithmetic and its application to physics, ethics, and theology (4–7), and the remaining mathematical sciences of geometry, music, and astronomy (8–10).[66] Only the first four books survive intact, but the manuscript from which all others derive was evidently the first volume of two, and its table of contents attests the arrangement of the work and the former existence of books 5–9. The existence of a tenth book, on astronomy, is an inference, for an encyclopedia of Pythagoreanism would surely deal with the heavens and would have ten, rather than nine, books. The plan and unity of the work has been obscured by the fact that modern editors published the four surviving books as separate works. Fragments of the later books, preserved by the eleventh-century Byzantine philosopher and bibliophile, Michael Psellus, show us what the later books must have contained. The voice is that of Psellus.

> You were surprised when, at our meeting yesterday, I said that there was another, physical number besides mathematical number. But if you only knew of the variety of number, you would have asked me about the

> intelligible, essential, and ideal number. For number of this <latter> kind is truly the highest and first. . . . As there are numbers fitting nature, so there are fitting <ethical> habits. And as there is a physical, so there is an ethical arithmetic. . . . The philosopher Iamblichus wrote an arithmetic of higher natures, not treating of the numbers in them mathematically, nor imaging the higher kinds through analogies, nor positing them as hypostatic, self-moved, intellectual, or essential numbers, but he says <that> as the genus of higher <natures> transcends all being, so is their number absolute and of itself. . . .
>
> Suitable and appropriate to the higher kinds is the higher kind of mathematical number, such as the one, limit, the determinate, equal, and such-like. As there is a physical cause of physical numbers, an ethical for ethicals, thus of divine number there is a uniform divine principle, prior as cause to the causes in all numbers, a uniform unity pre-existing even all divine unified number itself.[67]

Psellus goes on to discuss the divine henad, dyad, and triad. O'Meara argues that this discussion, fragmentary though it is in Psellus' excerpts, reflects an attempt to deal with Aristotle's criticisms of the doctrine of the Forms in the context of a Pythagoreanizing Platonism.[68] It certainly represents an attempt to incorporate Pythagorean concern with number within the framework of the complex metaphysics of Neoplatonism. Similar concerns are present in later Neoplatonist philosophies. Proclus, as is well known, wrote a commentary on the first book of Euclid's *Elements*, and incorporated concern with mathematics into his metaphysics.

Most often the Neoplatonists considered the question of Pythagorean numbers in the context of the existence of mathematicals, the theory identifying the Forms as numbers that Plato formulated in his old age, and the criticism of this teaching by Aristotle. Such concerns reached the Muslims by many channels. A rather disjointed rationalization of Pythagorean number metaphysics is preserved in Ibn al-Ṭayyib's *Commentary on the Golden Verses*.

> Pythagoras made numbers Forms and symbols *(muthulan wa-rumūzan)* for divine entities, especially the numbers falling between one and ten. He gave each of them a different cause and different effects. Ten-ness for him was the efficient cause of the world. . . . The first number is an indication of God since He has pure onenness. If another number is related to it, they are forms *(ṣuwar)* of secondary gods, according to what they say. They reserve unity for Zeus and name him by it. They call Athena by threeness and Apollo by sevenness, and likewise other gods. The first numbers are signs of the gods, the secondary [numbers] are the intelligible forms *(al-ṣuwar al-ma'qūla)* in existents, the tertiary numbers are the forms of the soul because they sustain the souls as father and generator of them from the numbers. The quaternary are the forms of

> natural things in the degree of matter and its rank by form. Since the ranks of numbers are the four numbers: divine, rational, of soul, and natural, it is necessary that the end of numbers be in fourness.[69]

More sophisticated Neoplatonic accounts of Pythagorean number theory reached the Muslims through other channels, the commentaries on Aristotle probably being the most important, and find their echoes in the discussions of the Forms in the standard texts of Islamic philosophy.[70]

The most conspicuous Pythagoreans in Islam were the Brethren of Purity—the Ikhwān al-Ṣafā'—authors of a set of "epistles" that together form an encyclopedia with a strongly mathematical bent. Although the philosophical system of the Brethren is Neoplatonism of a sort familiar from other Islamic philosophical systems, their explicit allegiance is Pythagorean. Their encyclopedia begins with arithmetic, not logic, for the Pythagoreans had shown that the fundamental truths of metaphysics could be attained through mathematical proofs.[71]

The Brethren addressed the question of the interpretation of Pythagorean number metaphysics in their thirty-second and thirty-third treatises, which deal with the first principles of beings according to the Pythagoreans and the Brethren of Purity respectively. The bulk of these two chapters is Neoplatonic rather than explicitly Pythagorean, a systematic cosmogony tracing the origin of the various kinds of creatures from God, but first the Brethren must address Pythagoras' puzzling assertion that numbers are the first principles of being. Pythagoras, they tell us, was

> the first to discuss arithmetic and the nature of number. He said that the nature of existents is in accordance with the nature of number. Thus, one who knows numbers, their rules, and their nature, genera, species, and properties, is able to know the number of genera and species of existents. He will understand the wisdom of their being as they are now and why they are neither more nor less numerous than they are.[72]

The Creator is one in every respect, but it is not in accord with divine wisdom for the universe to be one in all respects. Thus, things come into being variously dual, triple, quadruple, and so on. Among things that are dual are matter and form, substance and accident, dark and luminous, good and bad, male and female, and so on. Other classes of beings come in threes: length, breadth, and depth; line, plane, and solid; past, present, and future; and anything with a mean and two extremes. Classifying the world another way, the Brethren divided everything into universals and particulars and stated that there were nine universals, having respectively one through nine attributes: the Creator, who is one absolutely; the intellect, which has two powers; and so on through the soul (3), matter (4), nature (5), body (6), the spheres (7), the elements with their eight combinations, and the nine generated species.[73] Thus, for the Brethren things are not numbers, but they are numbered. Numbers are the first principles of being because the fundamental components of the universe all come in groups of one to nine and the structure of the universe to that extent parallels the relationships among the numbers.

For the Brethren of Purity, the Pythagoreans have a special relation with numbers, for they give each number its due whereas other sects concentrate on a single number. Thus, the dualists—the Zoroastrians and Manicheans—are especially interested in things that come in pairs. Christians concern themselves with triads. The "physicists" *(ṭabī'īyūn)*, presumably the Ionian Presocratic physicists, concern themselves with fours. "Physicist" carried troubling connotations of atheism for unsympathetic Islamic writers. The Ionians' association with four presumably refers to the four elements and the four fundamental properties of physical things: hot, cold, moist, and dry. The Khurrāmīya, an early Shi'ite sect, concerned themselves with fives, the Ismā'īlīs with sevens, musicians with eights, and Indians with nines. The Ismā'īlīs are sometimes known as the "Seveners," both because their origins are supposed to go back to the seventh successor of the Prophet and because of the use of the number seven in their sacred history and cosmology. I do not know the basis of the association of five with the Khurrāmīya, or of nine with the Hindus. According to the Brethren of Purity, only the Pythagoreans concern themselves with all the numbers.[74]

Mathematics plays no special role in the Illuminationist system. There are both biographical and philosophical reasons for this. Prior to Suhrawardī and for some time after, Islamic philosophers were usually physicians, astronomers, or mathematicians by profession. His commentator, Quṭb al-Dīn Shīrāzī, was all three. Suhrawardī was the first major Islamic philosopher to be primarily a Sufi by orientation. (Ghazālī might be included in this category, but I am inclined to see Islamic law and theology as his fundamental disciplines.) Thus, for example, while Suhrawardī is very interested in cosmology and the physical structure of the universe, he has little interest in the mathematical aspects of astronomy. Not being a physician he was equally uninterested in the details of biology. We will see, for example, that he was interested in vision purely from the point of view of epistemology and ignored both the geometrical and biological aspects of vision. Thus, Pythagoras interested him as a mystic rather than as a mathematician. As I have observed above, he had no experience with the magical ability of numbers to shape the physical world and thus no particular motivation to reify them or even produce a complex philosophy of mathematics.

Philosophically, there were good reasons for his rejection of the Pythagorean number metaphysics. Suhrawardī was a thorough nominalist in some important respects, in particular with regard to the *i'tibārāt 'aqlīya*, 'beings of reason'. These include, for Suhrawardī, existence, necessity, and contingency—and the numbers. Such concepts are ways of considering a thing, not something that really is in a thing:

> So too, unity is not a meaning added to the thing in concrete objects, for unity would be one thing among others and would itself have unity. Also one could say "a one and many ones" just as one can say "a thing and many things." Moreover, if the quiddity and the unity belonging to the quiddity are taken as two things, they are two, one of them the unity and the other the quiddity to which the unity belongs, so that each one of them would have a unity. From this follow absurdities.[75]

The numbers beyond one are even more tenuous entities:

> If such is the case with unity, number must also be something intellectual, for if number is made up of ones and unity is an intellectual attribute, number must also be so.
>
> Another consideration is that if four, for example, is an accident subsisting in man, either fourness must be complete in each one of the individuals, which is not the case, or else there must be something of fourness in each one, which can only be the unity. Therefore, either the totality of fourness must have no locus other than the intellect, or else neither fourness nor anything of fourness can be in each one. On this latter supposition also fourness is only in the intellect. It is obvious that if the mind links one in the east to another in the west, it will behold duality. If a man looks at a large group, he can count three or four or five, linking them together as his eye happens to fall upon them, and he can also count numbers like hundreds, scores, and the like.[76]

Obviously for Suhrawardī the Pythagorean number mysticism is not acceptable in a literal form. Suhrawardī, of course, has the option of declaring any of Pythagoras' views to be symbolic or rhetorical,[77] but the doctrine that numbers are the principles of being is too basic to be dismissed out of hand. Instead, he conflates it with his version of the doctrine of Platonic Forms. Thus he denies that Pythagoras meant that numbers were self-sufficient, active principles.

> Among the intellects and their luminous supernatural *(lāhūtī)* states are relations of number, as the divine Pythagoras said, "Numbers are the bases of existents." He did not mean that number was something self-subsistent and active *(fa''āl)*, but rather meant that in the celestial realm *(malakūt)* there are luminous essences that do not subsist in dimensions and that these are active holy identities *(annīyāt)* whose unity does not exceed their essences. . . . There are wondrous numerical relations among them from which wonders occur in bodies.[78]

Reincarnation and the World of Image

There are two other teachings that the Illuminationists associate with Pythagoras: reincarnation and the World of Image. Reincarnation—or, more exactly, metempsychosis—is an unquestionably authentic Pythagorean doctrine, indeed the only one that the skeptical Barnes will admit as both authentically attributed to Pythagoras and of philosophical interest.[79] The story is told, for example, that Pythagoras had been a son of Hermes in an earlier incarnation and had asked from his father the boon of remembering his earlier existences when he was reborn. Having once been the Trojan warrior Euphorbus, he recognized the shield that Menelaus had long ago taken from him on the battlefield and given to the temple of Apollo at Branchidae.[80] For Suhrawardī reincarnation is a theme linking the whole tradition of divine philosophy, both in Greece as represented by Empedocles, Pythagoras, and Plato, and in the Orient. Reincarnation was a decidedly dubious doctrine in Islamic terms, and Suhrawardī chooses to discuss it as a Buddhist doctrine, thus placing it as far away as possible.

The other teaching, the World of Image, is not so easily linked to Pythagoras, since so far as I can tell it is a philosophical doctrine that first emerges clearly in the writings of Suhrawardī himself. The existence of a realm of autonomous images, the "World of Image" or the "fourth realm." Suhrawardī himself calls it "the world of incorporeal figures" *('ālam al-ashbāḥ al-mujarrada)* or in one place "the eighth clime" and "Hūrqalyā." It is one of the doctrines that Suhrawardī's followers attribute to the ancients, usually mentioning Empedocles, Pythagoras, Socrates, and Plato.[81] The concept of a fourth world is not unknown before Suhrawardī; al-Mas'ūdī mentions it in *Kitāb al-Tanbīh wa'l-Ishrāf;* his four worlds are lordship, intellect, soul, and nature.[82] Suhrawardī's "fourth world" is an ontological plane in which images can exist that do not subsist in matter. It serves to explain both the prosaic, images in mirrors; the occult, jinn and magicians' tricks; and the eschatological, the rewards and punishments of the afterlife—and reincarnation. It is particularly associated with the celestial spheres, which are generally the loci of these immaterial images. Some justification for associating the doctrine with Pythagoras might be provided by Ibn al-Ṭayyib's statement that the purified souls of the blessed will live in the pure air just beneath the sphere of the moon.[83] On the other hand, Suhrawardī actually says the Ancients agreed on the existence of *three* worlds, which Quṭb al-Dīn identifies as the worlds of intellect, soul, and body.[84] Why Suhrawardī should not have mentioned the World of Image as a doctrine agreed upon by the Ancients is not clear. However, Suhrawardī certainly thought that Pythagoras had magical powers, and magical powers in his view involved the manipulation of the

World of Image. Therefore, the commentators are justified in attributing knowledge of the World of Image to Pythagoras and the other ancient divine philosophers.

CONCLUSION

A medieval philosopher seeking to reconstruct the Pythagorean philosophy was faced with choices, though perhaps not outright contradictions, and grave problems of interpretation. And borrowings from Pythagoras can take more than one form: a desire to make mathematics and science a primary interest, a mysticism of numbers, a primary concern with the realm of the intelligible. For Suhrawardī and his successors, Pythagoras was the founder and representative of a particular way of doing philosophy. He had sought to know the intelligible realm through intuition, an intuition perfected by a mystical discipline carried out in the context of an elite band of comrades in the mystical and philosophical search. Like Pythagoras Suhrawardī had spent his youth wandering in search of knowledge, had found mystical knowledge through his spiritual exertions, had made it the basis of a philosophical system, and had gathered a circle of disciples to share this quest. Like Pythagoras he had seen this knowledge as the foundation of sound government, and like Pythagoras he had attempted to govern a city by this wisdom—in the case of Pythagoras as a republic of philosophers, and in the case of Suhrawardī through its governor, the Ayyubid prince al-Malik al-Ẓāhir. In death too they shared a fate: each aroused the jealousy of the old elite, was overthrown, and met death. Even the death was by some accounts the same: death by starvation while confined. Each gave short shrift to the philosophy of things of this world in order to explore the higher realm. Each found symbolic expression to be the appropriate mode for expressing such truths, and each confined the inner teaching to an oral tradition within the school.

These parallels are not accidents, for Suhrawardī saw himself as being in a real sense the master of a revived Pythagorean school. Pythagoras, according to Diogenes Laertius, belonged to the "Italian school" of philosophers. Islamic scholars knew the school from Aetius (Pseudo-Plutarch) 1.3, "On the First Principles of Being." Aetius first gives the views of Thales, Anaximander, Anaximenes, Anaxagoras, and Archelaus of Athens. These, he says, were the *Yūnānīyūn*. In Arabic this word usually means "Greeks," but occasionally, as here, it means "Ionians," the word from which it derives. He then gives the views of Pythagoras, Heracleitus, Hippasus of Metapontum, Epicurus, Democritus, Empedocles, Socrates, Plato, Aristotle, and Zeno the Younger (the founder of the Stoics), identifying these as the "Italian school." Shahrazūrī approvingly quotes this in his biographical dictionary of philosophers.[85] The importance of this succession to the Illuminationists may easily be seen by examining the contents of Shahrazūrī's work, a self-consciously Illuminationist history of philosophy. Of the Ionians mentioned by Aetius only Anaxagoras, "mention of whom fills Aristotle's books," is given a separate biography. Of the "Italians" all have biographies with the exceptions of the comparatively obscure (to the Arabs) Heracleitus, Hippasus, and Epicurus. Whereas Diogenes Laertius lists Socrates, Plato, and Aristotle in the Ionian succession, Aetius and Shahrazūrī place them among the Italians. Arguments can obviously be made for both arrangements, but certainly the mystical and mathematical bent of Plato, particularly the Plato of the *Timaeus*, would seem to earn him a place among the Italians, and such late antique philosophers as Iamblichus and Proclus would place him in Pythagoras' succession.

It would seem to be the members of the Italian school who were the 'divine philosophers' among the Ancients. Suhrawardī and Shahrazūrī both are clear that the distinguishing feature of these philosophers was their reliance on mystical intuition and their tendency to use symbolic language to express their doctrines. Therefore, this school is Suhrawardī's, in the sense that he is reviving the approach of these ancient mystical philosophers.

CHAPTER 7

The Divine Plato

> *[The fifth to whom wisdom was attributed] was Plato. He associated with Socrates in order to acquire wisdom, but he did not confine himself to religious matters but dealt in all the sciences—physical, metaphysical, and mathematical. Eventually, he turned over instruction and teaching to his best students and retired from society in order to devote himself to worship of his Lord most high.*[1]

Suhrawardī considered himself to be a Platonist. Despite all that has been written about his having revived the wisdom of ancient Persia, it is plain to any dispassionate reader of his books that Plato is the key figure in his history of philosophy, a figure of such commanding wisdom as to merit without any question his title "Divine" *(ilāhī)*. The central question of the present book is, why did Suhrawardī choose to be a Platonist? This chapter addresses the questions of what Suhrawardī might have known about Plato, what he may have thought Platonism to be, and in what sense his mature philosophical system is Platonic.[2]

THE BIOGRAPHY OF PLATO IN ARABIC

Shahrazūrī, like other medieval Islamic authors, wrote about Plato on the basis of popular anecdote, slightly garbled information from sound Greek sources, and third-hand information about the dialogues. For Shahrastānī, as for Suhrawardī and indeed for the philosophers of Roman times, Plato was the last of the "Ancients," just as Aristotle was the first of the "Moderns."[3] Showing his dependence on a Greek source, he tells us that the name 'Plato' means "wide" or "broad." He was of noble birth, the son of Ariston and a descendant of Asclepius on both sides. If the underlying text is parallel to Diogenes Laertius, "Asclepius" is a garbled rendering of Poseidon, but for Muslim readers, this descent links him with the medical tradition.[4] His mother was a descendent of Solon the Lawgiver, who was well known to medieval Islam as an author of wise sayings and as a lawgiver, a *shāri'*, a secular Greek counterpart of a major Islamic prophet.

At first Plato studied poetry and language *(shi'r wa-lugha)*, an Arabization presumably of the lyrics and tragedy attributed to him in Greek sources, but he abandoned these amusements after hearing Socrates condemn poetry.[5] Shahrazūrī tells us that there were three influences on Plato's philosophy. From Socrates he learned the religious or metaphysical sciences. Prior to meeting Socrates he had followed the views of Heracleitus. Like Socrates he was also influenced by the Pythagoreans, with whom he studied in Egypt after the death of Socrates. He is said to have agreed with Cratylus on the prohibited matters, with Pythagoras on rational matters, and Socrates on political philosophy.[6] This last nugget is also found in Diogenes Laertius 3.8, which says, more plausibly, that it was "sensible matters" in which which he followed Cratylus, the Heracleitan, and this reading is supported by Ibn Abī Uṣaybi'a.[7] It is also said that he took the majority of his philosophy from Socrates and Timaeus.[8]

From some Greek source Shahrazūrī gives a description of Plato. He was swarthy in color, of middle height and erect posture, and quiet and restrained. He had a handsome face, a fine beard, little hair on his cheeks, blue-black eyes with lustrous whites, a black mole on his lower chin. He was subtle of speech, loved to sit in open places alone, and could usually be found by the sound of his weeping, which was audible two miles away.[9] His character and benevolence were well attested.

Shahrazūrī knew of Plato's journey to Sicily to instruct the tyrant Dionysius in philosophy and of its unhappy outcome.

After his return from Egypt, where he had studied after the death of Socrates, Plato built two schools where he taught, the Academy and the Lyceum. Having learned from the experience of Socrates and his own adventures in Sicily, he did not attempt to reform the Athenians, and thus he lived to the ripe age of eighty-one. Toward the end of his life he retired from teaching, giving responsibility for the Academy to Xenocrates and for the Lyceum to Aristotle.

Shahrazūrī has heard that the names of sixty-five of Plato's works have been recorded, and that these are organized in tetralogies *(rābū', pl. rawābī')*, each tetralogy being linked by a common subject and the tetralogies in turn being linked to each other. Of these works, however, he names only the *Phaedo*, whose subject is the soul, and "the spiritual and natural *Timaeus*." The *Phaedo* was known in relatively complete form in Arabic translation. The "spiritual and natural *Timaeus*" probably refers to two epitomes of the *Timaeus* by Galen, both available in Arabic translation. More interesting to Shahrazūrī is the fact that Plato wrote his philosophy in riddles *(yalghuz ḥikmatahu)* so that only the wise could understand his purpose.[10]

Shahrazūrī mentions Plutarch as a source for his knowledge of Plato's works, evidently referring to the *De Placitis* of Pseudo-Plutarch.[11]

Shahrazūrī's more thorough list of Plato's writings derives from a work attributed in other sources to Theon of Smyrna. This Theon is not to be confused with the later and better-known astronomer and mathematician, Theon of Alexandria, who is also known in Islamic sources.[12] Theon of Smyrna was an early-second-century Platonist best known for his extant *On the Mathematical Knowledge That Is Needed to Read Plato (Περὶ τῶν κατὰ τὸ μαθηματικὸν χρησίμων εἰς τὴν Πλάτωνος ἀνάγνωσιν; Expositio Rerum Mathematicarum ad Legendum Platonem Utilium)*, an elementary introduction to the mathematical sciences. Apart from this book Theon is poorly documented in the Greek sources. He himself says that he wrote a commentary on the *Republic*.[13] The *Fihrist* describes Theon as "a zealous Platonist" *(al-muta'aṣṣib li-Falāṭun)* and ascribes to him a work entitled "The Order in which the Books of Plato Should be Read and the Titles of What He Wrote." This is not the book ascribed to him in the Western tradition, but might be a portion of the *Republic* commentary cited by Proclus.[14] Elsewhere the *Fihrist* quotes him as saying that Plato was in the habit of naming his dialogues after characters in them and cites about eighteen dialogues by name and subject on Theon's authority.[15] Theon, with no book title mentioned, is quoted on Plato's ancestry by Proclus in his commentary on the *Timaeus* and by Qifṭī. Since Qifṭī quotes more of the passage than Proclus, it is obvious that the two authors had independent access to Theon's text, directly or indirectly.[16] Since the *Fihrist* only mentions the one work of Theon, it is reasonable to suppose that the quotation on Plato's ancestry, the quotation on the titles of Plato's books, and the list of the dialogues all derive from this book mentioned in the *Fihrist* itself. Since no such work is mentioned in Greek and since these passages do not come from the *Expositio*, it is plausible to assume that they come from the lost commentary on the *Republic*. Two of Plato's brothers are mentioned in the first lines in the dialogue, and so a commentator might naturally discuss Plato's family, as Proclus does in a similar context in his commentary on the *Timaeus*. Likewise, a commentary on the *Republic* would likely discuss the dialogue's place in Plato's overall project. Theon's commentary on the *Republic* would probably be useful to Proclus commenting on the *Timaeus* because Theon's particular interest was mathematics. The simplest explanation for the Arabic citations is that excerpts from the beginning of Theon's commentary on the *Republic* were translated into Arabic as a guide to reading Plato. We do have a commentary on the *Republic* by Proclus, but it is missing the section on the characters of the dialogue where we would have expected to find Theon cited again. Proclus' commentary does not contain a guide to the order of reading Plato's dialogues although it does discuss the place of the *Republic* among them.[17]

To add to the confusion, there were at least two other Platos who appear in Arabic literature. Arabic authors were also familiar with a "Plato the Physician"—"Aflāṭūn al-Ṭabīb" as opposed to our Plato, who was "Aflāṭūn al-Ḥakīm, "Plato the Sage"—who was the fifth of the "Eight Physicians" and appeared 735 years after the death of Parmenides, around the end of the third century C.E. Ibn Abī Uṣaybi'a, on the authority of Pseudo-John Philoponus, said that he integrated the three major medical schools of his time: the dogmatists, the empiricists, and the methodists. The *Fihrist* also identifies him as a source for Galen—which would, however, make his third century date impossible. Pseudo-Philoponus also mentions that he "burned the books of Thesallus," presumably the first-century methodist Thesallus of Tralles. The *Fihrist* lists him as the author of a book on cauterization *(kitāb al-kayy)* in one part; al-Nadīm does not know who translated it. It exists in manuscript. Sezgin lists it as a "pseudo-Platonic work," but this is hardly fair since the Arabic sources are clear that it is by a much later physician with the same name. Ibn Abī Uṣaybi'a mentions a number of physicians who were his students or who followed his tradition. Probably he is another of those physicians of late antiquity whose names are preserved, often impossibly garbled, only in Arabic sources.[18] A "Plato the Copt" from Ḥulwān in Egypt, the follower of the materialist "Ṭīsūs," appears briefly in Pseudo-Apollonius of Tyana.[19] He does not seem to be the philosopher Plato, the physician, or, as has been suggested, Plotinus.

If the matter is not sufficient confused already, two works of Galen translated into Arabic dealt with the medical aspects of our Plato's works: *The Medical Commentary on the Timaeus (Περὶ τῶν ἐν τῷ Πλάτωνος Τιμαίῳ ἰατρικῶς εἰρημένων, Kitāb fīmā Dhakarahu Aflāṭūn fī Kitābihi al-Ma'rūf bi-Ṭīmāwus min 'Ilm al-Ṭibb;*) and *The Book of the Opinions of Hippocrates and Plato* (*Περὶ τῶν 'Ιπποκράτους καὶ Πλάτωνος δογμάτων; Kitāb fī Ārā' Buqrāṭ wa-Falāṭūn; GAS*, 3:105). These two last works are preserved in Arabic only in quotations, though a nearly complete Greek version of the latter exists and is available in a handsome edition and translation.[20]

So who is this Plato known to the Muslims? Al-Qifṭī remarks that "the Greeks exaggerate about Plato, praising him and saying that his birth was divine and that he was born under a fortunate star. They tell stories about him that are more like tall tales, so I have omitted them."[21] In rational philosophy he followed Pythagoras, and in many ways his story is like that of Pythagoras. We read that he travelled in search of wisdom, bringing together several traditions. He was also connected with Egypt through his visit there and was supposedly a contemporary of Zoroaster. He was thus the figure in whom all the intellectual and spiritual traditions of the ancients met: the heir of the wisdom of the Greeks and the barbarians and the teacher of all the philosophers who came after him. Unlike Pythagoras and Socrates he knew the impossibility of reforming his countrymen, so he kept silent and thus lived a long life. He works were all written in riddles and symbols, though few in the Islamic Middle Ages had read them directly. But who could doubt that the wisdom of the ancients culminated in him?

Such a reverence for Plato was reinforced by other sorts of information. As the heir of Hermes, Plato also appeared as the author of texts on scientific and occult subjects. A work on geometry was attributed to him, *Kitāb Uṣūl al-Handasa* (The Elements of Geometry), translated by the famous Greek Christian philosopher, astronomer, and mathematician Qusṭā b. Lūqā, the Costa ben Luca or Constanbulus of the Latins.[22] There are several manuscripts of a work on the magical properties of letters on the basis of their numerical values, the *Kitāb al-Khāfiya* (The Book of the Secret).[23] He is cited as an authority for astrology by Māshā' Allāh and the *Picatrix;* a *Kitāb al-Fuṣūl* (Book of Chapters) and *Kitāb al-Nawāmīs* (Book of Laws) are mentioned. He is one of the authorities in the anonymous compilation *Asrār al-Qirānāt* (Mysteries of Conjunctions), compiled for the Caliph al-Ma'mūn.[24]

As a scientist, though, Plato was best known for alchemy. The illustrious physician and free-thinking admirer of the ancients

> Abū Bakr al-Rāzī—that is, Muḥammad b. Zakarīyā—claimed that it is not possible to master the science of philosophy, nor can any learned man be rightly called a philosopher, without mastering the knowledge of the art of alchemy. By it he would become independent of all men, whereas all others would be in need of him for his knowledge and his condition. . . . Rāzī claimed in another place in his books that a number of philosophers—Pythagoras, Democritus, Plato, Aristotle, and later Galen—used to practice this art.[25]

Plato's association with alchemy is not unreasonable given his detailed attempt at developing a chemistry in the *Timaeus*. More than a dozen works on alchemy are attributed to him in Arabic, in addition to works citing him with other ancient sages, like the *Turba Philosophorum*. The most important is probably the *Kitāb al-Rawābī'* (Tetralogien), which was translated into Latin in the Middle Ages. A work on "corrections to Plato" *(Muṣaḥḥaḥāt Aflāṭūn)*, "who in this art excelled all the philosophers who were his peers," is attributed to Jābir (the Latin Geber), in which the alchemical views supposedly taught by Plato to his student Timaeus are criticized and corrected.[26]

The doctrines of these works are not cited in the well-known summaries of Plato's views (although these works have not been studied enough that we would know), and their titles are not included in the Arabic lists of dialogues. They do, however, reinforce the view of philosophy and the philosopher that we saw when discussing Empedocles and Pythagoras: the philosopher as magician and master of supernatural powers. That Plato in particular should be associated with such arts is only fitting, given that he was the greatest of the Greek philosophers and that he was rightly held to have had a mystical side, in contrast to Aristotle and the Peripatetics. Though the occult works attributed to Plato will not directly figure in the discussions below, the reader should remember that they colored medieval Muslims' view of Plato.

PLATONIC MATERIALS IN ARABIC

Evidence for Translations

There is no unabiguous evidence of a complete Arabic translation of any Platonic dialogue before modern times. Suhrawardī, we can be reasonably sure, did not read any authentic work of Plato in its original form. Of course, we cannot say for certain that such translations did not once exist. The *Fihrist* actually mentions of number of translations, either that al-Nadīm saw himself or that he had heard of from trustworthy people, including the *Laws*, the *Sophist* with a commentary by Olympiodorus, the *Timaeus*,[27] "The *Book of Correspondences (Kitāb al-Munāsabāt)*,"[28] "Plato's book to Iqriṭun, on laws,"[29] "The *Book of Unity (tawḥīd)*, and his discourse *(qawl)* on the soul, intellect, substance, and accident," "The *Book of Beauty and Pleasure*, "The *Book of Education of the Young*," "extant letters," and *The Principles of Geometry*."[30] Other translations are attested less clearly,[31] "the *Republic*, which Ḥunayn b. Isḥāq commented on," "a discourse *(qawl)* which he called the *Timaeus*, corrected by Yaḥyā b. 'Adī." Other references to translations of specific dialogues can be found in the Arabic sources, as can identifiable quotations.

The difficulty is that no full texts are known, nor unambiguous evidence that Islamic authors had read full texts. In several cases, we have abridgments, epitomes, or paraphrases—notably Fārābī's summary of the *Laws*, Averroes' commentary on the *Republic*, and the translation of Galen's epitome of the *Timaeus*. There are quotations from some sort of continuous biographical narrative—omitting most of the philosophy—compiled from the *Apology*, *Crito*, and *Phaedo*.[32] Although it is possible that the dialogues did originally exist in full Arabic translation, it should give us pause that there is no scholarly agreement about the nature of the texts used by Fārābī and Averroes. Questioning the general consensus that

Fārābī's summary of the *Laws* was based on some late abridgment translated into Arabic, Parens argues that Fārābī may well have had access either to a good Arabic translation—presumably the translations mentioned in the *Fihrist* by Ḥunayn b. Isḥāq and Yaḥyā b. ʻAdī, both competent translators—or even to a Greek text.[33] But Parens has no direct evidence for Fārābī's access to a translation, only arguing that Fārābī would have wished to use as good a text as possible, that the quality of his commentary argues for familiarity with the text, and that there is no evidence to disprove the existence of a full translation or a good Greek text available to Fārābī. All this is so, but the case for a full translation of any dialogue remains unproved.

Another argument for the absence of integral translations of the dialogues can be made from the bewilderment we find in the Arabic sources about the genre of Plato's books. Theon, as quoted in the *Fihrist*, wrote that "Plato composed his books as discourses that he told about people (or 'on their authority'; *yaj'al kutubahu aqwālan yaḥkīhā 'an qawm*), and he named each book after the person it was written for."[34] Theon surely knew what he meant, but this explanation could not have been very informative to a medieval Arabic-speaking reader unfamiliar with the dialogue form. When Qifṭī transcribed the passage two and a half centuries later, he simply wrote that Plato "would name his books after the men who had requested them," a titling convention common in Arabic scholarship.[35]

Another approach to the puzzling genre of dialogue was to treat them as history. This has merit, of course, and even contemporary histories of Greek philosophy wrestle with the question of how far the dialogues can be trusted as sources for the life and views of Socrates and, to a lesser extent, other interlocutors like Parmenides. Such an interpretation would be natural to Muslims. Not only is it the obvious way to read the dialogues in the absence of other evidence, but Islamic scholars with their strong tradition of oral transmission would recognize the dialogues as a form of hadith.

Somewhat in the same vein are passages identifying characters in the dialogues as influences on Plato. No one seems to have thought of the dialogues as doxographies, but it is sometimes assumed that they recorded the teachings that Plato had absorbed. Shahrazūrī states that Plato took most of his views from Socrates and Timaeus,[36] while Shahrastānī mentions that he "studied with *(akhadha al-'ilm min)* Socrates, Timaeus, and two strangers: an Athenian stranger and an Eleatic stranger"[37]—the Athenian stranger of the *Laws* and the Eleatic stranger of the *Sophist* and *Statesman.* This interpretation of the dialogues actually contradicts the biographical tradition available to Islamic scholars, which specifically identified the primary influences on Plato as Socrates, Pythagoras, and Heracleitus, though the careful Qifṭī remarks that nothing is known of the views of the Heracleitans.[38]

The final explanation of the dialogues and the one of most interest to Suhrawardī and his school is that they were deliberate riddles. Phrases like "he wrote his philosophy in riddles *(yalghuz ḥikmatahu)* so that only the wise could understand him" and "in them he employed symbolism and obscurity" *(dhahaba fīhā ilā al-ramz wa'l-ighlāq)* appear in the biographies.[39] Such a notion is also found—rightly—in the Arabic accounts of Pythagoras. It would have appealed to Islamic readers, familiar as they were with various esoteric traditions in which knowledge was to be revealed only slowly to the learner. Islamic readers were also familiar with the notion that Plato's works as a whole comprised a course of philosophical education. His works were connected in "tetralogies" *(rābū')*, each dealing with a single theme and each connected thematically with the tetralogy that came before it.[40]

At the end of this chapter, I will return to the question of the Platonic dialogue, Platonic myths, and philosophical allegory. First, however, I need to discuss one dialogue that was comparatively well known to the Muslims, the *Timaeus*.

Galen's Epitome of the Timaeus

Fashion changes in reading Plato. Our age is inclined to see the *Republic*, with its sparkling conversation and dialectic brilliance, as the height of Plato's achievement. This taste has not been universal, and philosophers of Late Antiquity and the Middle Ages were more likely to respect the dogmatic seriousness of the *Timaeus* and the *Laws*.[41] The *Laws* need not detain us in the context of Suhrawardī—his politics were mystical, not practical—but the *Timaeus* needs mention, for according to Suhrawardī's commentators,

> [The philosophy of illumination] "is the very intuition of the inspired and illumined Plato, the guide and master of philosophy," because of what is said in his books, the *Timaeus* and the *Phaedo*, and in his epistles [or "essays," *rasā'il]*.[42]

The *Timaeus* existed in Arabic in the form of an epitome by Galen, part of a larger collection of epitomes of the dialogues. The bibliographical issues are confusing, and were confusing even when the *Fihrist* was written. The published Arabic version that we have is entitled "Epitome of the *Timaeus* on Natural Science." It is attributed to Galen, and the translation is attributed to Ḥunayn b. Isḥāq. Apparently this is the "Natural Timaeus" referred to by Ṣā'id, Shahrazūrī, and others, dealing with "the arrangement of the world of nature" and which is different than the "Spiritual Timaeus" dealings with "the world of soul, intellect, and lordship."[43] Whatever is the case, the epitome as we have it covers the entire dialogue. A "Medical Timaeus" is also sometimes mentioned.[44]

The *Timaeus* was important to the medievals, both Muslim and Christian, because it presented a comprehensive, rational account of the origin and structure of the universe with a clear place for God and creation. It was especially important to the Latins, for in the partial translation and commentary of Calcidius it was the only text of Plato and the most important text of ancient cosmology available to them up to the twelfth century. Thus, in Europe an important early stage in the development of medieval science was the attempt to reconcile the *Timaeus* with the account of creation in Genesis. By its existence it showed that rational investigation of the cosmos and, more important, the assertion that the cosmos was itself rational were compatible with monotheism. For Pythagoreanizing Neoplatonists like Suhrawardī, it also had the value of connecting Plato unambiguously with the Pythagorean tradition, for Timaeus, to whose account of the universe Socrates listens without interruption and whom the Islamic historians of philosophy count as a teacher of Plato, was a Pythagorean.

The *Timaeus* is a dialogue of medium length, about a quarter the length of the *Republic*—seventy-five pages in the standard edition.[45] Though it begins as a dialogue, it soon turns into a lecture by the visiting Pythagorean, Timaeus of Locri. It is set on the day following the day of the *Republic*, though it was written much later. It was to have been the first part of a trilogy. The second, the *Critias*, was to have contained an account of the ideal city, primeval Athens, and its defeat of Atlantis, but this dialogue is incomplete. The final dialogue, the *Hermocrates*, was never written. The *Timaeus* opens with a recapitulation of the *Republic* and a summary of the account of ancient Athens that was to come in the *Critias*, the story of the Athenian defeat of Atlantis that the Athenian lawgiver Solon learned from the priests of Egypt.

The bulk of the dialogue consists of Timaeus of Locri's lecture on the origin and operation of the universe. The ancients accepted the historicity of Timaeus on the basis of a work attributed to him entitled "On Soul of the World and Nature" (Περὶ φύσιος κόσμω καὶ ψωχᾶς), which was supposedly Plato's source when he was writing the *Timaeus*, but this work is universally recognized by modern scholarship as an epitome of Plato's *Timaeus*. The chief basis for rejecting Timaeus' historicity is that he appears nowhere else in the philosophical or historical record. The usual explanation is that Plato needed a Pythagorean with astronomical and medical knowledge, and there was no such real Pythagorean of the right age.[46] The pronounced Pythagorean character of the dialogue led the modern commentator A. E. Taylor to see the *Timaeus* not as the supreme statement of Plato's mature views but a genuine piece of fifth-century Italian Pythagoreanism:

> It is, in fact, the main thesis of the present interpretation of Plato's dialogue that the teaching of Timaeus can be shown to be in detail exactly what we should expect in a fifth-century Italian Pythagorean who was also a medical man, that it is, in fact, a deliberate attempt to amalgamate Pythagorean religion and mathematics with Empedoclean biology.[47]

This thesis is vehemently rejected by the other great modern English interpreter of the *Timaeus*, Francis Cornford. If Taylor's thesis is rejected, then the Pythagoreanism of the *Timaeus* must be Plato's own. This, of course, was the view of Plato held by the Neoplatonists and, much later, Suhrawardī.

The most important assumption of Timaeus' lecture is that the cosmos is divided into "being" and "becoming." The sensible physical world is becoming, a more or less imperfect copy of the intelligible world of being. Thus, even Timaeus' account of the universe can only be probable, "a likely story." In a sense, then, the cosmology and physics of the *Timaeus* are no more than a particularly rigorous and plausible myth, not unlike Plato's other myths. The point is important to us, for the distinction of being and becoming operates in Suhrawardī's *Philosophy of Illumination*, and Illuminationist cosmology can also be said to fall into the category of "likely story." The lecture itself has three parts: the "works of reason," the "works of necessity," and the "cooperation of reason and necessity." Perhaps these, with the introductory discussion, are the "four books" of the *Timaeus* referred to in Islamic sources.

In the "works of reason," Timaeus describes the creation of the universe by the demiurge: the form of the universe as a whole, the uniqueness of the universe, its spherical shape, its natural rotation, and the world-soul. There is a good deal of complex mathematics involved in the deduction of the geometry of the spheres and the motions of the planets. The "works of necessity" or of the "errant cause" deals with the nature of becoming. Plato's notion seems to be that the demiurge, his creator god, is to some extent constrained by necessity, which seems to mean the uncooperativeness of the raw material with which the demiurge must work. In this section Plato attempts to invent the equivalent of particle physics and chemistry. The material world is made in the "receptacle of becoming," an entity with no qualities of its own. The receptacle is resolved into triangles, which then form the four primary bodies. Plato sets up a very complicated system whereby these triangles and the bodies they form explain the properties of the elements and of material bodies, including the sensible properties like taste, odor, color, and sound. The final section, on the cooperation of reason and necessity, describes the physiology and pathology of the human body.

The *Timaeus* is a remarkable attempt to create a complete scientific system of the world, not just describing the features of the world but attempting to deduce them from first principles. Since Aristotle's physical system on the whole works better, the system of the *Timaeus* was generally supplanted by that of Aristotle in later times—but not always.

How would the *Timaeus* have appeared to Islamic scholars? Their best source would have been Galen's epitome, although there are many references to the *Timaeus* in Aristotle. Galen says that

> Plato's purpose in his book called the *Timaeus* is to discuss the coming to be *(kawn)* of the world and the living things in it. He does not distinguish the words 'world' *('ālam)* and 'sky' *(samā')*, since he means by 'sky' the round body that moves in a circle.[48]

After mentioning the introductory conversation on the war between ancient Athens and Atlantis, Galen continues:

> Thereafter, Plato makes the speaker to be Timaeus, but not in the question-and-answer format that is ordinarily used in the books of Plato. Instead, he makes Timaeus the only speaker. For this reason we cannot abridge what Timaeus has to say in this book in the way we have done when summarizing the meaning of other books of Plato. In the other books his discussion is long and diffuse, but in this book it is extremely condensed, very different from the laconic and obscure works of Aristotle and from the prolixity of Plato in his other works. Though you might imagine that there are some laconic and obscure passages, these are actually very few. If you think about it, you will discover that the cause [of not understanding the text] is not the obscurity of the text in itself . . . but rather that the text is obscure because it can only be understood by someone who has studied that particular science.[49]

Galen then begins to summarize the dialogue, which he does in a clear and workmanlike manner. He ends some thirty pages later with the simple note:

> This is all of the book entitled *Timaeus*. I hope to give a simplified account *(akhdh jumalihā wa-mawāqi'ihā)* of its mathematical portions in the following chapters *(maqālāt)*.[50]

The promise is not fulfilled in what is available to us in Arabic. Nor does Galen give a satisfactory account of the place of the *Timaeus* among the works of Plato or explain why Plato's physical science should be put into the mouth of Timaeus of Locri.

Fārābī in his *Philosophy of Plato* places the *Timaeus* immediately after the *Republic* and describes its content in terms of Plato's political philosophy.

> When this city [i.e., the city ruled by philosophers as described in the *Republic]* had been rendered perfect in speech, he next presented in the *Timaeus* an account of the divine and natural beings as they are perceived by the intellect and known by means of that science; [he showed] what distinguishes the sciences that ought to be set up in that city; how everything that is not yet known will be inquired into and a comprehensive investigation of it will be made in that city; and how there will be a succession of men who will investigate this science and preserve what is discovered of it, until all of it is found.[51]

In his *Attainment of Happiness*, which serves as an introduction to the *Philosophy of Plato* and the *Philosophy of Aristotle*, Fārābī also mentions the *Timaeus*, this time in the course of a discussion of the distinction between philosophy and religion. He has argued that according to the Ancients philosophy and religion dealt with the same subjects, differing only in the means by which the subjects were conceived and assented to. In philosophy the subjects are conceived by the intellect and assented to after demonstration. In religion conception is brought about by similitudes presented to the imagination, and assent through rhetorical persuasion. In the course of listing the kind of similitudes used in religion, Fārābī remarks that

> Religion . . . imitates the actions of natural powers and principles by their likenesses among the faculties, states, and arts that have to do with the will, just as Plato does in the *Timaeus*. It imitates the intelligibles by their likenesses among the sensibles: for instance, some imitate *matter* by *abyss* or *darkness* or *water*, and *nothingness* by *darkness*.[52]

In other words, Fārābī considers the *Timaeus* to be *religion*, not philosophy, for it deals with the likenesses of intelligibles rather than with those intelligibles as known by the intellect. It is a plausible story, exactly as Timaeus himself tells us in the dialogue, a similitude of the truth. In this Fārābī disagreed with Galen, who, as we have seen, held the *Timaeus* to be perspicuous, requiring no special interpretive tools apart from familiarity with the sciences under discussion.

Obviously, such an interpretation of the *Timaeus* would seem appropriate to Suhrawardī and to the Illuminationists who followed him, for they held that the Ancients, Plato included, had written in a more or less symbolic fashion. That the *Timaeus* in particular should be a symbolic text has some interpretive significance, since it completely contradicts Aristotle's physical system, even those parts that everybody believed to be sound.

Fārābī's understanding of the *Timaeus* raises a more important question for the interpretation of Suhrawardī's works. The counterpart of the *Timaeus* among Suhrawardī's works is *The Philosophy of Illumination* itself, particularly the second book, in which the metaphysics of light and darkness is expounded. Are we to understand its "science of lights" as another "likely story"? The *Timaeus* is an attempt to combine the earlier likely stories—the myths of other dialogues—with scientific rigor. Plato hoped to produce a plausible account of a reality that even in principle can only be known imperfectly. Suhrawardī's purpose in *The Philosophy of Illumination* is much the same. He too has his simple myths, recorded in his allegorical stories. Plato signifies the discontinuity of the great myth of the *Timaeus* from the rest of his work by putting it into the mouth of a Pythagorean stranger and making Socrates a passive listener. Suhrawardī signifies the discontuity of *The Philosophy of Illumination* from his other work by recasting it in new terminology and abandoning the language and methods of the Peripatetics. For Suhrawardī too his subject can only be expounded through similitudes, for the first principles of the science of lights and the full intellectual conception of its central subjects—the incorporeal lights—are not accessible to the ordinary consciousness. Suhrawardī "imitates the intelligibles by their likenesses among the sensibles," just as Fārābī said Plato had done in the *Timaeus*. Quṭb al-Dīn confirms this when he gives an account of the cosmos following the pattern (though not the technical terminology) of *The Philosophy of Illumination* in his semi-popular philosophical encyclopedia, *The Pearly Crown:* "These considerations about the first intellect are given merely as a possible example of how the many might emanate from the One without asserting that in reality it could not have been different."[53] In other words, the careful reader can infer that the cosmology of *The Philosophy of Illumination* is a plausible account of that which cannot be fully known or fully explained. It is to be distinguished from Suhrawardī's "Peripatetic" works because it reaches beyond them and abandons demonstrative rigor. It is to be distinguished from the allegories, which are written for beginners, in that it deals with the highest truths for the most advanced seekers.

Other Sources on Platonic Philosophy

There are or were other Platonic materials in Arabic. Nearly all of Aristotle was translated, with extensive selections from the Greek commentaries, so almost anything Aristotle said about Plato, along with much that the commentators said, was or might have been available to medieval Muslim philosophers, but there were few books specifically devoted to Plato. According to the *Fihrist* the early Muslim philosopher al-Kindī wrote several books relating to Plato. Among his "arithmetical works" is listed "A Treatise in Explanation of the Numbers Mentioned in His Book the *Republic*." Among his political works are "A Treatise on the Dialogue that Transpired between Socrates and Aeschines," "A Treatise on the Death of Socrates," and "A Treatise on What Transpired between Socrates and the Guards."[54] Also listed among his political works are treatises on "The Excellence of Socrates" and "The Words of Socrates," which could be anything but probably are the kind of wise sayings and stories found in the biographical literature. Kindī also wrote "A Treatise on What Is Said about the Soul, Abridged from the Book of Aristotle, Plato, and the Rest of the Philosophers."[55] The works relating to the death of Socrates were probably based on some sort of text like the harmony of the dialogues reconstructed by Alon. Probably Plato's opinions in Kindī's treatise on the soul come from some version of the *Phaedo*. The work on numbers in the *Republic* perhaps points to Theon of Smyrna.[56] The scantiness of these texts indicates that Kindī, at least, did not have access to a great deal of material on Plato. However, he lived in the ninth century in the early stages of the translation movement, so it is possible that more material became available soon after.

One source of information—not necessarily accurate—on the Greek philosophers is disappointing on Plato. *The Differing Opinions of the Philosophers on the First Principles and the Creator* of Pseudo-Ammonius *(Kitāb Ammūniyūs fī Ārā' al-Falāsifa bi-'khtilāf al-Aqāwīl fī 'l-Mabādi' wa fī 'l-Bāri')* is a treatise on the views of the Greek philosophers about God and the first principles of the universe attributed to Ammonius of Alexandria, known to the Arabs as the student of Proclus and teacher of John Philoponus. Its modern editor considers it to be a ninth-century Islamic work based partly on Hippolytus' *Refutatio Omnium Haeresium* and partly on Neoplatonic materials.[57] Pseudo-Ammonius does not devote a separate section to Plato, who appears agreeing or disagreeing with various philosophers about particular doctrines. Plato and Empedocles are said to have agreed, against Thales and Plutarch, that the Creator had a kind of motion.[58] He and Aristotle are said to have asserted in opposition to Plutarch and Anaxagoras that the will and the act have form *(ṣūra)* distinct from the willer and willed and the actor and effect.[59] Pseudo-Ammonius is often quoted, especially on the question of the nature of creation, but he does not seem to enter into Suhrawardī's understanding of Plato.

Shahrastānī wrote his heresiography around the time of Suhrawardī's birth. Plato, he tells us, was known for monotheism *(tawḥīd)* and wisdom and was the successor of Socrates after the latter was poisoned.[60] On Plato his sources were Pseudo-Ammonius, *Metaphysics* A, the *Timaeus* and the *Laws* (presumably the epitomes that were in circulation), a "Rāmūz" ("model") attributed to Plato, and probably the *Theology of Aristotle.* Implicitly admitting that he did not have direct access to works of Plato, Shahrastānī says that a number of Plato's students report his views on God and the creation of the universe. These students included Aristotle, Timaeus (!), and Theophrastus. They reported that he held that the world had an omniscient Creator who had no beginning in time. Before the creation of the world there was nothing but a Form *(mithāl)*, sometimes called 'matter' *(hayūlā)* and sometimes 'element' *('unṣur)*. What follows is a very Neoplatonic and monotheistic account of Plato, but one that preserves distinctive features of his views, notably the Forms and the preexistence of the soul. Shahrastānī's account is almost a mirror image of the account in Fārābī's *Philosophy of Plato*, for it is entirely metaphysical and does not deal at all with politics; even the quotation from the *Laws* deals with philosophical religion.

DIALOGUE, MYTH, AND ALLEGORY

Plato's Dialogues in Late Antique Philosophy

We now need to consider the dialogue as a philosophical genre. The question is important, for a continuous literary-philosophical tradition runs from Plato's dialogues to Suhrawardī's allegories.

The literary forms used for writing philosophy have changed through the ages in response to changes in philosophy. The most common have usually been the treatise on a specific science; the summa, covering an entire philosophical system; the essay, answering a single question; and the commentary. All except the commentary are already found among the works of Aristotle, and his followers soon supplied that lack. Fashions might change somewhat—commentaries and summas are now out of style and essays unusually popular—but the literary forms used by philosophers were already well established in Roman times.

In Plato's time the situation was still fluid, and other genres contended for the loyalty of philosophers. The Pythagoreans employed riddling symbols, as we have seen, but mostly kept silent about their doctrines. Empedocles and Parmenides, among others, wrote poems. Some Presocratics seem to have employed epigrams, though that often reflects that fragmentary form in which we have their works.

Plato's choice of the dialogue surely reflects three influences: the pedagogical and philosophical approach of Socrates, the secrecy of the Pythagoreans, and Plato's own early experience as a dramatist. The Arabic sources, like the Greek, tell us that when Plato fell under the influence of Socrates, he destroyed his youthful efforts at poetry. The early dialogues, full of the snap and vigor of the great teacher's conversation, are probably sufficiently explained as efforts to convey the experience of Socrates. Later the dialogues become complex dialectical enterprises in which Plato's own position is often obscure. Toward the end, in dialogues like the *Timaeus*, the dialectical and ironic sides of the earlier dialogues are entirely lost, and they become very much like philosophical treatises. Nonetheless, even in so untheatrical a dialogue as the *Timaeus*, Plato remains sufficiently cryptic that its two recent English commentators can disagree on so basic a question as whether or not the cosmology given there actually represented Plato's views.[61] Also, we know that Plato, like the Pythagoreans, had a private teaching given orally to his students—the famous "unwritten doctrines."[62]

During the lifetime of Plato and for a little while after, the dialogues must have been a well-understood part of a lively, mostly oral intellectual life. When Aristotle, with his twenty years of study with Plato, wrote of his teacher's doctrines, he obviously wrote from an intimate knowledge of what Plato actually thought and was not necessarily citing particular passages in the dialogues. He was the last who could do so; other ancient commentators on Plato could only make more or less plausible inferences about Plato's views based on the texts of the dialogues and indirect evidence of his unwritten doctrines. During antiquity attitudes toward and understanding of the dialogues changed greatly.

The dialogue as a literary form fell from favor in Greek. Aristotle wrote some, which were popular for a few centuries, but they were supplanted by the systematic treatises of the *Corpus Aristotelicum*. Diogenes Laertius records the names of dialogues by others, but we do not have them. The Neoplatonists did not write dialogues. An exception that proves the rule is Porphyry's *Exposition of Aristotle's* Categories *by Question and Answer*, which is really a catechism, not a dialogue.[63] So far as I know, none of the Greek philosophical classics after Plato were in dialogue form. The Romans, always behind the times in higher culture, did write some dialogues. Cicero's *The Nature of the Gods* (1st cent. B.C.E.) and Augustine's *Against the Academicians* and *The Teacher* (late 4th cent.) are examples. In the Middle Ages the dialogue form is not common, although Peter Abelard wrote one under the influence of Latin models. It was not until the Renaissance that the dialogue came back into fashion.[64]

Even the Platonists themselves forgot what the dialogues were intended to be and instead mined them for systematic doctrines. When we reach the far end of antiquity, we find Proclus writing learned commentaries on the dialogues—in effect, converting them into philosophical treatises—and his interest is especially in the dialogues most amenable to such treatment: the *Parmenides* and the *Timaeus*, for example, not the early

Socratic dialogues. The dialogue form is utterly unsuited for the systematic and dogmatic philosophy of the Neoplatonists—or, for that matter, for the philosophy of any of the philosophical sects of Hellenistic and Roman times. In the Middle Ages, Proclus' commentary on the *Parmenides* was translated into Latin, but the medievals displayed no interest in the underlying text of Plato.

Some later writers in Greek were still interested in writing philosophy in an indirect way, but for esoteric initiation. Thus, the closest things to philosophical dialogues that we find in Greek in Roman times are certain treatises of the *Corpus Hermeticum*. Though these works are often in dialogue form—though inclining to the monologous, as in the later Plato—their spirit is utterly different from the Platonic dialogue. They are the records of gods revealing the truth to their semidivine disciples. There is no irony, no ambiguity, no search for truth, no doubt about what viewpoint the author wishes to convey. They are catechisms for initiates, not philosophical explorations.

The Arabs thus did not have the Platonic dialogues as a literary example, and so Islamic philosophers did not write dialogues in the Platonic mode. Actually, there are two important exceptions, but they were written by enemies of the philosophers and reflect the Islamic hadith tradition, in which historical and doctrinal information is transmitted in the form of self-contained ancecdotes. The dialogue between the grammarian al-Sīrāfī and the Christian logician Mattā b. Yūnus, as reported by the litterateur al-Tawḥīdī concerns the usefulness of logic. Abū Bishr Mattā b. Yūnus, who died in 328/940, was an important translator from Greek into Syriac and Arabic, a Greek himself and the teacher of Fārābī. He translated or commented on a number of Aristotle's works. Abū Sa'īd al-Sīrāfī, d. 979, was a legal scholar who wrote mostly on grammar. Mattā defended logic as the tool of sound thought, but Sīrāfī derided it as reflecting Greek linguistic habits, arguing that Arabic grammar is sufficient and more useful for a speaker of Arabic. Sīrāfī, we are told, carried the day, and Mattā, whose Arabic was imperfect, retired in ungrammatical confusion.[65] The second "dialogue" features a teenaged Ibn 'Arabī, already a rising star among Andalusian Sufis and later to become the greatest theoretician of Islamic mysticism, and the elderly Averroes. In one of his books, Ibn 'Arabī tells how as a teenager he was taken by his father to meet Averroes, who had expressed curiosity about the young man's spiritual attainments. The dialogue consists entirely of a paradoxical series of "yes's" and "no's" as the two take each other's spiritual measures. In the end Averroes realizes that the young man has attained spiritual knowledge that is beyond all his syllogizing. Ibn 'Arabī reports that later he saw Averroes's coffin being carried slung on one side of a donkey, its weight being balanced by a box of

Averroes' books on the other. Ibn 'Arabī wonders to himself whether Averroes had obtained what he sought through his philosophical investigations. In the same spirit are the anecdotes in the biography of the Sufi sheikh Abū Sa'īd Abi'l-Khayr telling of Avicenna's conversion to Sufism under the influence of the sheikh.[66]

These two "dialogues" are unusual only because they involve philosophers and philosophical issues. In reality, they are not part of the literature of Islamic philosophy but rather parts of *adab*—Arabic polite literature—and Sufism respectively. In these literatures they have many parallels—though rarely involving prominent philosophers as interlocutors. Also, they purport to be historical testimony, which philosophical dialogues generally do not. Islamic philosophers did not normally use the Islamic reported-anecdote genre to transmit information, so they did not record debates in this form, as would sometimes happen in the religious sciences. Thus, despite the existence of these two famous counterexamples, Islamic philosophers did not reinvent the dialogue from Arabian materials—and, of course, they did not have the Platonic dialogues in their original forms to copy.

The Platonic Myths

Plato's dialogues are mostly conversation and debate (and sometimes lectures), but they also contain a series of brilliant myths. No one would take these myths literally, but they did serve as a model and legitimization for allegory, allegorical presentation of philosophy, and allegorical interpretation of myths and stories from other sources. This point deserves further discussion, since it is this side of Plato that does reach the Illuminationists. The myths in Plato are presented as "likely stories"; as imaginary history, as in the account of the Athenian defeat of Atlantis; as extended metaphors, as in the Myth of the Cave; as the results of visionary experience; and as sheer exuberant storytelling. However the myths are read, they do certainly legitimize allegory, allegorical interpretation, and esoteric modes of instruction within the Platonic tradition.[67] In fact, the influence of the myths extends in several directions, each of which reached the Islamic world and each of which finds expression in Suhrawardī's work.

The Tabula of Cebes as Philosophical Allegory

The work known as the *Tabula (Πίναξ)* of Cebes was probably written in about the first century C.E., a dating based mainly on linguistic evidence. Were I writing in the Renaissance or even in the nineteenth century, I would not need to introduce this work, but it is now thoroughly out of fashion along with most classics of didactic literature. The *Tabula* is an extended allegory, rather in the style of Bunyan's *Pilgrim's Progress*, in which classical ethics are expounded through the description and interpretation of a painting on a votive tablet in a temple dedicated to Cronus, the god of time. The work was traditionally attributed to Cebes of Thebes, a student of Socrates who is a minor character in the *Crito* and *Phaedo*. It is not pseudepigraphic in the usual sense, since the author makes no attempt to identify the work with its purported author. Some modern scholars believe that it was written by an obscure Cebes who came to be identified with the better-known Cebes of Thebes. Though Plato is the only philosopher cited by name, the work itself seems Stoic or Cynic.[68]

The *Tabula* opens with the narrator describing how he and and some friends, strangers to the place, are visiting the shrine and notice the tablet:

> For what was depicted seemed to us to be neither a walled city nor a military camp; it was, rather, a circular enclosure having within itself two other circular enclosures, one larger and one smaller. There was also a gate in the first enclosure. It appeared to us that a large crowd was standing before the gate, and within the enclosure quite a number of women were visible. Standing in [the entry way of] the [first] gate [and enclosure] an old man looked as though he were giving orders of some sort to the entering crowd.[69]

The visitors are puzzled by the picture, and while they are discussing it, they are approached by an old man who offers to explain it to them. As a youth he had known the man who had built the temple and dedicated the tablet, a foreigner who followed the Pythagorean and Parmenidean way of life. He warns the eager tourists that the explanation is not without danger. If they heed its message, they will be wise and happy, but if they do not, they will be worse than before. A sample of the old man's explanation will give a sense of the whole.

> "You must know, first of all, that this place is called Life, and the large crowd standing at the gate consists of those who are about to enter Life. The old man standing up here—who has a scroll in one hand and who appears to be pointing at something with the other—is called Daimon. To those who are entering he prescribes what they must do upon entering into Life. . . ."
>
> "Do you see, then, alongside the gate," he said, "a throne situated at the spot where the crowd enters? And sitting on it do you see a woman who is counterfeit in character and yet persuasive in her appearance, with a cup in her hand?"
>
> "Yes, I see, but who is she?" I said.
>
> "Deceit she is called," he said, "the one who leads all mankind astray."[70]

The old man goes on to describe in Bunyanesque fashion personifications of fortune, the vices, the consequences of vice, false education, true education, and so on, all portrayed in this elaborate picture.

The description of an impossibly complicated work of art is a familiar genre in Greek literature; this text brings to mind Homer's description of the shield of Achilles in the *Iliad*.[71] The description and interpretation of the picture are embedded in what is formally a dialogue. Though the form is not very different from Plato's Socratic dialogues and though there is philosophical discussion of a sort, the center of the dialogue is not the clash of opinions and argument but the explication of the picture by the authoritative guide. Nor is it like Plato's myths. The Myth of Er at the end of the *Republic* also tells how people enter life, make choices, and are blessed or ruined by the choices they make, but it concerns real people and the real universe, or at least purports to, whereas the characters in the painting at the temple of Cronus are only symbols. The myths are . . . myths, imaginative explanations of the real world. The *Tabula* is an allegory, a coded set of symbols, and we are not expected to suspend disbelief or identify with the characters.

In fact, the *Tabula* is a closed allegory. Every item in it has its precise meaning, explained to us by a guide who speaks with authority. It is a set of philosophical doctrines coded as a picture. Plato's myths speak to us as not only as symbols but as works of art with their ambiguities. Their meanings cannot be reduced to a set of philosophical concepts without leaving something left over. When Odysseus chooses the life of a "quiet, private man," he is not just Temperance or Prudence; he is a human being whose experience we understand and whose joy we can share. We do not share emotionally the triumph of the traveller in the *Tabula* when he finally receives the reward of happiness. This point is important, since it is this sort of closed allegory that is written by the philosophers of Islam.

The *Tabula* was rendered into Arabic by some unknown translator, probably in the tenth century. The text is preserved in what seems to be a quite accurate form in Miskawayh's *al-Ḥikma al-Khālida* (Eternal Wisdom), an ethical compilation that arranges wisdom literature by its county of origin—Persia, India, Arabia, Greece, and the Islamic world—and contains quite a number of significant texts.[72] This Arabic version was probably not widely read—the *Fihrist* does not know it—but Cebes and his *Tabula* do appear in the Islamic biographical literature. Shahrazūrī writes:

> Cebes the Socratic was one of the modern sages[73]. He was a companion of Plato. The only work of his that we have found is his *Tabula* [*Lughz*, lit., "riddle" or "puzzle"], which deals with the world[74] and the investigation concerning it. It urges man to reject the world and to consider it as

unimportant and explains the duty of man to abandon any thought of following desires in favor of pursuing perfect happiness and salvation from the evils that are in the world of sense.[75]

Most likely, Shahrazūrī or his source constructed this biography on the basis of the Arabic translation of the *Tabula*.[76] Cebes is also mentioned in an Arabic version of the *Phaedo*.[77] It is possible, as we will see in chapter 11, that his name is also preserved in anecdotes about the succession to Plato, but that his name and identity have been rendered unrecognizable by the ambiguities of the Arabic alphabet. There is also a short commentary on the *Tabula* by Abu'l-Faraj Ibn al-Ṭayyib, the same man who was responsible for the Arabic version of the commentary attributed to Proclus on Pythagoras' *Golden Verses*.[78]

The Islamic Philosophical Allegory

Allegories are not common in Islamic philosophical writing, though the few that there are have received a great deal of attention from modern scholars. Allegory is far more important in other genres, particularly Persian epics.[79] Philosophical allegories seem to have been written as a way of popularizing philosophy and should thus be ranked with vernacular philosophical encyclopedias and abridgments as literature produced for the use of the educated public, particularly the bureaucratic class. Charming though they are, I do not think that they are central to the philosophical enterprise of any of their authors, with the exception of Ibn Ṭufayl.

Islamic philosophical allegory first emerges as a distinct genre in the works of Avicenna with his *Salamān and Absāl*, *Epistle of the Birds*, and *Ḥayy b. Yaqẓān*. Suhrawardī is clear that his allegories were inspired by Avicenna's.

Salaman and Absal. A classical story translated into Arabic by the great Ḥunayn b. Isḥāq, this story became stock material for the Islamic philosophical allegorists—at least to the extent of the names being reused. Avicenna mentions the story in his *Book of Hints and Allusions (Kitāb al-Ishārāt wa'l-Tanbīhāt)*, that much-commented-on compendium of his mature philosophical views. "Should your ears happen to be struck by the story of Salāmān and Absāl, should their tale be among those that you hear, know then that Salāmān is a symbol of you and Absāl a symbol of your station in mystical knowledge—if you are worthy of it. The riddle will be unravelled if you are able."[80] Corbin refers to the story as "Hermetistic" and complains that the interpretation of the story given by the thirteenth-century philosopher Naṣīr al-Dīn al-Ṭūsī is "artificial and scarcely convincing."[81] This is certainly true, but Ṭūsī deserves sympathy in his thankless task. His predecessor in commenting on the *Hints*, the theologian Fakhr al-Dīn al-Rāzī, had not known the story at all and remarks plaintively, "It is not one of the well known stories. Rather, they are two names that the Sheikh made up for some reason. In such cases the intellect cannot ascertain the matter unaided." Rāzī then goes on to make some half-hearted guesses about the meanings of the names: Salāmān/Adam/rational soul and Absāl/Paradise/degrees of happiness.[82]

Ṭūsī's hermeneutical task was complicated by his discovery of Ḥunayn's translation of the story, a gothic tale of sex, violence, and the occult produced by some forgotten Hellenistic Anne Rice. The story is obviously Greek, and probably Egyptian, since there are some details having to do with the cult of the Serapeion temple in Alexandria that could scarcely have been known much after the fourth century. The story itself may ultimately be of Indian origin since the names Salāmān and Absāl can be given a plausible Indian etymology if a Pahlavi intermediate version is assumed.[83] The great antediluvian king Hermanus, son of Heraclius, has no heir. His exasperated court wizard points out that this is because he will have nothing to do with women. The wizard, Aqlīqūlās the Divine, takes the king's semen and produces a child by magical means and procures a beautiful eighteen-year-old girl named Absāl as wet-nurse. In due course Salāmān grows up and falls passionately in love with Absāl. The king wishes his son to follow in his path of celibate wisdom, so the lovers run away. Pursued by the king's magic, they try to drown themselves, but the king stretches out his powers to save his son. The boy's grief is so intense that the wizard uses his magic to summon Absāl back from the dead, a spell that requires him to vow to love no other woman. Just as Absāl is about to be brought back, Venus appears to Salāmān and he falls passionately in love with her. Evidently this breaks the spell. Eventually Salāmān tires even of Venus and abandons her for a life of celibate kingship. He has the story engraved on golden tablets where Aristotle eventually finds them at the time of Alexander's conquest of Egypt.

Ṭūsī interprets the story as a catalog of symbols drawn from the Avicennan Peripatetic tradition: the king is the active intellect, Salāmān the rational soul, Absāl the animal spirit, their love the soul's inclination towards bodily pleasures, and so on. It is, as Corbin complains, neither deep nor convincing. Corbin's explanation of Ṭūsī's failure—that he missed the Hermetic depths of the story—is not very convincing either.[84] The Hellenistic *Salāmān and Absāl* is an occult thriller, not a deep mystical parable, and Corbin's hermeneutic efforts, like Ṭūsī's, are unlikely to be very fruitful.

The point for us, however, is that Ṭūsī treats the story as a closed system of symbols, however unsuitable the raw material. An allegory for him is a sort of mnemonic symbolizing a well-understood intellectual system. Ambiguity is not welcome, and although multiple layers of symbols are acceptable, each layer is subject to the same kind of didactic unpacking. It was thus with considerable relief that Ṭūsī, two decades after he first wrote on this text of the *Hints*, happened on the story that Avicenna was really talking about, his own version of *Salāmān and Absāl*.[85] This story has almost nothing in common with the Hellenistic story. Salāmān and Absāl are half-brothers. Absāl was the younger, a paragon of intelligence and beauty, and so his half-brother's wife falls in love with him. His chastity much tried by the woman's importunities, he goes off to conquer other countries in his brother's name. Returning after many years, he finds his brother's wife still in love with him. When he again rejects her advances, she first attempts to have him slain in battle and finally poisons him. God, however, reveals his wife's treachery to Salāmān, who then poisons her and her accomplices. Ṭūsī's interpretations here are similar—an identification of the elements of the Avicennan system with the characters and events of the story—but the *ta'wīl* (symbolic interpretation) is less forced, and we have Avicenna's own testimony that the story is meant to be understood in some such way. The story, in other words, was written as an allegory, not just interpreted as one, though it retains some of the storytelling qualities of the original romance.

Avicenna's other allegories. When we come to the other allegories of Avicenna, their character as closed allegories is patent. For example, in his *Ḥayy b. Yaqẓān* the narrator and his three friends meet a sage in the gardens outside the city. The sage uses the science of physiognomy to tell the narrator that he is easily led, either to good or ill, by companions. He then tells the narrator that his companions are respectively dishonest, violent, and gluttonous. The sage then goes on for some pages describing the climes through which he had travelled. The narrator is the soul, so easily tempted, and his companions are the faculties of sensation, anger, and desire. We are back once again to the universe of the *Tabula* of Cebes, in which a static word picture is described and an intellectual system converted to images.

Suhrawardī's Philosophical Allegories

Suhrawardī wrote a number of allegories like the *Tabula* of Cebes and the allegories of Avicenna. He is explicit that they are of the genre of Avicenna's allegories.[86] Most are in Persian. They seem to be closely related to his other short Persian treatises, which have similar titles, deal with similar themes, but do so in direct rather than allegorical manner.

In *A Day with a Group of Sufis*[87] the narrator—Suhrawardī himself, we suppose—is sitting with some Sufis who are taking turns reading to each other from the lectures of their respective masters. When his turn comes, Suhrawardī describes asking his teacher about a problem in kinematics. He had been watching a jeweler work with a grinding wheel. What, he wonders, would be the motion of a bead dropped on a spinning disk? If there were concentric grooves at various distances from the center, how would the motions of the beads in the various grooves differ? The master explained that the beads would roll in a direction opposite to the motion of the disk and be carried around at differing rates. His master then goes on to describe a masterpiece of the gem carver's art, a jewel carved into a set of rotating nesting balls with a medallion engraved on each. Suhrawardī correctly guesses that this is a model of the celestial spheres, so his master goes on to explain various points of elementary geocentric astronomy: the presence of so many stars in the sphere of the fixed stars, the brightness of the sun, the borrowed light of the moon, and the relative motions of the spheres. The master explains that there are three kinds of people in relation to the heavens: those who only look with physical eyes; those who look with the eyes of the heavens, the astrologers; and those who look with the eye of proof *(istidlāl)*, those who find the truth *(muḥaqqiqān)*. When Suhrawardī expresses the wish to be among those who find the truth about the heavens, his master instructs him to give up pleasures and desires and undergo a forty-day retreat. If he is successful in purging himself, his inner eye will be opened and he will see what he sees. When Suhrawardī finishes his story, the other Sufis present express their admiration of his teacher.

In *The Sound of Gabriel's Wing*[88] Suhrawardī complains that a bigoted man, presumably a Sufi, had been deprecating the masters of the past in order to glorify the contemporary Sufi masters. When he criticized Abū 'Alī Fārmadī[89] for his answer to a question about the effects of the sound of Gabriel's wing, Suhrawardī puts him in his place. He tells the man that one night when he was just old enough to leave the women's quarters on his own, he was awakened by a nightmare and went into the men's part of the house. When dawn broke, he went to his father's *khānqāh* (Sufi monastery), which had doors opening both into the city and into the fields. Going out into the fields, he meets ten handsome old men. The first of them greets Suhrawardī and says that they are a group of those who are abstracted from the material world *(mujarradān)* who had come from "Nowheresville" *(nākujā'ābād)*, a place that cannot be pointed to. They spend their time tailoring, have memorized the word of God, and are travellers. The other nine old men are too exalted to speak to Suhrawardī, so the tenth is their spokesman. Suhrawardī sees a basin with eleven nested layers and a little sand and water in the middle and is told that each layer was made by one of the old men, his interlocutor having made the inner two, which are of inferior workmanship. The tenth old man explains that he and his fellows are not married, though each has a son and a mill that the son operates. The tenth old man is distinguished by having a four-level mill and a great many sons, who remain in that dangerous place for a time and then return to him. His children are the product of a sort of spontaneous generation in his Abyssinian slave girl, who conceives whenever the turning of the mill brings him into her sight. The old man then goes on to teach Suhrawardī a little of the art of tailoring, enough to patch his own cloak. He also teaches Suhrawardī a magical alphabet and the numerical values of its letters so that he could learn something of God's word. He explains the symbolism of Gabriel's wings, the right wing of pure light and the left tinged with darkness. When the day finally broke, the people of the bazaar began to appear and the old men vanished.

The Treatise of the Birds[90] is actually a translation of a work by Avicenna. It begins with an address to his brethren, asking them to listen so that he can convey something of his sadness. Suhrawardī tells how as a bird he was trapped by hunters and caged. One day some other birds escape and aid him to escape also. Though still bearing the remains of fetters on their legs, the birds fly across seven mountains to reach the court of the king on the eighth. There they are told that they must go back since only the one who put the fetters on their legs can remove them.

The Crimson Intellect[91] tells how the narrator was first created in the form of a falcon. He was trapped by the hunters Decree and Fate in the trap of Predestination using Free Will as bait. He is taken to another country and his eyes are sewn shut. He is held by four fetters under the supervision of ten custodians, five facing him and five facing away. One day the ten custodians happen not to be paying attention, and the falcon escapes and meets a luminous elder. The elder's true color is white, but he appears red to the falcon because he too had been captured and cast into a dark pit. He is a traveller who has seen many wonders, among them Mount Qāf, the Night-Brightening Pearl, the Tree of Ṭūbā, the Twelve Workshops, King David's chainmail, the Sword Balārak, and the Fountain of Life. The elder then interprets these entities as symbols of various parts of the universe.

In the State of Childhood[92] begins when the young Suhrawardī sees some children going to school. Puzzled about the "knowledge" that they are going to school to acquire, he meets their schoolteacher, who teaches him the alphabet. One day he is joined by an ignorant person. When Suhrawardī sees what the teacher has written on the slate, he becomes very excited and tells his companion all about it. His ignorant companion reacts with derision, and the teacher is no longer anywhere to be found. After long wandering Suhrawardī meets his teacher in a *khānqāh* and is told the importance of not telling the full truth to those unready for it. The physician must treat the patient with medicines appropriate to the stage of his disease. The teacher then tells him he must go first to the shore of the Great Sea to find the Night-Brightening Pearl. There he will find a cow that grazes at night by the sea. He is to eat the plant that the cow eats and then go to Mount Qāf to eat the fruit of the tree where the Phoenix nests. The teacher then explains the geometry of the phases of the moon, stressing how large the heavens are in relation to the earth. The teacher explains the dangers of possessions through the story of a man who attempted to build a fabulous palace, but died before its completion, being unable to persuade the angel of death to wait until it was done. He also told of a merchant whose ship was caught in a storm. As the ship is coming safely into port, he throws the rest of his possessions into the sea. The teacher finishes by telling him about spiritual maturity by analogy with the pleasure of sexual intercourse and the *samā'*, the Sufi dance, and its function.

On the Reality of Love, or the Companion of Lovers,[93] is a sprawling allegory on the relationships among Beauty, Love, and Sorrow, each of which comes to be for the sake of God's first creation, the intellect. At the time of creation the four natures were imprisoned by the seven planets within the prison of the six directions. After forty days Adam was created, and Beauty set out in search of him. Love and Sorrow then went in search of Beauty. Beauty returned to his own kingdom, leaving Love and Sorrow behind. Beauty once again came into the world in the time of Joseph, and Suhrawardī explains how Love, Sorrow, and Beauty took part in that famous story. On meeting Zulaykhā, Joseph's lover, Love tells of the pavilion of the City of the Soul, how it may be reached, and the contents of its nine stories. Suhrawardī concludes with discussions of love and beauty and their relation to the mystical path.

The Language of the Ants[94] is a collection of ten fables mostly about animals, and two short discourses. Each deals with the question of the true home of the soul. The first fable records a debate among the ants about the origin of dew. One of the leaders of the ants explains that things attempt to return to their origin, and as the sun warms the dew, they see that it ascends into the air.

The most elaborate of Suhrawardī's allegories is *The Story of the Occidental Exile*.[95] Unlike the other allegories, it is in Arabic, although the Corbin edition includes an old Persian translation and commentary. The introduction explains that it was inspired by Avicenna's allegories *Ḥayy b. Yaqẓān* and *Salamān and Absāl*. The narrator and his brother 'Āṣim ("guardian"), sons of al-Hādī b. al-Khayr al-Yamanī ("the guide, son of the good, of Arabia Felix"), travel from their home in Transoxania in order to hunt birds on the shore of the Green Sea. On reaching the town of

Qayrawān (in Tunisia), the people imprison them in a pit beneath a many-towered palace. Only at night were they allowed out, at which time they could go up into the palace and look out a small window where sometimes they would hear news from the land of the Beloved. One night the hoopoe bird, Solomon's messenger in the Qur'ān, brings them a letter from their father, telling them how to escape and warning them of the adventures and dangers that they would face on their journey home. After many adventures, the narrator reaches his father's hermitage on Mount Sinai. His father commends him on his escape but tells him that he must return to his Western exile in Qayrawān, for not all his fetters have been removed. The tale ends abruptly as Suhrawardī's spiritual state changes from exaltation to distress. He too finds himself among the ignorant in a Western exile, but an indescribable pleasure remains to him.

Why and for whom did Suhrawardī write these stories? None are dated, either in the texts themselves nor, so far as I know, in the manuscripts or other sources, so we cannot know for sure when in Suhrawardī's life they were written. Some things can be said:

— They are written for Sufi *murīds*, that is for beginners on the mystical path.
— They expound a Peripatetic, not an Illuminationist, cosmology.
— They therefore do not represent the pinnacle of Suhrawardī's thought but rather a beginning or lower intermediate level. Some may be juvenalia, written before Suhrawardī's thought took its mature Platonic form.

That they are written for *murīds* is clear from both form and content. The allegories have a didactic tone appropriate to a master addressing his younger disciples. Their tone is, for example, very different from that of the introduction to *The Philosophy of Illumination*, which sounds like the first among equals addressing his almost-peers. The fact that most are in Persian may also indicate a less educated audience, although there can be other explanations for the use of a vernacular in place of the learned Arabic. Two allegories—*The Sound of Gabriel's Wing* and *In the State of Childhood*—are presented as events from Suhrawardī's own childhood, while most of the others deal with the earlier stages of the Sufi path: the initial break with the world and the mystical experiences of the earlier stages of the Path. *A Day with a Group of Sufis* describes how his master urged him to mortify his flesh if he wanted to understand the truths of spiritual cosmology. Both *The Treatise of the Birds* and *The Crimson Intellect* describe the experiences of birds when they break free of their cage, it being clear in each case that the initial escape and flight is only the beginning of the spiritual quest. *In the State of Childhood* describes spiritual maturity by analogy to the pleasure taken in sexual intercourse by the experienced mature man; the reader is not expected to know from his own experience either mature spirituality or mature sexual intercourse. It raises the question of what knowledge is but, unlike *The Philosophy of Illumination*, gives no answer. *The Story of the Occidental Exile* exactly parallels the treatise of the birds, describing how the narrator escapes from his bonds but must return to where he was held prison to have the last of his fetters removed.

For Suhrawardī, as for other mystics, the beginning of the mystical Path consists of a break with the worldly life, a course of hardships deliberately undertaken to confirm the break with the world, and finally a brilliant mystical experience endorsing the rightness of the decision to abandon the world. It is these phases of the Path that are described in the allegories. Suhrawardī is clear, however, that these stages are not the whole of the path; the first ecstacy must be abandoned and the new mystic must return to the world. Thus the escapees of *The Treatise of the Birds* cross seven mountain ranges to meet their king on the eighth, Mount Qāf, but the king tells them they must return, though he sends along a herald to convince their former captors to remove the remnants of their fetters. The experience of the young man held captive in Qayrawān in *The Story of the Occidental Exile* is identical. In neither case is there a description of the second journey. The allegories make various points about mysticism—the importance of the Path, the hardships of its early stages, the transitoriness and purpose of the first experience of ecstasy—but they all relate to newcomers, not to advanced mystics.[96]

Another aspect of the allegories suggests that they are intended for students. Several give elementary expositions of cosmology and astronomy. *A Day with a Group of Sufis* explains the dynamics of the retrograde motion of the planets and describes a carved gem that is a model of the cosmos with its nesting spheres. *The Sound of Gabriel's Wing* also shows a model of the cosmos, this one in the form of a basin, and introduces the intellects and souls of the ten spheres. *The Crimson Intellect* gives an allegory of philosophical psychology and the metaphysics of fate. *In the State of Childhood* gives, among other things, a geometrical account of the phases of the moon. *The Story of the Occidental Exile* gives an account of the faculties of the mind. These are not sophisticated philosophical expositions, just simple allegories and models making the basic notions of philosophy and astronomy easy to grasp and remember. They certainly are not philosophically innovative.

The second point about these allegories is that they expound a Peripatetic, not an Illuminationist metaphysics. Of course, not all differences between Peripatetic (Avicennan) and Illuminationist philosophy lend themselves to allegorical expression—it is difficult to imagine how Suhrawardī would have allegorically expressed his rejection of the Peripatetic essentialist definition—but we would expect to find some distinctive aspects of his system expressed allegorically. Suhrawardī explains his difference with Avicenna and the Peripatetics about the Forms in terms of the number of immaterial intellects: the Peripatetics say that there are ten; Suhrawardī says that there are more, the additional ones being the Platonic Forms. In *The Sound of Gabriel's Wing* Suhrawardī meets ten old men, representing the intellects of the spheres. Nine of the ten have a single son each, the soul of that sphere. Only the tenth has more, but these "sons" are the souls of men. If this were an Illuminationist text, each old man would have many sons. The models of the universe described in *A Day with a Group of Sufis* and *The Sound of Gabriel's Wing* have no place for the Forms. The absence of any explicit reference to the Forms is decisive in identifying these works as Peripatetic since Suhrawardī himself says that it was the acceptance of the Platonic Forms that separated his juvenile from his mature philosophy. Nor is the doctrine of knowledge by presence reflected in the allegories; it is explicitly contradicted by references to the five internal senses. In his mature thought Suhrawardī denies that these senses represent distinct faculties. There are other features of Suhrawardī's mature thought that we do not find in the allegories: the World of Image *('ālam al-mithāl)*, the rejection of the Peripatetic distinction of matter and form, and the rejection of the external reality of existence and the other beings of reason *(i'tibārāt 'aqlīya)*.

So, the distinctively Illuminationist philosophical doctrines are not found in the allegories. Why should this be? One obvious possibility is that these are early works. The fact that they are in Persian would seem to indicate that they are from the period when Suhrawardī lived in Persian-speaking regions, which makes it more likely that they predate his conversion to Platonism. Quṭb al-Dīn remarks that Suhrawardī's juvenalia include the *Hayākil al-Nūr*, the *Alwāḥ-i 'Imādīya*, and "most of the short works *(rasā'il)*," which would probably include the allegories.[97] Another Persian work, the *Partaw-Nāma*, was written for a Seljuq ruler, thus placing it in the pre-Aleppo period, as was, it seems, the *Yazdān-Shinākht*, which is dedicated to one Muḥammad b. Maḥmūd al-Dārī.[98]

We are left with two possibilities for understanding the place of the allegories in Suhrawardī's works: either they are juvenalia or they deliberately omit the distinctively Illuminationist aspects of his work. Perhaps both are true, either because some are later works deliberately written to reflect an earlier stage of his thought or because he himself thought that the works ought not to be revised because it was appropriate for *murīds* to retrace his steps for themselves. In either case they are not *philosophically* innovative.[99]

This view is supported by one of the minor Arabic works: the *Epistle on the Creed of the Sages (Risāla fī l'tiqād al-Ḥukamā')*.[100] Suhrawardī says that he wrote this little book in response to the popular canard that the divine sages were atheists *(dahrīya)* who did not believe in a Creator or in the basic doctrines of religion.[101] Suhrawardī vigorously responds that they do believe in these fundamental doctrines of religion and gives a quite standard precis of Avicennan metaphysics. He softens the doctrines only to the extent of explaining how they are expressed in religious language and ending with a discussion of prophecy and mysticism. The work contains no distinctive Illuminationist doctrines—no reference to the Platonic Forms or the rejection of Avicennan ontology, for example. This is in contrast to the major Peripatetic works that do at least allude to such teachings. Since there is absolutely no foreshadowing of Illuminationist doctrine and since it explicitly asserts a view that Suhrawardī elsewhere states was characteristic of his juvenile philosophical thought—the doctrine that there are only ten immaterial intellects—it seems more plausible that this was a work of Suhrawardī's youth rather than an exoteric work of his mature period.[102]

Symbolic Expression Revisited

Plato, the Islamic sources tell us, wrote his philosophy in riddles and symbols, a habit he shared with Pythagoras, Empedocles, and Plato. Shahrazūrī explains that the Ancients used symbolic expression for three reasons: (1) to prevent philosophy being known by the unworthy and thus leading to evil; (2) to challenge the student; and (3) to sharpen the student's wit.[103] Quṭb al-Dīn adds a fourth reason: to make the text suitable for both the elect and the common people.[104] These reasons certainly would have been acceptable to Plato. He, after all, kept his full teaching unwritten, and the dialogues do indeed challenge the student, sharpen his wit, and suit inquirers on various intellectual levels.

After Plato's death the project of his dialogues soon ceased to be understood, but his dialectical project was pursued in other ways. One product of the Platonic tradition, as we have seen, was the philosophical allegory. In its ancient and medieval form it was a closed text with a fixed and limited meaning, decoded to expound a set of philosophical doctrines. The allegory served as a mnemonic, as a literary exercise, and as a rhetorical device for drawing students to deeper thought while conveying to the ordinary reader what he was capable of understanding.

A second product of the breakup of the Platonic dialectical project was the tradition of esoteric writing in philosophy. This really goes back to the

Pythagoreans, with their traditions of secrecy. Philosophical doctrines, some thought, ought not to be freely revealed lest the unworthy misunderstand them. In late antiquity there were many who saw the appropriateness of this. Boethius, for example, wrote:

> You asked me to state and explain somewhat more clearly that obscure question in my *Hebdomads* concerning the manner in which substances are good in virtue of existence without being substantial goods. You urge that this demonstration is necessary because the method of this kind of treatise is not clear at all. . . . But I think over my *Hebdomads* with myself, and I keep my speculations in my own memory rather than share them with any of those pert and frivolous persons who will not tolerate an argument unless it is made amusing. Wherefore do you not take objection to obscurities consequent on brevity, which are the sure treasure-house of secret doctrine and have the advantage that they speak only with those who are worthy.[105]

Among the Christians Origen insisted that the doctrines of the Church should be understood literally by the masses and philosophically by the intellectuals.[106] In Islam the philosophers of the Fārābian tradition worked out a systematic theory explaining how the teachings of religion were symbolic rhetorical expressions of philosophical truth; they discouraged philosophers from revealing their teachings openly. Fārābī, always the careful logician, remarked that the Pythagoreans often replaced a universal with a proper accident *('araḍ)* of a property *(khāṣṣa)* of the universal and says this technique was often used by the Presocratic physicists and Empedocles.[107] A more extreme example concerns the gnostics and the mystery religions in which the true teachings were hidden, to be revealed orally only to the initiated. For such thinkers—we cannot always call them "philosophers"—the deeper works should be written in such a way that only those supplied with the key can fully understand them.

The third product of the Platonic dialectical enterprise was the notion that books must be read esoterically. Plato's dialogues must be read with great care on the basis of deep knowledge in order to extract the wisdom that Plato had hidden so carefully. Plato, we are told, was unique among the thinkers of this tradition in using a scientific method along with the symbolic. Proclus writes in the *Platonic Theology* that knowledge of metaphysical entities can be conveyed in four ways:

1. Inspired utterances, as in the *Chaldaean Oracles;*
2. Symbolism, as in the Platonic myths and the Orphic writings;
3. Images, often mathematical, as in Pythagoras;
4. Dialectic, which is unique to Plato.[108]

Thus, any text on higher things can be read as philosophy by using esoteric techniques of interpretation. Just as Porphyry can give a Neoplatonic intepretation of the Cave of the Nymphs in the *Odyssey* and Iamblichus can investigate the "true" meanings of the doctrines of the barbarian sages, so too can Suhrawardī and other Muslim philosophers find philosophy in the Qur'ān through symbolic interpretation.

For Suhrawardī such concerns affect his whole project as a philosophical author. Suhrawardī was a Sufi, not a scientist, and the goal of his philosophy was to enable his reader to experience reality, not just to comprehend it. At the same time, his was a philosophy somewhat at odds with the beliefs of his time. Thus, he wrote for three kinds of people:

1. Those not yet ready to understand philosophical argument;
2. Those capable of understanding philosophical argument but not equipped to understand the highest aspects of his "Illuminationist" philosophy;
3. Those capable of learning the highest things from him.

He had to address each of these groups in a different way, and a work written for one group had to be written in such a way that it would not cause harm if it fell into the hands of those for whom it was not written. Thus we have, with respect to symbolic expression and the freedom with which Suhrawardī expresses his own distinctive teachings, four kinds of works:

1a. Popular "Peripatetic" works: These are books such as the *Temples of Light* and the *Book of Emanation* written, often in Persian, for a general audience. They do not contain Suhrawardī's distinctive and controversial teachings in a clear way. They also do not require advanced philosophical background to understand.

1b. The allegories: These are written for young Sufis. Their literary charm encourages these young people to persevere on the path. They contain elementary explanations of philosophy and cosmology, presented in a way that requires no philosophical background. They also contain discussions of mystical psychology sufficient to prepare the *murīds* for their experiences on the early stages of the Path. They contain little of importance for more advanced mystics or for philosophers.

2. The advanced "Peripatetic" works: These are the Arabic manuals of philosophy written around the same time as *The Philosophy of Illumination*. These are written for a dual audience: Peripatetic philosophers and intermediate students of the Illuminationist philosophy. They pre-

sume the Illuminationist doctrines though they do not always insist on them. The Peripatetics can read them as products of their own tradition, but a more careful reader will discover that they undermine the Peripatetic system. They are too long, difficult, and dull to disturb the faith of those incapable of comprending them.

3. *The Philosophy of Illumination:* The first half of this work belongs, in a sense, with the advanced Peripatetic works, although its criticisms of the Peripatetics are clearer and more pointed. The second half is written symbolically in the language of light and darkness. It is meant for the disciple, and its true interpretation is unwritten, being in the hands of "him who arises with the Book." If Suhrawardī knew what Proclus had said about the forms of expression in the *Platonic Theology*, he might justly have said that this book uses all four methods. Certainly, the work fits all four uses of symbolic expression mentioned by Shahrazūrī and Quṭb al-Dīn.

Thus, symbolic expression comes into play at the extreme ends of the spectrum of Suhrawardī's writings. On the one hand, it is a tool used to interest, instruct, and encourage the *murīds;* at the other it is the device used to keep his true doctrines out of the hands of the unworthy and the unready—and to express the ineffable. It is a literary project that both Plato and the Neoplatonists would have understood, for Iamblichus had explained the recapitulation of the *Republic* at the beginning of the *Timaeus* in terms of symbols.

> Some, (sc. Porphyry), taking the recapitulation of the *Republic* in an ethical sense, say that it reveals to us that we must enter upon the contemplation of the Universe in an ethically ordered frame of mind; others (sc. Iamblichus), consider that it has been placed before the whole physiological enquiry as an image of the organization of the Universe; for the Pythagoreans had the habit of placing before their scientific instruction the revealing of the subjects under inquiry through similitudes and images, and after this of introducing the secret revelation of the same subjects through symbols, and then in this way, after the reactivation of the soul's ability to comprehend the intelligible realm and the purging of its vision, to bring on the complete knowledge of the subjects laid down for investigation. And here too the relating in summary of the *Republic* before the physiological enquiry prepares us to understand the orderly creation of the Universe through the medium of an image, while the story of the Atlantids acts as a symbol; for indeed myths in general tend to reveal the principles of actuality through symbols. So the physiological theme in fact runs through the whole dialogue, but appears in different forms in different places according to the different methods of revelation.[109]

Like Plato, Suhrawardī had gone beyond the Pythagoreans by including both the symbolic and the scientific approaches. Proclus would have recognized the philosophico-literary project of Suhrawardī as being distinctively and properly Platonic: he begins with symbolic allegories to introduce the subject, moves on to scientific expressions of the same subject, and ends with loftier allegory, expressing the highest things.

ISLAMIC WRITERS ON PLATONISM

Fārābī on the Philosophy of Plato

The most important Islamic authority on Plato was al-Fārābī. *The Philosophy of Plato* is an essay on the themes of the dialogues and how the order of their themes corresponds to Plato's intellectual quest. It is the middle piece of a trilogy, the first being *The Attainment of Happiness*, on ethics, and the third *The Philosophy of Aristotle*, on the subjects of Aristotle's works. *The Philosophy of Plato* is something of a puzzle. It is a political work, explaining how Plato's works fit together into a systematic account of the nature and realization of human perfection and the highest happiness. It is not very long—fifteen pages in Arabic. An excerpt will show the style and method of the work:

> Then, after that, he investigated what this knowledge [through which happiness is attained] is and its distinguishing mark, its character, and that it is knowledge of the substance of each of the beings: this knowledge is the final perfection of man and the highest perfection he can possess. This is to be found in his book that he called the *Theatetus* (meaning *voluntary*).
>
> Then, after that, he investigated the happiness that is truly happiness, what it is, from which kind of knowledge it proceeds, which state of character it is, and which act it is. He distinguished it from what is believed to be happiness but is not. And he made it known that the virtuous way of life is what leads to the achievement of this happiness. That is to be found in his book that is called the *Philebus* (meaning *beloved*).[110]

Some of the descriptions are longer, up to a page or so. They generally are recognizably connected with the authentic dialogue, but, unlike the descriptions of Aristotle's works in *The Philosophy of Aristotle*, they do not indicate real familiarity with the text of Plato. The translations of the Greek names are probably not part of Fārābī's text. All of the dialogues commonly attributed to Plato are mentioned, almost always by name, with the possible exception of the *Minos*.

The book has Fārābī's dry, precise style and fits well with his system, but it would be interesting to know what Fārābī's source was. The order in which the books of Plato and Aristotle were to be read was a familiar topic, much loved by the pedagogues of late antiquity. It is tempting to identify Fārābī's source as the translation of Theon of Smyrna's book on the order in which Plato's dialogues should be read.[111] Theon was fairly early—second century—and Fārābī's account of Plato shows no trace of Neoplatonic influence. On the other hand, Fārābī says nothing about mathematics, which was evidently Theon's special interest—though Theon's commentary on the *Republic* could well have contained a list of the dialogues from the point of view of politics. The order in which Fārābī cites the dialogues has nothing in common with the order in which they appear in the lists supposedly cited from Theon, though these lists are so incomplete as to indicate that the author of the *Fihrist* did not necessarily have access to the text of Theon's work. The order in which Fārābī gives the dialogues, beginning with *Alcibiades Major*, is not the usual one, though Diogenes Laertius (3.62) mentions that one of the orderings of the dialogues starts with *Alcibiades Major.*

The point is moot for us, since the Plato of Fārābī's *Philosophy of Plato* is not the Plato of Suhrawardī. There is no mysticism or even metaphysics. The Forms are not mentioned. This is purely a political Plato, and Fārābī is writing in the exoteric tradition of the *Republic*.

Fārābī's Harmony of Plato and Aristotle

Fārābī's other work on Plato is far more interesting for our purposes: *The Harmonization of the Opinions of the Two Sages, Plato the Divine and Aristotle*, a treatise showing that Plato and Aristotle did not necessarily disagree as much as was usually thought.[112] This work is printed in the margin of Quṭb al-Dīn's commentary on *The Philosophy of Illumination*. The nineteenth-century Iranian editor was correct in his judgment—as he was excellent in his editing—for the disagreements between Plato and Aristotle are central to Suhrawardī's view of the history of philosophy and his place in it.

After the rediscovery of the *Corpus Aristotelicum* it was not uncommon for philosophers to assert the harmony of the views of Plato and Aristotle. In antiquity the motivations for doing so were varied: recognition of the complementary strengths of the two philosophical positions, desire to make use of Aristotle's systematic philosophy of this world as a supplement to Platonic metaphysics, and the general late antique taste for syncretism. The tradition of Neoplatonic commentary on the works of Aristotle is the most philosophically significant effort to bring about a harmony between the last of the Ancients and the first of the Moderns.[113] Porphyry started the tradition with a work entitled *On the School of Plato and Aristotle Being One.*[114] That Plato and Aristotle were in general agreement was the predominant view of the later Neoplatonists and went on to influence medieval thought. Of this curious doctrine Sorabji observes: "Not for the only time in the history of philosophy (the condemnation of 219 propositions in 1277 provides another example), a perfectly crazy position (harmony) proved philosophically fruitful."[115]

For Muslim philosophers, particularly in the earlier period when the ideological situation was still in flux, the need was to avoid intellectual scandal. Philosophy was a rival to the religion of Islam for men's ideological allegiance. Its claim to authority was based on its ability to give the students of philosophy true knowledge of the world as it is. If, however, the two greatest exponents of philosophy disagreed on important issues, the whole enterprise was put into doubt.

> I have seen that most people in our time are squabbling about whether or not the world had a beginning in time, claiming that the two great ancient sages disagreed about whether there was a first Creator and whether causes result from him. They also claim that these two sages disagreed about the soul and intellect, about recompense for good and bad acts, as well as about many issues of political philosophy, ethics, and logic. Thus in this treatise of mine I wish to begin to reconcile their two opinions and show how the purport of what each one says indicates this agreement, thereby showing the agreement of what the two of them believe and removing the doubt that arises in the hearts of those who study their books.[116]

There are a number of discreet caveats for the careful reader in this passage—and, for that matter, the careful reader of the full title of the book. Fārābī mentions specific doctrines, "opinions," and "believe," but he says nothing about "knowledge" or "philosophy." He cites works such as *The Theology of Aristotle* and Aristotle's letter of consolation to Alexander's mother that he does not mention among Aristotle's works in *The Philosophy of Aristotle*. That he knows Plato and Aristotle have fundamental disagreements is perfectly obvious from reading *The Philosophy of Plato* and *The Philosophy of Aristotle*, which have the two sages saying different things. Moreover, Fārābī knew the *Metaphysics* and the other major works of Aristotle very well, and thus knew Aristotle's criticisms of Plato.[117] The philosophical import of the disagreements between Plato and Aristotle is explained on the next page.

> The definition and quiddity of philosophy is the knowledge of existents insofar as they are existent, and these two sages created philosophy, originated its first principles and premises, and completed its final parts

> and branches. They are relied upon in all matters of philosophy, whether great or small, are the final arbiters in matters simple and obscure in every branch of philosophy. . . . Since statements and beliefs are only true when they correspond to the existents that they refer to, and since there is contradiction between what these two sages say about most branches of philosophy, the explanation must be one of these three possibilities: (1) The definition explaining the quiddity of philosophy is incorrect, (2) the universal or predominant opinion about the philosophizing of these two is incorrect, or (3) the knowledge of those who hold that there is disagreement about principles between these two is in some way deficient.[118]

Fārābī argues that since the first two possibilities are clearly false, the third must be true. Now, there are a number of odd features about Fārābī's argument here. His argument for the preeminence of Plato and Aristotle as philosophers is based on what Islamic lawyers would call *ijmā'*, "consensus," but he goes out of his way in the next paragraph to argue that the consensus of those who do not form their own judgment counts as the judgment of a single individual. Moreover, once we get into the substance of the book, it is not always entirely clear that Fārābī is showing that Plato and Aristotle are in agreement—only showing that their respective positions are each reasonable interpretations of the evidence. Also, Fārābī ignores certain of the most important and notorious disputes between Plato and Aristotle: Aristotle's theory of matter, for example. Fārābī's book thus is dialectal or rhetorical, not demonstrative—an exercise in public relations. Fārābī is covering up the scandal of philosophy, that its greatest exponents are not in agreement about its doctrines.

Whatever Fārābī's intentions were in writing this book, it shows that early Islamic philosophers knew of important disagreements between Plato and Aristotle. This fact was certainly known to Suhrawardī, who discussed these differences in his books. In his view, the later Peripatetics delved deeply into the trivialities of their master's system, neglecting the important intuitive component of philosophy characteristic of Plato's system. Aristotle, Suhrawardī tells us, was good, Plato was better, and the Peripatetics were and are worse.

From Suhrawardī's point of view, it is the first and second explanations of the apparent disagreements between Plato and Aristotle that are correct. The first possible explanation of the disagreement was that the definition of philosophy was wrong. Fārābī says that philosophy is "the knowledge of existents insofar as they are existent," a definition that presumably derives from Aristotle's definition of metaphysics as the "science which investigates being as being."[119] Suhrawardī holds that this definition applies only to one kind of philosophy, discursive philosophy *(baḥth)*, but there is also "intuitive philosophy"—*ta'alluh*, literally, self-divinization. Peripatetic philosophy is discursive philosophy, whereas Platonism is both discurisive and intuitive.[120] The second century Platonist Alcinous wrote in his *Didaskalikos*, a textbook of Plato's doctrines: "Philosophy is a striving for wisdom, *or* the freeing and turning around of the soul from the body, when we turn towards the intelligible and what truly is; and wisdom is the science of things divine and human."[121] To this we may compare a definition given by the fourteenth-century writer of textbooks, al-Sharīf al-Jurjānī, obviously under Illuminationist influence: "Philosophy: making oneself resemble God insofar as it is possible for human beings in order to acquire eternal happiness . . . by acquiring knowledge and shedding bodily qualities."[122] Fārābī's definition is wrong because it omits one kind—the more important kind—of philosophy. Second, Aristotle has been overrated in comparison to Plato: "Even though the First Teacher [Aristotle] was very great, profound, and insightful, one ought not exaggerate about him so as to disparage his master."[123] So, there are real disagreements between the two, and it is likely that in a given case Aristotle was wrong and Plato right. The *sophismata* in *The Philosophy of Illumination* are devoted to exploring these differences.[124] Thus, Suhrawardī rejected the fundamental argument underlying Fārābī's attempt at reconciling Plato and Aristotle. Whether Fārābī would have agreed that he himself had actually reconciled Plato and Aristotle is a question that we can leave to the Farabists.

Fārābī's work contains a useful list of the significant disagreements between Plato and Aristotle as they were understood by early Islamic philosophers. Since many of them reappear in one way or another in Suhrawardī, some as important philosophical issues, I will summarize them here.

Ascetic versus worldly way of life: Plato had lived a life withdrawn from the world but had written extensively on politics, whereas Aristotle had lived a worldly and political life. This, Fārābī says, is because Plato in his own life followed the principle that an upright soul was the first priority, whereas Aristotle, realizing the strength of his own character, felt free to carry out the social and political admonitions of Plato.

The permissibility of writing philosophy: Plato, in a compromise with his earlier view that philosophy ought not to be written, eventually came to write his philosophy in symbols and riddles. Aristotle, on the other hand, wrote everything out clearly. However, the careful reader of Aristotle's books will find them no less full of devices to conceal their full meaning: omitted premises or conclusions and the like.

Primary substance: Plato holds that the intelligible is what is most worthy of being considered substance, but Aristotle holds that it is the sensible. They are dealing with different sciences, since Plato is discussing metaphysics and the things that do not change while Aristotle is discussing the sciences of generated beings and logic.

Division versus essentialist definition: Plato employed division, a form of induction, when devising definitions, whereas Aristotle used combination *(tarkīb)*, that is, combining genus and differentiae.

The mixed modal syllogism: Plato and Aristotle are said to have disagreed about the modality of the conclusion of a syllogism in which the major premise is necessary and the minor contingent. Plato is credited with the view that the conclusion is contingent and Aristotle with the view that it is necessary.

The negative minor premise: Plato is said to have used syllogisms of the first and third figures with negative minor premises, forms that Aristotle said yielded no valid conclusions. Fārābī says that these cases involve infinite propositions, those where the predicate, not the proposition as a whole, is negated.

Contraries: Plato is said to have asserted that a contradictory is more opposed than contraries: that is, '*x* is black' and '*x* is white' are more opposed than '*x* is black' and '*x* is nonblack'. There may be some confusion in the text, but Fārābī seems to be saying that Plato held that cases like virtues as means between vices cannot be explained by Aristotle's square of opposition.

Vision: Plato, as is well known, believed that vision occurs by visual rays whereas Aristotle believed that vision occurs by rays from the object entering the eye. Fārābī says that this notorious disagreement results from interpreting the respective positions in extreme ways.

The mutability of moral traits: Plato asserted that moral qualities were innate, whereas Aristotle thought they were changable. In actuality, moral traits in adults can be changed but only with difficulty, a view that both Plato and Aristotle would agree to.

Whether seeking knowledge requires preexisting knowledge: Plato held that knowledge was recollection, a view that Aristotle denied. However, Aristotle admits the need for preexistent knowledge and the existence of universals acquired by the mind through the contemplation of particulars. This is close to what Plato said, especially since they were discussing the question in different philosophical contexts—Plato in relation to the immortality of the soul, and Aristotle in relation to logic.

Whether the world is eternal, and whether it has a Creator: The common view was that Plato asserted in the *Timaeus* that the world began in time and had a Creator, whereas Aristotle said in the *Topics* and *De Caelo* that it has no beginning in time and no Creator. In fact, this view misinterprets Aristotle, who clearly asserted the createdness of the world in the (pseudo-Aristotelian) *Theology*. The work of [Pseudo-]Ammonius reports the views of both on the Creator.

The Forms: Aristotle is well known to have criticized the doctrine of

Forms in the *Metaphysics* on the grounds that Plato's arguments, if accepted, would show that there were forms of mathematicals, artifacts, accidents, and so on. On the other hand, in his *Theology* Aristotle affirmed the existence of Forms. Since it is unlikely that Aristotle would contradict his own views, there must be another explanation, which is that both Plato and Aristotle refer to ideas in the mind of God.

Reward and punishment in the afterlife: In the *Republic* Plato said that there was reward and punishment after death whereas Aristotle is thought to have denied that the soul would receive recompense. However, Aristotle's letter of consolation to the mother of Alexander the Great shows that he did believe in such reward and punishment.

A number of these disagreements will be of relevance in coming chapters where we discuss Suhrawardī's views on several disagreements between Plato and Aristotle.

Abū Bakr al-Rāzī

The ambiguous figure Abū Bakr Muḥammad b. Zakarīyā al-Rāzī, the Latin Rhazes (864–925 or 932), was the most notorious early Islamic anti-Aristotelian.[125] He was a freethinker, whose philosophical works survive even to the limited extent that they do because his contemporaries and successors felt the need to refute him. He retained some respect, however, because of the thoroughness and brilliance of his medical works, which survive in much greater quantity. We can scarcely claim that the Illuminationists saw him as a predecessor; Suhrawardī does not mention him, and Shahrazūrī primly quotes Ṣā'id al-Andalusī: "Al-Rāzī did not understand metaphysics very deeply, nor did he understand its ultimate goal. For that reason his views were confused and he subscribed to stupid and vile opinions, condemning groups whom he did not understand."[126] Shahrazūrī's biography begins not with the customary testimony to the subject's excellence and learning but with the acid observation that he had begun as an artisan, but having injured his eyes with the vapors generated in his alchemical experients, he turned to medicine so as to be able to cure them.

Rāzī's connection with Plato is decidedly vague. While it is true that he often cites Plato and is firmly anti-Peripatetic, he actually claims allegiance to the "Ancients" and to Socrates rather than to Plato. Since he is an atomist and a rational hedonist, we are reminded more of Democritus and Epicurus than of Plato. Ibn Taymīya attributed Rāzī's theory of the "Five Eternals" to Democritus. Democritus was not especially important as a philosophical source, but he was important to the alchemists and is also linked with the Pythagoreans in late antiquity and Islam through the herbalist Bolus of Mendes.[127] Moreover, given the miserable fragments that we have of Rāzī's philosophical writings, it is difficult to be sure what to make of him. Nonetheless, he provides in certain respects the closest early Islamic counterpart to Suhrawardī's anti-Aristotelian project.

The most important parallel is simply the nature of his project. Islamic philosophers, of course, knew of the disagreements among the ancient philosophers, but they generally chose not to emphasize them. Partly this was because they believed that these philosophers were engaged in a valid and at least partly successful search for the truth. Therefore, the true parts of their respective beliefs ought to be harmonized. Also, as the example of Fārābī makes clear, they knew that the philosophical enterprise in Islam was a fragile and poorly rooted shoot; exposing the scandal of its deep internal disagreements to its enemies would put the whole project in danger. Rāzī and Suhrawardī both chose to throw caution to the winds and champion the Ancients against the overwhelming authority of Aristotle.

Rāzī's most famous doctrine was the five eternals, his teaching that God, soul, time, space, and matter all existed together without beginning and are the first principles of everything that is. Soul, desiring matter, is drawn into time and space, setting matter into motion. The goal of soul is thus to return to the spiritual world. This reminds us of various Greek theories, but most especially of the *Timaeus*. In the dialogue Plato allows a number of first principles: the Demiurge, the creator's "Model," the "Receptacle," the World-Soul, and Reason and Necessity. Rāzī is known to have written a commentary on the *Timaeus*—or more probably Galen's epitome of the work.[128] How close the parallels might have been is difficult to say.

The *Timaeus* commentary is lost, and the doctrine of the five eternals was the most disgusting of all Rāzī's dubious doctrines, rank gnostic polytheism, since only God—and perhaps the Qur'ān—could be eternal. Medieval authors allude to it with a shudder and hurry on, looking nervously over their shoulders lest some taint attach to them. Even authors who used a Neoplatonic cosmology, Suhrawardī included, made clear that the eternity of the universe was of a derived sort, unlike the eternity of God, which was essential and innate. There are nonetheless certain similarities between Rāzī's metaphysics and Suhrawardī's. The latter also based his universe on a small number of universal entities—substantial and accidental light and darkness—but as a Neoplatonist he makes absolutely clear that all of these entities are based on a single being, the Light of Lights. He specificially condemned dualism of the gnostic sort—"the heresy of Mani," for example—precisely because it posited more than one first principle.[129]

Thus, Suhrawardī could not have seen himself as a follower of Rāzī. The great physician was too free a thinker, too willing to reject entirely the role of religion, too eager to dismiss the real achievements of the Peripatetics. Moreover, Rāzī was an atomist, a position that ran completely contrary to Suhrawardī's fundamental metaphysical and epistemological positions. With the atomism came irreligion, whereas Suhrawardī was a pious, if unconventional, mystic. Perhaps Shahrazūrī was right, that Rāzī did not adequately understand the positions he was criticizing. Nonetheless, Rāzī and Suhrawardī did represent two instances of the same kind of philosophical enterprise, the conscious revival of non-Aristotelian thought as a corrective to the dominance of the Peripatetics in philosophy and of literalist theologians in religion. Rāzī's influence was negligible and ephemeral, leaving behind only the memory that there were dangerous but alluring paths one might walk beyond the safe and familiar highways of Kalam and Peripatetic philosophy. These paths, Rāzī and Suhrawardī both knew, had first been explored by the philosophers before Aristotle.[130]

WHY DID SUHRAWARDĪ BECOME A PLATONIST?

These were the Platonic materials that medieval Islamic philosophers had to work with, at least the ones that have survived and been rediscovered for us to examine. They were doctrinal and were not tied to the Platonic texts as we know them. Franz Rosenthal has observed:

> What aroused most interest concerning Plato, and continued in Islam in full vigour, was not the exterior form of his work as preserved by the faithful labours of philologists, but *certain thoughts of his* which strongly incited Islamic philosophy and which found there an enthusiastic reception and a vivid echo, although their author may sometimes have been forgotten.[131]

These "certain thoughts" were not altogether coherent. In this the medieval Muslims were in no different position from we are. Modern philosophers still argue about the "real Plato."

But there is a larger question. The identification of possible textual influences does not tell us why Suhrawardī chose to become a Pythagoreanizing Neoplatonist in a philosophical environment that was overwhelmingly Neo-Aristotelian. Though the term 'Islamic Neoplatonism' is casually used in contemporary scholarship, its use in each case must be justified. The elements of Avicenna's philosophy are overwhelmingly Aristotelian, despite some emanationist elements in his metaphysics. He himself testifies that the critical event in his intellectual development was his encounter with Aristotle's *Metaphysics* and Fārābī's commentary on it.[132] His logic is firmly Aristotelian, as is his psychology. The arrangement of his systematic works on philosophy follows the traditional arrangement of the Aristotelian corpus. Suhrawardī identifies Avicenna's school as *Mashshā'ī*—Peripatetic. Even today, the Iranian philosophers who support the views of Avicenna against those of Suhrawardī and Mullā Ṣadrā are known as "Peripatetics." Suhrawardī, on the other hand, asserts that the critical event in his own intellectual development was the rejection of Aristotelian epistemology—his acceptance of the doctrines of knowledge by presence and the Platonic Forms. His logic rejects such key Aristotelian concepts as essential definition. His systematic philosophical works are arranged quite differently from the traditional Aristotelian arrangement. He falls on one side of a line, and most of the earlier Islamic philosophers, notably Avicenna, fall on the other. Why? He himself attributes his Platonism to mystical experience. As we will see, the logic of his philosophical positions also drives him to his Platonism.

Suhrawardī's defense of the Ancients against the Peripatetics of his time involved both an approach to the practice and writing of philosophy and certain specific issues, several of which I will discuss in coming chapters: Platonic logic, the problem of vision, and its epistemological counterpart, knowledge by Presence. But before turning to the philosophical details of Suhrawardī's Platonism, it is necessary to say something about Aristotle.

CHAPTER 8

Aristotle and the Peripatetics

THE HISTORICAL ARISTOTLE IN THE ISLAMIC TRADITION

In theory, medieval Muslim scholars could have a sound and accurate knowledge of Aristotle and his life. Almost all of his books were in Arabic, usually in more than one translation, the *Politics* being the main exception. For most books there was at least one Greek commentary available in Arabic. The biographical material on Aristotle in Arabic gave a reasonably accurate account of Aristotle's life. There was some obscurity—Muslim writers sometimes confused Aristotle's father with Nicomachus of Gerasa, the author of a well-known textbook of arithmetic—but in general the Islamic portrait of Aristotle was accurate enough and easily available in biographical dictionaries of philosophers and physicians.[1] There were two practical limits to Islamic knowledge of Aristotle.

First, the Arabic translations of his works and their commentaries quickly passed out of circulation. They were confusing, difficult to understand, out-of-date philosophically, and not very systematic. They were soon replaced by more systematic and modern synthetic works written in Arabic. The key figure in this process was Avicenna, whose works were the basis of all the philosophical encyclopedias and textbooks written later. Today the bulk of the translations are lost, although we do have at least one Arabic version of most of Aristotle's works. The commentaries and related literature exist today only in fragments. Although this loss is regrettable, its long-term cultural consequences were not as serious as might be thought. Though Avicenna incorporates non-Aristotelian ideas, he presents a generally faithful account of Aristotle. Where he does diverge from Aristotle, it is in the interests of greater systematization or to incorporate more modern philosophical ideas like Stoic propositional logic and Neoplatonic metaphysics. And, indeed, the changes are often for the better. Nonetheless, the underlying philosophical system is thoroughly Aristotelian, using Aristotle's logic, his division of sciences, and his philosophical working principles. Suhrawardī called this system and its later variants 'Peripatetic' (Mashshā'ī) and did so justly.

The second limit to medieval Islamic understanding of Aristotle is more serious. The *Corpus Aristotelicum Arabicum* included a number of widely read pseudepigrapha: purported letters to Alexander the Great (notably, the *Mystery of Mysteries*), an account of Aristotle's death *(The Book of the Apple)*, and, most important, a collection of excerpts from Plotinus' *Enneads* known as *The Theology (Uthūlūjiyā) of Aristotle.*[2] Not everyone accepted the authenticity of these works, but they were influential. Since Suhrawardī seems to explain their incongruity with the rest of Aristotle's works as being the result of a change in his views in his old age, I will refer here to these works as "the old Aristotle."

For 'Āmirī Aristotle was the fifth and last of the Greeks "to whom wisdom was attributed." At least in the case of Aristotle, this "wisdom" is not some higher knowledge but philosophy pure and simple. Aristotle was the last of those called "sage" without qualification, and his knowledge was all-embracing.[3]

Certain biographical details were of special interest to Muslim scholars, but they are identical or parallel to those of particular interest to the Greeks. Aristotle was Plato's star pupil and was known by the title *rūḥānī*, "spiritual." Plato nicknamed him "the mind." He was one of the two who led the teaching after Plato's retirement. (The distinction between the Academy and the Lyceum was not clear to Muslim historians, who seem to have thought of the situation as a division of labor rather than an ideological schism.) Most especially, they knew that Aristotle had been the teacher of Alexander the Great. Even if they had not possessed purported letters from Aristotle to Alexander, the relationship would have been of interest since Alexander appears in the Qur'ān as Dhu'l-Qarnayn, "possessor of two horns," and the romance of Alexander had been translated into Arabic. The Islamic tradition is almost unanimous that "Dhu'l-Qarnayn" is Alexander, and the story is such that there is no real reason to doubt it. There is no consensus on the strange name "possessor of the two horns," but there are coins showing Alexander with ram's horns. The presence of Alexander in the Qur'ān had the curious effect of turning him, a little uncomfortably, into a prophet. The great fundamentalist Ibn Taymīya, a bitter enemy of all things Greek and philosophical, complains that ignoramuses have venerated Aristotle as the vizier of a prophet, when all the sound historical sources show that Dhu'l-Qarnayn could not have been Alexander and that Aristotle was an idol-worshipping polytheist like the rest of the pre-Christian Greeks. He is almost ranting by the time he reports that certain Sufis have identified Aristotle with Khiḍr, the mysterious teacher of Moses in Qur'ān 18—but Ibn Taymīya's indignation only serves to document the general respect that Aristotle enjoyed.[4]

THE PROBLEM OF SUHRAWARDĪ'S "OLD ARISTOTLE"

In the previous section we dealt with the "real" Aristotle—the Aristotle of the *Corpus Aristotelicum*—and with Suhrawardī's quarrel with the "Peripatetics," the somewhat faithful followers of the teachings of the historical Aristotle—chief among them Avicenna. This Aristotle, the first of the "Moderns" for both later Greek philosophers and Islamic writers on the history of philosophy, was perfectly familiar to Suhrawardī, at least through the writings of Avicenna and most probably through the Arabic translations of some of Aristotle's own works. The difficulty is that this is not the only Aristotle who appears in Suhrawardī's works; there is another Aristotle who is very much a Platonist and thoroughly in sympathy with the views of the "Ancients." Suhrawardī and his followers are aware of the contradictions in doctrines but attribute the differences to Aristotle's having returned to the doctrines of Plato late in his life.

> It is reported that Aristotle said he gave up his denial of reincarnation and returned to the view of his teacher Plato the Divine and the other ancient sages. The view that is well known from his books is due to political expediency, or else he was led to it by reason *(naẓar)*. Thus, he accepted reincarnation after having rejected it. The general view among the Peripatetics is the denial of reincarnation, though every school of sages and every religion has a firm tendency towards reincarnation.[5]

It is not necessarily a silly notion; we need only consider the amount of ink and paper that has been spent in this century dealing with "development" in Aristotle's thought and in trying to arrange his works in chronological order. Suhrawardī's solution seems obviously wrong to us only because we happen to know that the works he was relying on are not representative of a return by Aristotle to Platonism—written during the fourth of Jaeger's three stages, we might say—but of a return to Platonism in the later Greek philosophical tradition. We are also less likely to give credence to what Aristotle tells us in our dreams. There is also a mysterious reference to "eleven doctrines that Aristotle concealed out of prudence."[6]

Apart from his famous dream of Aristotle, which was mentioned in the first chapter and which I will analyze in detail in connection with the problem of Platonic epistemology, Suhrawardī's chief textual authorities for the views of the late Aristotle are—probably—the *Book of the Apple*, and—certainly—the *Theology*. Each explicitly claims to represent Aristotle's views in the period after the composition of the familiar exoteric works.[7] Both were generally, though not universally, accepted as authentic in the Middle Ages, both in the Middle East and in Europe.

The Book of the Apple

The notion that Aristotle changed his views on the hereafter late in his life inevitably suggests the influence of *The Book of the Apple (De pomo)*. This curious work purports to be an account of the conversation between the dying Aristotle and his grieving disciples. Its name comes from the apple whose scent keeps the great philosopher alive long enough to deliver fifteen pages of advice. It is obviously modeled on the *Phaedo*, whose literary brilliance is, however, lacking. The resemblance is close enough that manuscripts occasionally replace Aristotle's name with that of Socrates.[8] The precise origin of the work is unknown. It could well have been written in Greek, though a reference to "the book of Hermes" led Margoliouth to suggest a Harranian Sabian origin.[9] Since the passages most plausibly Sabian are near the end and not too well integrated into the whole, it looks to me more like an Islamic translation of a Sabian recension of a late Greek text. It has also been suggested that Kindī was in some way responsible for its composition. It is first attested in Arabic in the tenth century in the *Epistles of the Brethren of Purity*,[10] and it is quoted, in Arabic, in a Persian work by the eleventh-century Isma'ili philosopher and missionary, Nāṣir-i Khusraw.[11] The *Fihrist* does not mention it, which is odd if it were translated through the usual channels, nor do the usual biographical sources on Aristotle. There are few manuscripts of the Arabic work. Even Shahrazūrī does not mention it. In Barcelona in 1235 Rabbi Abraham ben Chasdai produced a heavily adapted Hebrew translation that was in turn translated into Latin in 1255, supposedly by King Manfred of Sicily. This Latin translation had great popularity in the thirteenth and fourteenth centuries, surviving in nearly a hundred manuscripts.

The intellectual importance of the work lay mostly in the fact that it seemed to bring Aristotle into line with the monotheistic religions on two key points, the immortality of the soul and the creation of the world, especially in Rabbi Abraham's recension. In Europe it figured in debates about whether Aristotle had achieved salvation, being quoted in such contexts into the sixteenth century. The work was not so well known in the Islamic world, where the *Theology* was a far more important text for settling such issues. Maimonides specifically identified it as spurious. Perhaps Averroes also considered it spurious, for he ignored it, so far as I know, though the Hebrew translation shows that it was available in Spain during his lifetime. On the other hand, it was translated into Persian in 1630, a date that indicates an association with the revival of philosophic thought known as the School of Isfahan.[12]

On these grounds it would be tempting to declare *The Book of the Apple* irrelevant to Suhrawardī's understanding of Aristotle, were it not for three considerations: first, Shahrazūrī's statement that Aristotle had changed his views on reincarnation late in his life; second, parallels between the Aristotle of this book and the Platonic Aristotle of Suhrawardī's dream; and, third, the similarity between its philosophical program and Suhrawardī's.

At the beginning of *The Book of the Apple*, Aristotle's disciples come to see him at his sickbed. Though he is obviously near death, his happiness and intellect are undimmed. They are puzzled as to why they should be the ones who are unhappy when it is Aristotle who is about to die. He replies, "The joy that you perceive in me does not arise from my cherishing any desire for life, but from my confidence about my condition after death." They ask about his grounds for confidence. Though the text records only the dialogue and does not reflect on its context, a reader familiar with the doctrine of the soul generally attributed to Aristotle in medieval Islam would find the disciples' question quite reasonable. Aristotle had notoriously denied the immortality of the soul—or at least he had provided no sure grounds for believing in it—so this confidence must have come from new discoveries on Aristotle's part. His reasons must wait, however, for Crito, one of the disciples, interrupts to remind his fellows that they are under strict orders from the doctor not to let Aristotle talk. Aristotle asks for an apple and tells them that there is no point in being alive if one cannot talk about philosophy.

Aristotle's argument for the immortality of the soul is based on epistemology. Wisdom—philosophy—is acknowledged by the disciples to be the highest good. Aristotle compels them to admit that the body is a hindrance to the acquisition of wisdom; wisdom properly pertains to the spirit. Since the body and its affairs are detrimental to the spirit's acquistion of wisdom, it follows that the separation of the spirit and the body is preferable to their connection. The disciples admit that this argument is valid—it is valid, of course, only if the substantiality of the soul is assumed—but they complain that their acceptance of the argument has not given them the same confidence in the face of death that Aristotle obviously has. Aristotle must start the argument again, explaining that the troubles imposed on the man of wisdom and his lack of interest in the pleasures of the body make death preferable to him. He goes on for some pages, answering the queries of his disciples and urging them to adopt a life of philosophy. Certain features of this argument are worthy of mention.

First, this work is not philosophy, properly speaking, since it is not demonstrative; it does not proceed by rigorous arguments from premises known with certainty to conclusions that are equally certain. Instead, its arguments are rhetorical. Arguments for the superiority of the life of wisdom are based on popular wisdom, appeal to the authority of sages like

Hermes and Plato, and analogy. For example, Aristotle says, "When one of the humors dominates the body, it enkindles the body as a flame enkindles firewood, bringing out the light of the soul just as fire brings light and heat out of wood."[13] *The Book of the Apple* is a sustained piece of wisdom literature, not a philosophical investigation of literary brilliance like the *Phaedo*. It nevertheless has merit and stands rightfully though modestly with more distinguished examples of its genre: the *Tabula* of Cebes, various books of the Hebrew Bible, and *The Pilgrim's Progress*.

Second, although *The Book of the Apple* is not philosophy as such, it does properly belong in the philosophical curriculum. It is a work encouraging the promising student to enter and persevere in the laborious path of the philosopher and is thus like Suhrawardī's allegories in purpose and form. It would not be appropriate for it to use rigorous demonstrative arguments, since the students for whom it is written are not yet capable of understanding them. What they are capable of understanding is analogy, which is explicitly discussed as a method of proof, "judgment from the present on the absent,"[14] here presented as a sort of weak induction. Rhetorical power is important, since the students must be encouraged. Finally, the work ends with a discussion of the textbooks the students ought to read: the "book of Hermes" for first philosophy and theology; the *Politics;* the *Physics* for natural science; the *Ethics* for good and bad actions; and for logic, the *Categories*, *De Interpretatione*, and the *Prior* and *Posterior Analytics*.[15]

Third, "Aristotle" appeals to the authority of the barbarian sages, grounding philosophy in revelation:

> DIOGENES. To whom was this thing, I mean wisdom, first made clear?
>
> ARISTOTLE. The minds of men are far from being able to attain to any thing so grand without teaching; just as their eyes are far from seeing without the light of a lamp.
>
> DIOGENES. From whom did the philosophers learn it?
>
> ARISTOTLE. The heralds and ambassadors of the different ages in the different regions of the globe were constantly summoning mankind thereunto; and the first person on earth to whom that knowledge came by revelation was Hermes.
>
> DIOGENES. Whence came it to Hermes?
>
> ARISTOTLE. His mind was taken up to heaven and it came to him from the Archangels, who had got it from the record of God. From him it came to the earth, and was received by the sages.[16]

This is exactly the account of the origin of philosophy assumed by Suhrawardī, even Hermes, who is a key figure for the Illuminationists.

Thus, *The Book of the Apple* is a text embedding Aristotle in a context that is fundamentally Neoplatonic and eclectic. It makes clear that Aristotle's works and ideas are to be understood in a Platonic context—historically because it shows that he died in a state of Platonic grace and intellectually because both its content and its recommendations for further reading show that the physical doctrines of Aristotle are to be understood in a Platonic and Hermetic metaphysical context. Its implicit program is exactly as laid out by Suhrawardī, that the student should master the science of lower things through the exacting but unexalted methods of the Peripatetics and pursue higher things through the ways of Plato.

The Theology of Aristotle

A number of Neoplatonic texts existed in Arabic, some widely circulated and some barely known. By far the most important was the so-called *Theology of Aristotle*. The text entitles itself

> The book of Aristotle the Philosopher, called in Greek *Theologia*, being the discourse on the Divine Sovereignty *(rubūbīya);* the interpretation *(tafsīr)* of Porphyry of Tyre, translated into Arabic by 'Abd al-Masīḥ Ibn Nā'ima of Emessa and corrected for Aḥmad ibn al-Mu'taṣim bi'llāh by Abū Yūsuf Ya'qūb ibn Isḥāq al-Kindī.[17]

The Arabic names given here are plausible. Ibn Nā'ima, the Latin Abenama, was a Christian, not especially important but attested in the *Fihrist* as a translator of Aristotle and active in the first half of the ninth century. Abū Yūsuf al-Kindī is the famous philosopher, who died in 866. Al-Mu'taṣim reigned from 833 to 842, and Kindī was the tutor of his son Aḥmad. Kindī is known to have commissioned translations of authentic works of Aristotle.

As European scholars have known since the nineteenth century, the *Theology* is actually a collection of excerpts from *Enneads* 4–6, strung together with connecting material. It is unknown in Greek. Cases have been made for both Greek and Arabic origins and for a Syriac intermediary text. Some have argued that it actually does go back to some epitome by Porphyry, although that scarcely matters for our purposes. The most recent thorough treatment is that of F. W. Zimmermann, who argues—plausibly, so far as I can tell—that the *Theology* is a portion of a compilation on philosophical theology prepared for al-Kindī and his circle that also included selections from Proclus' *Elements of Theology* and some short texts of Alexander of Aphrodisius. He argues that the original translation of the *Enneads* was made directly from Greek by Ibn Nā'ima as a very free adaptation, a form popular in the early stages of the translation movement. This original large compilation of Plotinus, Proclus, and Alexander was dispersed, probably physically, late in the ninth century and was the basis of the *Theology*, the *De Causis*, the so-called "Sayings of the Greek Sage," and several other greater and lesser pieces of Neoplatonica. The longer version of the *Theology*, which is so far unpublished in Arabic but which was the basis of the Latin translation, was prepared by an unknown editor from the familiar shorter *Theology* shortly before 900.[18] Zimmermann's case is very tightly argued, but it is bold and speculative. He is also perhaps too inclined to explain all features of the text in terms of its transmission history; at least, such is the case at the one point where I feel qualified to second-guess him.[19]

To a non-Peripatetic philosopher such as Suhrawardī, the *Theology* would have appeared to be the most extensive example available in Arabic of a work of Greek "divine philosophy." Consider the following passage from the first chapter *(maymar)* of the *Theology*. It appears under the heading, "A statement of his that is like an allegory of the universal soul."

> Often have I been alone with my soul and have doffed my body and laid it aside and become as if I were naked substance without body, so as to be inside myself, outside all other things. Then do I see within myself such beauty and splendour as I do remain marvelling at and astonished, so that I know that I am one of the parts of the sublime, surpassing, lofty, divine world, and possess active life. When I am certain of that, I lift my intellect up from that world into the divine world and become as if I were placed in it and cleaving to it, so as to be above the entire intelligible world, and seem to be standing in that sublime and divine place. And there I see such light and splendour as tongues cannot describe nor ears comprehend. When that light and splendour overwhelm me and I have not strength to endure it, I descend from mind to thought and reflection. When I enter the world of thought, thought veils that light and splendour from me and I am left wondering how I have fallen from that lofty and divine place and am come to the place of thought, when my soul once had the power to leave her body behind and return to herself and rise to the world of mind and then to the divine world until she entered the place of splendour and light, which is the cause of all light and splendour. Wonderful it is too how I have seen my soul filled with light, while she was still in my body like her appearance, not leaving it.[20]

This passage is not easily related to Aristotle, of course, and the medievals might well have wondered whether even a deathbed conversion to Platonism would have elicited such language from the pedantic Stagirite. In the *Theology* itself, it is not clear who exactly is talking, since the phrase "a statement of his" points away from the supposed author of the book, and "his" has no obvious referent in the text. Of course, the speaker is not Aristotle, and the Plotinian treatise from which it is drawn, "The Soul's

Descent into Body," is clearly a commentary on Plato's words on the subject, although the text does not say so explicitly.

Suhrawardī recognized that this passage refers to Plato, not Aristotle, and when he quotes or alludes to this passage, he says that he is quoting Plato.

> Of himself Plato said that in certain of his spiritual conditions he would shed his body and become free from matter. Then he would see light and splendor within his essence. He would ascend to that all-encompassing divine cause and would seem to be located and suspended in it, beholding a mighty light in that lofty and divine place. The passage of which this is a summary ended with the words, "but thought veiled that light from me."[21]

Zimmermann spends several pages puzzling over how Suhrawardī and the editor of the long version of the *Theology* knew that the passage referred to Plato, not "Aristotle." He proposes that the Greek manuscript of the *Enneads* 4.8 had a title mentioning Plato, which neither the existing Greek manuscripts nor the Arabic *Theology* have, and that Suhrawardī and the editor of the longer *Theology* had access to a version of the proto-*Theology* that made explicit reference to Plato.[22]

No such assumption is needed. This passage has nothing in common with the Aristotle known from his works and the Arabic biographical literature and could scarcely be mistaken for authentic Aristotle by anyone with even a minimum of philosophical sophistication. Moreover, the context of the passage gives strong indications to an informed reader that it is not the views of Aristotle that are under consideration. A few lines earlier the author of the *Theology* had said:

> As for what we ought to mention to those who will accept nothing except by syllogism and demonstration, we have completed a brief discussion of its reality and truth. As for the things that we ought to mention to those who will only accept the evidence of the senses, we will mention them at the beginning of our discussion of that on which the Ancients and Moderns *(al-awwalūn wa'l-ākhirūn)* agreed. That is that the Ancients agreed that when the soul becomes defiled and under the control of the body's lusts . . .[23]

"Those who will accept nothing except by syllogism and demonstration" are obviously the Peripatetics, also referred to here and elsewhere as "Moderns" (elsewhere also *muta'akhkhirūn*).[24] The discussion of the fallen soul would have pointed immediately to Empedocles, Pythagoras, and Plato. The allegory of the universal soul is followed by a passage in which Pythagoras is quoted in support of the views just expressed by "him." The text next describes at some length Plato's accounts of the soul, at one point citing Empedocles in support of a particular point. Based on what comes after, a careful reader would probably conclude that it was Plato's views on the soul that were being discussed and that some disturbance in the text had resulted in loss of the lines making clear that Plato was the relevant "Ancient."

There is more. The "allegory of the universal soul" says, "I remember Heracleitus, for he ordered that one should seek and inquire about the sublime substance of the soul and should desire to ascend to that sublime and exalted world."[25] Heracleitus is not a particularly prominent figure in the Islamic account of Greek philosophy, but he was known and was known in particular as one of the three sources of Plato's philosophy.[26] He is much more naturally associated with Plato than with Aristotle, and cannot be associated with Pythagoras or Empedocles. The natural interpretation would be that this passage represents Plato quoting his teacher or teacher's teacher. It is true that the sources usually say that Heracleitus was Plato's teacher in "sensible things" *(maḥsūsāt)*, but "Aristotle" has just told us that he is beginning with "those who will only accept the evidence of the senses." Moreover, from Suhrawardī's point of view, Plato's mystical experience *is* the evidence of the senses, albeit in the special mode of the intuition of the mystics. There is also the evidence of the title, "A statement of his that is like an allegory *(ramz)* of the universal soul." As we have seen, Plato was known to have expressed his philosophy through symbols *(al-ramz wa'l-ighlāq)*.[27] The word *ramz* would immediately have suggested Empedocles, Pythagoras, or Plato, and it is clear from the context that the passage is not by Pythagoras. Finally, there is the assumption that if the *Theology* is an authentic work of Aristotle, it represents the period of his reconversion to the Platonism of his youth. If that is so, then an unnamed speaker is most likely to be Plato.

In short, *pace* Zimmermann, it would have been surprising if Suhrawardī or any other reasonably informed medieval reader had attributed this passage to anybody except Plato; there is no need to propose an emendation of the *Enneads/Theology* manuscript tradition to explain the identification. On the other hand, the fact that the passage is included in a book supposedly compiled by Aristotle would indicate that Aristotle endorsed this account, so in the *Intimations* immediately after a paraphrase of this passage Suhrawardī remarks: "The First Teacher [Aristotle] spoke from his own experience of these mighty lights."[28]

This passage is obviously of philosophical significance to Suhrawardī, as is indicated by the fact that he quotes or cites it at least three times in his published works. We will see how he uses the notion of mystical or philosophical intuition it when we examine the problem of knowledge by presence in chapter 10.

Suhrawardī therefore is justified on two grounds when he makes philosophical use of *The Theology of Aristotle* and its fascinating collection of Neoplatonic doctrines. First, he has reason to think that the book contains citations of the teachings of the Ancients, including Plato, Empedocles, and Pythagoras. Second, he had reason to believe that this book represented the most mature period of Aristotle's thought. We should not forget, though, that Suhrawardī was first and foremost a philosopher and so he was quite capable of being drawn to the *Theology* on the basis of the interest of its ideas, quite apart from any ancient authority it might or might not have. And the interest of these ideas was considerable, for the *Theology* summarized the central doctrines of Neoplatonism: the fall of the soul, its substantiality, and its knowledge, the supernal beauty of the intelligible world, the atemporal emanation of the many from the One, the Platonic Forms, and many other themes.[29] *The Theology of Aristotle*, in short, was the most developed example of the Divine Philosophy available to Suhrawardī.

SUHRAWARDĪ'S CRITIQUE OF THE PERIPATETICS

With such Neoplatonic materials to work with and having probably read the *Metaphysics*, Suhrawardī would naturally have distinguished between Aristotle and the "Peripatetics." 'Peripatetic'—περιπατητικός—means "walking around," in particular while teaching. The title was applied to the followers of Aristotle, supposedly because Aristotle was in the habit of lecturing while walking around.[30] The Arabs rendered the name literally as "Mashshā'ī," "constantly walking." They too thought that it had something to do with lecturing and walking, although they were not so sure of the details—some sources mention that Plato had lectured while riding a horse and Aristotle had been in the habit of walking at his stirrup. Still, everybody understood 'Peripatetic' to refer to the followers of Aristotle, particularly those concerned with his exoteric system.[31]

For many medieval European thinkers the system of Aristotle—"the Philosopher"—represented the highest attainment of unaided human reason. Though Suhrawardī stoutly opposed the Peripatetics, he would not have disagreed.[32] When he uses the name "Peripatetic," he refers mainly to Avicenna and his followers, though, of course, he knew that they carried on an older tradition. They were not necessarily to be identified with Aristotle himself, for they were not so much followers of Aristotle as philosophers who followed Aristotle in a particular way. Suhrawardī held that there were several things wrong with the Peripatetics. First, they pursued only speculative philosophy and neglected intuitive philosophy. In other words, they relied only on unaided human reason and not on the mystical intuition used by Empedocles, Pythagoras, and Plato. Second, they devoted excessive attention to secondary aspects of logic, science, and philosophy. Thus, for example, they devised elaborate rules for handling various composite forms of the syllogism when researchers actually need only simple, very general rules for avoiding error. Finally, they were excessively concerned with worldly matters and thus neglected the more important spiritual matters.[33] In short, they were pedants and court functionaries, not divine philosophers. The model for these criticisms is certainly Avicenna, one of the few Islamic philosophers whom Suhrawardī quotes by name. In his *Healing*, Avicenna systematizes Aristotle's logic, working out, for example, all the valid forms of the modal syllogism. Avicenna repeatedly sought court patronage and political advancement. His death, supposedly due to complications caused by sexual excess, scarcely exemplified the ideal of the Illuminationist philosopher: "The ancient philosophers like Plato, Aristotle, and others, were ascetics. Abū 'Alī [Avicenna] did not follow their practices or distinguishing qualities. He loved drinking wine and the satisfaction of his lusts. Those who came after him followed the example of his vice and addictions."[34]

Though some recent scholars have claimed at least the later Avicenna as a mystical philosopher, it is clear that Suhrawardī would not agree, for he quotes the book in which mystical concerns are most obviously present—the *Hints and Admonitions*—and nonetheless treats it as a purely exoteric work. For example, Suhrawardī quotes the definition of *ḥadd*, "essential definition" from the *Hints*.[35] My impression is that this book is Suhrawardī's chief source for Avicenna's thought, though the maddeningly vague citations of other authors in Suhrawardī's books means that more research will need to be done before we know for sure. The extreme example of the mystical interpretation of Avicenna is Corbin.[36] The problem arises from the fact that toward the end of his life Avicenna wrote a book called the *Kitāb al-Inṣāf (The Book of Fair Judgment)* in which he undertook to decide between the views of the "Eastern" (Mashriqīyūn) and the "Western" philosophers. Except for a few fragments this book was lost in one of Avicenna's brushes with disaster. He also wrote a *Logic of the Easterners*, which is extant. The question is what is meant by this Eastern or "Oriental" philosophy. If *mashriqīya*, "eastern," is vocalized *mushriqīya* "illuminationist," as can be done without changing the Arabic consonantal outline, it is possible to connect it with Suhrawardī's *ishrāqī* philosophy, though it is not very convincing morphologically and there is not much in the way of corroborative evidence. I am inclined to see the *Fair Judgment* as a comparison between the views of the philosophers of eastern Iran with those of Baghdad. I also think—as Suhrawardī evidently did—that the mystical aspects of Avicenna's philosophy were not particularly central, so I will not pursue the supposed link between Avicenna's "Oriental philosophy" and Suhrawardī's Illuminationism.

Philosophically, the tension between Illuminationist and Peripatetic methods and doctrines provides much of the interest in Suhrawardī's system. It might be thought that Suhrawardī simply was rejecting Peripatetic doctrines in favor of Platonic ones, but that is not exactly the case. The relationship may be understood in terms of Suhrawardī's biography, in terms of the relationship between the two philosophical schools, in terms of lower and higher approaches to knowledge, and in terms of the truth or falsity of specific doctrines.

Biography

Suhrawardī was a Peripatetic before he was an Illuminationist. He was trained in the Peripatetic philosophy and advocated it in his youth. This philosophy was certainly in Avicenna's tradition. In time Suhrawardī rejected it, partly because he had encountered problems, particularly in epistemology, that the Peripatetic philosophy could not solve, but more fundamentally because his dream of Aristotle and his mystical apprehension of the Platonic Forms had awakened him from his Peripatetic slumbers and convinced him of the superiority of the philosophy of the Ancients and especially of Plato. In this context the Peripatetic philosophy is the doctrine of his youth that he rejected in his maturity.

Philosophical Schools

In another sense, as I will argue in detail in connection with Stoicism, Suhrawardī saw the Peripatetics and the Illuminationists as separate and rival philosophical schools—the two rival wings of the Platonic tradition. Each school had its own set of doctrines, and Suhrawardī considered certain Peripatetic doctrines to be wrong. Such a view is implicit in Suhrawardī's account of his conversion. It is also the view of later philosophers like Mullā Ṣadrā, who dismissed the Illuminationists as "followers of the Stoics."

Lower and Higher Forms of Knowledge

Suhrawardī, however, also saw a dialectical relationship between Peripatetic and Illuminationist philosophy, for he continued to write in the Peripatetic mode long after his conversion to Platonism: "Before I wrote this book and during the times when interruptions prevented me from working on it, I wrote other books in which I have summarized for you the principles of the Peripatetics according to their method."[37] The Peripatetics were not "wrong" in the sense that a Thomist would consider a Marxist wrong. Rather, the Peripatetic philosophy was a sort of curtailed philosophy, one that used only reason and failed to use mystical intuition as a philosophical tool. If correctly done it was sound, but it was prone to error, having no intuitive faculty to guide it, a willfully blind philosophy tapping its way through the world with a stick, and it could not attain the highest truths. On the other hand, it did not require the personal ethical and spiritual attainments necessary to carry out the Illuminationist philosophy. It was thus suitable for the beginner and for those unwilling to endure the fasts and mortifications necessary for the adept of the Illuminationist philosophy. It is not unlike the sixth century Alexandrian curriculum that put students through three years of Aristotle before they began reading Plato's dialogues.[38] It is in this sense that certain of Suhrawardī's books are "Peripatetic," for they use reason but not mystical intuition. The distinction is not absolute. For example, the Platonic Forms are a doctrine of the Illuminationist but not the Peripatetic system. Nonetheless, when Suhrawardī discusses a related issue in the *Paths and Havens*, one of his "Peripatetic" works, he hints at the Illuminationist view.[39]

Specific Doctrines

Suhrawardī also disagrees with specific doctrines: the Aristotelian rejection of the Forms, the reification of beings of reason, the intromission theory of vision, and certain other points. These are discussed in the *sophismata* of *The Philosophy of Illumination*. These doctrines raise other questions about the dialectical relationship between Peripatetic and Illuminationist philosophy. First, Suhrawardī deals with these doctrines in the context of the Peripatetic philosophy itself, showing that in Peripatetic terms these particular doctrines are unsound. It is a strategy similar to that used by Ghazālī in his *Incoherence of the Philosophers*.

> Let it be known that it is our purpose to disillusion those who think too highly of the philosophers, and consider them to be infallible. Since I have undertaken to expose the incoherence and contradiction involved in philosophical thought, I will approach them in order to attack them, not to defend something of mine own.[40]

Second, they are doctrines that can be known through mystical intuition. They are thus the key points of difference between Peripatetic and Illuminationist philosophies. Finally, these doctrinal distinctions provide the framework for Suhrawardī's philosophical polemic, which is couched in terms of his differences with the Peripatetics.

These differences will provide the framework for the following chapters, in which I will discuss in detail several specific differences that Suhrawardī saw between the Illuminationists/Platonists and the Peripatetics.

CHAPTER 9

Plato versus Aristotle (i): The Critique of Peripatetic Logic

In *The Philosophy of Illumination* Suhrawardī reduces logic to "a small number of very useful rules. These are sufficient for the intelligent and for those who seek illumination. Whoever wishes to learn the details of this science—which is merely a tool—should consult the more detailed books."[1] Indeed, the treatment of logic in this work is not far from being a parody of traditional logic, a country bumpkin's triumphant reduction of all the ponderous complication of Aristotelian logic to Barbara, modus ponens, and modus tollens, all expressed in deliberately naive terminology ('univeral meaning', 'individualizing word', 'definitely necessary propositions') that replaces the traditional jargon. Suhrawardī does wander from his simplistic neologisms, reverting to the standard logical terminology he learned in school and much of his presentation can be traced to Avicenna's *Hints*, but he has made his point: the simple cases in logic are self-evident, and any intelligent person can reduce the complicated cases to the simple ones by use of his common sense.

We might thus read the logic of *The Philosophy of Illumination* as no more than an exercise in semi-satirical dialectic, by which he ridicules and deflates the claims of the Peripatetics to know deeper truth through subtle logical methods unavailable to amateurs. But Suhrawardī was not an amateur. He had mastered traditional logic and its twelfth century critiques while still a student, and he dealt with it in detail in his other works.[2] What he does include in his logic is significant, for it provides a logical foundation and a parallel to his metaphysics and ontology later in the same work.

Three areas seem significant to me: definition, about which both Hossein Ziai and I have written elsewhere; his reduction of all propositions to necessary affirmative propositions; and his stress on propositional logic.

DIVISION AND THE REJECTION OF ESSENTIALIST DEFINITION

In the last chapter of the *Sophistical Refutations*, Aristotle proudly wrote:

> It is manifest that we have completed what we set out to do, starting from the beginning and reaching an end appropriate to the subject. One ought

> not to ignore something that is unique to this art, in contrast to all other existent arts. In those arts, there was always something already done, ready to take from others, so that the labor could be undertaken little by little, divided with other people who came before. . . . But as for this art [logic], it was not the case that part existed and part did not, so that it could be added to now. Rather, absolutely nothing at all of it existed.[3]

This claim was accepted by Muslim historians of philosophy.

> The only books I know, ancient or modern, composed on any science that completely cover that science and explain all its parts are these three: first, the *Almagest* on this science of astronomy and the motion of the stars; second, Aristotle's book on the science of logic; and, third, the *Kitāb* of Sībawayh of Basra on the science of Arabic grammar.[4]

Of course, there was a Platonic logic, although it was not presented as the orderly mind of Aristotle would have wished. Later logicians then clarified the logical disputes between Plato and Aristotle in terms of what became the standard logical categories, those of Aristotle. Fārābī, the reader will recall, listed four disputes between Plato and Aristotle on subjects related to formal logic. Several of those points relate to issues raised by Suhrawardī as points of disagreement with the Peripatetics.

Division and Definition

"Knowledge," wrote the thirteenth-century Peripatetic Najm al-Dīn Dabīrān al-Kātibī al-Qazwīnī in the introduction to his standard textbook of logic, "is either conception only or conception together with assent."[5] Conception is an idea unaccompanied by a judgment; assent is the judgment that an idea is or is not the case. 'Paul Bunyan's blue ox' denotes a conception; 'Paul Bunyan owned a blue ox' denotes an assent. In Islamic Peripatetic logic, conceptions are acquired by definitions and assents by syllogisms. Suhrawardī's most important disagreement with earlier Islamic logicians concerns the construction of definitions and their role in conveying conceptions.

Aristotle's logic of science is a "top-down" system, a deductive logic of terms, in which the sciences are deduced from prior, necessary, better known, and more general propositions and from the essential properties of the things studied in the sciences. He does indeed mention induction, but he can scarcely be said to have presented a real theory of inductive reasoning—and dialectic is a complication that I have no intention of dealing with. But his heart is in deductive reasoning—valid arguments, we would say—which he considers the standard to which real sciences must be held. In other words, to construct a science we must have both conceptions of the entities that form the subject matter of that science and assents relevant to those entities. The conceptions, moreover, must reflect the real essences of the entities studied; a science of zoology, for example, must start from the real essences of animals. To build a theory in this way is splendid and unquestionably valid—if we can be sure that we have acquired the relevant conceptions and assents. But Suhrawardī thinks that we cannot always acquire conceptions and assents in this way and that knowledge by presence is sometimes required.[6]

Aristotle and the Peripatetics claimed that an essential defintion *(ὅρος, ḥadd)* must be composed of the proximate genus and the differentiae. This is a stronger criterion than simply requiring that the definition identify the thing defined. The classic example is man, which is defined as "a rational (i.e., language-using) animal," where 'animal' is the proximate genus and 'rational' is the differentia, the essential property that distinguishes man from all other animals. It is distinguished from a definition like "man is a laughing biped," which, though equally effective in distinguishing man from other things, does so with properties that are accidental to the essence of man: bipedal, which is a common accident shared with other animals, and laughing, which is an accident thought to be proper to man.

Suhrawardī sees problems with this theory of conception. First, suppose that we have constructed an essential definition. How then do we know that we have included all the differentiae? True, by Aristotelian standards we do not know the thing unless we do know the differentiae, but if so, how do we know that we actually know the thing? But the rot goes even deeper, endangering the possibility of any knowledge. If such definitions must be known, either explicitly or implicitly, before we can know the thing, we can know nothing. The differentia is by definition specific to the thing being defined, so how can we know the differentia without first knowing the thing we are defining, particularly if it doesn't happen to be a sensible property? What is worse, there is sometimes disagreement about what the essential properties are. The Peripatetics would include matter and form in the definitions of air and water, whereas the Islamic theologians would include indivisible atoms. Ordinary people, who know air and water perfectly well, have no opinion on either view or may even have an incorrect opinion about what air and water are—yet still they know air and water.[7] Obviously, two or even all three of the parties are ignorant of the reality of air and water in some sense, but they all certainly know them. The issue is even more obvious in the case of definitions of sensible qualities. 'Black' is defined by the Peripatetics as "a color that collects vision,"[8] but what could this possibly mean? Leaving aside the formal question of whether this definition fits the genus/differentia model, it is perfectly obvious that nobody knows black by knowing this definition; we know black by seeing black things. If we have not seen black things—if we are born blind, for example—we cannot know black, no matter what definition is given to us.

Suhrawardī was not the only one to object to logic in general or to see essential definition in particular as a fatal flaw in the Aristotelian system. The Neoplatonists had criticized Aristotelian term logic.[9] Sīrāfī, in his famous debate with the Christian logician Mattā b. Yūnus, objected that logic was not universal laws of thought but simply Greek grammar repackaged for export. Ghazālī, who knew logic and philosophy well, held that logic was unobjectionable in itself but led the unwary to assume that the metaphysical reasoning of the philosophers was as rigorous and reliable as their logic indicated it ought to be, which was not the case. The great fundamentalist Ibn Taymīya, writing about a century after Suhrawardī, saw much the same objections to Aristotelian definition and wrote refutations of Greek logic.[10] At first he presumed that Ghazālī was right but then he came to understand that logic itself was pernicious.

> I had always known that Greek logic was neither needed by the intelligent nor useful to the stupid, but I had assumed that all of its premises were correct, since I had seen the truth of many of them. Then it became clear to me later that a number of them were erroneous, and I wrote something about that. . . . That itself was not my purpose; rather my purpose was to write against them concerning metaphysics, but it had become evident to me that many of their fundamental principles in metaphysics and logic were among the sources of their errors in metaphysics, for example, the compounding of quiddities from attributes that they call 'essential' and their restriction of the modes of knowledge to definitions and demonstrative syllogisms.[11]

In other words, if logic falls, so too do the pernicious doctrines of the philosophers on metaphysics.

Suhrawardī was not a skeptic, however, and definition has a place—a Platonic place—in his system. It was well known to Islamic philosophers that definition was an important point of disagreement between Plato and Aristotle. Thus, Fārābī wrote:

> Also, [Plato and Aristotle] are supposed [to disagree] about division and combination in constructing definitions *(al-qisma wa'l-tarkīb fī tawfiyat al-ḥudūd).* Plato thought that definitions could only be constructed by means of division, and Aristotle thought they should be constructed by demonstration and combination.[12]

Plato, like his teacher Socrates, was deeply interested in what things really were, an interest that led him to two philosophical pursuits of interest to us: the construction of definitions and the theory of Forms. Socrates went around Athens pestering the people whom the Arabs called *a'yān*, "notables," asking them about the true meaning of various words they thought they understood: justice, piety, courage, self-restraint, and the like. In his later dialogues Plato reflected on this method and called it "division" *(διαίρεσις)*.[13] The *Sophist* and the *Statesman* contain famous examples of Plato's mature method of division. In the *Sophist* the first example given is that of the fisherman. Angling is an art; it is acquisitive, not separative or productive; it acquires by capture, not exchange; and so on. For Plato the art of constructing definitions by division was not arbitrary; the divisions had to be made at the "natural joints."[14] In other words, the division used to form a definition had to correspond to the divisions among the various Forms.

Fārābī saw—or professed to see—this procedure as a matter of taste in philosophical method: Plato thought that it was simplest to construct definitions by working from the more general to the more specific, whereas Aristotle preferred to work from the specific to the general. They were on the same set of stairs, but Aristotle went up and Plato down. In the end they covered the same distance. If one looks carefully at Aristotle's arguments, one finds that he actually does use the method of division extensively, although he does not necessarily refer to Plato when he does so.[15]

Suhrawardī does not accept this rosy history of the methodology of constructing definitions. We do not need to discuss his critique of definitions here in detail, since Hossein Ziai has thoroughly analyzed the matter,[16] but some discussion is in order. Suhrawardī does not explicitly refer to Plato's method of division in *The Philosophy of Illumination*, but he would have been aware of it. There are two problems to discuss: what is wrong with the Peripatetic theory of definition, and what alternative method is there for acquiring conceptions. The problem with Aristotelian definition is, simply put, that it is circular. Aristotelian definition is *essential* definition; it purports to tell us about real kinds in a way that reveals to us the real structure of the thing. But to understand the definition, we must already know the thing. Such definitions work well for biological taxonomy, but not for anything else. We can know dogs by knowing the properties of the genus *canis* and the differentiae—tooth structure, for example—that distinguish the species *canis domesticus* from the other canines. This is not quite the same as knowing dogs.[17]

But what is the alternative to essential definition? Lexical definition is valid but uninteresting, an arbitrary assignment of a name, and Suhrawardī, like both Plato and Aristotle, is interested in real kinds. "We only have definition by means of things that specify by conjunction *(bi'l-ijtimā')*."[18] Suhrawardī means that a certain number of properties in combination identify the thing, distinguishing it from everything else. To define something, one need merely specify a group of properties that collectively apply only to the thing defined. 'Rational animal' and 'laughing, largely hairless biped' serve equally well to divide off man from everything else in the world. Suhrawardī's theory of definition thus calls for the identification of things in the world, not for the exposition of their reality as such. The affinity of this theory of definition with Plato's theory of division is obvious enough. But if Aristotle's definition claims too much for itself, this theory would seem to claim too little, merely carving out little chunks of reality with a dialectical penknife. How does Suhrawardī's theory of definition by conjunction differ in any meaningful way from lexical definition?

To answer this question, we must go back to Plato's theory of division. Division, for Plato, was part of the larger science of dialectic. Division was not an arbitrary procedure; there were right and wrong ways of dividing reality, "natural joints" to be found by the philosopher-butcher. These natural joints reflect distinctions among the Forms and the fact that there really are essential attributes of things. How exactly these joints are to be found is not always very clear in Plato, though it seems to involve discussion and debate. Suhrawardī accepts the Forms as the sources of order in the world and as the causes of natural kinds, but like Porphry and some other Neoplatonists who sought to use Aristotle's logic without adopting his metaphysics, he is quite a radical nominalist. The way in which he finds the natural joints will be seen below in the discussion of knowledge by presence.

THE SIMPLIFICATION OF THE SYLLOGISM

Suhrawardī sought to reduce the complexity of logic by reducing the number of its component parts. The logic of inference in Aristotle's syllogistic is complicated because there are many kinds of syllogisms, some valid and some not, and there are many kinds of syllogisms because there are many kinds of propositions. If there were fewer kinds of propositions, there would be fewer kinds of syllogisms. If there were only one kind of proposition, there would be only one kind of valid syllogism. Thus, if Suhrawardī can reduce all propositions to the necessary universal affirmative: 'Necessarily all A is B', the four figures of the syllogism with their 256 moods will be reduced to one: a modalized version of Barbara: 'Necessarily all A is B, and necessarily all B is C; therefore necessarily all A is C'.

The simplification of the proposition is effected by including the mode, quality (affirmation or negation), and quantification in the terms. First, he iterates the modality, converting the proposition 'Contingently, all humans are literate' into 'It is necessary that all humans are contingently literate'. Although he is working with terms rather than propositions, the result is not greatly different from those contemporary interpretations of modal logic that allow the inference 'It is possible that ϕ implies that it is necessary that it is possible that ϕ' ($\Diamond\phi \supset \Box\Diamond\phi$, a characteristic axiom of the S5 system of modal logic). Negation can be eliminated by replacing the predicate with an infinite term; 'Man is not stone' becomes 'Man is non-stone'. Existential quantification is a little trickier, cases like 'Some animal is rational'. In this case, Suhrawardī tells us, we must give a name to the class of rational animals, say 'D'. We can then convert the proposition into 'All Ds are rational'.[19] At first sight, this would seem to be an obvious, if somewhat simple-minded, way to formalize reasoning. Oddly enough, I have not been able to find anyone else who has used such an approach. That it simplifies logic is questionable; it only moves the complication from the syllogism back to the stage in which propositions are formulated.

Whether or not Suhrawardī is right that he has simplified logic, whether this logical procedure is even valid, such a move is hardly innocent and has deep implications for his metaphysical system. For Aristotle, contingency was built into logic. He was a biologist, a museum curator, a collector of specimens and facts. Having rejected the heavenly Forms of his teacher Plato, he grounded his universals in his knowledge of the particular. His is, to start with, a logic of terms—of propositions that apply predicates to subjects—a logic suited to the needs of the biologist seeking to identify and analyze natural kinds into orderly categories. In a way, his treatment of syllogisms reflects his tastes as a collector, identifying the 256 possible and twenty-four valid forms of the syllogism. Of the twenty-four forms, only one, Barbara, yields a universal affirmative proposition. The other twenty-three yield universal negations and existential affirmatives and negations. The third figure—the one in which the two premises have the same subject—yields only existential propositions. The introduction of modality complicates the issue, but it is still only the modalized Barbara that yields a necessary, universal, affirmative conclusion. Other figures, moods, and modalities yield lesser results. But this complication is very much to Aristotle's taste. Apart from the satisfaction of producing an orderly classification of diverse forms, his logic reflects his universe in which necessity must be carefully teased out of a mass of contingent facts.

One large motivation to use term logic vanished with Suhrawardī's rejection of Aristotelian essentialism and essential definition. Aristotle's logic was developed to serve his approach to science, a science in which the essences of things were the proper objects of study. Term logic, as Aristotle formulates it, is particularly useful for unpacking statements of essences and thus requires essentialist definition. Uncoupled from this particular approach to science, Aristotelian term logic often seems uncomfortably tautological, a fact seized upon by Islamic theological critics like Ibn Taymīya. Suhrawardī rejected Aristotelian essentialism and held that essences could be known, if at all, only through direct acquantance. It was in principle impossible to create definitions that were both complete and actually conveyed new knowledge. Detached from its scientific context, term logic loses importance in Suhrawardī's thought and can be reduced to his "few simple rules."

Moreover, for Suhrawardī contingency is an illusion—or at best a relation, the product of our limited view of the universe from within time. The Light of Lights just *is*—absolutely, eternally, necessarily. Everything else is generated by necessity from it, directly or indirectly. These generated beings are contingent in the sense that they do not exist necessarily of themselves, but they are necessary through the Light of Lights and could not be other than they are. The contingency of contingent beings is a fact to be understood in the context of their ultimate necessity. Modern modal logic distinguishes necessity and possibility by making them quantifiers over possible worlds. A proposition is possible if it is true in some possible world w of the set of all possible worlds W, and necessary if it is true in all such possible worlds. If it is true in the actual world w^*, it is therefore possible but might or might not be necessary, depending on its truth in all other possible worlds. For Suhrawardī there is only *one* possible world, so w^* is the only member of W. All true propositions are therefore necessary, and all false propositions impossible. Contingency does retain meaning in two senses: as applying to change within time and as referring to ontological dependence. However, both these kinds of contingency are contained within a larger structure of necessity. Time is required to express the full complexity of the interrelations of the immaterial lights. In modern terms we might say that the complexity of the lights generated from the Light of Lights requires four dimensions for its full expression, but from the point of view of God, the angels, and the mystics who have transcended the material world, the universe can be seen to be a static structure determined in all its aspects by the necessity of the Light of Lights and its eternal activity. As for ontological contingency, it is necessity when expressed in terms of modal logic. From the point of view of Suhrawardī's modal logic, it is certainly justifiable to reduce possible propositions to necessary ones, for the Illuminationist philosopher will eventually see the illusoriness of contingency through mystical intuition.

This ontological theory is paralleled by Suhrawardī's syllogistic. Whereas Aristotle's modal syllogistic with its large and untidy collection of valid and invalid forms reflects his complicated world in which contingency and necessity intermingle, Suhrawardī's modal syllogistic contains only one mood, the clear and austere Barbara, further restricted to necessary propositions. But it is Barbara that best reflects the structure of Suhrawardī's universe, with its systematic unfolding of the simple and necessary into the multiple and contingent—or, more properly, the necessary by another.

Suhrawardī's differences with Aristotle (or, more accurately, the tradition of Aristotelian term logic, since the introduction of the fourth figure of the syllogism was a post-Aristotelian innovation) are not simply formal. He holds that the arguments used to establish the validity of the second, third, and fourth figures are invalid. The problem is that these proofs are based on conversion, which in turn is based on ecthesis and reductio ad absurdum. The validity of each of these last two, however, is based on the other, this introducing a circularity into the justification for the other figures of the syllogism. Suhrawardī maintains instead that the validity of the various figures of the syllogism can only be established by "reflection or inspection."[20]

But are we even justified in expressing Suhrawardī's modal theory in terms of modern modal logic? I do not think so. As has been mentioned, mainstream modern modal logic converts modal statements—'It is possible that X' or 'It is necessary that X'—into statements about possible worlds—'There is some possible world where X' or 'In all possible worlds X'. The advantage of this system is that it converts the somewhat mysterious notions of necessity and possibility into statements using the well-understood notions of all and some. The disadvantage of this method is that it is difficult to know what the possible worlds are.[21] The question for us, then, is whether Suhrawardī's modal logic can be translated into possible worlds language. It cannot, for reasons having to do with his logic and metaphysics.

Suhrawardī describes modality in *The Philosophy of Illumination* in terms of both the necessity of the copula and the essence of the entity:

> The relation of the predicate of a categorical proposition to its subject either must exist—in which case it is called 'the necessary'—or must not exist—'the impossible'—or may either exist or not exist—'the possible' or 'the contingent'. An example of the first is 'man is animal'; of the second, 'man is stone'; and of the third 'man is literate'. By 'possible' most people mean that which is not impossible. For when they say 'not impossible' they mean by it the possible, and when they say 'not possible' they mean by it the impossible. However, this is not our usage, for what is not contingent according to this usage may be either what has to exist or what cannot exist. If the necessity or impossibility of something depends on something else, then if that other thing is removed, then neither the necessity nor the impossibility remains, and the thing is contingent in itself.

> The contingent is necessary by virtue of that which necessitates it and is impossible on condition of the non-existence of that which necessitates its existence. When one examines the thing itself in the two states of existence and non-existence, it is contingent. . . .
>
> By 'necessary' we mean only that which it has by virtue of its own essence. That which is necessary on condition of a time or state is contingent in itself.[22]

Mumkin can be translated as either 'possible' or 'contingent'. In Arabic it has the same ambiguity that the English 'possible' has, for it can mean either that which is not impossible or that which is neither necessary nor impossible. The term is translated 'contingent' here, which accurately renders its technical Arabic meaning, but this makes Suhrawardī's explanation of the difference between popular and technical logical usage unnecessary. By 'necessary' Suhrawardī means one of two things, either that an entity has sufficient reason for existing or that an attribute is essential to its substance. Something is contingent if it exists, or could exist, due to a cause other than its own essence, whether as a substance whose existence is caused by something else or as an accidental attribute. Neither notion lends itself to translation into the possible worlds language of modern modal logic.

The first difficulty is that necessary and contingent entities are not mutually exclusive categories. In fact, there is only one necessary entity that is not also contingent: God, the one being that is necessary by essence. Every other existent entity is contingent in itself but necessary by another. This might not, at first, seem to be an insuperable problem. Take, for example, the proposition 'Socrates exists'. Socrates, like all existent beings other than God, is contingent in himself and necessary by virtue of the causes that brought him into being: an act of sexual intercourse between his parents, and so on. To say that Socrates is contingent is to assert that there is at least one conceivable world in which Socrates exists and another in which he does not. To say that he is necessary by another is to say that Socrates exists in all conceivable worlds in which the circumstances leading to his birth and survival obtained. So far, so good; the combined necessity and contingency of Socrates is no more than an equivocation; 'possibly' means only "for all I know." But let us take another example: 'The proximate light exists'. The proximate light is the first emanation from the Light of Lights, or God. For Suhrawardī this being is necessary and contingent in exactly the sense that Socrates is, yet its existence is a logically necessary consequence of the existence of the Light of Lights. Thus the proximate light exists in all conceivable worlds, but it is contingent because it is an effect and its existence is dependent on another—not because there is a conceivable world in which it does not exist. The same is true of the third light, of the Platonic Forms, of the spheres, and so on down to the humblest thorn bush growing in the desert. The only difference between the proximate light and Socrates is that in the first case we can understand the necessity of its existence and in the second case we cannot. Since there is only one possible world, Suhrawardī's notion of contingency as causal and ontological dependence cannot be expressed in terms of the possible worlds version of modal logic.

We might attempt to salvage the situation by distinguishing beings that are outside time from those that are within time, restricting modal logic to the latter—the so-called "statistical interpretation" of modality with its "principle of plenitude," that no genuine possibility can remain forever unrealized.[23] By this interpretation a possibility is a state of affairs that holds at at least one point in time. This will not do either since it does not correspond to Suhrawardī's use of modal terms. Consider the propositions 'Socrates is rational', 'Socrates is bipedal', 'Socrates is white', 'Socrates is in the law court', and 'Socrates is in the Holy Land'. In Suhrawardī's view the first is necessary and the rest contingent, for Socrates is a man and he is thus by essence rational. Although all men are bipedal, this is not part of the essence of humanity, at least according to the Islamic logicians, and Socrates is white due to accidental causes external to his human essence, though he is always white. He is in the agora due to purely temporary causes, and there might have been contingent causes that took him to the Holy Land, but in actual fact there were not. In all possible worlds where he exists Socrates is a rational being because that is his essence as a human being. Yet it is not easy to argue that there is a truly possible world in which Socrates is not white. There is certainly not a time in which he is some other color. If we say that we can imagine a world in which Socrates is African, how can we reply to the objection that this is not a real possibility but only a figment of our imaginations, possible only in the sense that flying horses are possible? Yet if we restrict possible worlds to worlds that could be realized, we have only the possibilities that can be realized at some moment in time—which do not include Socrates' blackness.

It is not surprising to find that Suhrawardī's modal logic cannot be made compatible with the contemporary modal logic of possible worlds, for the underlying metaphysical assumptions are very different. For Suhrawardī contingency is not a matter of realized and unrealized possiblities but of ontological dependence. Modern philosophers have recognized that the notion of possible worlds in modal logic raises major metaphysical questions, and so possible worlds have had their share of critics among contemporary philosophers. What is somewhat more surprising is that Suhrawardī's modal logic seems not to be the same as the so-called temporal-modal logic of mainstream Islamic logicians, at least insofar as this logic is known to modern scholars.[24] But to sort out this question would require a detailed study of Suhrawardī's logical works in the context of the even less known history of logic in the time after Avicenna.

PROPOSITIONAL LOGIC

Suhrawardī in *The Philosophy of Illumination* also stresses propositional logic. This logic was primarily a Stoic invention, a rival to the logic of terms developed by Aristotle. By late antiquity the distinction between the two forms of logic was no longer very clear, and there was a tendency to assimilate propositional logic to term logic. Islamic logicians, possibly following Galen, tended to treat propositional logic as a special case of the categorical syllogism. Avicenna devoted several chapters at the end of the *Posterior Analytics* of his *Shifā'* to propositional logic.[25] But Suhrawardī puts it first. Why?

Suhrawardī is not so modern as to draw a sharp distinction between propositional and term logic, so the metaphysical point I am going to make is somewhat vitiated by the fact that he reduces propositional logic to term logic. Nonetheless, there is some interest in seeing how he goes about it. He offers two techniques for assimilating propositional logic to the syllogism. The first is the hypothetical syllogism, which allows "if-then" and "either-or" (exclusive disjunction) statements. A hypothetical syllogism, as he sees it, has either of the two forms:

	If AB, then CD	or	AB or CD
but	AB		
therefore,	CD	or	not CD

It differs from the categorical syllogism by having four different terms, two of which are in both premises. He probably assumes strict implication in the first case and certainly assumes exclusive disjunction in the second. This is an obvious extension of Aristotle's theory of the syllogism and is already used by Galen and Avicenna.[26] The second approach, decidedly odder and probably dubious, converts hypothetical propositions into categorical propositions (i.e., a proposition in which a predicate is applied to a subject). A hypothetical proposition like 'if the Sun is shining, then it is day' becomes 'the rising of the Sun implies the existence of day'.[27]

For Suhrawardī propositional logic is peculiarly well suited to the logical demands of his metaphysical system. Term logic was invented to unpack essences and deals with propositions of a particular internal structure. The variables of propositional logic are whole propositions, quite apart from their specific content, and so propositional logic is useful for exploring how one fact or state of affairs is the cause of another. Proclus had made the same point, arguing that hypothetical syllogism—that is, propositional logic—was better suited than term logic to carry out Platonic dialectic.

> For the most part we use hypothetical deductions, which direct our attention especially well to the connection of things—their interrelations and their mutual divisions. But we shall use categorical too when we need to argue for the conditional or for the minor premise in each hypothesis.[28]

It is such a relation that is Suhrawardī's fundamental ontological principle: *al-imkān al-ashraf*, "the most noble contingency." "One of the Illuminationist principles is that if a baser contingent exists, a nobler contingent must already have existed."[29] In other words, every state of affairs on a lower level of existence corresponds to some state of affairs on a higher plane. Such relationships must be explored by propositional logic, not by a logic of terms. Having rejected key features of Aristotelian essentialism as it applies to logic, Suhrawardī is thus pushed towards giving greater importance to propositional logic.

A full understanding of what Suhrawardī meant to do with his logic will need to wait until the logical portions of his Peripatetic works are all published and studied, especially the massive *Paths and Havens*. My interpretations here are speculations based on his critiques of Peripatetic logic in *The Philosophy of Illumination*. Nor is it always clear that his distinctive logical doctrines are exploited in the rest of his philosophy. He certainly does not write in the peculiar modalized categorical propositions that have been described above. However, in certain cases the logical doctrines clearly are important elsewhere in his philosophy. His critique of definition is closely related to his epistemological concerns. The categories, which are omitted in the logic, reappear in metaphysics, where his addition of a new category of intensity is central to his metaphysical project.

The most important role played by the critique of Aristotelian logic in Suhrawardī's works is probably polemical. Ghazālī had written:

> To be sure, the philosophers themselves are guilty of a kind of injustice in the case of this science of logic. This is that in logic they bring together, for apodeictic demonstration, conditions known to lead undoubtedly to sure and certain knowledge. But when, in metaphysics, they finally come to discuss questions touching on religion, they cannot satisfy those conditions, but rather are extremely slipshod in applying them. Moreover, logic may be studied by one who will think it is a fine

> thing and regard it as very clear. Consequently he will think that the instances of unbelief related of the philosophers are backed up by demonstrations such as those set forth in logic. Therefore he will rush into unbelief even before reaching the metaphysical sciences.[30]

Ghazālī had seen that logic was the glittering pride of the philosophers and that the prestige it gave to philosophy was a major source of the power that philosophy had over the minds of men. So logic had to be cut away from metaphysics lest it mislead indirectly. Ibn Taymīya, two centuries after Ghazālī, sought to extirpate logic, root and branch, in the name of religion. Suhrawardī's program is different, but he knows that to puncture the pretensions of the Peripatetics, it is necessary to remove logic from its pedestal—not destroy it, as Ibn Taymīya wished to do, but merely put it in its place. He had to explain why those who did not have the books of the *Organon*—the Ancients and the Sufis notably—could nonetheless know the truth, how Plato could demonstrate without knowing how to construct a demonstration, as Olympiodorus had said. And so "We have reduced the famous 'tool' that guards thought from error to a small number of very useful rules. These are sufficient for the intelligent and for those who seek illumination."[31] In the end it was Ghazālī's approach that prevailed, and the Islamic logic of the last six centuries has lost its metaphysical associations and has been a semantically oriented discipline, closely aligned with grammar, and pursued as a tool of jurisprudence.

CHAPTER 10

Plato versus Aristotle (ii): Platonic Epistemology

Later Islamic philosophers considered the doctrine of 'knowledge by presence', *al-'ilm al-ḥuḍūrī*, to be one of Suhrawardī's distinctive contributions to philosophy.[1] Knowledge by presence is the doctrine that knowledge can only occur by the unveiled presence of the thing known before the conscious subject. In other words, whatever machinery is posited to explain how something is known or perceived, it is ultimately only known through direct contact with a self-conscious subject. Suhrawardī not only stresses the subjective aspect of knowledge; he also tends to reject all forms of intermediate machinery—for example, rejecting all of the physiological and mathematical aspects of optics in favor of a theory of direct awareness of the thing seen. In this latter move, he was not followed by his more science-minded followers, but the central role of consciousness in perception and knowledge remained a characteristic feature of his school.[2]

In discussing knowledge by presence, I will deal first with sensation, concentrating on vision, which is the paradigmatic case for Suhrawardī. I will then discuss the application of the theory to intellectual knowledge and the specific place of the theory in the foundations of Illuminationist philosophy. I will then return to the general epistemological issues in Platonism, comparing Suhrawardī's views with those of Plato in the *Seventh Epistle*.

THE PROBLEM OF VISION

The great rival accounts of vision in antiquity and the Middle Ages were the extramission and intromission theories, associated with the mathematicians, including Pythagoras, and Aristotle respectively. Each had advantages and grave defects.

The intromission theory made the commonsensical assertion that vision occurs by something coming into the eye but has difficulty explaining *what* comes into the eye: How does the mountain know to send an image to the eye? How does it happen that the image is exactly the right size to fit into the eye? If the mountain is sending out images in all directions, why do we not see some sort of image stew, with the images of the mountain, the houses, the trees, and so on, all interfering with each other and getting jumbled together as they cross each other? What, physically, is it that comes to us from the mountain? The extramission theorists, who were usually mathematicians, assert that something—the 'visual cone'—goes out of the eye and contacts the thing seen. Mathematically, this theory works well, since it is easy to draw diagrams of how the visual cone contacts the object, why distant things appear small, why the mountain's image is just the right size to fit in the eye, and so on, but it has its own set of problems. While it is easy enough to imagine the visual cone going out to contact something close at hand, it is harder to imagine it going out instantaneously to the farthest part of the universe—but it must be instantaneous, since if we look at a star, there is no delay before we see it. Also the extramission theory does not do a very good job of explaining why light makes things visible. To deal with such difficulties some theorists, Empedocles and Plato included, offered intermediate theories. Plato says that vision occurs when the fire leaving the eye (the visual cone) interacts with the fire in the air (light) and with fire coming off the object seen (color). This had the unfortunate effect of reintroducing some of the problems of the intromission theory.[3]

The question of vision is one of the disagreements between Plato and Aristotle that Fārābī treats in detail in his *Reconciliation*. Fārābī admits that "concerning the nature and manner of vision, the opinion attributed to Plato differs from the opinion attributed to Aristotle in that Aristotle believed that vision occured by the eye being affected while Plato believed that vision occurs by something coming out of the eye and meeting the object seen."[4] Fārābī asserts that the disagreement only appears to be absolute due to the quarrelsomeness of the commentators, whom he denounces in distinctly religious language:

> The commentators of the two sects busied themselves splitting hairs in respect to this issue, advancing foolish and dogmatic arguments. They perverted the sayings of the masters, concealing the truth that was originally intended. They twisted the meanings of the text to justify their vile views and avoided the path of fairness and truth.[5]

Fārābī then goes on to summarize the major arguments on both sides. The supporters of Aristotle argued that what came out of the eye must be either air, light, or fire. But there is already air between the eye and the object, and no more is needed. If it is light, why is additional light needed to see things? Why can we not see in the dark? Why isn't it easier for a group to see something, since presumably the thing looked at by many is illumined by the light of many eyes? If it is fire, why does it not behave like other fire, rising by nature, being quenched by water, and the like? In general, why don't the visual rays of many eyes interfere with each other?

To such objections the Platonists reply that there are equal objections to Aristotle's theory. What exactly is it that is "affected" in order to make vision possible—the intermediate air or the pupil of the eye? If it is the pupil, how can it accept many colors at once? Why can we see the very distant stars instantaneously (although the same objection, of course, applies more strongly to Plato's theory)? Plato's theory can explain how a distant lighted thing can be seen in darkness; Aristotle's theory requires that the intervening distance be lighted. Plato can also explain why it is easier to see nearby objects than distant ones.[6]

Fārābī now argues that much of the disagreement results from an excessive concern with the partially figurative language used by Plato and Aristotle. 'Coming out' was not used by the Platonists in the usual bodily sense, nor does Aristotle's 'being affected' mean anything apart from a change in quality.

> When we consider this matter with the eye of fairness, we realize that there is a power connecting the eye and the thing seen. If someone criticizes the disciples of Plato for saying that a certain power comes out of the eye and meets the thing seen, he must realize that it is equally blameworthy to say that the air carries the color of the thing seen to the eye, with which it comes in direct contact. Exactly the same objections made to the assertion that such a power exists and comes out of the eye can be made to the view of the followers of Aristotle that the air carries colors and their bodies to the eye.[7]

The basis of the problem, Fārābī concludes, is simply that the philosophers did not have language available to them sufficient to convey the subtleties of their meanings.

The reader of Fārābī's *Reconciliation* will learn from this passage that there are fundamental and quite valid objections to both prevalent theories of vision but that the ancient philosophers had something in mind that was subtler, incapable of expression in Greek, and valid. We are to understand that the problem with both theories is their attempt to explain vision in purely physical terms. Suhrawardī agrees.

Vision is the paradigmatic case of knowledge by presence for Suhrawardī. For him, as for many others, it is the noblest of the senses:

> Five outer senses have been created in man and the other perfect animals: touch, taste, smell, hearing, and sight. The objects of vision are noblest, for they are the lights of the planets and the like. The objects of

> touch are more important to animals, for that which is most important is not necessarily that which is noblest. The objects of hearing are subtler in another respect.[8]

Suhrawardī has a clear definition of the mechanism of vision:

> Since you know that vision is not by the imprinting of the form of its object in the eye nor by something emerging from the eye, it can only be by the illuminated object being opposite a sound eye—nothing more. Imagination and images in mirrors will be explained later, for they have great importance. Being opposite amounts to the absence of a veil between that which sees and that which is seen.[9]

In other words, vision is consciousness of the thing seen. There is no imprinted form transferred to the eye, no visual cone emerging from the eye. No matter or even accidents are exchanged between the eye and what it sees. A healthy eye is a condition of vision, as is an unobstructed line of sight, but the eye is not a machine for processing images. The connection of his theory of vision with his theory of light is very simple. Light is that which is manifest in itself and manifests another. What physical light is manifest *to* is a sound eye. Since it is a property of a lighted thing to be visible, no mechanism is needed to explain how the eye is able to see.

His treatment of vision is in the same spirit as his treatment of logic. He takes a technically complex discipline that happens to have questionable first principles and deals with its problems by replacing the whole theory with an almost satirically simple mechanism. His followers and commentators understood perfectly well—as probably he did himself—that a more complex mechanism was needed to explain vision. The oversimplification of the mechanism of vision serves to clarify his fundamental point: that perception is a matter of consciousness, not of lens, retina, and imprinted images. What makes vision actual is the consciousness of the thing seen by a self-conscious subject. No matter what mechanism is posited to explain vision, there remains a gap across which a mind directly contemplates the object of perception.

Suhrawardī's critique of the other two systems echoes the standard objections, although there are some novel features.[10] It also raises some interesting questions about his use of his sources and his relation to the Avicennan Peripatetics since, on the whole, his criticisms of the earlier tradition of philosophical optics are not very different from those of Avicenna. Suhrawardī does not mention the names of those whom he is attacking, but the commentator Quṭb al-Dīn identifies the Ancients, the Peripatetics, and the "mathematicians," by which are meant respectively Plato, Aristotle and the Islamic Peripatetics, and the practitioners of mathematical optics, starting with Euclid.[11] Suhrawardī makes no attempt to defend the extramission theory as it was usually attributed to Plato, and he does not mention Plato (or the Peripatetics) by name, referring only to "them." The commentators, who presumably knew who was being criticized, understood the sharpest criticisms of the extramission theory as referring to the practitioners of mathematical optics and did not mention Plato in that connection.

Suhrawardī first addresses the question of the physical nature of light. Light is not a body, he argues, for it does not behave like other bodies. When we close a window, the light already in the room does not remain. Particulate light, like any other kind of projectile, would reflect from—that is, bounce off of—hard rough surfaces more easily than damp soft surfaces. If light is a body emerging from a luminous object, it would always emerge only at right angles to the surface, rather than going in all directions from every point. Finally, particulate light from many lamps ought to pile up in thick layers, with the thickness depending on the degree of illumination. None of this is the case.

Turning to the question of light in Aristotle's intromission theory, Suhrawardī challenges the Peripatetic theory of color. Aristotle had rejected the idea that light was a body travelling from the object seen to the eye. Rather, vision, he thought, occurs by the ability of transparent media like air to transmit colors to the eye. Light is the actualization of the transparency of the medium, and color the property of the surface of bodies by which they affect the transparent medium.[12] This implies that there is no difference between the color of an object and the 'ray'—by which Suhrawardī means the illumination of a surface by a light, not a line of light traveling through the air or the aether.[13] Suhrawardī argues that such a theory identifies whiteness and brightness and darkness and blackness, yet we can, for example, tell that snow is whiter than ivory, even if the snow is in shadow and the ivory in sunlight. Suhrawardī argues that the illumination of a surface is distinct from its color. He admits, however, that the point is not quite settled and excuses himself on the grounds that the issue is not critical to his system.[14]

When we examine the functioning of vision according to the extramission and intromission theories, we find more difficulties. The extramission theory is physically implausible for the reasons usually mentioned by its critics. The planets and stars would not be seen simultaneously, but would turn on one by one as the visual cone reached them. Since the visual cone is part of the body, we ought to be able to choose not to see even though our eyes are open. We ought to see more easily through porous solids like earthenware than through impervious materials like glass. Finally, this body must emerge from the eye and fill half the universe instantaneously, an implausible assumption.

On the other side are the Peripatetics and their theory of imprinting.[15] Suhrawardī consistently rejects 'imprinting' *(inṭibāʿ)* as an explanation for any sort of knowledge. The problem is that we do not experience images; we experience real things as real things. We do not experience a small image of a mountain imprinted on the retina, nor do we infer the size of the mountain from the small image; we experience the mountain as a thing far too large to fit into the retina or the brain.[16] The image in a mirror is obviously not "in" the mirror in any normal sense. The image has depth, but it obviously doesn't fit into the thickness of the mirror nor is it in in the air. It is not the form of the thing reflected since the image in the mirror is smaller than the thing of which it is the reflection.

Suhrawardī generalizes this theory of sensation by presence to cover hearing. The conventional—and correct—Peripatetic explanation of sound was that it is vibrations in the air. Plato gave a similar theory of sound in the *Timaeus*. The physical aspects of sound are less mysterious than those of vision, for although we cannot normally see sound waves in the air, it is easy to see the vibrations that cause the vibrations in the air—in the string of a musical instrument, for example. Suhrawardī raises some half-hearted objections to the physical explanation of sound: that air will not hold a shape and that disturbing the air around the ear ought to destroy sound. He is willing to admit that sound might be conditioned on vibration or air, though he does not think that these issues are relevant to the subject at hand. His real objection is that we do not experience vibrating air; we experience *sound*, a simple sensation that cannot be reduced to something else. The primacy of experienced sound is shown by the fact that sound cannot be defined to a deaf person and cannot be explained in terms of other senses. Sound is a simple entity.[17] Suhrawardī confirms his theory by reference to cases in which sounds are not associated with vibrations in the air, in particular the sounds heard by mystics and Pythagoras' music of the spheres. In these cases, the sounds obviously have completely different causes. For this reason, it can be said that the immaterial intellects hear and see. "The heavens possess hearing not conditioned on ears, sight not conditioned on eyes, olfaction not conditioned on nostrils. This is the most noble contingency."[18]

ALEXANDER OF APHRODISIUS ON VISION

I do not know of any exact parallel among ancient or medieval philosophers to Suhrawardī's rejection of both intromission and extramission as explanations of vision in favor of a theory of vision by direct unmediated intuition.[19] There is, though, a short essay attributed to Alexander of

Aphrodisius on the mechanism of vision entitled "An Essay *(maqāla)* in Refutation of Those Who Hold That Vision *(ibṣār)* Is by Extramission of Rays *(bi'l-shu'ā'āt al-khārija)* When They Go Out of the Eye."[20] It is lost in Greek but survives in a unique manuscript containing a collection of short philosophical texts, most attributed to Alexander. The manuscript's attribution is confirmed by references to the text in both the *Fihrist* and Ibn Abī Uṣaybi'a.[21] There is no particular reason to doubt the accuracy of its attribution to Alexander—though its authenticity is irrelevant for our purposes—since other short texts attributed to Alexander in Arabic are extant in Greek, including two of the texts in this collection.

Alexander of Aphrodisius occupies an interesting place in the Illuminationist history of philosophy. He flourished around the beginning of the third century, and his reputation is based on a series of major commentaries on Aristotle. Five survive in whole or in part, the most important being the commentary on the *Metaphysics*, and another ten are attested in fragments. These commentaries were sufficiently impressive and faithful to win him the title "the interpreter" (ὁ ἐξηγητής). He also wrote original works on various problems raised by the Greek philosophical tradition. A considerable number of his works were translated into Arabic. The *Fihrist* lists fifteen, in addition to his commentaries on the *Categories*, *Prior Analytics*, *Topics*, *Sophistical Refutations*, *Physics*, *De Caelo*, *On Generation and Corruption*, *Metaphysics*, and *Meteorology*, though it is not always clear how complete or in what form these translations were.

The Muslims thus knew him as a Peripatetic *par excellence*. The Spanish historian of science Ṣā'id al-Andalusī wrote, "Many after Aristotle followed his method and commented on his works. The most illustrious of them are Themistius, Alexander [of Aphrodisius], and Porphyry. These three were the most knowledgeable about Aristotle's books best and were the most reliable authors on philosophy after him."[22] It is thus a little surprising to find that the portrait of Alexander in Shahrazūrī's *Delight* is by no means negative. He knows that Alexander is much admired by the Peripatetics, observing that, "All the Peripatetics honor him. Abū 'Alī Ibn Sīnā (Avicenna) esteemed and praised him. Likewise, the Shaykh (Avicenna) also lauded Themistius, expressing extravagant gratitude to him." He goes on to quote a remark from Avicenna's *Inṣāf*, a mostly lost work in which Avicenna discussed at great length the disagreements between the Easterners and the school of Baghdad, that he found it much more profitable to read the works of Alexander, Themistius, and Philoponus than those of the Baghdad philosophers, with the exception of Fārābī.[23] This ought to be, in Illuminationist terms, the kiss of death, but Shahrazūrī goes on to cite with sympathy several of Alexander's better-known teachings. Of his reputation in general he writes, "Alexander was one of the great scholars, both in his opinions and his scientific views. His writings are sound, and what he has to say is reliable. He agrees with Aristotle in all his opinions, but he goes beyond him."[24]

Most of the text on vision consists of arguments against the extramission theory of vision attributed to Plato and the mathematicians. The arguments are familiar and resemble those used by Fārābī in discussing extramission; indeed, it seems likely that this work was an important source for the Muslims' knowledge of the arguments against extramission. At the very end of the text Alexander adds: "Therefore, vision does not occur by any motion. Since vision is not by motion, it also does not occur by rays falling on something, nor by the motion of the form to the eye, nor by both together."[25] This is puzzling. "Rays falling on something" in this context must be the extramission theory, although it could refer to some forms of the intromission theory, including our modern theory of light and Ibn al-Haytham's theory, in both of which rays travel from the lighted thing to the eye. "The motion of the form to the eye" must refer to some form of intromission, in which the form is carried from the thing to the eye. Alexander's arguments had proven the implausibility of the view that vision occurs by a ray emerging from the eye and did so by stressing the physical impossibilities involved. This last sentence seems to tell us that these arguments also make it impossible for vision to be by the physical transfer of anything from the object to the eye.

To a Peripatetic, perhaps this last sentence would have gone unnoticed, a casual rejection of varieties of the intromission theory opposed to Aristotle's. For Suhrawardī, however, it would have raised fundamental questions about the nature of vision. If the mechanical theory of vision given in the *Timaeus* is physically implausible, yet the physical difficulties recur in the opposite theory, then the entire problem would have to be rethought and reformulated in completely new terms. And that is what he did.

KNOWLEDGE BY PRESENCE

Suhrawardī's theory of knowledge by presence is an extension of his theory of vision: "All the incorporeal lights see, and their vision does not reduce to their knowledge, but rather their knowledge reduces to their vision."[26] The Buddhist logicians held that every instance of knowledge is self-consciousness,[27] a sentiment with which Suhrawardī would have been in complete agreement. The problem that interests him is not the conventional epistemological/psychological problem of how experience gets processed into knowledge but the basis of the subjective experience of knowing: 'how do *we* know' rather than '*how* do we know'.

The Peripatetic logicians in "the introductions to the handbooks of logic," to use Quṭb al-Dīn's derisive expression,[28] had divided knowledge into 'conception' and 'assent', images in the mind either alone or accompanied by a judgment. Such knowledge is 'renewed' *(mutajaddid)*,[29] in the sense that it does not deal directly with the thing known but rather concerns the image of that thing. Starting from the obscure hints of *De anima* 3.4, Avicenna had developed a theory of intellection in which the mind becomes what it thinks. Avicenna had been less concerned with the problem of conscious knowledge than with explaining knowledge of abstract entities. In his epistemological theory the mind progressively shucked off the material accoutrements of the forms it acquired. At its highest level, knowledge of abstract entities like a mathematical triangle, the immaterial intellect actually becomes the form that it has acquired through the contemplation of the products of sensation. The triangle contemplated by the intellect is not any particular triangle, but just the abstract form of triangle. The intellect cannot know particulars because particularity requires matter. For example, the intellect cannot know the difference between right and left.[30] To know that difference requires a material organ within which a material form can in some way be imprinted.

This problem lands Avicenna in serious difficulties when it comes to knowledge of particulars. How, for example, can God know individuals or, in general, contingent facts? God, after all, has no material organs in which there could be forms of Zayd and 'Amr. Also, what about the immortality of the individual and reward and punishment in the afterlife? It may be argued, and Avicenna does, that immortality is made possible by the actualization of the intellect. What then of those whose intellects are not actualized by the contemplation of geometry and other such abstract sciences? More seriously, souls according to Avicenna are individualized by being in particular bits of matter. When they shed that matter, what happens to their individuality? Avicenna argues that the intellects have been in some way tinged by their association with particular bodies, but this solution was not very convincing to theologians like Ghazālī, who remained convinced that the philosophers denied the immortality of the individual soul and the resurrection of the body.[31]

Suhrawardī's solution is to completely change the terms of reference. He has, as it happens, dramatized the transformation of his views in his famous account of the dream of Aristotle in the *Intimations*, the first of the "Peripatetic" works, a book meant to be read as a propaedeutic to *The Philosophy of Illumination*.[32] The dream is most often cited for Aristotle's assertion that the Sufis, not the Peripatetics, are the true philosophers of Islam, but the bulk of the text is concerned with the explication of the theory of knowledge by presence.

The story of the dream occurs in the first section of a chapter entitled "On the Discussion of Incoporeality, Providence, Fate and Predestination, and Beatitude" in a section dealing with "apprehension and renewal" *(al-idrāk wa'l-tajaddud).*[33] 'Apprehension' *(idrāk)* refers to all kinds of mental awareness, including knowledge, sensation, and imagination. 'Renewal' in this context is conceptual knowledge. Suhrawardī is puzzled that the philosophers disagree on the nature of apprehension, with some saying that it occurs by the one who apprehends becoming what is apprehended and others saying that it occurs by union *(ittiḥād)* with the active intellect, the incorporeal mind of the lowest sphere that is the source from which the mind obtains intelligibles. Both theories are full of problems. It is difficult to know in what sense the one who apprehends becomes what is apprehended. Union with the active intellect raises issues of individuation. Also, how is it that having been united with the active intellect with respect to one kind of knowledge, we are not then omniscient? Suhrawardī notes that he has taken these arguments from "the most learned of the moderns"—that is, Avicenna—who used them to criticize Porphyry's account of intellection, "abusing him at length in a way that does not befit the learning of either." Yet, Suhrawardī points out, Avicenna's account of the union of the soul with the intelligible leads to exactly the same difficulties. Another issue arises when we realize that an individual can be known either as an individual or as a complex of universals, as when we know Zayd as a tall black man who is the son of a certain man. This account identifies him but does not make it impossible that there should be another man fitting the same description.[34]

The dream occurred, we are told, at a time when Suhrawardī had been working hard on the problem of knowledge but had made little progress. When Aristotle appears, Suhrawardī asks him the solution to the difficulty. "Consult yourself, and it will be solved for you," the great philosopher replied. Not surprisingly, Suhrawardī asks for clarification. Aristotle explains that the key to the problem is self-apprehension. When we know ourselves, it does not happen through a form of the self or through a faculty. To posit an intermediary by which one's knowledge of oneself is acquired would lead to an infinite regress. If such self-knowledge were by universals—by concepts, in other words—it could never be knowledge of the self in the full sense, since there is nothing in a universal concept that makes it impossible to apply to another. Thus, in this particular case, one's own essence is the intellect, the intellecting one, and the intellected. The same arguments apply to our knowledge of our own bodies and our knowledge of such mental states as are dependent on physical organs—the imagination, for example. Though neither the body nor the mental faculties dependent on bodily organs are identical with our souls, we know them directly. Since it is through faculties dependent on physical organs that sense-data are presented to the soul, it is obvious that all our knowledge is of this form: direct apprehension conditioned on lack of concealment of the known from the incorporeal knower. Suhrawardī asserts that the ability of the knower to apprehend itself and others is stronger to the degree of its incorporeality. If this is so, it follows that the apprehension of the Necessary Existent—God—is strongest.

Knowledge is, therefore, a relation between the knower and the known and, like any other relation, does not introduce multiplicity into the essence or substance of the knower. Therefore, it is possible for the Necessary Existent to know particulars without compromising its own unity. This is the more true since a relation of origination and sovereignty *(iḍāfa mabda'īya tasalluṭīya)* exists between the Necessary Existent and the creatures.

Aristotle then ties up a loose end connected with the critiques of the Peripatetics. "Contact" and "union" between souls and with the active intellect are possible only in the intelligible world after separation from the body, since they are conditioned on a lack of concealment of the souls from each other.

This theory is fundamental to the metaphysics of the second part of *The Philosophy of Illumination.* The "incorporeal lights" are structurally identical with the essence that knows itself in Aristotle's description.

> Nothing that has an essence of which it is not unconscious is dusky, for its essence is evident to it. It cannot be a dark state in something else, since even the luminous state is not a self-subsistent light, let alone the dark state. Therefore, it is a non-spatial pure incorporeal light. . . .
>
> A detailed explanation: The self-subsistent, self-conscious thing does not apprehend its essence by an image of its essence in its essence. If its knowledge is by an image and if the image of its ego is not [the ego] itself, the image of the ego would be an "it" in relation to the ego. . . .
>
> You [i.e., as a self-subsistent incorporeal light] are never unconscious of your essence or your apprehension of your essence. Since this apprehension cannot be by a form or by something superadded, you need nothing to apprehend your essence save that essence, which is evident in itself [and] not absent from itself. Therefore, it must apprehend its essence due to what it itself is in itself, and you can never be unconscious of your essence or any part of your essence. That of which your essence can be unconscious—organs such as the heart, liver, and brain, and all the dark and luminous barriers [i.e., bodies] and states—do not belong to that part of you that apprehends. Therefore, that in you which apprehends is not an organ or anything to do with a barrier, since otherwise you would always be aware of these as you are always and unceasingly aware of your own essence. . . .
>
> If you examine this matter closely, you will find that that by which

> you are you is only a thing that apprehends its own essence—your "ego." All else that apprehends its own essence and ego shares with you in this. Apprehension, therefore, occurs neither by an attribute nor by something superadded, of whatever sort. It is not a part of your ego since the other part would still remain unknown. Were there something beyond consciousness and awareness, it would be unknown and would not belong to your essence, whose awareness is not superadded to it.[35]

In other words, the incorporeal lights are self-conscious knowing subjects by virtue of being incorporeal lights. They know other entities in the same way.

This is Suhrawardī's famous teaching of knowledge by presence *(ḥuḍūr)*. The key, as "Aristotle" told him, is the self's knowledge of itself. All kinds of knowledge require a direct, unmediated relation between the knowing self and the object of knowledge. In the case of the self, the object is the self itself. In the case of sensible entities, the sensible object is present unveiled to the mind with the physical organ being a condition of sensation. What is known in the first instance is the individual, whether the individual is a physical thing or an intelligible reality.

Yet it must be said that the theory is more radical still, as we can see from his account of vision. We would expect that he would explain vision as the direct awareness by the self of the form as presented to it by the organs of vision. The visual images would be projected by the optical nerve on a screen in the brain, and the self would watch them. But this would be a form of the loathesome imprinting theory. Rather, he thinks that the images in the physical organs are in some way a condition that makes possible our direct awareness of the objects of vision. We see the mountain as being the size that it is, he argues, not as an image small enough to fit into the eye. Behind this argument are the difficulties faced by the traditional intromission theory of vision.

To solve such difficulties and to explain a host of phenomena involving forms not imprinted in matter Suhrawardī posited the "World of Image," the *'ālam al-mithāl* that so interested later Islamic thinkers. Aristotle and others had successfully explained material forms as being, as it were, the shapes of matter, but they could not explain the protean forms found in mirrors, nor ghosts, nor the wonders produced by magicians. Suhrawardī argued that there were two possible relationships between forms and bodies. In the more familiar case, the forms are shapes of bodies, a particular set of extensions and qualities. In the other case, the body is the "locus" *(maḥall)* of the form but not necessarily its place. Such are the forms of the World of Image. The body, in some mysterious way, is the condition for the form's appearance, but the form is not in the body in the way that the form of the dog is in the body of the dog. Instead, the locus makes it possible for the form to be manifest to us—but we see the form, not the locus. Our brain and our organs of sensation are such loci. They make it possible for us to see or hear or smell the forms, but the forms are not imprinted in them in the way that they are in their bodily instances.[36]

Suhrawardī's theory of knowledge by presence is deeply nominalist and empiricist. The Peripatetic theory of knowledge had explained knowledge of universals with some success, but it had profound difficulties with the knowledge of particulars and with the origins of our knowledge of universals. Aristotle seems to have assumed—as did Socrates and Plato in different ways—that essences and universals could be found by thoughtful contemplation of particulars. Drawing on the tradition of Greek commentaries on the *De anima*, Fārābī and Avicenna developed theories of intellection in which the intellect *became* the objects of its knowledge. Yet it could not become particulars in the same way, and the theory enforced an arbitrary and very awkward distinction between knowledge of individuals and knowledge of universals. The awkwardness became scandal when the philosophers were asked to explain God's knowledge. It was bodily organs that allowed Avicenna to explain how we knew, for example, right hand from left, but God has no bodily organs, nor does the soul after death—thus the accusation that the philosophers held that God could not know particulars.

Suhrawardī solved this problem by making all real knowledge into knowledge of particulars. God, just like us, can know particulars because particulars are present to him. Presence, though, does not explain universals. To some extent, this is less of a problem for Suhrawardī than it might be since he has separated out the causal functions of universals through his version of the theory of Forms. He does not need to make universals real since the Forms/lights/angels/intellects are the causes of the various sorts of regularity in the world. Rabbits remain rabbitish because the immaterial intellect that is the lord of the species rabbit causes them to be rabbittish, but there is no form in individual rabbits that actually causes that rabbit to be rabbittish. That rabbit, like everything else, is just self-subsistent magnitude and qualities. There is no "secondary substance" in it that we would come to know by inspection.

It is not clear to me whether Suhrawardī thinks we have direct knowledge of rabbittishness, perhaps through the active intellect, or whether he would be content with a Humean empiricism. It does not matter greatly since he has given a satisfactory explanation both of how we know individuals and of how it happens that there is regularity in the world for us to discover. Moreover, he has done so without the epistemological overkill of Aristotle's theory, which requires us to recognize the essences of species more or less on sight.

The issue is clearer when we consider more abstract universals, the *i'tibārāt 'aqlīya* or "beings of reason."[37] These are such concepts as existence, quiddity in general, necessity, contingency, and the like that we acquire not from the contemplation of individual entities but rather from the contemplation of conceptions. We commonly say that a thing—say, our rabbit—has existence, but what do we then mean? The rabbit surely does not have existence in the same sense that it has ears or the accident of whiteness. Suhrawardī's answer is based on a critique of Avicenna's use of such notions in his metaphysics. Avicenna's view might be unkindly chacterized as a naive realism. As a general matter, he presumed that for any given mental distinction there is a corresponding real distinction. Thus he could know through introspection that there is a difference between knowing *what* a thing is and knowing *that* a thing is. He then assumed that there is a real distinction between the quiddity of a thing and its existence and could then go on to make metaphysical and ontological arguments based on the properties of existence, quiddity, necessity, and so on. Such argumentation was essential for establishing his basic metaphysical theorems, such as the existence of God. Avicenna had distinguished between the existence and the quiddity of the thing, so it is natural to suppose that existence is something added to the quiddity. If so, does this not mean that the existence of the rabbit formerly did not have existence and now does? A vicious regress results. It is easy to show that other such concepts are vulnerable to the same arguments.[38]

Suhrawardī argues that beings of reason are creations of our minds. *I'tibār* means to posit or to consider something. He believes that such universals do not have independent existence in concrete reality but are products of our reflection on things. That they are not arbitrary constructions—like hippogriffs, say—is obvious enough. To say that something has existence is to say something true or false about it; the thing either is there or is not there. Likewise, to say that it is contingent is to say that it does not have to exist in the world. Nonetheless, there is nothing in our rabbit that is either existence or contingency. Such concepts seem to be like the categories of Kant, products of the creative activity of our minds that are nonetheless neither arbitrary nor dispensible. The Latins distinguished between a 'distinction of reason' and a 'being of reason', the former being the act of making such a distinction and the latter its object. 'Distinction of reason' might be a satisfactory rendering of Suhrawardī's *i'tibār 'aqlī*, which is, after all, a verbal noun, were in not for the fact that Suhrawardī seems to use the term not for the act of intellectual considering but for the objects of that consideration.[39]

Suhrawardī certainly believed his epistemology to be Platonic in some fundamental sense. In Suhrawardī's account of his dream, Aristotle breaks off his explanation of epistemology and "began to praise his teacher, the divine Plato, so lavishly that I was bewildered."[40] Suhrawardī might have known of the Platonic inscription over the door of the Sabian assembly hall in Harran: "He who knows himself is deified," *man 'arafa dhātahu ta'allaha*.[41] There are several points of contact worth discussing. Proclus holds that knowledge of the self is the fundamental principle of Platonism and of all philosophy.[42]

His connections are closer to Porphyry and the Neoplatonists who followed him. Like Suhrawardī they had given up on identifying the Platonic Form with the universals that we know, splitting the universal into three: the Platonic Form, which is the cause of the species; the form that actually constitutes the thing; and the universals in our minds, which are constructed by our minds. They thus no longer needed to maintain an extralogical distinction between real and unreal classes. So, like Suhrawardī, they were formalist in their logics and nominalist in their epistemologies. Beginning with Porphyry they also distinguished between terms or names of first and second imposition, the former being names given to external things and the latter names given to classes of names, 'genus' and 'verb', for example. The distinction is not unlike Suhrawardī's between concepts drawn from experience and beings of reason.[43]

More generally, Plato tended to speak of knowing in terms of seeing, especially when he was speaking of knowledge of the Forms and of first principles. In various places Plato writes of the ascent of the soul and its vision of the Forms.[44] The allegory of the cave was known to Muslims.[45] It is, as usual, unclear exactly what texts might have been available to Suhrawardī, but he certainly did know the account of Plato's vision of the intelligible world in *The Theology of Aristotle*, which is perfectly in the spirit of Plato's ascent narratives.[46] The commentators think that Suhrawardī's theory of memory was Platonic, in that he held that memory involved retrieval of forms from the intelligible world, not the inspection of the contents of the rear cavity of the brain, as had been the Peripatetic view.[47] There are various accounts of mystical experience associated, with considerable justice, with Plato. For Suhrawardī these show that Plato relied on mystical intuition in philosophy and therefore imply the theory of knowledge by presence. A particularly suggestive connection is the famous digression on epistemology in the *Seventh Epistle*.

EPISTEMOLOGY AND THE *SEVENTH EPISTLE* OF PLATO

There are thirteen letters attributed with varying degrees of plausibilty to Plato in the ancient tradition. Hardly anyone now believes that they are all authentic, but Diogenes Laertius knew a collection of thirteen letters and did not doubt their authenticity. Testimony to the existence of letters of Plato goes back much further, to the third century B.C.E. The Muslims knew of these letters, for the *Fihrist* laconically remarks of Plato: "There are extant letters of his."[48]

The most important of these letters and the one most commonly accepted as authentic is the seventh, an autobiographical essay about forty-five pages in length. It purports to be a letter to his friends in Sicily, consoling them after the assassination of the Platonist politician Dion and the collapse of the political ambibitions of Plato's friends in Syracuse. It is interesting in part because Plato's—or more exactly, Dion's—experience of teaching philosophy to young tyrants was similar to that of Suhrawardī. More will be said of this later. If it is authentic, it was written in the last decade of Plato's life. It seems unlikely that the full text of the *Seventh Epistle* was available in Arabic; at least, it does not seem to be extant. The biographies contain information that ultimately derives from it, but it is much more likely that some Greek biography was the intermediary. The testimony of the *Fihrist* indicates that something was in circulation, but it does not sound as though the author was familiar with them. There are also vague references to what could be the *Seventh Epistle* in Fārābī's *Reconciliation*. Perhaps it is best to assume that as in the case of the dialogues, some sort of epitome of the *Epistles* was translated.

For our immediate purposes the relevant feature of the *Seventh Epistle* is the so-called "philosophical digression," a five-page discussion of epistemology and the writing and teaching of philosophy. When Plato arrived in Syracuse on his third and last visit to Sicily, his purpose was to educate the young tyrant, Dionysius the Younger, as a philosopher-king. Later, after his return to Athens, Plato heard that Dionysius had written a book containing the philosophical teachings that he had picked up from Plato and other teachers. Plato was disgusted since the highest teachings of philosophy cannot be written down.

> For this knowledge is not something that can be put into words like other sciences; but after long-continued intercourse between teacher and pupil, in joint pursuit of the subject, suddenly, like light flashing forth when a fire is kindled, it is born in the soul and straightway nourishes itself.[49]

The theme of true knowledge as illumination returns at the end of the digression: "Only then, when reason and knowledge are at the very extremity of human effort, can they illuminate the nature of any object."[50]

The core of the digression is an account of the bases of true knowledge. Plato writes:

> For every real being, there are three things that are necessary if knowledge of it is to be acquired: first, the name; second, the definition *(λόγος)*; third, the image *(εἴδωλον)*; knowledge *(ἐπιστήμην)* comes fourth, and in the fifth place we must put the object itself, the knowable and truly real being *(ὁ δὴ γνωστόν τε καὶ ἀληθές)*.[51]

Plato goes on to explain what he means, using the example of a circle. It has a name, 'circle', and a definition composed of nouns and verbs. Third are the 'images', the real circles that we draw or meet with. The fourth category embraces knowledge, reason, and right opinion *(ἐπιστήμη καὶ νοῦς ἀληθές τε δόξα)*, which are grouped together because each is in the mind *(ἐν ψυχαῖς)*, not in words (the first and second) or bodily shapes (the third). The fifth is presumably the intelligible realm of Forms, however Plato may have conceived it at this late stage in his career. The four yield misleading or incomplete knowledge, for they are more likely to tell us about the properties of the thing than reveal its being. Moreover, all the particular circles possess properties that the truly real intelligible circle does not possess. Thus, someone who wishes to speak about the fifth—or, even worse, write about it—will find himself exposed to the objections of the ignorant.[52]

In light of what Suhrawardī has to say about the same subject in the introduction to *The Philosophy of Illumination*, Plato's account of the qualities needed for true philosophical learning is worth quoting.

> By the repeated use of all these instruments, ascending and descending to each in turn, it is barely possible for knowledge to be engendered of an object naturally good, in a man naturally good; but if his nature is defective, as is that of most men, for the acquisition of knowledge and the so-called virtues, and if the qualities he has have been corrupted, then not even Lynceus could make such a man see. In short, neither quickness of learning nor a good memory can make a man see when his nature is not akin to the object, for this knowledge never takes root in an alien nature; so that no man who is not naturally inclined and akin to justice and all other forms of excellence, even though he may be quick at learning and remembering this and that and other things, nor any man who, though akin to justice is slow at learning and forgetful, will ever attain the truth that is attainable about virtue. Nor about vice, either, for these must be learned together, just as the truth and error about any part of being must be learned together, through long and earnest labor, as I said at the beginning. Only when all of these things—names, definitions, and visual and other perceptions—have been rubbed against one another and tested, pupil and teacher asking and answering questions in good will and without envy—only then, when reason and knowledge are at the very extremity of human effort, can they illuminate the nature of any object.[53]

For the commentator on Suhrawardī, several points are striking. First are the references at both the beginning and end of the digression to knowledge of reality as illumination. Second, the reference to *εἴδωλον*, "image" or "idol," seems a likely explanation of the peculiar expression, *rabb al-ṣanam*, "lord of idol," which is one Suhrawardī's terms for the Platonic Forms.[54] The notion that true knowledge cannot be taught directly will be discussed shortly. The implied distinction between discursive and true knowledge will also be of interest.

Plato seems to be talking about dialectic as a means to attain knowledge of the intelligible. Such knowledge is not discursive, so it cannot be reduced to a set of propositions and written down. It must be elicited by interaction with a teacher. This knowledge is, in addition, accessible only to those of good character. The vicious person will fail to see that his character is unsuitable for attaining it and will be deluded into thinking that he can or actually has acquired it. For the Peripatetic, whose system starts at the bottom with the particular, such difficulties do not arise. In constructing syllogisms, as Avicenna often explained, "intuition" *(ḥads)* is needed to find the correct middle term and thus understand the cause, but once this middle term has been found, the syllogisms can easily be written down in a treatise, and anybody with "quickness of learning" and "a good memory" can easily follow them.[55] And, indeed, the Peripatetics throughout the history of their school have been distinguished by their willingness to write everything down—in systematic detail, at endless length, and without attention to dialectical subtlety.

This complex of doctrines—the impermissibility and impossibility of writing down true knowledge, the essential position of a living teacher and a community of philosophers, and the importance of virtue in attaining knowledge—are interdependent and central to the Platonic philosophical vision. Each can be inferred from the others, and all are based on the fundamental Platonic philosophical positions of the distinction of the sensible and intelligible and the primacy of the intelligible.

Suhrawardī discusses these ideas in the introduction to *The Philosophy of Illumination*. He had not wished to write down the Illuminationist philosophy, thinking that the works he had written in the Peripatetic mode would be sufficient for those who wished to learn from books, but his friends and disciples had pestered him to write down the philosophical discoveries that had resulted from his mystical intuitions and visions. He had refused, but, he adds mysteriously, there was "an incumbent obligation, a prior word, and a command given from a place, disobedience to which will lead to straying from the path" that compelled him finally to accede to this request. We would naturally suppose that this "command" was the voice of the young Ayyubid prince, but the commentator Shahrazūrī identifies it as the obligation of the learned and judges in Islam to guide those capable of receiving guidance.[56]

Suhrawardī, as deep as his identification with the Ancients might have been, was still writing from within the monotheistic revealed religion of Islam, so he tempers Plato's absolute elitism and clearly defined intellectual classes. Moreover, he is a Sufi, an Islamic mystic, part of a tradition with a long history of anti-intellectualism and untutored saints.

> In every seeking soul there is a portion, be it small or great, of the light of God. Every one who strives has intuition, be it perfect or imperfect. Knowledge is not confined to some one people, so that the doors of heaven are shut behind them and the rest of the world denied the possibility of obtaining more. Rather, the Giver of Knowledge,[57] who stands at the "clear horizon,"[58] is not stingy with the unseen. The most evil age is the one in which the carpet of striving has been rolled up, in which the movement of thought is interrupted, the door of revelations bolted, the paths of visions blocked.[59]

If all people are capable of receiving some measure of divine truth, then it is the obligation of the possessor of truth to give each of them as much of that truth as his capacity allows. His disagreement with Plato on this point is not so much of kind as of degree. Plato, urged by Dion and his supporters to come help educate a philosophically promising young tyrant, thinks himself obliged to go, despite misgivings, because the good that might have been accomplished by putting his ideas into practice was so great.[60] Apart from that, he could keep his true teachings for his disciples, releasing only his entertaining dialogues to the public. Indeed, it can be argued that this passage is the only place in his writings where Plato writes openly of his philosophical views, without *ramz* or *ighlāq*.[61]

The issue of philosophical elitism and esoteric writing is important in Islamic philosophy. Suhrawardī's older contemporary Averroes urged on philosophers a policy like Plato's, drawing sharp distinctions between grades of people. Averroes argued that the vast majority of people were capable of understanding only rhetorical arguments with a minority capable of understanding dialectical argument. A tiny minority was capable of understanding demonstrative arguments—that is, philosophy. These three groups were the ordinary believers, the theologians, and the philosophers. The prophet was capable of expressing philosophical truth in symbolic language accessible to the masses, and the theologians were capable of expounding this revelation but not of understanding its full philosophical significance. Philosophers ought not to try to teach philosophical doctrines to the dialectical or rhetorical classes, since any attempt to do so would just shake their faith in religion without giving them real philosophical understanding in its place.[62] The most vivid portrayal of this view is in the allegorical novel *Ḥayy ibn Yaqẓān* by Averroes' teacher Ibn Ṭufayl. Ḥayy, a self-taught philosopher who grew up alone on a desert island, attempts to teach philosophy to the pious people of a neighboring island, with disastrous results.[63]

Platonic philosophical elitism is very much present in Suhrawardī's thought, though he allows for the use of philosophical and non-philosophical means of obtaining wisdom. He distinguishes between the philosopher proficient in "discursive philosophy" *(al-baḥth*, lit., "investigation") and the one proficient in "intuitive" or "divine philosophy" *(ta'alluh*, lit., 'becoming God'; cf. *al-ilāhī*, "the divine," the attribute applied to Plato).[64] A wise man can be proficient in either or both. Suhrawardī identifies the stereotypical Peripatetic philosopher as being "proficient in discursive philosophy" and the Sufi saints, some of whom he includes in his spiritual pedigree, as being "proficient in intuitive philosophy." Mastery of intuitive philosophy requires undergoing the disciplines of the mystical path, since the intuition *(dhawq)* involved is that by which the intelligible beings are beheld directly. It is for this reason that the intuitive philosopher is superior to the discursive philosopher, even if the intuitive philosopher is of only middling attainment and the discursive philosopher has mastered his subject. In this he differs from the view implied in an anecdote about the meeting between Avicenna and the Sufi saint Abū Sa'īd Abi'l-Khayr:

> Three days [Avicenna and Abū Sa'īd] were with one another in private, talking. After three days and nights Avicenna departed. His students asked him: "How did you find the Sheikh?" He replied: "Everything I know he sees!" And when the Sufis and the Sheikh's disciples came before the Sheikh, they asked him: "Oh Sheikh, how did you find Avicenna?" He replied: "Everything I see, he knows."[65]

Suhrawardī does not think that the discursive philosopher can know all that the mystic can see.

The highest attainment is that of the philosopher who combines proficiency in both discursive and intuitive philosophy. The object of the highest level of philosophy is to know the "fifth thing," "the object itself, the knowable and truly real being."[66] This is a strange formulation that has puzzled commentators. Name, definition, and knowledge about the thing seem to belong together as degrees of knowledge, as do the instances and the Form as objects of knowledge, but how do the two classes fit together? We might say that these are the various ways in which a thing—a circle, to use Plato's example—can be: in a name, in a definition, in the mind, in concrete instances, or as it is in itself, as a Form. Yet Suhrawardī had insisted that knowledge by presence was a doctrine of the Ancients, and of

Plato, so let us try to give this passage an Illuminationist reading. If all these are kinds of knowledge, then what kind are they in terms of Suhrawardī's epistemological system? Name and definition are simple enough. The name is a conventional label. The definition is a formula composed of words sufficiently precise to mark off the thing from everything else and allow us to identify the thing in the world and the conception in the mind. This is description or definition by division *(rasm)*. Both are discussed in the logic of *The Philosophy of Illumination*. Third are the actual embodied instances of the thing, which we know through our senses—or, since we are treating all five as kinds of knowledge—our sensible knowledge by presence, vision most commonly, of the instances of the thing. The fourth thing is discursive knowledge about the thing—assents, the other subject of Islamic logic. This level would include both our ordinary knowledge about the world and discursive Peripatetic philosophy. The fifth is presential knowledge of the thing in the intelligible world, direct perception of its Form. Discursive philosophy cannot itself give knowledge of the fifth kind, for it is based only on logic and concepts, not on intuition of the intelligible realities.

Discursive philosophy is nonetheless necessary. Plato, in a formulation that Suhrawardī would certainly have endorsed, held that knowledge of the fifth was attained by a sudden illumination coming after prolonged study of the first four and discussion with the teacher and other philosophers "when reason and knowledge are at the very extremity of human effort." Discursive knowledge provides a preparation for the sudden illumination, a framework that the teacher can use to prepare the student's mind. For Suhrawardī it is also a means of interpreting the experience of the intelligible world, which is why he can write books of philosophy both for those with, and those without, mystical experience. It is true that the person with this experience is always superior to the person without it, even if the latter possesses discursive philosophy and the former does not. However, among those of equal mystical experience, it is the one with discursive philosophy who is superior, since he has the tools to understand his experience.

The term 'knowledge by presence' blurs the identity of Suhrawardī's epistemology with that outlined in the *Seventh Epistle* since it seems to imply the separateness of the knower and the known. If we use the fomulation often used by later Islamic philosophers—'the identity of the knower, knowledge, and the known'—the similarity is clearer. It all goes back to a progressively closer approach to the thing itself. First, we know its name, then we know what its name means, then we know about it, more or less. But it is a higher thing to actually know the thing by direct acquaintance, so first we know the thing as instantiated around us, and then perhaps in the end we know the thing as it is in the intelligible world. The direct apprehension, whether of the instantiated thing or of the Form, comes after discursive knowledge because it is a more direct and real knowledge of the thing. The knowledge of the Form is the philosophical/mystical intuition that distinguishes the Illuminationist philosopher from the Peripatetic. Words, λόγοι, can perhaps guide us, but they are not the same as the direct knowledge attained only "through long and earnest labor."[67]

One last point relating to the epistemology and philosophy of education of the *Seventh Epistle* remains to be noted, the role of the teacher. Suhrawardī allowed a little more role to the book than Plato had, since he, more than his ancient master, considered everyone to have some portion of capacity. Nonetheless, the role of the teacher is essential, and Suhrawardī is insistent that *The Philosophy of Illumination* can only be understood with the aid of "him who arises with the Book." Presumably, this is the "divine philosopher proficient in both intuitive philosophy and discursive philosophy."[68] During his lifetime "he who arises with the Book" was certainly Suhrawardī himself, and after his death Suhrawardī's appointed successor. Given Suhrawardī's abrupt death, there seems to have been no such person appointed, so our understanding of Suhrawardī's work is entirely dependent on the text. And, so, perhaps our understanding of Suhrawardī's thought is forever warped and limited.

Of course, we do not know that Suhrawardī had read the *Seventh Epistle*; probably he had not. Nonetheless, his Platonism is sufficiently authentic that we can do an Illuminationist reading of the *Seventh Epistle* and obtain results that are faithful both to the text and spirit of Plato and to the distinctive doctrines of Suhrawardī's Illuminationism.

INTUITION AS A BASIS OF PHILOSOPHY

At the beginning of the seventh book of the *Republic*, Plato puts the famous allegory of the cave into Socrates' mouth. I will cite the allegory from Averroes' *Commentary on the Republic*, rather than from the text of Plato, to give a clearer picture of how this allegory appeared to well-read Muslim philosophers of Suhrawardī's day. The work is an epitome, rather than a commentary and, according to Averroes, eliminates the dialectical arguments, leaving only the scientific ones. Averroes says that he wrote it because he had been unable to find a copy of Aristotle's *Politics*.[69] The work survives only in a Hebrew translation.

> We say that Plato compares the relation of this kind of people, as regards their knowledge, to the rest of the multitude. He says that the

> multitude resemble humans who have lived in a cave since childhood, never having left it. They turn to look carefully at what is in the cave without turning their faces to the mouth of the cave. At the cave's mouth there are images of the other kinds of beings, and at their backs [a fire], so that they see nothing of those images other than their shadow on the hollow of the cave. This being their situation, these grasp nothing of the knowledge of things other than the shadow of [an image of] beings falling on the hollow of that cave. They think that true beings are nothing more than those [shadows]. As for the wise, why they are those who go out to the cave's mouth, into the sparkling light, and see things as they truly are in the sunlight. Just as a man who suddenly goes forth from a cave into the sunlight finds that his eyes are grown dim and that it is impossible for him to look at something, so is it impossible for this class of humans—i.e., those who are disposed to knowledge—that we rush them to inquiry in the sciences since they find it hard to abstract the intelligible and to look at it. The cunning device adopted with them is to lead them upward gradually step by step so as to look at things, first by means of the light of the stars and the moon, to the point that they are able to look at them in the presence of the sun.[70]

Averroes' cave is simpler than Plato's, but the essentials are there: to attain true knowledge it is necessary to *see* the objects of knowledge in a way that is not possible for the ordinary run of mankind. Seeing the objects of intellection does not yield a knowledge that contradicts ordinary knowledge, but it does make sense of ordinary experience in a way that is impossible for those who have not stepped outside of daily experience. Avicenna and Ghazālī had both raised questions about the relationship of mystical experience to philosophical investigation, and Sufism and Sufi theory were becoming important in Spain. Clearly the intellectual claims of mysticism were important and were foreshadowed by Plato, but how exactly were they to be reconciled with philosophy?

This problem was on the minds of other twelfth-century Spanish philosophers. Ibn Bājja cites the *Republic* in his political essay, *The Governance of the Solitary*, and mentions the allegory of the cave in his *Treatise on Conjunction*, an essay on the intellect.[71] At the beginning of his philosophical novel, *Ḥayy b. Yaqẓān*, Ibn Ṭufayl ponders the issues raised by the allegory of the cave in a discussion of the role of mystical experience in philosophical investigation.

> My dear and noble brother, you have asked me to explain to you everything that I can about the eastern wisdom of Avicenna. . . . Your question, praise be to God, created in me a spiritual state whereby I was able to attain a mystical insight that I had never before attained. I was brought to a state so extraordinary that no tongue can describe nor any exposition

> describe, for it is of a plane and a world quite different from theirs. . . . Should it be experienced by one not versed in the sciences, he will speak of it in a way that cannot be understood.[72]

Ibn Ṭufayl compares this level to the intellectual perfection that Ibn Bājja describes:

> There can be no doubt that Abū Bakr [Ibn Bājja] attained this degree by means of speculative investigation and investigation through thought, but the degree that we previously alluded to is something different. There is nothing that is revealed in the one that is contrary to what is revealed in the other. The former differs in its greater clarity and in the way that one perceives by means of something that can only metaphorically be called a faculty.[73]

In terms of the allegory of the cave, Ibn Ṭufayl is trying to explain the difference in the knowledge of the intelligent people in the cave and those who have gone outside into the sunlight. All of the latter are in some sense superior to those who have not gone out, although only those with "scientific skill" will be able to explain their experience precisely. Ibn Ṭufayl's counterpart of the allegory of the cave is the allegory of the man born blind. As he grows up, he learns his way around his city and in the end knows the city as well as anyone who can see. The only exception is color, for he can know colors only by description and cannot understand what they are. If his sight is suddenly restored, he will go around the city and discover nothing that he did not already know. The difference is a greater vividness and a pleasure in sight and color. The blind man, Ibn Ṭufayl tells us, is like the rational philosopher, and the colors are like the experiences of the mystic or of the philosopher who attains holiness.[74]

Ibn Ṭufayl claims a limited role for mystical experience. The mystic knows nothing that the speculative philosopher cannot also know; he only knows it with with greater clarity and pleasure. If the experience of the blind man and of Ḥayy, the hero of the novel, is any guide, mystical experience is a confirmation and reward of laborious study. The blind man already knows the city, and knows of colors, so when he is given his sight, he runs around the city enjoying the pleasure of *seeing* the city, the vividness and pleasure of light and color, but there are no new propositions whose truth he learns. Ibn Ṭufayl has thus explained the nature of mystical experience and given it a place in his epistemological system, but he did not give it an independent role in philosophical investigation. That task was carried out by Suhrawardī.

With his doctrine of knowledge by presence, Suhrawardī must face the question of the relationship between direct experience and theoretical knowledge on the levels of both Becoming and Being. 'Presential illumination', to use one of his terms, gives us direct knowledge of individuals. We know what black is because we can see it; if we cannot see it, we do not know it in any meaningful sense. We know the positions of the stars because we can observe them, and we have the reports of others who have observed them in other places and times. Mystical intuition works much the same way. Plato knew that there were Forms because he had seen them. If we are prepared to undergo the same spiritual preparation, we too can see them. Suhrawardī differs from Ibn Ṭufayl and Averroes in holding that some philosophical truth is only accessible through mystical intuition. The Forms are one example, for he admits that the arguments both for and against the Forms are rhetorical, not demonstrative. The commentator Quṭb al-Dīn remarks that the science of lights treats of the First Principle, the (celestial) intellects, and souls. That which is based upon it includes most of physics, some of metaphysics, and, in general, that which is known by intuition.[75]

Suhrawardī seems to conceive of mystical experience as a philosophical tool that can settle certain questions and, in general, provide useful guidance in philosophical investigation. He likens it to astronomical observations, insisting that the reports of the mystical experiences of the great sages be given credence in the same way that the observations of reputable astronomers are.[76] Philosophical speculation provides the means by which this experience can be interpreted, but it is also the case that mystical intuition can take us further than speculation alone can. That is why *The Philosophy of Illumination* differs in its doctrines from the works of the Peripatetic philosophers and why its characteristic doctrines are not necessarily spelled out in Suhrawardī's so-called "Peripatetic" works.[77] Suhrawardī, in other words, has provided an independent and logically clear place in his epistemology for mystical experience.

SUHRAWARDĪ'S PLATONISM IN REVIEW

With this we come nearly to the end of our survey of Plato and Platonism in the thought of Suhrawardī and his Illuminationist followers. It has occupied almost half of this book. In Suhrawardī's philosophical history, what came before Plato—Hermes, Empedocles and Pythagoras, the oriental sages of Egypt, Persia, India, and China—represent philosophical mythology. What comes after—Aristotle and the Peripatetics—represents a turning away from the true methods of divine philosophy. The central philosophical themes of Suhrawardī's thought fall within his discussions of Plato and the Platonic disputes with the Peripatetics. Plato himself bridges the mythological and philosophical aspects of the Illuminationists' history of philosophy. It is his Platonism that is critical for judging Suhrawardī as a philosopher, so at this point a recapitulation is necessary.

Suhrawardī as a Pythagoreanizing Neoplatonist

In 1950 the famous classicist W. H. D. Rouse selected and translated a collection of dialogues for students. He included the *Apology*, *Crito*, *Phaedo*, *Ion*, *Meno*, *Symposium*, and *Republic*.[78] Fifteen hundred years earlier another great professor, the Neoplatonist Proclus, selected the following dialogues for commentary: *Alcibiades I*, *Cratylus*, *Timaeus*, *Republic*, *Parmenides* (extant), and *Phaedo*, *Gorgias*, *Phaedrus*, *Theaetetus*, and *Philebus* (lost). He also wrote commentaries on the first book of Euclid's *Elements*, the *Chaldaean Oracles* and Plotinus' *Enneads*.[79] These two selections of dialogues tell us something important about how differently Plato was understood a thousand and more years ago. Only two dialogues are in both collections, the *Phaedo* and the *Republic*. The modern translator's choices are all from the early and middle periods of Plato's career; Proclus' largely from the middle and late periods. The choice of works that survive shows that the tastes of Proclus' readers and their scribes ran even more strongly to the late period of Plato's dialogues. Of the three non-Platonic texts that Proclus commented on, none, with the occasional exception of the *Enneads*, are among the classics now read by college students.

The point, as the attentive reader will have already seen, is that the so-called Neoplatonists—who, of course, considered themselves to be Platonists, period—and the medieval admirers of Plato were far more interested in the later, more systematic, and less dialectical dialogues than are most modern readers and admirers of Plato. Their Plato was a Pythagoreanizing Plato. The plausibility of this view may be shown by the fact that Plato himself chose to present his scientific account of the universe in the mouth of the Pythagorean Timaeus and that his lecture, *On the Good*, which presented the "unwritten doctrines," seems to have reduced metaphysics to mathematics in a very Pythagorean way. This Pythagorean interpretation of Plato was the norm from the rise of the Neoplatonists up through the Renaissance and finds its defenders still.[80]

This strain of Platonism is characterized by an emphasis on the mystical and mythical side of Plato, an acceptance and rationalization of myth, and a tendency to see Plato as part of an Orphic and Pythagorean tradition with affinities to oriental wisdom. The Socratic side of Plato is forgotten. Paradoxically, because this intepretation of Plato put him on a higher plane than more prosaic philosophers, it makes a firm place for Aristotle as the philosopher of the things of this world.

The Nature of Suhrawardī's Platonism

Suhrawardī too belonged to this tradition of Pythagoreanizing Neoplatonism, but with his own peculiarities. Suhrawardī was solidly in accord with those Neoplatonists who made Pythagoras and Plato central to the history of philosophy, who were fascinated by oriental and ancient wisdom, and who made mysticism central to the theory and practice of philosophy. Like them he saw Aristotle's thought as a worthy but limited propaedeutic to the Platonic philosophy. He differed from most Neoplatonists in his rejection of the mathematical side of Pythagoreanism and Platonism, a rejection that he justified by invoking the Neoplatonic principle of symbolic interpretation of revealed wisdom.

In certain ways, Suhrawardī was solidly in the tradition of Plato himself. We have examined here his critiques of Peripatetic logic and and his Platonic epistemology. We might also have discussed his criticism of Aristotelian hylomorphism and his defense of the Platonic Forms and metempsychosis. In each case, though, he gives the doctrines his own twist—for example, turning Platonic Forms into angelic intellects, thus stripping them entirely of their epistemological functions and making them into cosmological efficient causes of the forms of sublunar beings.

Suhrawardī and Islamic Peripateticism

The reverse of Suhrawardī's Platonism was his critique of the Islamic Peripatetics: Avicenna and his followers. Like so many Neoplatonists, he did not reject Aristotle entirely and composed a series of philosophical works within the Peripatetic frame of reference; these are his equivalents of the commentaries on Aristotle's works written by such Neoplatonists as Porphyry and Simplicius. On the level of philosophical mythology, he distinguished Aristotle from the Peripatetics by invoking the "old Aristotle," the Aristotle of the *Book of the Apple* and the *Theology*, who had been reconverted to Platonism. But he did have fundamental criticisms to make of the Peripatetic philosophy of his own time, aiming shrewd and well-argued blows at several weak points in the foundations of the Peripatetic system: essential definition, the foundations of knowledge, the nature of body, the bases of the rejection of the Forms, their account of vision and sensation in general, and their unexamined habit of assuming that real distinctions corresponded to mental distinction.

The Robust Integrity of Major Philosophical Positions

I have argued that Suhrawardī's position, his own twists nothwithstanding, fell solidly within a particular tradition of Plato interpretation, but it is also clear that he had access to only a limited selection of texts from this tradition. In other words, he had a reasonably good understanding of the implications of the basic Pythagorean and Platonic positions and of major features of the Neoplatonic synthesis such as the central roles given to

Pythagoras, Plato, and Oriental sages, the role of symbolic interpretation in understanding these philosophers, the essential role of mystical experience, the primacy given to the intelligible over the material, and so on. It is possible to identify textual connections to explain how Suhrawardī knew of these various features, but there is clearly something more robust at work. Suhrawardī has not simply picked and chosen at random among fragments of ancient thought and philosophy that happened to reach him; he has given his own version of a very well known philosophical standpoint.

Suhrawardī's system is a project parallel to those of philosophers like the late Plato, Iamblichus, and Proclus and of later figures like Bruno and Thomas Taylor the Platonist. (Taylor was a nineteenth-century amateur of Greek Neoplatonic and Neopythagorean literature at a time when it was out of fashion. He published a large number of excellent translations, mostly of neglected Neoplatonic works.) In other words, whenever the hegemony of Aristotelianism has weakened, interpretations of the history of philosophy have emerged in which Pythagoras and Plato play central roles, in which symbolism and symbolic writing are central means of philosophical expression, an eclectic orientalism is a major source of inspiration, and a Neoplatonic interpretaton of Plato forms the central philosophical core. The reason, I think, is that this complex of doctrines represents a coherent philosophical position, one with its own internal logic and consistency, that appeals to philosophers of a particular bent. It thus is periodically reinvented whenever conditions are favorable and a sufficient number of texts come back into circulation. These texts need not be comprehensive or systematic; to a sympathetic and careful reader like Suhrawardī even a quite fragmentary collection of material is sufficient to trigger the reinvention of the position. Nor is this the only such position to emerge from antiquity. Aristotelianism, the dialectical and political Platonism of the early and middle dialogues, Stoic ethics, and the atomism of Democritus and Epicurus seem to have, to a greater or lesser extent, a similar coherence and perennial appeal.

This fact has implications for the study of the history of philosophy, for it tends to reduce the value of the study of the transmission of ideas and raise the value of the study of the inner logic of philosophical systems. If it is the case that the great philosophical positions have an inner logic and robustness and if they are likely to be rediscovered regularly given even fragmentary sources, then philological analysis is not likely to be decisive in explaining philosophical developments. If a few bones are sufficient for a thoughtful philosopher like Suhrawardī to rediscover the dinosaur of Pythagoreanizing Neoplatonism, then there are almost always enough materials at hand to explain how a given position reemerges—and there are enough materials at hand at the times when it does *not* reemerge. Instead, the development and change of philosophical systems must be explained by an intellectual logic. What led the early Platonists to gradually abandon the political and dialectical sides of the master's work? Why did a Pythagoreanizing Platonism emerge as a powerful force in the late Plato, in the Neoplatonism of the Roman period, in postclassical Islamic philosophy, and in the European Renaissance? What is the cause of the enormous vitality of Aristotelianism and of its periodic rejection? Understanding the loss, rediscovery, and circulation of texts is part of the answer, but not the only one. While Renaissance Neoplatonism might be explained in terms of the rediscovery of non-Aristotelian texts, neither the original rise of Neoplatonism nor the Neoplatonism of Suhrawardī can be explained in that way. In other words, the critical problem is not understanding how ideas pass from one philosopher to another, though this is indispensible in its own sphere, but understanding the internal logic and dynamics of particular philosophical positions, how they develop, why they cohere, and why they appeal to the philosophers, times, and places that they do.

Before we leave the subject of Platonism for good, there is one last question to answer: what, in the view of the Illuminationists, was the fate of the Platonic philosophy after the master's death. That leads us to a very peculiar use of the term 'Stoic' in the later tradition of Islamic philosophy.

CHAPTER 11

The Stoics: The Heirs of Plato's Esoteric Teachings

THE PROBLEM: MULLĀ ṢADRĀ'S IDENTIFICATION OF SUHRAWARDĪ AS A STOIC

In his *Book of Prehensions* the seventeenth-century Iranian philosopher Mullā Ṣadrā writes:

> We say: that which is brought into being by essence is not the quiddity, contrary to the views of those who—like the martyred Sheikh [Suhrawardī] and his followers . . .—are followers of the Stoics. Likewise, it is not the quiddity that becomes existent, which is the well known Peripatetic view.[1]

While the view described as "Stoic" is characteristic of Suhrawardī and his school, it seems very odd to describe him as a follower of the Stoics *(al-Riwāqīyīn)*. One would have expected "Illuminationists" *(Ishrāqīyīn)*, Suhrawardī's own name for his school. So far as I know, Suhrawardī never calls his school "Stoic" or even mentions the word. As we have seen, he identifies himself as a follower of the "divine philosophers," of whom the greatest was Plato. I quickly eliminated my first suspicion, that this was a copyist's error, for though the two words are close enough in Arabic to make an error possible, the commentators confirm the reading, although they say nothing in explanation. I found a similar passage—the translator notes it as an oddity—in Mullā Ṣadrā's *Wisdom of the Throne* and some more in his massive *Four Journeys*.[2] Moreover, copyist errors would likely go the other way, since 'Illuminationist' is a term more commonly associated with Suhrawardī than 'Stoic'. Nor is this identification unique to Mullā Ṣadrā. The modern Persian lexicographer Dihkhudā defines 'Stoic' as "the Illuminationist philosophers, who acquire knowledge through unveiling of the states of minds,"[3] a clear reference to Suhrawardī's use of mystical intuition as a source for philosophy. We can assume, then, that Mullā Ṣadrā and others actually did identify the Illuminationist philosophers of Islam as Stoics. Why?

Stoic ideas provide a minor but persistent counterpoint to the predominant Aristotelian tradition in late antique and medieval European and Islamic philosophy. The scholars of medieval Islam knew the name 'Stoic', but they knew little in detail about the school. The Stoics died out as a school in the third century and, except for ethics, had been largely without influence for a century or two before that. Like us, medieval Muslim authors knew the Stoics from fragments contained in Greek works unsympathetic to them, notably the works of Galen and the commentaries on Aristotle. In Muslim sources the Stoics are a somewhat mysterious and distasteful group, condemned by all the best late classical authors.[4] Due to accidents of transmission and the tendency of Arabic translations and their copyists to garble unfamiliar Greek names, the knowledge of Muslims scholars was less complete and even more confused than ours. Naturally, there was a good deal of unrecognized Stoic influence through late antique authors, an example being the hypothetical syllogism. After translations of Greek philosophical and scientific works had been superceded in general use by works of Islamic authors, Muslim scholars knew only what happened to be preserved in biographical dictionaries, heresiographies, and standard treatments of particular topics. In general, the school affiliations of Greek philosophers were not well understood by Muslim scholars, and so even on the rare occasions when the biographical dictionaries discuss individual Stoics, it is usually not clear to the reader that the individual Greek being discussed was a Stoic.

But why should a seventeenth-century Iranian philosopher choose 'Stoic' as a term for a postclassical school of Islamic philosophy? First, we need to look at the doctrines that Mullā Ṣadrā calls "Stoic." In the passages I have found they are:

1. The primacy of essence.[5] This doctrine is an outgrowth of Avicenna's famous distinction of quiddity and existence. Certain later philosophers such as Mullā Ṣadrā had held that the foundation of all being was undifferentiated existence. Suhrawardī, as we have seen, had denied that there was anything outside the mind corresponding to existence in general, holding instead that general existence—as opposed to the existence of individual entities—was a construct of the mind, a being of reason. Later philosophers called Suhrawardī's position 'primacy of quiddity' and that of his opponents 'primacy of existence'. This issue is the most important point of dispute between later Illuminationists and their opponents.

2. That such notions as existence and necessity are *i'tibārāt 'aqlīya*, beings of reason, and thus do not have referents outside the mind, a

more general statement of the previous doctrine.[6] In this case Mullā Ṣadrā does not reject the Illuminationist/"Stoic" criticisms outright but argues that they can be reconciled with Aristotle's view by a deeper understanding of the issue.

3. That God's knowledge of contingents is by the presence of the contingents, not by something in God's essence. Mullā Ṣadrā also expresses this by saying that God knows things by the things themselves, not by something in himself.[7] This doctrine is the application to God of Suhrawardī's theory of knowledge by presence.[8]
4. That God's knowledge is identical with his essence and his creativity. Therefore, there is no providence in the sense of God's having prior knowledge of his creation. Mullā Ṣadrā here compares the views of the materialists, Islamic theologians, Avicenna and the Peripatetics, and Suhrawardī—who, he says, follows the Persians and the Stoics. Mullā Ṣadrā evidently holds Avicenna's view.[9]
5. That the Stoics, in opposition to the school of Democritus and the Islamic theologians, reject atomism.[10] This is not a criticism of the Stoics and Suhrawardī since Mullā Ṣadrā also rejects atomism in both its Greek and Islamic versions.
6. That the Stoics rely, at least in part, on mystical intuition: "I resolved to compose a book containing the scattered things that I found in the books of the Ancients, containing a summary of the views of the Peripatetics and a selection of the intuitions *(adhwāq)* of the Illuminationists among the Stoic sages, with additions not found in the books of the philosophers of past generations."[11]

There are three common features of these passages. First, all the passages mentioning the Stoics either identify Suhrawardī explicitly with this school or are phrased in ways that unmistakably point to him. Second, all the references to the Stoics deal with authentic doctrines of Suhrawardī, well known from his books and identified by Suhrawardī himself as distinctively Illuminationist doctrines. Third, most of these doctrines are points of major disagreement between Mullā Ṣadrā and Suhrawardī. Where they are not, they are cases where "the Stoics" agreed with other ancient authorities acceptable to Mullā Ṣadrā, as in the denial of atomism. The obvious conclusion is that Mullā Ṣadrā believed that a number of the points on which he disagreed with Suhrawardī were due to the latter's adherence to the Stoa. This explains the fact that most of Mullā Ṣadrā's references to Suhrawardī do not refer to the Stoics. When he discusses Suhrawardī's views on the Platonic Forms, he refers to Plato and the ancient Persians, as does Suhrawardī himself, but he does not mention the Stoics.[12] He discusses Suhrawardī's views on how the separate intellects know[13] and his identification of body with magnitude,[14] in both cases without mentioning the Stoics. These are issues on which he either agrees with Suhrawardī or at least does not consider his errors to be particularly dangerous.

From this we may draw a further conclusion: Mullā Ṣadrā approved of Plato and disapproved of the Stoics—or at least felt no obligation to approve of them. Accordingly, he approved of Suhrawardī's doctrines when he thought that they were authentically Platonic and blamed the Stoics for the doctrines of which he disapproved.

THE TRANSMISSION OF STOIC IDEAS

We are now back to the primary question: Why should Mullā Ṣadrā have thought that Suhrawardī's Illuminationist school was Stoicism? To know that, we must find out what Mullā Ṣadrā might have known about the Stoics. Most Islamic accounts of the history of philosophy include a mnemonic listing the seven Greek philosophical schools. It comes from a work of Ḥunayn ibn Isḥāq, the famous translator, and is found in various sources, including a history of philosophy written by Quṭb al-Dīn al-Daylamī, a contemporary of Mullā Ṣadrā.

> The Greeks had seven philosophical schools, the names of which were formed from seven different things. . . . The followers of Chrysippus are known as the Stoa, taking their name from the place where they taught philosophy, the portico of the temple in Athens.[15]

The other schools mentioned are the Pythagorean, Cyrenaic, Cynic, Sceptic, Epicurean, and Peripatetic. Muslim historians of philosophy did not find this especially helpful since all but the Pythagoreans and Peripatetics were even more obscure than the Stoics.

More interesting are stereotyped accounts that in one way or another associate the Stoics with Plato. Shaykh Bahā'ī, Mullā Ṣadrā's own teacher, reports:

> Plato's disciples are divided into three groups, namely, Seekers of Illumination, Stoics, and Peripatetics.
>
> The Seekers of Illumination *(Ishrāqīyūn)* among them have cleared the tablets of their intellect from all records of earthly existence. Hence the rays of the lights of truth from the tablets of the Platonic soul have illuminated them without the mediation of remarks and the intervention of allusions.
>
> The Stoics *(Riwāqīyūn)* are those who used to sit in the portico of his house and derived wisdom from his remarks and allusions.
>
> The Peripatetics *(Mashshā'ūn)* are those who used to walk alongside

> his stirrup and receive the pearls of his wisdom. Aristotle belonged to them, and it is frequently claimed that the Peripatetics are those who used to walk alongside Aristotle's stirrup, not Plato's.[16]

Ja'far Kashfī, a mid-nineteenth-century Shi'ite theologian of esoteric bent, laid out a scheme in which the Peripatetics, Stoics, and Illuminationists corresponded to progressively more profound approaches to the interpretation of the Qur'ān.[17] In both passages the Illuminationists are the highest school and the Peripatetics the lowest. The heresiographer Shahrastānī, in a book that we know Mullā Ṣadrā had read, identifies three philosophical schools stemming from Plato: "the Peripatetics, the Stoics, and the followers of Aristotle."[18] He also reproduces a supposed summary of Stoic views that goes back to Pseudo-Ammonius.[19]

The identification of three schools evolving from Plato's teaching is a late innovation, and the Illuminationists are not mentioned in this way in any early source that I know of. Earlier texts portray the Stoics and the Peripatetics as two rival sects stemming from Plato or place the Stoics vaguely, possibly even before Plato. The historian Mas'ūdī (d. 957) mentions the Stoics twice in lists of eminent Greek philosophers, once after Plato and Themistius and once between Empedocles and Homer, but without any clear indication of chronological priority.[20] If the statements of Ibn Juljul, writing in 987, and Ibn Khaldūn, in 1377, are typical, Muslim scholars in North Africa and Islamic Spain thought that the Stoics were identical with the Peripatetics or were a subsect of them.

> The Peripatetic philosophers, in particular the Stoics, possessed a good method of instruction in the intellectual sciences. It has been assumed that they used to study in a stoa, which protected them from the sun and the cold. Their school tradition is assumed to have passed from the sage Luqmân and his pupils to Socrates of the barrel, and then, in succession to Socrates' pupil, Plato, to Plato's pupil, Aristotle, to Aristotle's pupils, Alexander of Aphrodisias and Themistius, and others.[21]

The reference to Luqmān probably indicates that this account is intended to expand 'Āmirī's list of the five Greek sages. They are named "Stoics," Ibn Khaldūn explains elsewhere, because Aristotle used to teach while walking under a shady porch.[22]

In addition to these accounts of Stoicism as a school, there were also scattered references to particular Stoic doctrines. These were derived from the Greek commentaries on Aristotle and from some later authors such as Pseudo-Plutarch (i.e., Aetius) and Galen. Medical sources, especially Galen, also refer to the *Rūḥānīyūn*—"Pneumatists," a Greek medical school closely linked with the Stoics and identified with them in at least one Islamic source.[23] These references were generally hostile to the Stoics;

for example, Chrysippus "was a philosopher famous in his time in the land of Greece who taught a first philosophy whose principles are not proven and whose springs were poisoned."[24] Since no Muslim scholar made a concerted effort to collect these testimonies, they gradually dropped out of the tradition and were mostly forgotten.[25]

Finally, there is a curious text attributed to Ibn Waḥshīya, the tenth-century author or supposed translator of a number of occult and semi-occult works, the most famous being the *Nabataean Agriculture*, which claims to be a translation of a compendium of Mesopotamian agricultural and magical lore. In his book on alphabets, real and imaginary, he mentions that the illuminationists *(ishrāqīyūn)* were the descendants of the sister of Hermes and gives an alphabet that he attributes to Hermes.[26] Ibn Waḥshīya has been discussing hieroglyphics, which he (and the learned editor: this was before Champollion) believed to be occult symbols used by the followers of Hermes. He identifies four grades of initiates, of which the teachings of the two lowest survive. One group was the aforementained Illuminationists, the descendants of Hermes' sister. They intermarried with those not of their caste so there are those who understand their language and symbols. The other caste are the Peripatetics *(Mashshā'ūn)*, the descendants of the strangers who mingled with the descendants of Hermes. It was they who introduced the worship of the celestial bodies in place of the worship of the one true God (*ilāh al-ilāhīya*, probably a misprint for *ilāh al-āliha*, literally, "God of gods").

The conclusion—or at least one plausible conclusion—to be drawn by a careful, relatively late Islamic philosopher like Mullā Ṣadrā is that the Stoics and the Peripatetics were rival schools of Platonism but that the views of the Stoics were rejected by later Greek philosophers. Such a view would have been the more plausible in that the various Arabic lists of Greek philosophical schools did not list the Platonists among them as a separate school, implying that the legacy of Plato was carried on by one or more of the schools explicitly mentioned. This view would have been reinforced by the predominance of Aristotle commentaries among the philosophical literature translated into Arabic.

With this material we can suggest why Mullā Ṣadrā sometimes refers to Suhrawardī and the Illuminationists as "Stoics." His sources would have led him to believe that there were two significant philosophical schools among the followers of Plato: the Peripatetics and the Stoics. He also accepted Suhrawardī's claim that the Illuminationists were an ancient school associated with Plato.[27] Since the Illuminationists were not mentioned in his early sources and clearly were not to be identified with the Peripatetics, they must have been the Stoics. It is possible that he found confirmation of the identification in a tradition quoted by Shahrastānī:

> Plato would teach philosophy while walking out of respect for it. Aristotle followed that practice, so he and his followers are called Peripatetics. The Stoics *(aṣḥāb al-riwāq)* are the people of the porch *(ahl al-miẓāll).* Plato had two teachings: the teaching of Kalīs, which is spiritual, dealing with that which cannot be perceived by vision but only by thought; and the teaching of Kā'is, dealing with material things.[28]

It was well known that the Illuminationists used mystical intuition as one basis of their philosophy and that the Peripatetics did not but were greatly interested in the natural sciences. Perhaps he also knew about Ibn Waḥshīya's identification of the Illuminationists and the Peripatetics as two Hermetic schools. Therefore, Mullā Ṣadrā would have identified the Stoic/Illuminationist tradition with the teaching of "Kalīs" concerning spiritual things. It is not clear who is meant by 'Kalīs' and 'Kā'is'. I suspect that 'Kā'is' is 'Qābis', that is, Cebes, whose *Tabula* was discussed above. It deals with ethics, is obviously exoteric, and could thus be considered to deal "with material things." 'Kalīs' may possibly have been Calanus, the Indian sage who joined Alexander's court and who is identified as a Pythagorean in Arabic tradition. He appears in Pseudo-Apollonius' *Mystery of Creation,* a magical text that Suhrawardī cites, under the name Kālūs or Kābūs asking pointed questions about the omnipotence of God.[29] The "teaching of Kalīs" perhaps then dealt with metaphysical matters, such as are found in the *Timaeus.* Identifications of lesser-known Greek names are often problematic in Arabic due to the ambiguity of the medieval Arabic script.[30]

Mullā Ṣadrā does seem to have drawn a distinction between the "Stoic" teachings of Suhrawardī and his Platonic and Persian teachings. He explicitly states that the teachings of Suhrawardī concerning the Forms are Platonic[31] and relates his teachings on the Forms and on the use of the principles of light and darkness to the Persian sages.[32] The epithet 'Stoic' by this account would seem to be reserved for those aspects of Suhrawardī's teachings with which Mullā Ṣadrā disagreed and which he did not wish to attribute to Plato. In short, "Stoic" is a derogatory epithet reserved for non-Peripatetic, non-Platonic aspects of the Illuminationist system when Mullā Ṣadrā happened to disagree with them.

ILLUMINATIONISM AS STOICISM

Suhrawardī, to the best of my knowledge, nowhere explicitly mentions Stoicism. I have already cited possible sources for Suhrawardī's knowledge of the Stoics as a school. For Stoic doctrines, three texts come to mind for Suhrawardī's information on Stoics, each of which has been repeatedly cited throughout this book: Pseudo-Plutarch (i.e., Aetius), *De Placita Philosophorum*; Pseudo-Ammonius, *On the Opinions of the Philosophers (Fī Ārā' al-Falāsifa)*, and Shahrastānī's *Book of Religions and Sects (Kitāb al-Milal wa'l-Niḥal)*. None of these works are directly cited by Suhrawardī, but each most likely was available to him. One of the surviving Arabic manuscripts of *De Placitis* was written in Bagdad during his lifetime. The Pseudo-Ammonius was written in the ninth century, but it was quoted often by later authors, and the surviving manuscript dates from the fourteenth century. It was directly known to Shahrastānī, who reproduces whole its section on the Stoics. Shahrastānī wrote only a few years before Suhrawardī's birth. His work became very popular and is preserved in many manuscripts and in Persian and Turkish translations. Suhrawardī could have known the Stoics through a variety of other texts as well, but Shahrastānī gives a useful combination of historical and doctrinal information, was likely to have been known to Suhrawardī, and presumably represents the state of Islamic knowledge about Stoicism in Suhrawardī's century.[33]

The following is a tentative reconstruction of the development of Suhrawardī's view of his relationship to Stoicism:

1. Suhrawardī knew that there had been a line of major philosophers in Greece—the "pillars *(asāṭīn)* of wisdom"—including Empedocles, Pythagoras, Socrates, and Plato.[34] These were 'Āmirī's succession of "those to whom the Greeks attributed wisdom." This series of philosophers, roughly corresponding to the "Italian school" of Greek historians of philosophy, are the 'Divine philosophers' among the Ancients, whose school Suhrawardī claimed to be reviving.
2. After his death, Plato's school divided. Some authorities mention three schools—the Peripatetics, Stoics, and Aristotelians—but most two—either Peripatetics and Stoics, or the teachings of Kalīs and Kā'is, which latter dealt with spiritual and material things respectively.[35]
3. The Peripatetic school corresponds to the teaching of Kā'is, probably Cebes. The Peripatetics were represented in the Islamic world by Fārābī, Avicenna, and their followers. These Islamic Peripatetics are the subject of scathing criticism in Suhrawardī's works, especially in *The Philosophy of Illumination*.
4. Suhrawardī then deduced that the Stoics or the followers of Kalīs represented the Platonic teaching dealing with spiritual things. This would have found confirmation in the well-known texts associating Kalīs/Calanus with Pythagoreanism in India and with Hermes in Pseudo-Apollonius. The fact that information about them and their

teachings was so sparse would confirm the impression that their teaching was esoteric and secret. And it was well known that Plato had unwritten doctrines.

5. Suhrawardī identified himself with a "spiritual" or "divine" tradition in Greek philosophy: Empedocles, Pythagoras, Socrates, Plato, Kalīs/Stoics. These were the philosophers who relied on both intuition and reason and who often expressed themselves in symbols.[36]
6. From the Stoics came the name 'Illuminationist' that Suhrawardī gave to his school. It is the antonym of *aṣḥāb al-maẓalla*, "companions of the shadowed place." Suhrawardī would have considered such a name pejorative and hardly appropriate for a school of philosophers who gazed on the immaterial light of God and who were sometimes known as *rūḥānīyūn*, "the spiritualists." This would explain why he was so willing to place his own school under a new name in a past whose general features were reasonably well known to his contemporaries.
7. It should also be noted that the Stoics are occasionally called *aṣḥāb al-usṭuwān*, "the companions of the columns." It seems more likely to me that *usṭuwān* is a transcription of some form of 'Stoic', though it is possible that some clever translator, thinking of classical collonaded porches, came up with it as a rendering of 'Stoic' that was both translation and transcription. Be that as it may, *usṭuwāna*, pl. *asāṭīn*, "column," is the term that Suhrawardī and his school use to refer to the greatest of the ancient sages: Hermes, Pythagoras, Empedocles, Socrates, Plato, and sometimes Aristotle. *Aṣḥāb al-usṭuwān* can thus also be translated as "the followers of the ancient sages."[37]

This account is speculative. Since Suhrawardī was not in the habit of quoting sources, it is unlikely that it can be demonstrated by direct evidence from his own pen, and the Illuminationist tradition as represented by Shahrazūrī and Quṭb al-Dīn Shīrāzī seems to have nothing to say about the Stoics. Moreover, we know that there were aspects of his teaching that he did not write down, so any or all of this could have fallen into that category. Since there was evidently no oral tradition that survived Suhrawardī's death, it is quite possible that the commentators would not have known about a Stoic connection. The chief virtue of my theory is that it answers some questions about Suhrawardī's system: Why did he so confidently assert the existence of an ancient Illuminationist school? And where did the name 'Illuminationist' come from? The theory also has the virtue that it can be confirmed or disproven fairly easily by the discovery of additional texts explaining how the Stoics fit into the history of Islamic philosophy. The limitation of this account is that Suhrawardī obviously saw himself mainly as a Platonist, so Stoicism would have been to him only a particular tradition of Platonism. He certainly was not a Stoic in a full and authentic sense.

We can now at last return to the original question: why did *Mullā Ṣadrā* think that Suhrawardī was a Stoic? If my theory is correct, it is possible that the fact—that is, my theory that Suhrawardī considered himself a Stoic—reached him through some channel not presently known to us. On the other hand, he too knew the texts on ancient philosophy that Suhrawardī had read and would have had no difficulty in following the same line of reasoning as I have. Since these were mostly points of disagreement with Suhrawardī, he would have wished to make the opposite historical deduction—that the Stoics were not Platonists—and to remind his readers of the derogatory connotations of the name 'Stoic'. The only explanation that we can so far give with some confidence is that Mullā Ṣadrā certainly would have seized any opportunity to delegitimize Suhrawardī's claim that his essentialist doctrines were those of the divine Plato. Thus, by labelling Suhrawardī as a Stoic, Mullā Ṣadrā could defend his own claim that his mystical existentialist philosophy corresponded with the views of Plato, the greatest mystical philosopher of the ancient world.

SUHRAWARDĪ'S SYSTEM AND THE HISTORY OF PHILOSOPHY: RECAPITULATION

It is time to summarize what we have covered so far. The principal point that I have tried to make is that Suhrawardī's system is a coherent response to a well established philosophical tradition: Pythagoreanizing Neoplatonism. His allusions to his predecessors evoke the texts and ideas that provide the context of his system. The central figures in this tradition are Pythagoras, who is in many respects the prototype of the kind of philosophical project that Suhrawardī wishes to carry out, and Plato, who is his intellectual master. His Plato is the Timaean Plato of the late antique Neoplatonists. The curious complex of philosophy, mysticism, mythology, and the occult that we find in Suhrawardī would have been instantly recognizable to Porphyry, Iamblichus, Proclus, and the others of their school. There is no reason to believe that Suhrawardī is following them by means of extensive texts; rather this complex of Neoplatonic and Neopythagorean ideas form a coherent whole that has been repeatedly reinvented down through the history of Platonism, that indeed has much in common with certain Renaissance and early modern philosophies and even with aspects of the New Age movement of our own time. Suhrawardī, however, has his own peculiarities, notably his thoroughgoing nominalism. Despite the mystical and occult trappings, the heart of his system is philosophy, a philosophy that was sufficiently rigorous and compelling to become the point of departure for most later Islamic philosophy. His key positions, most of which are discussed in the *sophismata* of *The Philosophy of Illumination*, form the major part of the agenda of philosophical debate among later philosophers like Mullā Ṣadrā. These positions include most notoriously his rejection of the reality of existence—the famous "primacy of quiddity"—the Platonic Forms, the rejection of essentialist definition, knowledge by presence, and a number of other doctrines, most of which have been discussed above. His recasting and allegorization of metaphysics in terms of light had less long-term philosophical influence, but its influence in poetry, mysticism, and the rhetoric of later Iranian philosophy was immense. Long after his death it even reshaped the Zoroastrians' view of their own ancient past.

Suhrawardī has usually been interpreted as a mystic and an advocate of the Persian tradition. He was certainly a mystic, but the mysticism, as befits a Platonist, is firmly placed in a rational setting and put in the service of epistemology.

PART 3

Aftermath

CHAPTER 12

Politics, Plato's Seventh Epistle, *and the Failure of Suhrawardī's Political Ambitions*

"His knowledge was greater than his prudence." So wrote Ibn Abī Uṣaybi'a of Suhrawardī, echoing the judgment of some of those who had known him. His teacher Fakhr al-Dīn al-Mārdīnī had feared that Suhrawardī's rashness would be his undoing, and such proved to be the case.[1] But for Shahrazūrī Suhrawardī's fate was due to the jealousy of lesser minds:

> The 'ulamā' of Aleppo gathered and listened to him talking about his investigations into the excellences of the sages, showing the stupidity of their opponents, debating them and silencing them in the assemblies. He also performed wonders (*'ajā'ib*) by the power of the Holy Spirit. They agreed out of jealously to declare him an infidel, attributing to him a claim to prophethood, and incited the Sultan [al-Malik al-Ẓāhir] to kill him, but he refused. They then wrote to Saladin, saying among other things, that he was going to corrupt the religion.[2]

In fact, he was reenacting a drama that his masters Pythagoras, Socrates, and Plato had played out, a drama driven by contradictions at the heart of Platonism.[3]

Our sources do not tell us why Suhrawardī came to Aleppo in 579/1183. Perhaps it was because the city had just been taken from the Zangids by Saladin, and Saladin favored Shāfi'īs, the legal school to which Suhrawardī belonged, over the previously dominant Ḥanafīs. No elaborate explanation is really needed; travelling in Mesopotamia and Syria as he did, he would naturally have passed through Aleppo, particularly if he wanted to avoid Crusader territory. When Suhrawardī arrived, incognito and shabby, he took lodgings at the Ḥallāwīya Madrasa, at that time the leading Ḥanafī school in Aleppo.[4] There he joined in the debates among the jurists. Iftikhār al-Dīn al-Hāshimī, the head of the *madrasa*, realized that he was a learned man and politely sent his son with a suitable set of clothes. Rejecting the proffered gift, Suhrawardī gave the boy an enormous gem and asked him to auction it in the bazaar. When the boy secured a bid of thirty thousand dirhams, Suhrawardī smashed the stone, thus proving that his poverty was voluntary.[5]

The thirty thousand dirham bid had come from the prince-governor himself, al-Malik al-Ẓāhir, the son of Saladin. The prince sent in search of the gem and found that it had belonged not to Iftikhār al-Dīn as he had supposed but to a poor dervish. He took Suhrawardī, whose reputation he already knew, and installed him in great state in the citadel. He sponsored debates between Suhrawardī and the 'ulamā' of the town in which, our sources agree, Suhrawardī always triumphed. We do not know if Suhrawardī remained there during the two and a half years (1184–86) that the city was ruled by Saladin's bother, al-Malik al-'Ādil or if he followed al-Malik al-Ẓāhir. It was in Aleppo, we may assume, that Suhrawardī completed *The Philosophy of Illumination*, on 15 September 1186, less than three weeks after al-Malik al-Ẓāhir had reassumed the governorship; that evening the sun, the moon, and the five planets were in conjunction in Libra.

Suhrawardī's ascendancy over the prince led to trouble, and the established 'ulamā' of the town, or at least an influential party of them, wrote to Saladin complaining. If, as seems likely, Suhrawardī spent some of the time when al-Ẓāhir was out of office with the prince in Damascus, perhaps we have an explanation for the willingness of Saladin and the Damascus 'ulamā' to take alarm at charges of heresy levelled against him. Saladin wrote back ordering his son to put Suhrawardī to death. The prince reluctantly did so, later taking his revenge on those responsible.

But what was it that aroused the anger of the 'ulamā' and the fears of Saladin, and what were the charges laid against Suhrawardī? The biographers give a variety of answers and the chroniclers add a few more.

> According to Yāqūt they accused Suhrawardī of heresy and atheism *(ilḥād, zandaqa)* and warned Saladin of the danger to the religious beliefs of his son and the people of the province.
>
> Ibn Abī Uṣaybi'a, citing Ibn Raqīqa, says that he was accused of unbelief *(kufr)* and of being a danger to the the faith of al-Malik al-Ẓāhir and of the people in whatever place he happened to be. Another of Ibn Abī Uṣaybi'a's sources accuses Suhrawardī of becoming arrogant after his triumphs in debate and acting as though he were superior in rank to the other 'ulamā'.
>
> Ibn Khallikān says he was accused of "corrupted belief" and *ta'ṭīl*, the heresy of denying the reality of God's attributes. This was, it seems, due to his following the ancient sages. Most people in Aleppo, says Ibn Khallikān, thought that he had been an atheist and believed in nothing.
>
> Ibn Shaddād, the qāḍī of Aleppo, accused him of denying revelation

> *(sharā'i'*, lit., divine laws), and lists "the philosophers, the *ma'aṭṭila*, the *dahrīya*, and those who rejected *(yu'ānid)* the Law" as particular objects of Saladin's hatred.[6]
>
> 'Imād al-Dīn al-Iṣfahānī says that he claimed that God was capable of creating a prophet after Muḥammad.[7]
>
> Shahrazūrī says that his execution was motivated by jealousy. Specifically he was accused of being an infidel, claiming prophethood, and corrupting religion, both of the prince and potentially of the people in whatever place he was exiled to. Shahrazūrī mentions a report that some of his friends called him 'Abu'l-Futūḥ Rasūl Allāh—"father of victories, messenger of God." Since his opponents did not understand his view, they thought that his philosophy was snake oil.[8]

The list boils down to

1. jealousy;
2. atheism or some other form of unbelief;
3. being a danger to the religious faith of the prince-governor and the populace.

What sense can we make of these charges? That they were motivated in part by jealousy is surely true but not very interesting philosophically. The 'ulamā' are always jealous of each other and of potential outside rivals, but this jealousy does not usually result in death sentences, even less often in death sentences that the civil authorities are willing to carry out.

Suhrawardī's supposed "heresy," "unbelief," and "atheism" are explicable on various levels. For one thing, philosophers in general were often suspected of atheism or unbelief. Ghazālī in his *Incoherence of the Philosophers* identifies three philosophical doctrines as sufficient to justify a charge of unbelief: the eternity of the world, the denial of God's knowledge of particulars, and the denial of the resurection of the body.[9] Suhrawardī did believe that God knows particulars, but on the other two charges he would have stood justly condemned. The charge of *ta'ṭīl*, the denial of the reality of God's attributes, would have been justified, for Suhrawardī considered God's attributes to be relations and without reality of their own. *Ta'ṭīl* is a charge most commonly made against the rationalist Mu'tazilite theologians, with their uncompromising rejection of anthropomorphism. It is also made against some Isma'ili philosophers, though the Isma'ilis themselves deny it.[10] The contradictory charges of claiming prophethood and denying revelation, along with the related charge of admitting the possibility of a prophet after Muḥammad, are more problematic. Suhrawardī did claim to have experienced mystical intuition, and even hostile sources say that he could work wonders, but the same was true of any self-respecting Sufi master. And there is no reason to deny that he was a pious Muslim. In sum, charges could be laid against Suhrawardī, at least if one were willing to accept the usual accusations against philosophers, and perhaps a combination of clerical jealousy at Suhrawardī's triumphs and his own lack of tact and wisdom would be sufficient to explain why these charges were taken to Saladin. They are not, however, sufficient to explain why Saladin took notice or why he insisted on Suhrawardī's execution. That must depend on the third charge: corrupting the religion of the prince and people.

Suhrawardī spent several years in Aleppo under the protection of al-Malik al-Ẓāhir and perhaps some time in Saladin's Damascus, surely long enough to know the danger he was in. Why did he stay? After all, he had spent his adult life wandering, learning, and teaching. We might expect that his extreme asceticism and his metaphysical interests would have led him to shun the courts of kings as sources of corruption and distraction. He was not an urbane scientist like Quṭb al-Dīn Shīrāzī, his follower a century later, in need of royal patronage in order to conduct his scientific work. But like so much else in Suhrawardī's life, his stay in Aleppo makes sense in the context of his philosophy.

There is a political doctrine implicit in the Illuminationist philosophy, a doctrine that finds open expression in the introduction to *The Philosophy of Illumination*. Suhrawardī distinguishes between 'discursive' and 'intuitive' philosophy *(baḥth, ta'alluh)*. The philosopher who is proficient, or even intermediate, in intuitive philosophy is superior to the one proficient in discursive philosophy. The term that I translate as 'intuitive philosophy', *ta'alluh*, literally means 'becoming a god' and is so used in the rendering of Greek terms relating to divinization.[11] In Suhrawardī's thought it means mystical attainment and is mostly likely intended to allude to the expression *ḥakīm ilāhī*, 'divine sage', the title he applies to Plato and others among the Ancients. Suhrawardī continues:

> Should it happen that in some period there be a philosopher proficient in both intuitive philosophy and discursive philosophy, he will be the ruler by right and the vicegerent of God. Should it happen that this not be the case, then rulership will belong to a philosopher proficient in intuitive philosophy but of middle ability in discursive philosophy. Should these qualities not coincide, rulership belongs to a philosopher who is proficient in intuitive philosophy but who lacks discursive philosophy. The world will never be without a philosopher proficient in intuitive philosophy. Authority on earth will never belong to the proficient discursive philosopher who has not become proficient in intuitive philosophy, for the world will never be without one proficient in intuitive philosophy, one more worthy than he who is only a discursive philosopher, for the

> vicegerency requires direct knowledge. By this authority I do not mean political power. The godly leader may indeed rule openly, or he may be hidden—the one whom the multitude call 'the Pole'. He will have authority even if he is in the deepest obscurity. When the government is in his hands, the age will be enlightened, but if the age is without divine rule, darkness will be triumphant.[12]

The reference to the Pole links this passage with the Sufi doctrine of the hidden saints who are the secret rulers of the world, of whom the Pole is the senior member. There is thus a hierarchy of saints responsible for preserving the well-being of the world, a sort of secret government composed of unheralded individuals of high spiritual attainment. Much Sufi folklore concerns meetings with these individuals, and many prominent Sufis were rumored to belong to this hidden brotherhood. Abū Rayyān believes this passage is the probable source of the accusation that Suhrawardī believed that God could send another prophet.[13] The commentators soften the meaning of this passage, stressing its allegorical and spiritual character, but for once their insight—or perhaps their courage—fails them, for the exoteric political implications of the passage are obvious. The sage proficient in intuitive philosophy is the legitimate ruler, whether or not he is recognized. A ruler who does not have such intuitive philosophy is not legitimate, for he does not have the knowledge necessary to rule. If the state is ruled openly by a philosopher proficient in both speculative and intuitive philosophy, "the age will be enlightened."

Al-Malik al-Ẓāhir, Shahrazūrī tells us, "loved" Suhrawardī and "believed in him."[14] The exact nature of the relationship between the two men is not specified in the sources, but the accusations of corrupting the prince's religion leave little doubt that the prince was both Suhrawardī's patron and his disciple. That Suhrawardī's ambitions included political power is confirmed by a story preserved by Ibn Khallikān.

> Shaykh Sayf al-Dīn al-Āmidī . . . said, "I met al-Suhrawardī in Aleppo. He said to me, 'Without doubt I will rule the earth.' I said to him, 'But how will that be?' He said, 'I had a dream in which I drank the water of the sea.' I said, 'Perhaps this means the fame of knowledge and what is connected with that.' But I saw that he did not turn away from what he had thought, and I realized that he had much knowledge and little prudence."[15]

Suhrawardī sought to be, or to be the counsellor of, a philosopher-king. His earlier associations with other rulers indicate that this ambition predated the meeting with al-Malik al-Ẓāhir.

Yet the implied accusation of rashness and the specific accusations of arrogance made by others miss the philosophical point. For him wisdom in politics as in other aspects of life comes from the intelligible world. Political wisdom comes not from the shrewdness of the worldly and experienced king but from the inspiration vouchsafed to the enlightened individual. He was, after all, both a Muslim and an Iranian. The ideal regime of Islam was neither a democracy nor the shrewd monarchies of such rulers as Mu'āwiya and al-Manṣūr; it was the primitive theocracy of Muḥammad and the early caliphate. It is also quite possible to see Shi'ite, and indeed Isma'ili, influences in this aspect of his philosophy. The Iranian tradition provides him with an alternative but complementary model—the wise vizier, two of whom, Frashostar and Burzurgmehr, are mentioned by name in *The Philosophy of Illumination.* Each model of wisdom in politics had produced its golden age: the heroic age of early Islam and the great ages of the Iranian kings with their philosopher-viziers at their sides. Pythagoras partook of both traditions. The Muslims knew the story of his ideal philosophic republic, and there was a pseudepigraphic letter available in Arabic translation supposedly written by Pythagoras to Hiero, "the tyrant of Sicily," in which the philosopher boasts of the self-sufficiency of his own life and rejects the tyrant's overtures.[16]

The intellectual validity of these models of good government could be derived from the most basic principles of Suhrawardī's Platonic philosophy. When presented with an opportunity to put his political teachings into practice, he would have considered himself obliged to take it. Since he also considered himself to have revived the deepest, long obscured wisdom of the Ancients, the urgency of putting it into political effect would have been that much greater, especially since the political decay of the Islamic world was so far advanced.

Plato, Suhrawardī's true master, had reasoned the same way fifteen centuries before.[17] Dion, the Syracusan statesman and admirer of Plato, had written to urge Plato to come and undertake the instruction of the young tyrant Dionysius II. "What better opportunity can we expect than the situation which providence has presented us with?" he asked Plato. He pointed out that his own nephews and followers could be persuaded to accept Plato's principles and way of life, thus providing a further good influence on Dionysius, "so that now, if ever, might we confidently hope to accomplish that union, in the same persons, of philosophers and rulers of great cities."

Plato was well aware of the risks, having visited Sicily before. He first went to Sicily at about the age of forty to visit the Pythagorean communities and as a distinguished visitor was naturally invited to the court of Dionysius I. He was deeply shocked by the luxury and moral laxity of Syracuse, and he surely was not impressed by the character of Dionysius, a ruthless and successful tyrant of a sort familiar to other times. There he first met Dion, then only a young man but of a character to impress Plato. The trip ended badly; Plato was auctioned in the slave market of Aegina, where one of his students bought his freedom (though it is not clear that the tyrant was responsible for this indignity). Twenty years later Dion urged Plato to come to Syracuse again to undertake the instruction of the young new tyrant. When Plato arrived, he found his misgivings confirmed. The court was riven by factions, with courtiers whispering to the young tyrant that Dion and his friends aimed to distract him with useless instruction—geometry lessons seem to have particularly rankled—while they gained control of the city. Dionysius subjected himself to the philosophical regime for a while, but then he exiled Dion in disgrace, keeping Plato as a well-treated but involuntary guest. Plato was finally allowed to leave in 367, when a war in Sicily distracted Dionysius' attention. Nonetheless, Plato seems to have maintained civil relations with the tyrant, perhaps in hopes that his and Dion's goals might eventually be realized.

In 361 Plato began receiving reports of Dionysius' renewed interest in philosophy, and Dion urged him to return. Plato was naturally reluctant. "What tipped the scales eventually was the thought that if anyone ever was to attempt to realize these principles of law and government, now was the time to try, since it was only necessary to win over a single man and I should have accomplished all the good I dreamed of."[18] "And the age will be enlightened," Suhrawardī later said under similar circumstances. Also Plato feared being taken as a mere theoretician, and he would have borne the blame for negligence if the opportunity was lost and disaster followed. On arriving in Syracuse Plato tested Dionysius' commitment to philosophy and found it wanting. Abandoning the goal of transforming the tyrant into a philosopher-king, he attempted to reconcile Dionysius and Dion. This too failed, and Plato had to ask the intercession of the Italian Pythagoreans to gain the tyrant's permission to return to Athens.

Dion, angered by Dionysius' treachery, gathered a small band of idealists to attack Syracuse, overthrow the tyranny, and reestablish the democracy under Dion's leadership. To everyone's astonishment, the expedition was successful and Syracuse was taken. Unfortunately, the leaders of the new government soon quarreled, Dion's haughtiness having made him unpopular. In the end Dion was murdered, the event that occasioned the *Seventh Epistle*. Syracuse fell into civil strife that lasted until after Plato's death.

As Pythagoras discovered in aristocratic Croton, Socrates in democratic Athens, and Plato in autocratic Syracuse, philosopher-kings are not necessarily popular. Saladin, for one, did not like them. He was a pious Sunnī Muslim and had met them before in the form of the Isma'ilis: the Fatimid rulers of Egypt and the "Old Man of the Mountain," the leader of the so-called "Order of Assasins." He had destroyed the Fatimid state, which he had once served. Shortly before conquering Aleppo in 1183 and putting it under his son's rule, he brought the Old Man of the Mountain to heel. In 1187 he destroyed the Kingdom of Jerusalem at the battle of the Horns of Hattin. When the complaints of the Aleppo jurists reached his ears, he was awaiting the Christian counterattack, the Third Crusade in 1191 with its formidable leaders Richard Lion-Heart of England and Philip Augustus of France.

What Suhrawardī was teaching al-Malik al-Ẓāhir would have sounded distressingly like Isma'ilism to Saladin. The Isma'ilis were the most enthusiastic philosophers among the Muslims, and such doctrines as *ta'ṭil*, universal cycles, and reincarnation could easily be connected with the Isma'ilis. Ghazālī had said that the Isma'ilis were followers of Pythagoras, as the *Epistles of the Brethren of Purity* certainly indicate, and Ṣā'id had said that they were followers of Empedocles.[19] The notion that mystical wisdom gave sovereignty had an Isma'ili flavor and was subversive in itself, especially if we accept the story of Suhrawardī's prophetic dream of univeral dominion. Aleppo, moreover, was strategically important, an anchor of Saladin's line of communication to the east. Petty Muslim states had made common cause with Crusaders before, and Suhrawardī's rumored claim of prophethood would have freed al-Malik al-Ẓāhir of any obligation to support Sunnī Islam against the Christians. In such a context, Saladin's anxious and repeated orders to have the seditious philosopher killed make perfect sense. He was acting rationally to protect his state from the dangers of rule by the wise.

Platonists have repeatedly tried to put their principle of rule by philosopher-kings into practice. The results have never been encouraging. The prototype, the Pythagorean regime in southern Italy, was overthrown by popular revolution. Socrates—whose project was, after all, the moral reformation of Athens—was put to death by the democracy for corrupting the youth, precisely the offense for which Suhrawardī died. His teaching, as the democrats pointed out, produced not just the great philosopher Plato but also the political opportunist and traitor Alcibiades—and Plato too was tainted by an early association with the tyranny of the Thirty. Plato's attempts to reform Syracuse by instructing its tyrant in philosophy and supporting the philosophically inclined Dion twice ended in fiasco. The *Seventh Epistle* is his attempt to justify his political adventures to the democratic party in Athens and Syracuse. Other Platonist political disasters might be added to the list. Julian the Apostate and his Neoplatonic supporters were unable to rescue Rome from Christianity or eventual ruin. The last Neoplatonic professors of Athens went to Persia in hope of finding a wise king in Khusraw Anūshīrwān but returned disappointed. To this list we must add Suhrawardī's failure in Aleppo and perhaps also all the dismal failures of autocratic utopianism in the modern world.

The failure is not, as Plato would have us believe, due to the inadequacy of the raw material—the fickleness of the young men presented to Platonist philosophers for education. The failure arises from a contradiction at the heart of Platonism. The basic insight of Platonism is that the world known by the senses is a world of becoming and that the true world of being is the ideal intelligible realm of the Forms. Platonism, as Suhrawardī knew very well, is the exploration of this ideal realm. The things of our world are only copies of the ideal archetypes. There can be no real knowledge of the world of becoming, only opinion. Even Plato's greatest attempt to describe the world, the *Timaeus*, is avowedly only a "likely story."[20] But this is, if anything, even more true of political philosophy. The *Republic* describes not a realized state but a "city in thought." How then can an ideal city be realized in the world of becoming? There is no particular reason to believe that those at home in the world of being will be the best guides in the world of becoming. It seems likely that Plato himself realized the force of this difficulty, for his last work, the *Laws*, describes a second-best city, a more realistic political project than that of the *Republic*. Morrow argues that the project of reform described in the *Seventh Epistle* was not the establishment of a republic of philosophers but only the more modest project of the restoration of constitutional government and moral reform.[21]

In fact, Suhrawardī's project goes beyond even the idealistic politics of the *Republic* and the Sicilian adventure; it is based on the Pythagorean and Neoplatonic notion of "demonic" or "divine men." For Suhrawardī sovereignty belongs to the man who is *muta'allih*, "divinized." The idea occurs in Hierocles' commentary on the *Golden Verses*.[22] Hermias in his *Commentary on the Phaedrus* wrote: "And indeed he thought it right to call the divine men gods in the *Sophist*, for the wise and divine men are as gods in relation to men. And so he was wont often to credit his works to the divine men, in the *Phaedrus* to Pythagoras, in the *Charmides* to Zalmoxis, a wise man, and the story of Atlantis in the *Timaeus* to the Egyptians."[23] Such divine men are at the intersection of human intellect, politics, and metaphysics. Suhrawardī's political doctrine is that of the late antique Neoplatonists and—Saladin was right about this—the Isma'ilis.

If there is a contradiction involved in bringing the ideal city into the world of becoming, it is scarcely surprising that the record of Platonic political ventures is so dismal. Plato understood the moral pressures at work on the young Dionysius II keeping him from realizing the philosophical ideal. We have no such document from Aleppo to tell us how Suhrawardī's political project came to fail, but some of the elements that led to Plato's failure in Dionysius' Syracuse were clearly present: political factions, the jealousy of rival schools of thought, the temptations of luxury, and the impracticality of cloistered philosophers. Suhrawardī lacked the caution and political prudence that barely preserved Plato from personal disaster in the end. He was younger, and Plato admits that his youthful politics were not always wise.[24] Suhrawardī did not understand that the king possessing political power is inevitably a creature of the world of becoming. Perhaps it is true that the Pole—God's hidden vicegerent, the master of intuitive and discursive philosophy, if there is such a person—is the rightful but unrecognized ruler of the world, and perhaps, as the Sufis believe, he and his secret court wander the world setting things aright. Nonetheless, it was Saladin, famed as the epitome of the wise king by his European enemies, who understood the philosophical issue correctly. He knew that to confuse the intellectual and spiritual ascendancy of the philosophers and saints with the worldly power of kings is to invite mischief.

And so Suhrawardī had to die.

CHAPTER 13

The Philosophical Heritage of Suhrawardī

THE TRANSMISSION OF HIS BOOKS AND IDEAS

"One Friday after prayer at the end of Dhu'l-Ḥijja 587 [January 1192], al-Shihāb al-Suhrawardī was brought out dead from prison in Aleppo, and his disciples dispersed."[1] Who these disciples were, we do not know; none of the biographers preserves a list, and Suhrawardī does not appear in the biographical dictionaries, so far as I know, as the teacher of any scholar of the next generation. One Ḥakīm Ibrāhīm b. Abi'l-Faḍl b. Ṣadaqa was a witness to the miraculous vision of Damascus that Suhrawardī conjured up one day in Aleppo, and "one of the Persian jurists" was a witness to the incident in which the Turkoman pulled off Suhrawardī's arm—but who these people were, we do not know. Sadīd al-Dīn Ibn Raqīqa was a friend, but not necessarily a disciple or transmitter of Suhrawardī's teachings. Suhrawardī certainly intended his books to be accompanied by an oral teaching delivered by an authorized expounder of his teachings "him who arises with the Book." "Let no one seek to peruse the mysteries of this book without repairing to my successor, him who possesses the knowledge of the Book!"[2] But Shahrazūrī claims that Suhrawardī never found the intellectual peer whom he sought, and there is no reference to a successor. It is quite clear from *The Philosophy of Illumination* that there was a group of "brethren" to whom it was addressed. That a book has been written at the request of one or more friends is, of course, a hoary convention, but in *The Philosophy of Illumination* the brethren seem a little more tangible than usual, especially since their existence as a group is confirmed by historical sources.[3] Shahrazūrī knows of no adequate expounder of Suhrawardī's thought in the decades between the master's death and his attempt to resurrect the Illuminationist philosophy; certainly, Shahrazūrī's investigation was purely a matter of searching libraries, not of joining a living tradition.[4] So, in the absence of further evidence, we may assume that Suhrawardī's school as a living community died with its founder.

His books lived and continued to be read. Suhrawardī's reputation had preceded him to Aleppo. Perhaps this refers simply to his reputation for spiritual and magical attainments, but his books were already in circulation. The philosopher 'Abd al-Laṭīf al-Baghdādī (1162–1231), then a student in Mosul, read three of Suhrawardī's works—the *Intimations*, the *Lamaḥāt*, and *Ma'ārij al-Quds*. Though his teacher, the mathematician Kamāl al-Dīn ibn Yūnus (1156–1242), was enthusiastic about them, 'Abd al-Laṭīf thought they simply provided further evidence of the ignorance of the people of his own time.[5] Shahrazūrī, probably writing in the middle of the thirteenth century, refers to the popularity of Suhrawardī's books, especially his poetry and *The Philosophy of Illumination*, and lists nearly fifty works attributed to Suhrawardī.[6] This list includes all the major works and some minor works that now seem to be lost.

Another particular attests to the popularity of Suhrawardī's works in the thirteenth century. Two scholarly editions of *The Philosophy of Illumination* were already in circulation. Shahrazūrī used as the basis of his commentary a text that went back to a manuscript read to Suhrawardī himself for correction. Quṭb al-Dīn, who evidently had access to several manuscripts, used as the basis of his commentary a more polished text, though he also cites the edition used by Shahrazūrī and acknowledges its authority. In other words, in the first half of the thirteenth century unknown scholars took the trouble to produce two very professional editions of *The Philosophy of Illumination* following different editorial methods, the first a careful reproduction of the text as it was in the hands of Suhrawardī's students and the second a philosophically sophisticated "corrected edition," in which the Arabic and a variety of minor lapses of content were corrected.[7] Thus the thirteenth century saw the production of two editions of and two commentaries on *The Philosophy of Illumination*. In the fourteenth century at the far end of the Islamic world the Granadan vizier Lisān al-Dīn b. al-Khaṭīb (d. 776/1375) included a paraphrase of parts of *The Philosophy of Illumination* in a book on Sufism, attributing the views expressed to "the author" *(al-mu'allif)*, one of "the people of lights among the Ancients" *(ahl al-anwār min al-aqdamīn)*.[8]

Other works of Suhrawardī were in circulation. Shahrazūrī and Quṭb al-Dīn cite his Peripatetic works; indeed, these works were probably the major basis of their interpretations of *The Philosophy of Illumination*. Ibn Kammūna (d. 683/1284) wrote a commentary on the *Intimations*, as did the Shi'ite scholar 'Allāma al-Ḥillī in the fourteenth century. The *Temples of Light*, one of Suhrawardī's early works, received at least seven commentaries, including one in Turkish and one in verse. There were also commentaries on the *Lamaḥāt*, one of the early philosophical compendia, the *'Imādī Tablets*, a collection of prayers *(munājāt)*, a work entitled *The Forty Idrīsian Names (Arba'ūn Ism al-Idrīsīya)*, and several of the allegories. It would be fair to say on the basis of the bibliographical evidence that his shorter "Peripatetic" works received steady interest in the Iranian philosophical tradition, that interest in *The Philosophy of Illumination* tended to wax and wane, and that when *The Philosophy of Illumination* was the subject of commentaries, the commentators were thoroughly familiar with the Peripatetic works and the issues raised in them. One last bibliographical fact shows the mature Iranian philosophical judgment on Suhrawardī and his place in the history of philosophy. At the end of the nineteenth century the first printed edition of *The Philosophy of Illumination* was published as a lithograph in Iran. It took the form of an excellent edition of Quṭb al-Dīn's commentary, with Mullā Ṣadrā's supercommentary in the margins. When the supercommentary ends, it is followed by Fārābī's *Reconciliation of the Opinions of Plato and Aristotle*. This edition has been ever since a textbook for students of philosophy in the religious academies of Iran.

MARĀGHA TO THE SCHOOL OF ISFAHAN

The bibliographical history of Suhrawardī's influence is paralleled by a philosophical history, one still very imperfectly known.[9] A simplistic but useful way to consider the situation would be to divide Suhrawardī's intellectual followers into those interested in part one of *The Philosophy of Illumination*—the critique of the Peripatetics—and those interested in the introduction and part two—the mythical history of wisdom and the doctrines of light and darkness. The first were the philosophers of Iran, and the second, the Zoroastrian-oriented *Dasātīrīs* of Mughal India and the Iranian nationalists and Western intellectuals influenced by them. The interests of the first were philosophical in the usual sense and were expressed in the ordinary philosophical terminology of classical Islamic philosophy; the interests of the second were gnostic and mythological and were expressed in the specifically Illuminationist terminology of *The Philosophy of Illumination*.

The present chapter is concerned mainly with the first group, of whom the most important were the group of seventeenth-century Iranian philosophers known now as the School of Isfahan. Despite its importance, the story of the reception of Suhrawardī's thought by the later Iranian philosophical tradition is far too complicated a subject to deal with in detail here, but certain features of this reception do need to be mentioned.

First, it cannot be said too clearly that the Iranian philosophers of later centuries understood Suhrawardī not as a gnostic but as a philosopher, albeit one with strong mystical proclivities. They too fit this description. For the most part the School of Isfahan philosophers and their successors in the three centuries since were not physicians or astronomers, as their predecessors through the thirteenth century usually had been; they were mystics and religious scholars. Nonetheless, they were philosophers first and foremost, interested in rational argument and philosophical analysis above all else.

Second, it was Suhrawardī who set the agenda for the philosophers of the School of Isfahan, narrowing the focus of the Avicennan tradition to a particular set of issues raised mostly in his critique of the Peripatetics. The most important were the theory of knowledge by presence and his rejection of the reality of pure existence, but the World of Image, his critique of Peripatetic logic, and the interpretation of symbolism were also important issues. In these questions, Suhrawardī had supporters like Mīr Dāmād, but the later debate was shaped above all by the towering figure of Mullā Ṣadrā. It was he who formulated the doctrine of the primacy of existence, the teaching that there is an underlying unity to all being, in direct contradiction of Suhrawardī's positing of the individual existent as the fundamental ontological unit. Later Iranian philosophers split over the issue—whether existence or quiddity was primal—and remain divided over it to this day, though the followers of Mullā Ṣadrā seem to be in the ascendant.

Third, Suhrawardī's influence was exercised not only, or even mostly, through *The Philosophy of Illumination.* All of his books were studied. Moreover, the commentators and early Illuminationists, particularly Shahrazūrī, had immense influence in determining how Suhrawardī would be read. Philosophers like Shahrazūrī and Quṭb al-Dīn Shīrāzī were thoroughly trained in the Avicennan tradition and ensured that Suhrawardī would be understood in terms of the larger Islamic philosophical tradition.

We cannot go much further. When Suhrawardī lived, four centuries had passed since the first Arabic translations of Greek philosophical works. Three centuries had passed since Kindī, the first major Islamic philosopher. A century and a half had passed since the death of Avicenna. But eight centuries have passed since, during which the system developed by Suhrawardī was elaborated, criticized, and modified by a continuous tradition of philosophers in the Iranian world. Mullā Ṣadrā has been studied by modern scholars, although hardly in the detail that he deserves. A little work has been done on Sabziwārī, a nineteenth-century follower of Mullā Ṣadrā. Not much more has been done. The philosophy of Mīr Dāmād, an Illuminationist and the teacher of Mullā Ṣadrā, is very imperfectly known. Most of the other figures of the School of Isfahan, their predecessors and their successors, are little more than names to us. Relatively few works have been published and almost none have been translated or studied in detail in Western languages. We can expect that our view of Islamic philosophy and of Suhrawardī's place in it will change considerably as this long tradition becomes better known.

Why should we care, you might ask. First, Suhrawardī is a philosopher of considerable importance in Islam, the common ancestor of the two main surviving philosophical schools in modern Iran. Second, these issues raise questions about our interpretation of other parts of the Islamic tradition. It has, for example, become common to refer to "Islamic Neoplatonism," in which are included all manner of thinkers who incorporate some sort of emanationist scheme into their metaphysics. Thus, the term is applied to such varied philosophers as Fārābī, Avicenna, Suhrawardī, and Mullā Ṣadrā. The term is decidedly problematic, considering that, for example, Suhrawardī was in the habit of referring to Avicenna and his school as "the followers of the Peripatetics." Third, the appearance of a self-consciously non-Peripatetic school in Islamic philosophy raises suggestive parallels with the European Renaissance, in which trends of thought such as Platonism and Hermetism played an important role. Above all, everything we now know indicates that this later Iranian philosophical tradition possesses great philosophical richness and subtlety and that it will repay our study.

MYSTICISM AND THE DECLINE OF SCIENCE IN ISLAM

With that wonderful disregard of practicality characteristic of curricula throughout history, the undergraduates in the new universities of thirteenth-century Europe were required to study advanced logic and Aristotelian natural philosophy. Those who completed this daunting program of study and received the degree of master of arts were made to stay on for a few years instructing the younger students in these subjects. Often these young teachers were simultaneously doing advanced work in the faculties of theology, law, or medicine. They were not allowed to teach or write on theology, only on logic and natural philosophy, which explains why medieval European philosophers typically did their writing on logic while they were relatively young. It was only to be expected that these young masters of arts should often intrude into subjects that their elders thought were properly the domain of fully trained theologians. It was only to be expected that their elders should make regular—and quite ineffectual—efforts to keep them in the place that God had ordained for graduate students.

In the Condemnations of 1277 the bishop of Paris and his theological advisors rejected 219 propositions supposedly held by masters of arts at the University of Paris. The underlying issue seems to have been whether God could do what is impossible in nature—whether God could do what Aristotle had said He could not. The theologians were thus arguing for God's unfettered freedom to create as He willed. They did, however, hold that

God was bound by the laws of logic and thus could not do anything that involved a logical contradiction, that God could do what was naturally impossible but not what was logically impossible. It has been argued that this distinction was deeply fruitful in paving the way for the rise of science in the West by encouraging thought experiments on subjects such as the motion of the universe as a whole and the possible existence of other worlds. Such a view of things was a middle way between the deductive rationalism of the Aristotelians and an extreme occasionalism that would have made investigation of laws of nature a futile exercise.[10]

Such a middle path made sense from the point of view of medieval Christian theologians. On the one hand, fettering God with Aristotelian philosophy rendered religion subservient at best and intellectually irrelevant at worst. On the other hand, the theologians had good reasons to keep God within the domain of reason. The doctrines of the Church were understood by reason; what sense would subtle theologizing about the Trinity make if contradictory propositions about it could simultaneously be true? Likewise, the Church as an institution required revelation—the expression of God's arbitrary will—as the basis of its spiritual authority. Nonetheless, only the view that God was rational could preserve the Church from challenge by rivals claiming independent spiritual authority—mystics, for example, with their claim of direct contact with the source of the Church's authority—and, of course, Muslims. The Church required logic to support its own preeminence, but not too much lest it be subordinated to philosophy, and it could do without Aristotelian natural philosophy, if necessary. The arts masters of medieval Europe thus spent their energies speculating on physical science. They could do so in the knowledge that things might be other than they were but that the universe would nonetheless make sense. Two centuries later the Scientific Revolution began in Europe, pulling together ideas polished by these young medieval natural philosophers.

But why did Islam not follow a similar path and carry out a Scientific Revolution before Europe? It had started practicing science before Europe and remained far ahead of Europe until the thirteenth century. It too had the works of Aristotle—and theologians condemning Aristotelian rationalism. Nonetheless, Islam eventually spawned a subtle metaphysics based on mysticism, not modern physical science. Why? Three intellectual factors combined to lead Islamic thought away from the paths that might have led to an Islamic scientific revolution.

First, Muslim philosophers, Suhrawardī included, were firmly wedded to the notion of a world without beginning in time. Avicenna's analysis of contingency in an eternal world turned Islamic thinkers toward an analysis of creation based on ontological hierarchies, not temporal chains of causality. Thought about the creation of the world led them to metaphysics and ontology, not to natural philosophy. Thus, Suhrawardī was inspired by Plato to speculate on the entities of the intelligible world, not to attempt to reconcile the cosmogony of the *Timaeus* with the account of the creation of the world in scripture, as some of his Christian contemporaries had done.

Second, Muslim theologians adopted an extreme occasionalism that did not bind God to the laws of nature at all. At its most radical, Islamic Kalam theology postulated a universe destroyed and recreated in every instant in accordance with God's arbitrary will. Moreover, the supreme Muslim science was religious law, not theology. No one thought that the times of the five daily prayers could be deduced from reason or could even be explained rationally, except in a very general way. Clearly, God's will expressed as law was arbitrary. Nor were there central Islamic institutions needing the security of reason to protect them from alternative religious challenges. The authority of Islam was protected by the nearly universal recognition of the validity of Islamic law, not by doctrinal uniformity or the rational explication of dogma. It is true that Muslim theologians had begun to make serious use of philosophy by the thirteenth century, but by then the interest of Muslim philosophers in natural science was on the wane.

Third, we might ask of the theologians of Paris: who would assert that God is not bound by the laws of logic? The answer is Muslims in general and Muslim mystics in particular. Medieval Muslims displayed an extraordinary tolerance for religious contradictions. There were four equally authoritative schools of law, seven official texts of the Qur'ān, each with two official versions, "sober" and "drunken" mystics who acknowledged the appropriateness of each other's approaches, etc. Muslim scholars practiced different sciences with quite contrary principles without trying to bring them into systematic agreement. For example, Quṭb al-Dīn Shīrāzī, the commentator on Suhrawardī, wrote a large Persian philosophical encyclopedia called *The Pearly Crown.*[11] The core of the work is a systematic survey of the rational sciences, but it also has a very long "appendix"—the equivalent of more than a thousand printed pages—in which he includes a translation of a treatise on Kalam theology by Fakhr al-Dīn al-Rāzī; two accounts of political science, one based on "purely rational principles" and one not; and an account of monistic metaphysics translated from the work of a member of Ibn 'Arabī's school. It does not seem to occur to Quṭb al-Dīn that his three wildly different accounts of reality and two accounts of politics are contradictory, and he seems calmly to assume that different sciences have different methods and different conclusions. Why medieval Muslims should have been so tolerant of intellectual contradictions is a fact that has never been adequately explained, but a fact it is and one that seems to have kept Muslims from creating universal systems within which all of religion and reality could be explained in a single logical structure.

But those most indifferent to the demands of logical consistency were the mystics. Within Christianity the mystics caused some disquiet, even though they were bound within orders at least nominally subordinate to the Pope, and their theologians were watched carefully for heresy. In Islam there were no such limits. Islam values orthopraxy, not orthodoxy, and there was no central religious hierarchy to license and regulate mystical orders. Muslim mystics were free to speculate as wildly as they wished, and they would cause little offense as long as they scrupulously obeyed the laws of Islam, which usually they did. The most influential mystical theology was that of Ibn 'Arabi, who rejected all notion of logical consistency as applying to God. For him each creature has its own God, the sum of the divine attributes expressed in that creature. Any sort of theological formulation inevitably failed to capture more than a particular view of the truth about God. Logic did not apply to God, and so the world is beyond capturing by logic. In a sense, for Ibn Arabi each creature had its own logic. Mystical attainment allows one to see more clearly and to see into a realm that Aristotle's philosophy had shown only dimly, but what it shows is the world of metaphysical entities, not the messy and irredemiably inconsistent world we live in. Our world consists of paradoxes beyond which the mystic must pass. Suhrawardī taught later Muslim philosophers that the resolution of these paradoxes was the proper task of the brightest and purest souls. His followers were to take subtle scholastic speculation far beyond what was achieved in Europe. The cost was a near-total loss of interest in the things of this world and a withering of the tradition of Islamic science.

The discovery of mysticism by the philosophers thus coincided with a loss of interest in natural philosophy. Suhrawardī omitted physics from *The Philosophy of Illumination.* Philosophy collapsed into logic and metaphysics, with physics and mathematics dropping out. Even logic seems to have lost its power and interest since the philosopher cannot bring it into the intelligible realms. Logic became almost exclusively the domain of the jurisconsults and their students, who valued it for its usefulness in semantic analysis of legal texts.[12] By the time of the School of Isfahan in the seventeenth century, philosophy was thus further reduced to metaphysics, and the prime tool of discovery was mystical experience.

But in another sense Suhrawardī's project was not a retreat from reason, and his rationalized mysticism was the framework within which the philosophers understood the wild speculations of Ibn 'Arabī. He had constructed a science of mystic lights, a disciplined intellectual structure whose principles were known by mystical intuition but which were explicated by reason. While its principles were significantly different from those of the sciences of the Peripatetics, it nonetheless claimed to be a science, not gnosticism or the simple recording of the experiences of ecstacy. And, of course, it is different from modern physical science, which also claims to give an account of reality based on empirical experience. Contemporary critics of science have sometimes proposed that modern science is simply one rhetorical system among others, that its claims to be a privileged path to truth are arrogant and unjustified. If that is so, then the system of Suhrawardī and his followers provides an unusually good test case.

In medieval Europe rational philosophy was both accepted and restricted. It was accepted in the sense that it was seen as the rightful handmaiden of theology. Philosophy, both metaphysics and natural philosophy, thus had a secure place in the educational curriculum and the scholarly community. On the other hand, since theology was central to medieval Christianity in a way that it never was to medieval Islam, philosophy was tightly controlled by the church. The paradoxical result was that the central intellectual discipline of Christendom—dogmatic theology—was restricted to the highest levels of the educational system. That left a gap at the lower levels, those taught by the masters of arts of the new universities. Given the careers for which most university students were destined, in the government usually, one would have expected the basis of the curriculum to be subjects like rhetoric, history, and law. Instead, through the historical accident of the rediscovery of Aristotle coinciding with the foundation of the universities, natural science became a major part of the undergraduate curriculum. Curricula often being quite illogical, many people ended up doing science. The result was that European philosophers saw science and natural philosophy as a promising field in which to search for answers to the most important philosophical questions. The result, three centuries later, was the Scientific Revolution.[13]

In Islam the calculation was different. First, since there was no particular reason to restrict the study of Islamic law, it remained the basis of Islamic education in a way that Christian theology was not in medieval Europe. Science and natural philosophy, though they attracted a handful of the best minds, remained subjects outside the mainstream of Islamic education, particularly since they had never quite escaped the taint of heresy and unbelief. Muslim philosophers, moreover, had made a decision with far-reaching effects. Suhrawardī and others convinced them that mysticism was the most promising tool available for solving the great philosophical problems. Whereas most Islamic philosophers of the ninth through thirteenth centuries had been physicians, astronomers, or both, most later Islamic philosophers were were mystics and religious scholars. There were many exceptions, but the pattern was clear. In the view of most Islamic philosophers after the thirteenth century, mysticism was the most promising tool of philosophical research available to them, one that could solve the great problems that reason had posed but been unable to answer. They used mysticism to develop a subtle philosophy in which metaphysics, ontology, and epistemology were the central disciplines. Even today the philosophers of this tradition—and there are still many, mostly in Iran—consider physical science to be of limited philosophical interest. Whether they were right to take the path of mysticism is a question that no historian has the right to answer.

THE PROBLEM OF CONSCIOUSNESS AND THE RECURRENCE OF METAPHYSICS

Like Descartes, Suhrawardī thought that consciousness was the fundamental metaphysical fact. Self-awareness could not be epiphenomenal to something that was not itself conscious. Suhrawardī, though, did not think that consciousness could be just one ingredient among many in the universe. If there is something self-aware in the universe, that entity must be the starting-point both for our knowledge of the world and for the being of the world as a whole. Consciousness is the fixed point around which everything else turns. Despite Suhrawardī's acceptance of the mind/body distinction, despite his famous use of light and darkness as the fundamental metaphysical principles of being, he is not a dualist. His philosophy of illumination is "not the dualism of the infidel Magi," he firmly tells us.

And he is right to question dualism. It would be easy for us to imagine a universe—as our ancestors actually did—in which everything is alive and conscious, in which it is the nature of substance to be self-aware: "All things are full of gods." In such a universe the problem of dualism does not arise because existence implies consciousness. Likewise, we can imagine a universe in which nothing is conscious. It is the clockwork universe of Newton and the molecular biologists, but it is not the universe we actually live in. No matter how well we understand brain functioning and its relationship to conscious states, the mind is not reducible to the brain; the question "what is it like to *be* a brain?" has no answer, whereas, "What is it like to *have* a brain?" does. We have brains, but we are not brains. Indeed, if brain states are consciousness, we are once again in the animist universe of our ancestors where activity implies life. We can approach consciousness from two directions: (1) its relationship to its material organs, and (2) its internal structure. Each path has been fruitfully explored, by biologists and psychologists respectively. We can now even relate some states of our material organs to our subjective states, the contents of our conscious minds, but at the end of each path remains the simple inexplicable fact of our awareness of our selves, our bodies, and our conscious states.

Suhrawardī argued—rightly, I think—that consciousness is in principle inexplicable either in terms of its own states or in terms of any material organs. Aristotle told him in his dream that to solve the problem of knowledge, he would have to look to his own self, to his consciousness, and so he did. Likewise, he chose to solve his metaphysical problems in terms of consciousness—or, to use his own language, immaterial light. He was not a solipsist, so he argued that we are all immaterial lights generated from higher immaterial lights. Surely we cannot be lights/conscious minds coming to be from inert matter; to be an immaterial light is not to be a brain. Consciousness is active and matter is not, so consciousness must be the cause of activity in the universe. His universe is closer to the animist universe in which everything is alive and aware. He argues that men and animals have souls, and souls are immaterial lights and thus conscious. His Platonic Forms are also alive and conscious; they rule and keep in being the natural kinds of the world. Everything has in some way a conscious mind associated with it that makes it what it is. He is enough of a dualist to accept the distinction between the soul and the matter that embodies it, yet even this matter is directly generated from the immaterial lights. The respective matters of the spheres are, as it were, shadows of the immaterial lights, their dark backs facing away from God, the Light of Lights. How exactly this might be is not easy to tell, and it is probably unfair to ask Suhrawardī to explain it in rigorous physical terms. The cosmology of *The Philosophy of Illumination* is a Timaean "likely story," a great myth or allegory showing as much of the inner structure of the universe as we are able to grasp. Yet the centrality of consciousness in this system is not a speculative part of the "likely story"; it is fundamental to Suhrawardī's whole way of philosophizing and thus part of his permanent contribution to metaphysics.

We have not solved the riddle of consciousness in our day, only learned enough more to deepen our confusion. Suhrawardī's warning that consciousness cannot be generated from or explained by matter remains valid. The sciences of psychology and brain physiology attempt to explain the functioning of our minds, and their practitioners sometimes try to dismiss consciousness itself as epiphenomenal to brain functioning. Such a move, however, places the cart before the horse. Everything else we know, as Aristotle told Suhrawardī, presumes the knowledge of our selves—our consciousness. It is not the reality of the mind that can be doubted; it is the reality of the brain. Any satisfactory metaphysics, epistemology, or philosophy of mind, Suhrawardī warns us, must start with the reality of consciousness.

But if the consciousness of the individual is to be explained, rather than just left as a solipsistic brute fact, and if it is to be explained without denying the reality of the external world, are we not then driven to indulge in metaphysical speculations of the sort that Surhawardī gave us in the second book of *The Philosophy of Illumination*? Perhaps we are. If the mind is not an emergent property of the matter of the brain, and if we are to accept the reality of inanimate matter, do we not need to explain where the conscious mind comes from—and where and what it is? Suhrawardī's metaphysical system cannot stand as it is, of course, for we no longer have need of immaterial souls of the spheres to drive the planets in their courses nor of Platonic Forms to keep rabbits and louseworts breeding true. God, the Light of Lights, on the other hand, remains a possibility. When Bertrand Russell was sent to jail in World War I, the warden, when Russell said that he was an atheist, asked how to spell it and commented, "Well, there are many religions, but I suppose they all worship the same God."[14] It is a story that might have been told by Rūmī. The incident is emblematic, for philosophers have never quite been able to put to rest the question of God's existence, one way or the other. Muḥammad-Bāqir al-Ṣadr, a modernist Shi'ite philosopher executed by Saddam Hussein in 1980, wrote a book constructing an elaborate proof of God's existence based on Russell's theory of probability.[15] I do not know what an Illuminationist metaphysics would look like if rewritten in the light of modern science, but I suspect that the old questions of cosmology, God, angels, and all the rest may still lie in ambush, waiting for the moment when we incautiously admit that materialistic science, however clever it might be, cannot explain the simple experience of the subjective reality our own inner being.

APPENDIX I

Henry Corbin and Suhrawardī Studies

The most prominent interpreter of Suhrawardī in modern scholarship was the late French orientalist Henry Corbin (1903–78). Corbin was given a copy of Quṭb al-Dīn Shīrāzī's commentary on *The Philosophy of Illumination* by Louis Massignon. Corbin later came to see this as a sort of mystical initiation into the Illuminationist tradition. Though Corbin published his first article on Suhrawardī in 1935, a translation of the allegory *The Sound of Gabriel's Wing (Āwāz-i Parr-i Jibrā'īl),* his serious work on Suhrawardī began a few years later. He had gone to Istanbul in 1939 to collect manuscripts of Suhrawardī's works and was trapped there by the outbreak of war. His visit of a few months having lengthened to six years, he prepared a critical edition of *The Philosophy of Illumination* and two other minor works. At the end of the war he went to Tehran, where in 1946 he published *Les motifs zoroastriens dans la philosophie de Sohrawardî* in French and Persian. Later he published the metaphysical chapters for Suhrawardī's three "Peripatetic " works, arranged for the publication of the allegories and Persian works and then translated them, and translated *The Philosophy of Illumination.* A volume of his *En Islam Iranien* was devoted to Suhrawardī.[1]

Though there had been occasional studies of Suhrawardī by Western scholars, Corbin was the first to devote major effort to him. He and his excellent editions were responsible for Suhrawardī's popularization in Western scholarship. One must treat Corbin's interpretations of Suhrawardī with great caution, however, for he was as much a part of the Illuminationist tradition as an objective student of it. Pursuing his own philosophical (or theosophical, as he would probably have preferred) project, he introduced his own ideas into his interpretations. There are several serious limitations in Corbin's interpretation of Suhrawardī: First, he was not much interested in the systematic philosophical aspects of Suhrawardī's thought. Thus, he devoted great attention to Suhrawardī's symbolism but neglected the systematic works, which he dismissed as "Peripatetic." His edition of Suhrawardī omits the logical and physical sections of the Peripatetic works, and his translation of *The Philosophy of Illumination* omits the section on logic, though this is where the systematic critique of Avicennan

Peripateticism is to be found. Second, his renderings of key terms are tendentious. *Ḥikmat al-ishrāq*, which I render as "philosophy of illumination," Corbin translates as *sagesse* or *théosophie orientale*. Such renderings enable him to discuss at length concepts like "the orient of light" that are not present in the text. Third, Corbin—and even more, his nationalist Iranian admirers—saw Suhrawardī primarily in the context of the Persian spiritual tradition—much more an heir of Zoroaster than of Plato or Aristotle. This he does by building a great deal on a few unrepresentative passages. There are other such errors caused by overemphasizing minor texts at the expense of the context as a whole. I have discussed these issues at length above.

Nevertheless, Corbin deserves great credit for his tireless labors to reveal Suhrawardī's importance. Current scholarly interest in later Islamic philosophy is due in considerable part to his influence, and a good deal of other scholarship follows Corbin's scholarly methods.

APPENDIX II

Suhrawardī's Dream of Aristotle

Suhrawardī's dream of Aristotle is often cited, almost always for the passage at the end in which Aristotle identifies certain Sufis as the true heirs of the divine philosophers among the Ancients. In fact, the main point of the account is to show the relationship between Suhrawardī's theory of self-consciousness and his epistemology, and it occurs in a chapter discussing those subjects. In view of its importance for Suhrawardī's intellectual development and for the theme of the present book, it is worth presenting in a full English translation. It has previously been translated by Mehdi Ha'iri and partially by Mehdi Amin Razavi.[1]

The dream occurs in his *Intimations (Talwīḥāt)*, which he describes as a "short work," one of those "in which I have summarized for you the principles of the Peripatetics according to their method."[2] Apart from the use of standard philosophical terminology, the doctrine presented in the dream account is identical with that of *The Philosophy of Illumination*. The translation is literal.

STORY AND DREAM

For a long time I was extremely busy with intense thought and mystical exercise. I could not solve the problem of knowledge, and what was said in the books did not any make sense to me. One night a sudden trance resembling sleep came upon me. I was in a state of veiling pleasure, shining thunderbolt, and flashing light when the shape of a man appeared before me. I looked at him and realized he was that aid of souls and leader of philosophy, the First Teacher [Aristotle] with an appearance that astonished me and a splendor that dazzled me. He greeted me with such courtesy that my astonishment ceased, and my alarm was changed into affection. I complained to him about the difficulty of this problem, and he replied, "Consult your self, and it will be solved for you."

"How is that?"

"When you apprehend your self, is your apprehension of your essence by your essence[3] or by something else? If the latter, then you would either have another faculty or else an essence apprehending your essence, but either would result in an absurd regression. So when you apprehend your essence by your essence, is it by virtue of some effect of your essence in your essence?"

I said, "Yes."

He said, "If the effect does not correspond to your essence, then it is not its form, and so you would not have apprehended your essence."

"But the effect is the form of my essence."

"Is it your form of a self absolutely or is it particularized by other attributes?"

I chose the second, and he said, "Every form in the soul is universal. Even if it is composed from many universals, it is still not in itself impossible for it to be shared. If we assume that it is impossible for it to be shared, then there must be something else that prevents its being shared. But you apprehend yourself, which by essence cannot be shared. Therefore, this apprehension of the self cannot be by the form."

I said, "It is the notion of 'I' that is apprehended."

He replied, "There is nothing about the notion of 'I' as the notion of 'I' that prevents it from being shared. You know that 'particular' qua its being one particular and not another is universal. 'This', 'I', 'we', and 'he' all have [71] intelligible universal meanings qua their immaterial notions and do not identify a particular."

I said, "How then is it?"

"Since your knowledge of your essence is not by a faculty distinct from your essence, you therefore know that you and nothing else are what apprehends your essence and that it is not by an effect or an effect corresponding to your essense or an effect not corresponding to it. Thus your essence is the intellect, the intellecting one, and the intellected."

I said, "Tell me more."

He said, "Do you not apprehend that which you control in a continuing apprehension that you cannot escape from?"

"Yes."

"Is this due to the occurence of an individual form in your essence? You already know the absurdity of that."

"Rather it occurs by extracting universal attributes."

He said, "And you move your particular body and know that it is a particular individual body, but what you take from the form itself does not prevent its being shared, so your apprehension of it is an apprehension of your body in such a way that its notion cannot be conceived to belong to another."

He continued, "Have you not read in my books that the soul thinks with the aid of the cognitive faculty, which is what separates and combines the particulars and arranges the middle terms?[4] The imaginative faculty has no contact with universals because it is corporeal. If the soul has no awareness of particulars, how can it combine their premises? How can it extract the universals from the particulars? In which thing does it employ the cognitive faculty? How does it take from the imagination, and what does the combining by the imaginative faculty teach it? How does it aid thought in knowledge of the result? Moreover, the imaginative faculty is corporeal; how does it apprehend itself? Is the form in the soul taken from it universal? You know that your imaginative faculty and your faculty of estimation are two existent individual things, yet you know that the estimation denies the two."

I said, "Guide me! May God requite you with good among the people of knowledge."

He said, "Since you know that it does not apprehend itself [72] by an effect corresponding to it, nor by a form, know that intellection is the presence of the thing to the incorporeal essence—or if you would rather, I could say that it is the lack of concealment from it. The latter is better since it includes the apprehension both of itself and of another since while the thing is not present to itself, it is nonetheless not concealed from itself. As for the soul, it is incorporeal and not concealed from itself. It apprends its own essence to the degree of its incorporeality and is not concealed from itself. Since it is not present to its eye, like the heaven, the earth, and other such things are, its form must be present to it either as particulars, in which case the form would be in faculties present to it, or as universals, in which case it would be in its essence. This is because some entities apprehended are universal and cannot be imprinted in bodies. What is apprehended is the form itself that is present, not that which is extraneous to the conception. If you say of that which is extraneous that it is apprehended, it is said in a secondary sense. Its essence is not concealed from its essence, nor is its body whether as one collectivity nor as faculties apprehending its body as a collectivity. Just as the imagination is not concealed from its essence, neither is the imaginal form. The soul apprehends it due to its presence, not by forming an image of it in the the soul itself. The greater is its incorporeality, the greater and more intense its apprehension of its essence. If its rule over the body were stronger, the presence to it of the faculties and parts of the soul would be more intense."

Then he said to me, "Know that knowledge is a perfection of existence with respect to its notion, and it does not necessitate multiplicity. Thus it necessarily exists in the Necessary Being." He indicated what I have explained in the general chapter above.[5] "The essence of the Necessary Existent is incorporeal and so is sheer existence. All things are present to it in a relation of origination and control *(iḍāfa mabda'īya tasalluṭīya)* because all of them are correlates of its essence, and neither its essence nor any correlate of its essence is concealed from it. Its lack of concealment from its essence and the correlates of its essence, along with its incorporeality [73] are its apprehension, as we explained with respect to the soul. Thus the issue of knowledge in every sense goes back to the lack of concealment of something from the incorporeal, whether it is a form or something else. Relations are possible with respect to the Necessary Existent, as are negations, without affecting its unity. The multiplicity of its names are due to these negations and relations. Therefore, 'not even the weight of a mote' escapes from his knowledge 'in the heavens and the earth.'[6] If we ruled something other than our bodies in the way that we rule our bodies, we would apprehend it in the same way that I have said we apprehend our bodies without need for a form. From this it is clear that It knows all things and apprehends the numerical instances of existence without need of a form or image. It is the same as their presence to it and their being ruled by it." Then he said to me, "This is enough for you on the subject of knowledge." Then he guided me to matters that I have explained in detail in this book.

I said to him, "What is the meaning of contact and union of souls with each other and with the active intellect?"

He replied, "So long as you are in this world of yours, you are veiled. When you are separated from it and are perfected, you will have this union and contact."

I said, "We used to criticize the sects of the brethren of abstraction and the sages for their use of the expression 'contact' since it can only apply to bodies."

He replied, "Know that in your mind you intellect absolute contact between two incorporeal intelligible bodies. Do you apprehend the intelligible organs of one animal along with contact?"

"Yes."

"Is there a definite direction or an individual extension in your mind?"

"No."

"It is only an intellectual contact, so the souls also find an intellectual—not a bodily—contact and union among themselves in the higher world. You will know it after you are separated from your body."

Then he began to praise his teacher, [74] the divine Plato, so lavishly that I was bewildered and said, "Have any of the philosophers of Islam reached his station?"

"No, nor to a part of a thousandth part of his rank."

Then I began to list a number of those with whom I was familiar. He showed no interest in any of them, but when I reached Abū Yazīd al-Bisṭāmī, Abū Muḥammad Sahl b. 'Abd Allāh al-Tustarī, and others like them, he seemed to be delighted and said, "These are in truth the philosophers and sages. They did not stop with formal knowledge but went on to the knowledge that comes from presence, contact, and witnessing. They are not distracted by the connections of matter. They have "the nearness and the good end."[7] They move as we move and speak according to whay we say."

Then he departed from me and left me weeping at his departure. How grievous was that state!

NOTES

PREFACE

1. Harvard Middle Eastern Monographs 26; Cambridge: Harvard Center for Middle Eastern Studies, 1992.

2. Islamic Translation Series; Provo: Brigham Young University Press, forthcoming.

3. Marshall G. S. Hodgson, *The Venture of Islam: Conscience and History in a World Civilization* (Chicago: University of Chicago Press, 1974), 1:57–60.

4. See pp. 33–35 below. On the concepts of wisdom and philosophy in this period, see Jean Jolivet, "L'idée de la sagesse et sa fonction dans la philosophie des 4e et 5e siècles," *Arabic Sciences and Philosophy* 1 (1991): 31–65.

5. Hodgson, *Venture*, 1:44–45, 49.

6. Edward Said, *Orientalism* (New York: Pantheon Books, 1978).

7. For a survey of the literature of mysticism as a religious category, see E. Samuel Brainard, "Defining 'Mystical Experience'," *Journal of the American Academy of Religion* 44.2 (Summer 1996): 359–83.

CHAPTER 1. THE PROBLEM OF SUHRAWARDĪ

1. Suhrawardī, *Kalimāt al-Taṣawwuf*, ¶55, in Suhrawardī, *Three Treatises*, ed. Najaf-Gholī Ḥabībī (Lahore: Iran-Pakistan Institute of Persian Studies, 1397/1977).

2. For Corbin's views of Suhrawardī, see *Suhrawardī d'Alep: Fondateur de la doctrine illuminative* (Paris: G. P. Maisonneuve, 1939), *Les motifs zoroastriens dans la philosophie de Sohravardī* (Publications de la Société d'Iranologie 3; Tehran: du Courrier, 1946), *En Islam iranien*, 4 vols. (Paris: Gallimard, 1971), vol. 2: *Sohravardī et les Platoniciens de Perse*, and the *prolégomènes* to each of his following critical editions of Suhrawardī's works: *Opera Metaphysica et Mystica I* (Istanbul: Maarif Matbaasi, 1945); *Opera Metaphysica et Mystica II* (Tehran: Institut Franco-Iranien, 1954); *Opera Metaphysica et Mystica III* (Tehran: Institut Franco-Iranien, 1970). See also Corbin's translations in *SAe* and *Le Livre de la Sagesse Orientale: Kitāb Ḥikmat al-Ishrāq*, ed. Christian Jambet (Paris: Verdier, 1986). A short account is his *History of Islamic Philosophy*, trans. Liadain Sherrard (London: Kegan Paul International, 1993), 205–20. For a comprehensive discussion of Corbin's views, see Daryush Shayegan, *Henry Corbin: La topographie spirituelle de l'islam iranien* (Paris: Éditions de La Différence, 1990), especially

134–38, 192–201. For a critique of the "theosophical" interpretation of later Islamic philosophy, including Suhrawardī, see Hossein Ziai, "Explaining the Philosophical Meaning of Ṣadr al-Dīn Shīrāzī's 'Metaphysical Philosophy,' *Ḥikmat-e Mota'āliyeh*," *Iranshenasi* 5.2 (Summer 1993): 354–64.

An interpretation similar to that of Corbin is given by S. H. Nasr, *Three Muslim Sages* (Cambridge: Harvard University Press, 1964), chapter 2; idem, "Suhrawardī," in *A History of Muslim Philosophy*, ed. M. M. Sharif (Wiesbaden: Otto Harrassowitz, 1963), 1:372–98. Nasr also gives a religious significance to Suhrawardī's life and teachings. See, in this regard, idem, *An Introduction to Islamic Cosmological Doctrines* (revised edition; Boulder: Shambhala, 1978.), chap. 12. Ian Richard Netton, *Allāh Transcendent: Studies in the Structure and Semiotics of Islamic Philosophy, Theology, and Cosmology* (Exeter Arabic and Islamic Series 5; New York: Routledge, 1989), 256–68, 288–306, gives a similar interpretation while attempting to interpret Suhrawardī in terms of contemporary semiotic theory.

3. The best rigorous modern philosophical study of the Illuminationist tradition and its successors is Toshihiko Izutsu, *The Concept and Reality of Existence* (Studies in the Humanities and Social Relations; Tokyo: Keio Institute of Cultural and Linguistic Studies, 1971); though it is mainly concerned with the nineteenth-century philosopher Sabziwārī, it deals with the whole earlier ontological tradition. On Suhrawardī specifically, see my *SML* and Ziai, *ZKI*; idem, "Shihāb al-Dīn Suhrawardī," "The Illuminationist Tradition," and "Mullā Ṣadrā: His Life and Works," in Seyyed Hossein Nasr and Oliver Leaman, eds., *History of Islamic Philosophy* (Routledge History of World Philosophies I:1; London: Routledge, 1996), 434–96, 643–62. Older works from a philosophical perspective include Muhammad Iqbal, *The Development of Metaphysics in Persia* (Lahore: Bazm-Iqbal, 1959 [1908]), 96–116; A. Dānā-Sirisht, *Khulāsa-i Afkār-i Suhrawardī wa Mullā Ṣadrā* (Tehran, 1934); Muḥammad-'Alī Abū Rayyān, *Uṣūl al-Falsafa al-Ishrāqīya* (Beirut: Dār al-Ṭalaba al-'Arab, 1969), and idem, "al-Ishrāqīya Madrasa Aflāṭūnīya Islāmīya: Munāqashat Qaḍīyat al-Maṣdar al-Īrānī," in Ibrāhīm Madkūr, ed., *al-Kitāb al-Tidhkārī: Shaykh al-Ishrāq Shihāb al-Dīn al-Suhrawardī* (al-Maktaba al-'Arabīya 159; Cairo: Wizārat al-Thaqāfa, 1394/1974), 37–62. There are, of course, many more articles.

4. *ShS*, 6–7.

5. I have used and consistently cited two editions: Aḥmed, *ShNA*; and Abū Rayyān, ed., *ShNR*, which appears to be superior to the Aḥmed edition, of which Abū Rayyān was seemingly unaware. Toward the end of this project another edition came to my attention: ed. 'Abd al-Karīm Abū Shuwayrib (1st ed.; [Tripoli, Libya?]: Jam'īyat al-Da'wa al-Islāmīya al-'Ālamīya, 1988). It was done on the basis of two Islanbul MSS, but it is sharply criticized by Abū Rayyān, 44–50. The seventeenth-century Persian translation of *Nuzhat al-Arwāḥ* by Maqṣūd-'Alī Tabrīzī has recently been published by M. T. Dānish-Pazhūh and M. S. Mawlā'ī (Tehran, 1986) and differs (considerably at times) from the Arabic text. Part of the notice on Suhrawardī in this text has been translated in *MVT*, 1–4. Thackston's translation is based on the partial edition of S. H. Nasr in *SMj*, 3:13–30. This edi-

tion includes the Arabic text as well as the Persian translation of Tabrīzī. I have cited both the Aḥmed and the Abū Rayyān editions and have preferred the readings of Abū Rayyān unless otherwise noted. I have not used the Tabrīzī Persian translation. The *Nuzhat* is based on earlier works, al-Mubashshir b. Fātik's *Mukhtār al-Ḥikam (Los bocados de oro*, ed. 'Abd al-Raḥmān. Badawī [Madrid, 1377/1958]) being the most important but not the only source.

6. An edition was planned in Iran in the 1960s, but it never was completed. See also Hossein Ziai, "The Manuscript of *al-Shajara al-Ilāhīya*," *Iranshenasi* 2.1 (Spring 1990): 89–108, and the introduction to *ShS*.

CHAPTER 2. SUHRAWARDĪ'S LIFE AND WORKS

1. I know of five major medieval biographies of Suhrawardī, all dating from the early and middle parts of the thirteenth century, written by authors who were one to three generations younger than Suhrawardī. They are:

- Yāqūt al-Ḥamawī, *Kitāb Irshād al-Arīb ilā Ma'rifat al-Adīb al-Ma'rūf bi-Mu'jam al-Udabā' aw Ṭabaqāt al-Udabā'* (1st ed.; Cairo: Maṭba'a Hindīya, 1925), 7:269–72.
- Ibn Abī Uṣaybi'a, *'Uyūn al-Anbā' fī Ṭabaqāt al-Aṭibbā'*, ed. A. Müller (Königsberg, 1884), 1:168–71; the edition by N. Riḍā (Beirut, 1968), 641–646 differs slightly from Müller's.
- Ibn Faḍl Allāh al-'Umarī, *Masālik al-Abṣār fī Mamālik al-Amṣār*, ed. Fuat Sezgin (Publications of the Institute for Arabic-Islamic Science, Ser. C, 46; Frankfurt am Main: Institute for the History of Arabic-Islamic Science, 1988), 9:86–93, which is based largely but not entirely on Ibn Abī Uṣaybi'a.
- Ibn Khallikān, *Wafāyāt al-A'yān wa-Anbā' Abnā' al-Zamān*, ed. Iḥsān 'Abbās (Beirut: Dār al-Thaqāfa, 1968), 6:268–74; trans. W. M. de Slane, *Ibn Khallikan's Biographical Dictionary* (Oriental Translation Fund 59; Paris, 1843–71).
- *ShNA*, 2:119–43; *ShNR*, 600–22.

A slightly later account, significant for its sympathy to Suhrawardī, is al-Dhahabī, *al-'Ibar fī Khabar Man Ghabar*, ed. Ṣalāḥ al-Dīn al-Munajjid (al-Turāth al-'Arabī 10; Kuwait: Wizārat al-Irshād wa'l-Anbā', 1963), 4:263–64. It is based on Ibn Khallikān.

A source for several of the accounts is Ibn Shaddād, the biographer of Saladin and advisor to al-Malik al-Ẓāhir, who was actually involved in Suhrawardī's condemnation; see Bahā al-Dīn Ibn Shaddād, *Sīrat Ṣalāḥ al-Dīn: al-Sīrat al-Yūsufīya*, ed. Jamāl al-Dīn al-Shayyāl (1st ed.; Cairo: al-Khānjī, 1962), 10; trans. *The Life of Salah ud Din Ayyubi* (reprint Rawalpindi: Army Book Club, 1983), 10–11.

A later account, citing skeptical Sufis, is 'Abd al-Raḥmān Jāmī, *Nafaḥāt al-Uns*, ed. M. 'Abidī (Tehran: Iṭṭilā'āt, 1375/1996), 584–86.

As is to be expected, the early biographies are interdependent to a considerable degree, though each has information not shared by the others. Yāqūt, Ibn Abī

Uṣaybi'a, and Ibn Khallikān all cite Ibn Shaddād. Ibn Khallikān and Ibn Faḍl Allāh cite Ibn Abī Uṣaybi'a. Shahrazūrī is dependent on either Ibn Abī Uṣaybi'a or on his source Sadīd al-Dīn Ibn Raqīqa, though he seems to have his own sources as well. Viewpoints differ, ranging from Ibn Shaddād's pious hatred of the heretic to Shahrazūrī's frank adulation, with the rest of the sources expressing some degree of cautious reserve.

There are many modern accounts of Suhrawardī, but no really satisfactory historical or bibliographical study. In addition to the works mentioned in ch. 1, nn. 2–3 above, see Nasr, *Sages*, 52–82; George Sarton, *Introduction to the History of Science* (Carnegie Institution Publication 376; Washington, D.C.: Carnegie Institution, 1931), 2/1:361–62; *GAL*, GI:247, SI:781. Most of the modern editions and translations of Suhrawardī's works also contain more or less extensive accounts of his life and works. Most do not add anything new.

2. Ibn Abī Uṣaybi'a, ed. Müller, 2:23.

3. Ibn Abī Uṣaybi'a, ed. Müller, 1:263, 299–301. He too enjoyed the patronage of al-Malik al-Ẓāhir, shortly after Suhrawardī's death.

4. *ShNA*, 2:123; *ShNR*, 603; Hossein Ziai, *EIr*, *s.v.* "Ebn Sahlān al-Sāvī."

5. *ShNA*, 2:124–25; *ShNR*, 605, citing the conclusion of *SMM*, ¶225, in *SMj*, 1:505. This dates the *Mashāri'* at or just before the time of his arrival in Aleppo.

6. *ShNA*, 2:123–24; *ShNR*, 604. Ibn Taghribirdī (ninth cent.), an unfriendly source, goes on at length about the filthiness of his person and dress; *al-Nujūm al-Zāhira fī Mulūk Miṣr wa'l-Qāhira* (Turāthunā; Cairo: Wizārat al-Thaqāfa, n.d.), 6:114–15.

7. *ShNA*, 2:124; *ShNR*, 604–5.

8. Ibn Abī Uṣaybi'a, ed. Müller, 2:204. The works he saw were the *Lamaḥāt*, the *Talwīḥāt*, and *Ma'ārij al-Quds*.

9. See pp. 52–53 below.

10. *ShNA*, 2:126; *ShNR*, 605–6; Ibn Khallikān, ed. 'Abbās, 6:273; Dhahabī, 4:263. The source for the story of Suhrawardī's death by starvation is an account of Suhrawardī's adventures in Aleppo narrated by Sadīd al-Dīn Maḥmūd Ibn Raqīqa, who was a friend of Suhrawardī and another student of Suhrawardī's teacher Mārdīnī. Since Ibn Abī Uṣaybi'a was born about the time that Suhrawardī was killed and died in 1270 and since the story is given in shorter form in Yāqūt, who died in 1227, it is likely that both biographers are citing a written source by Ibn Raqīqa. Ibn Raqīqa does not seem to have been a witness to the events, but Mārdīnī enjoyed the patronage of al-Malik al-Zāhir shortly after Suhrawardī's death, so it is likely that he was the source of Ibn Raqīqa's information; Ibn Shaddād, *Sīrat*, ed. Shayyāl, 10.

Al-Malik al-Ẓāhir was governor of Aleppo from its capture in June 1183 until the following January when he was relieved by Saladin's brother, al-Malik al-'Ādil, and again beginning in late August 1186. If all the dates are accurate, then Suhrawardī must have come to Aleppo in the second half of 1183. It is thus probably significant that the completion of *The Philosophy of Illumination* was on 15 September 1186, the evening of a great conjunction of all seven planets, less than three weeks after al-Malik al-Ẓāhir's return to Aleppo. The gap in al-Ẓāhir's governorship perhaps explains an anecdote placing Suhrawardī in Damascus; al-Ẓāhir had spent the intervening three years with his father, at least part in the Ayyubid capital of Damascus; Ibn Abī Uṣaybi'a, ed. Müller, 2:168; Ibn Khallikān, ed. 'Abbās, 6:269. If Suhrawardī was in Damascus in these years, it may explain the alacrity with which Saladin issued the order for his death.

11. Ibn Khallikān, ed. 'Abbās, 6:273; cf. 6:269; Ibn Abī Uṣaybi'a, ed. Müller, 2:167; Yāqūt, *Irshād*, 7:270; *ShNA*, 2:126; *ShNR*, 607.

12. *HI*, ¶2–3.

13. The longest list is given by *ShNA*, 2:128–29; *ShNR*, 608–9. Shorter lists are given in Ibn Khallikān, ed. 'Abbās, 6:270; Ibn Abī Uṣaybi'a, ed. Müller, 2:170–71; Yāqūt, *Irshād*, 7:270; and in later standard bibliographical sources like Ḥājjī Khalīfa's *Kashf al-Ẓunūn* with its supplements; see *GAL*, 1:437–38, S1:781–83, 819. More detailed information on manuscripts, including commentaries, is given in Hellmut Ritter, "Philologika ix. Die vier Suhrawardī: Ihre Werke in Stambuler Handschriften," *Der Islam* 24 (1937): 270–86. It is noteworthy that Suhrawardī's works are on a narrow range of themes—philosophy, mysticism, and possibly magic. Most scholars of his time wrote on many topics, if for no other reason than to show the breadth of their knowledge.

14. The third book, metaphysics, of each of these works is published in *SMj*, 1. The logic of one of these works is published as *Manṭiq al-Talwīḥāt*, ed. 'Alī-Akbar Fayyāḍ (Intishārāt-i Dānishgāh-i Tihrān 270; Tehran, 1334/1955). Following *ZKI*, 9, I render these titles in the text as the *Intimations*, *Apposites*, and *Paths and Havens* respectively.

15. This is the view of Mehdi Amin Razavi, *Suhrawardi and the School of Illumination* (Curzon Sufi Series; Richmond, Surrey: Curzon, 1996), which I have reviewed in *International Journal of Middle East Studies* 30.4 (1998): 615–17.

16. *KAP*, 158.

17. *HI*, ¶6.

CHAPTER 3. A SUMMARY OF THE ILLUMINATIONIST PHILOSOPHY

1. The interpretation given in this chapter was worked out in my *SML*, particularly chapters 2 and 3.

2. *ZKI*, 44–45.

3. The distinction goes back to Aristotle and is used by Quṭb al-Dīn Shīrāzī; see his Illuminationist encyclopedia *Durrat al-Tāj li-Ghurrat al-Dibāj*, ed. Muḥammad Mishkāt, Ḥasan Mishkān, and Māhdukht Humāyī (Tehran: Majlis, 1939–46; Shirkat-i Intishārāt-i 'Ilmī wa-Farhangī 247; [Tehran]: Wizārat-i Farhangī wa-Āmūzish-i 'Ālī, 1990), 1, pt. 1:74, 136–38, 151–53, pt. 3 passim, written in the early fourteenth century.

4. See my *SML*, 45 ff.

5. See *SPI*, passim.

6. *QDS*, 16.

CHAPTER 4. SUHRAWARDĪ ON ANCIENT PHILOSOPHY

1. *SMM*, ¶144, in *SMj*, 1:401. Actually, Suhrawardī himself does not use the word *ishrāqī* very often, usually as an adjective describing philosophical doctrines, and rarely uses *ishrāqīyūn*, "illuminationists," the form that would refer to adherents of his philosophy.

2. *HI*, ¶6, 15, 21, 25, and so forth.

3. *ShS*, 4.

4. *HI*, ¶4.

5. See chap. 11 below.

6. On this passage, see pp. 57–59 above.

7. *QDS*, 12, commenting on *HI*, ¶2.

8. *HI*, ¶4.

9. An exception might be Porphyry's history of philosophy, whose biography of Pythagoras is preserved in Greek and is cited in the Arabic biographical dictionaries; see *Fihrist*, 514, and pp. 52–59 below.

10. See p. 190 (on the Stoics).

11. *RMP*.

12. Qur'ān 31:12.

13. *KAA*, 70, my translation. "The niche of prophecy," undoubtedly alludes to the Light Verse, Qur'ān 24:35. "God is the light of the heavens and the earth. The likeness of His light is as a niche, within it a lamp, the lamp in a glass, the glass like a shining star."

14. *KAA*, my translation.

15. 1.1.1, translated from the Arabic version of Thābit b. Qurra in Nicomachus of Gerasa, *Ṯābit b. Qurra's Arabische Übersetzung der 'Αριθμητικὴ 'Εισαγωγή des Nikomachos von Gerasa*, ed. Wilhelm Kutsch (Recherches . . . de l'Institut de Lettres orientales de Beyrouth IX; Beirut: Imprimerie Catholique, n.d) [*Kitāb al-Madkhal ilā 'Ilm al-'Adad*], 1.

16. See my "Explaining Away the Greek Gods in Islam," *Journal of the History of Ideas* 59.3 (1998): 389–403.

CHAPTER 5. EMPEDOCLES

1. On theurgy see Gregory Shaw, *Theurgy and the Soul: The Neoplatonism of Iamblichus* (Hermeneutics: Studies in the History of Religions; University Park, Penn.: Pennsylvania State University Press, 1995).

2. The classic criticism of Aristotle's treatment of his predecessors is H. F. Cherniss, *Aristotle's Criticism of Presocratic Philosophy* (Baltimore: Johns Hopkins University Press, 1935). On this problem as it relates to Empedocles, see *KAP*, 3–5.

3. Fragment 112, translated by Brad Inwood, *The Poem of Empedocles: A Text and Translation with an Introduction* (Phoenix Presocratics 3; Toronto: University of Toronto Press, 1992), 203.

4. On Empedocles' life and technical achievements, see *HGP* 2:128–34.

5. *KAP*, 233–92.

6. The starting point for reconstructions is "Diels-Kranz," H. Diels and W. Kranz, *Die Fragmente der Vorsokratiker* (tenth ed.; Berlin: Weidmann, 1961). The most recent English rendering is Empedocles, ed. and trans. Inwood, which gives translations of the testimonia and the ancient contexts of the fragments, along with a reconstruction of the poem in Greek and literal English—"poem" because Inwood believes that there was only one poem, not two as commonly believed. In this he follows Catherine Osborne, "Empedocles Recycled," *Classical Quarterly* 37 (1987): 24–50. If so, this fits well with the tendency of more recent scholarship to question the legitimacy of the distinction between the "religious" and the "scientific" Empedocles. On the general question of the "inconsistencies" between the two sides of Empedocles and the supposed two poems, see the summary in *HGP* 2:123 ff.

7. Fr. 111, trans. Inwood, 211.

8. Fr. 110, trans. Inwood, 211.

9. As does *HGP* 2:123–24.

10. *KAP*, 241–49.

11. *KAA*, 70–71, 78–81. *RMP*, 203–8, comments on the biographical information.

12. This sentence in not in the Aḥmed text but is paralleled in Shahrastānī's account of Empedocles, which has been added in Abū Rayyān's version of the text. I have omitted a lengthy account of Empedocles' theology that also derives from Shahrastānī or his source. Shahrastānī's account is a different expansion of al-'Āmirī's account; see his *SMN*, 2:68; his account of Empedocles is 2:68–73.

Abu'l-Fatḥ Muḥammad b. 'Abd al-Karīm al-Shahrastānī (479/1086–548/1153) is the most important medieval Islamic heresiographer, whose book far surpasses its rivals in thoroughness, accuracy, and temperateness. Unlike most such works, it also treats non-Islamic religions, sects, and schools of thought. It has been widely read from Shahrastānī's time to our own. It is a splendid reference work, of a quality sufficient that Kīlānī, its modern editor, saw fit to add a hundred page supplement bringing it up to date. For our purposes it is an ideal tool for discovering what was known and thought about pre-Islamic philosophers and religion in Suhraawardī's own century. The two English translations cover only the Islamic sections. Carmela Baffioni has produced a series of annotated translations of the sections on some of the pre-Islamic philosophers: "Una 'storia della filosofia greca' nell'Islām del XII secolo," *Elenchos* 2 (1981): 355–74 (Thales and Anaximenes); 3 (1982): 87–107 (Anaxagoras and Empedocles); 4 (1985): 93–132, 261–345 (Pythagoras); 6 (1985): 409–52; 7 (1987): 381–429 (the first sages); *Sulle tracce di sofia tre "divini" nella Grecia classica* (Saggi Bibliopolis 36; Naples: Bibliopolis, 1990) (Socrates, Plato, Aristotle).

13. *ShNR*, 171–72, 174–75. Abū Rayyān's text differs considerably from Aḥmed's, mainly by the addition of material for which there are parallels in Shahrastānī.

14. This last identifies Shahrazūrī's account as deriving from some account

dependent on Ṣā'id al-Andalusī. Miguel Asin Palacios elaborated on the notion that Ibn Masarra was an Empedoclean; see his *Abenmasarra y su escuela: Orígenes de la filosofía hispano-musulmana* (Madrid: E. Maestre, 1914), trans. Elmer H. Douglas and Howard W. Yoder, *The Mystical Philosophy of Ibn Masarra and his Followers* (Leiden: E. J. Brill, 1978), conveniently summarized by R. Arnaldez, *EI2*, s.v. "Ibn Masarra." S. M. Stern has since attacked the association of Empedocles with Ibn Masarra, pointing out that the identification is based only on a misunderstanding by Ṣā'id, a not especially reliable source for such things; see "Ibn Masarra, Follower of Pseudo-Empedocles—An Illusion," in *Actas, 4 Congresso de Estudos Arabes e Islâmicos, Coimbra—Lisboa 1968* (Leiden: E. J. Brill, 1971), 325–37, reprinted in *Medieval Arabic and Hebrew Thought* (London: Variorum Reprints, 1983), chap. 5. *KAP*, 381–82, has once again defended the Pseudo-Empedoclean interpretation of Ibn Masarra.

15. *ITP*, 4–6. On this text, see p. 61 below.

16. S. M. Stern, *EI2*, s.v. "Anbaduḳlīs," 483.

17. *AA*, 1.3.20; 104. *De Placita Philosophorum*, known to the Muslims as *Kitāb Fulūtarkhus fī Ārā' al-Ṭabī'īya allatī Taqūl bihā al-Ḥukamā'* (The Book of Plutarch on the Opinions Expressed by the Philosophers about Physics]. This work is an abridgment of a doxography by Aetius. The Greek original of Aetius has been recontructed by H. Diels, *Doxographi Graeci* (Berlin: G. Reimeri, 1879; several times reprinted), 26–444; Italian translation by L. Torraca, *I Dossografi Greci* (Padua: CEDAM, 1961), 15–223. The version known to the Arabs was an abridgment attributed to Plutarch, which, being spurious, is often omitted from editions of the *Moralia*. The most recent English translation that I am aware of is in *Plutarch's Morals*, ed. William Goodwin (Boston: Little, Brown, and Co., 1878), 3:104–93. The Pseudo-Plutarch was translated into Arabic by the well-known Christian scholar Qusṭā b. Lūqā (fl. ca. 900). This Arabic version has been published twice: "'al-Ārā' al-Ṭabī'īya' al-Mansūb ilā Fulūtarkhus," in Aristotle, *Fī 'l-Nafs*, ed. 'Abd al-Raḥmān Badawī (Cairo: al-Nahḍa al-Miṣrīya, 1954), and *AA*, which contains a German translation and extensive notes and indices. One of the existing MSS was copied in 1161, during Suhrawardī's lifetime, and the work is often cited by authors of the 11th through 15th centuries.

18. Qifṭī, ed. Lippert, 16.

19. *SMM*, ¶168, in *SMj*, 1:432.

20. They are published in D. Kaufmann, *Studien über Salomon b. Gabirol* (Jahresbericht der Landes-Rabbinerschule in Budapest, 1898–99; Budapest, 1899), 1–63.

21. *ShNA*, 1:51; *ShNR*, 174–75.

22. *DPsA*, V.1–21 and *passim; SMN*, 2:68–73

23. Syrianus, *In Metaphysica Commentaria* 11.28–31, ed. W. Kroll, in *Commentaria in Aristotelem Graeca* (Berlin: Georgii Reimeri, 1882–1909), 6/1; cited in *OPR*, 137.

24. *SMN*, 2:68–73. A summary of these doctrines is given by R. Arnaldez in *EI2*, s.v. "Ibn Masarra." An Italian translation of Shahrastānī's account of Empedocles with some commentary is given in Baffioni, "Storia," 3 (1982): 93–107.

25. *SMN*, 2:71–72.
26. *KAP*, 332–34, 378ff.
27. *HI*, ¶4; cf. *ShS*, 4–5.
28. *SMM*, ¶168, in *SMj*, 1:433.
29. *SMM*, ¶223, in *SMj*, 1:502–3; cf. *ShS*, 595. See also *Phaedo*, 81A on "practicing death."
30. *HI*, ¶274.
31. See chapters 6–7 below; cf. *SMj*, 1:156, 463–64; *HI*, ¶165–66; *ShS*, 392, 398, 551–52; *QDS*, 373, 511–12.
32. *HI*, ¶6. On this notion see *SML*, 34–35.
33. *HI*, ¶235; cf. *ShS*, 529–30; *QDS*, 477; *SMN*, 2:71
34. *HI*, ¶4; *Kitāb al-Talwīḥāt al-Lawḥīya wa'l-'Arshīya*, ¶86, in *SMj*, 1:111–12; *SMM*, ¶168, in *SMj*, 1:433; cf. *ShNA*, 1:22; *ShNR*, 96. See chap. 7 below.
35. *HI*, ¶147.
36. E.g., *HI*, ¶152–53, 156–57.
37. *SMN*, 2:71–72. There is another accurate account of the doctrine in *ITP*, 84, 86, but this work was seemingly not widely known.
38. Aristotle, *Physics* 1.4, 187a12–17, 1.5, 188b34; *AA*, 1.3.20; *DPsA*, V.
39. *SMN*, 2:69–70.
40. *SMN*, 2:70.
41. *SMN*, 2:71; *HI*, ¶242.
42. *Rhetoric* 3.5, 1407a33–36; cf. *KAP*, 53. On the question of symbolic language in philosophy, see chapters 6–7 below.
43. *HGP*, 2:123.
44. *HGP*, 2:122.
45. Ibn Abī Uṣaybi'a, ed. Müller, 2:168–69.
46. *HI*, ¶5–6.
47. *ShS*, 3.
48. *HI*, ¶6.
49. *HI*, ¶259.
50. *ShNA*, 2:124; *ShNR*, 604.
51. *HI*, ¶5.

CHAPTER 6. PYTHAGORAS

1. *PSL*.
2. As does Guthrie in *HGP*, 1:146–72, who meticulously sorts the evidence by date. His actual exposition of Pythagoras' life and thought is in practice heavily dependent on the late, mostly Neoplatonic accounts. The most ambitious attempt to make sense of early Pythagoreanism is W. Burket, *Lore and Science in Ancient Pythagoreanism*, trans. Edwin L. Minar Jr. (Cambridge: Harvard University Press, 1972).
3. The Arabic recension known to my authors is Shahrazūrī's version (*ShNA*,

1:92–103; *ShNR*, 185ff.). Since the proper names are much garbled and the narrative somewhat so in the Arabic versions, I have mostly made my summary from the Greek version. The major features of the story, nonetheless, are quite clear in the Arabic. Other recensions of the Arabic versions are in Ibn Fātik, 52ff., which is evidently Shahrazūrī's source, and Ibn Abī Uṣaybi'a, ed. Riḍā', 63–66. The Greek text is in "Vita Pythagorae," in *Porphyrii Opuscula Selecta*, ed. A. Nauck (2nd ed.; Leipzig, 1886; reprinted Hildesheim: Olms, 1963); and *Porphyre: Vie de Pythagore, Lettre à Marcella*, ed. and trans. Édouard des Places (Paris: Budé, 1982), 9–86. English translations are by Guthrie in *PSL*, 123–35, which I have used, and by Morton Smith in Moses Hadas and Morton Smith, *Heroes and Gods: Spiritual Biographies in Antiquity* (New York: Harper & Row, 1965), 105–28. Cf. Franz Rosenthal, "Arabische Nachrichten über Zenon den Eleaten," *Orientalia*, n.s. 6 (Rome, 1937), reprinted in Franz Rosenthal, *Greek Philosophy in the Arab World: A Collection of Essays* (Aldershot, U.K.: Variorum, 1990), §I., 43–56, which has a comparison of the Arabic and Greek versions of Porphyry's biography.

4. Hermann S. Schibli, *Pherecydes of Syros* (Oxford: Clarendon Press, 1990). On Hermodas, see *Paulys Real-Encyclopädie der classischen Altertumswissenschaft*, ed. G. Wissowa, W. Kroll, and K. Mittelhaus (Stuttgart: J. B. Metzler, 1894–1970; Munich: A. Druckenmuller, 1973–74), 15, col. 859.

5. For a defense of the plausibility and relevance of Pythagoras' Egyptian connection, see Anthony Preus, "Greek Philosophy: Egyptian Origins" (Research Papers on the Humanities and Social Science 3; Binghamton: Binghamton University Institute of Global Cultural Studies, 1992). A more general discussion is Christos Evangeliou, "The Origin of Hellenic Philosophy," in *The Hellenic Philosophy: Between Europe, Asia and Africa.* (Studies on Ancient Greek and Islamic Philosophy 5; Binghamton: Binghamton University Institute of Global Cultural Studies, 1997, 97–156).

6. The critics of the critics of the traditional accounts have complained—justly, I think—that many criticisms of the sources seem motivated less by implausibilities in the sources but by the failure of the sources to show us the Pythagoras we would have wanted—the intrusion of "magic" into the "scientific" Pythagoreanism; *KAP*, 292–96.

7. On the Arabic Pythagoras in general, see Franz Rosenthal, *EI2*, s.v. "Fīthāghūras."

8. *ITP*, 2, 4; translation mine.

9. *KAA*, 71. See also the commentary on this passage, *RMP*, 208–9, where the late antique parallels are analyzed.

10. *ShNA*, 1:89–92; *ShNR*, 182–85.

11. For example, in Miskawayh, *al-Ḥikma al-Khālida: Jāvīdān Khirad*, ed. 'Abd al-Raḥmān Badawī (Dirāsāt Islāmīya 13; Cairo: al-Nahḍa al-Miṣrīya, 1952), 225–28; trans. Franz Rosenthal, in *The Classical Heritage in Islam*, trans. Emile and Jenny Marmorstein (Berkeley: University of California Press, 1975), 118–20. An edition of this translation is found in M. Ullman, unpublished dissertation, Munich, 1959).

12. See, for example, the passage on divine numbers quoted on p. 76 below. On Ibn al-Ṭayyib's use of *istithmār* for his notes on Greek texts, see Franz Rosenthal, "The Symbolism of the *Tabula Cebitis* according to Abû l-Faraj Ibn al-Ṭayyib," *Recherches d'islamologie: Recueil d'articles offert à G. Anawati et L. Gardet par leurs collègues et amis* (Louvain, 1977), 274, 276.

13. L. G. Westerink, "Proclus commentateur des *Vers d'or?*" in G. Boss and G. Seel, eds., *Proclus et son influence* (Zurich: GMB Editions du Grand Midi, 1989), 61–78; discussed in *OPR*, 230–32.

14. *ITP*, 6.

15. *ITP*, 8, 10.

16. *ITP*, 18, 20, 76, 82, 84, 92, 94, 100, 102.

17. *ITP*, 76, 78.

18. *Alberuni's India*, trans. Edward C. Sachau (London: Trübner, 1888), 1:36; *Kitāb al-Bīrūnī fī Taḥqīq Mā li'l-Hind* (Dairatu'l-Ma'arifi'l-Osmania Publications 9; Hyderabad: Osmania Oriental Publications Bureau, 1958), 27.

19. Hans Daiber, *Neuplatonische Pythagorica in arabischem Gewande: Der Kommentar des Iamblichus zu den* Carmina aurea: *Ein verlorener griechischer Text in arabischer Überlieferung* (Koninklijke Nederlandse Akademies van Wetenschappen Verhandelingen, Afdeling Letterkunde, Nieuwe Reeks, Deel 161; Amsterdam: 1995).

20. Iamblichus, *Neuplatonische*, 40.

21. *SMj*, 1:12.

22. *GAS*, 3:20–22, on medicine; 4:45–46, on alchemy; 5:75–76, on mathematics. He is among the Presocratics who appear in the famous *Turba Philosophorum*.

23. *AA*, passim. It would be interesting to know the extent to which the doctrines recorded by Aetius actually affected Islamic scientific and philosophic thought.

24. *Metaphysics* A.5. *OPR*, chs. 5–10, traces the efforts of late antique philosophers after Iamblichus to rationalize Pythagorean number metaphysics, culminating in the subtle analyses of Proclus. The reader should remember that I am reporting views attributed to Pythagoras, particularly in Arabic sources, and not venturing an opinion as to Pythagoras' "authentic" views, whatever they might have been.

25. *ShNA*, 1:19; *ShNR*, 92–93.

26. *DPsA*, XV:6–13.

27. The obvious interpretations were already proposed in antiquity. *KAP*, 284, suggests that it was connected with the rituals of dream interpretation.

28. Iamblichus, *On the Pythagorean Life*, trans. Gillian Clark (Translated Texts for Historians 8; Liverpool: Liverpool University Press, 1989), 45–47; cf. Iamblichus, "Life of Pythagoras," in *Pythagorean Sourcebook*, ch. 23.

29. The following account is largely based on Dominic J. O'Meara's fascinating study, *Pythagoras Revived*, which contains detailed studies of Iamblichus, *On Pythagoreanism*, and of Proclus, and shorter accounts of Pythagoreanizing in Numenius of Apamea, Nicomachus, Anatolius, Porphyry, Hierocles, and Syrianus.

30. *OPR*, 148, 198–200.

31. *Platonic Theology* 1.20.19–25; trans. *OPR*, 199. The most recent edition and translation is Proclus, *Théologie platonicienne*, ed. and trans. H. D. Saffrey and L. G. Westerink (5 vols. to date; Budé; Paris: Société d'Édition, 1968–87). The only English translation is *The Platonic Theology*, trans. Thomas Taylor (Kew Gardens, N.Y.: Selene Books, 1985).

32. *OPR*, 119–24.

33. *KAA*, 70; cf. *ShNA*, 1:26, 90; *ShNR*, 182.

34. *OPR*, 25–28, 93–95; cf. Diogenes Laertius 1.1–11, who will have none of it.

35. *Epistula ad Anebo* 35, trans. *OPR*, 26; cf. Iamblichus, *De Mysteriis*, ed. Gustavus Parthey (Berlin: F. Nicolai, 1857; reprinted Amsterdam: Adolf M. Hakkert, 1965) 260.3–9; trans. Thomas Taylor, *Iamblichus on the Mysteries of the Egyptians, Chaldeans, and Assyrians* (2nd ed.; London: Theosophical Publishing Society, 1895), 299; Stephen Ronan, ed., *Iamblichus of Chalcis on the Mysteries: De Mysteriis Aegyptiorum* (Hastings, East Sussex: Chthonios Books, 1989), which contains the translations of Taylor and Alexander Wilder in parallel columns, along with the Porphyry's *Ad Anebo*, 19, 130. For a defense by a modern Egyptologist of this esoteric tradition of interpretation of the Egyptian mysteries, see Jan Assmann, *Moses the Egyption: The Memory of Egypt in Western Monotheism* (Cambridge: Harvard University Press, 1997).

36. Cited with slight modifications from the translation of "An Epistle Ascertaining the Reality of the World of Image," in *SML*, 206; cf. the Arabic text, 241. On the general question of the World of Image, see *SML*, 149–59, 196–271.

37. 14:13.

38. 14:1.

39. Iamblichus, *De Vita Pythagorica* 115, trans. *HGP*, 1:95; trans. Clark, 67.

40. *Republic*, trans. Allan Bloom, 530D.

41. *HGP*, 1:300.

42. *De Caelo* 2.9, 290b30–291a26.

43. *In Metaphysica* 39.24, commenting on 985b32 ff.; cited in *HGP*, 1:296.

44. 14:9–10.

45. Qur'ān 12:111.

46. *HI*, ¶258. Shahrazūrī cites the *Mashāri'* by name in this portion of his commentary and in all likelihood took his explanation from there.

47. *ShS*, 572. The music of the spheres is probably alluded to in the philosophical Hermetica, as in *Aesclepius* 13.

48. Since there seems to be some disturbance of the text, I have quoted this from *QDS*, 537, who adapts *ShS*, 572, which reads, "However, the Pythagoreans held that there is air between the two [spheres] and that it is excluded from us. We do not hear their sounds because our hearing is filled with it [the air; *athbatū al-hawā' baynahumā wa-khurūjahā 'annā wa-'adam samā'inā aṣwātihā li'mtilā' asmā'inā minhu*]." When confronted with textual problems, Quṭb al-Dīn tends to prefer readings that make clear philosophical sense, a trait that is quite obvious in the edition of *The Philosophy of Illumination* that is embedded in his commentary.

49. *ShS*, 574; not needing nutrition, they do not have taste. He does not men-

tion smell, Shahrazūrī says. It is not clear what passage Shahrazūrī is thinking of, possibly *De Caelo* 2.2 or 2.12, which do testify that the heavens are alive but do not, so far as I can tell, say that the heavens have hearing and sight but not taste. There was, however, an ancient tradition, affirmed by Simplicius and Olympiodorus but denied by Alexander of Aphrodisius, that Aristotle had held that the spheres were alive and had sight, hearing, and possibly touch but not taste or smell; see Harry Austryn Wolfson, "The Problem of the Souls of the Spheres, from the Byzantine Commentaries on Aristotle through the Arabs and St. Thomas to Kepler," in *Studies in the History of Philosophy and Religion*, ed. Isadore Twersky and George H. Williams (Cambridge: Harvard University Press, 1973), 1:38–40. It is thus likely that Shahrazūrī's statement derives ultimately from one of the commentaries on Aristotle. Plato, *Timaeus* 33C, denies that the world has eyes or ears on the grounds that there is nothing outside to see or hear. On the history of the question of whether the heavens are alive, see Edward Grant, *Planets, Stars, and Orbs: The Medieval Cosmos, 1200–1687* (Cambridge: Cambridge University Press, 1994), 469–87.

50. *ShS*, 574.

51. The assertoric demonstration proves the truth of a proposition; the causal demonstration shows why it is the case.

52. *ShS*, 574.

53. *Republic* 627B.

54. *SMM*, ¶185, in *SMj*, 1:452–53. The saying of Pythagoras is perhaps a paraphrase of Aetius 1.33.8, "The principles are numbers."

55. Jonathan Barnes, *The Presocratic Philosophers* (The Arguments of the Philosophers; revised edition; London: Routledge, 1982), 101.

56. Barnes, *Philosophers*, 378–96.

57. *HGP*, 1:181.

58. *HGP*, 1:150–53. Aristoxenus, a student of Aristotle, wrote that "the rest of the Pythagoreans used to say that not all his doctrines were for all men to hear"; Diogenes Laertius 8.15.

59. See p. 63 above.

60. Aetius 1.3.8–10, corresponding to Diels, 281a–283a. When this text is quoted, unless otherwise noted it is my translation of the Arabic edition of *AA*.

61. 985b23–985a2.

62. 987a15–16, my translation of the translation of Naẓīf b. Yumn contained in Ibn Rushd, *Tafsīr Mā Ba'd al-Ṭabī'a*, ed. Maurice Bouyges (Bibliotheca Arabica Scholasticorum, Série Arabe vi; 2nd ed.; Beirut: Dar El-Machreq, 1967), 1:54.

63. Ibn Rushd, *Tafsīr*, 1:60.

64. See pp. 90–95 below.

65. See chapter 7, note 46 below.

66. This account of the plan of the work is based on *OPR*, 30–35 and passim.

67. *OPR*, 219, 223, 227. O'Meara edits and translates the fragments of books 5–7 as preserved by Psellus on 217–29 and analyzes them on 53–85.

68. *OPR*, 78.

69. *ITP*, 76, 78; my translation.

70. The most widely cited Islamic discussion of the Forms and the mathematicals is Avicenna, *Kitāb al-Shifā': al-Ilāhīyāt*, ed. Ibrāhīm Madkūr (Cairo: al-Hay'a al-'Āmma li-Shu'ūn al-Maṭābi' al-Amīrīya, 1380/1960), 303–24, which is based on Aristotle, *Metaphysics* M. Expanding on Ibn Sīnā's discussion are *al-Muthul al-'Aqlīya al-Aflāṭūnīya*, ed. 'Abd al-Raḥmān Badawī (Institut Français d'Archéologie Orientale du Caire, Textes et Traductions d'Auteurs Orientaux 12; Cairo: Dār al-Kutub al-Miṣrīya, 1947), and Mullā Ṣadrā, *al-Ḥikma al-Muta'āliya li'l-Asfār al-Arba'a* (Qom, al-'Ilmīya, n.d.), 2:46–81.

71. *RIS*, 1:48.

72. *RIS*, 3:178–79.

73. *RIS*, 3:179–80, 202.

74. *RIS*, 3:180–81, 199–200.

75. *HI*, ¶61

76. *HI*, ¶¶61–62.

77. *al-Talwīḥāt*, ¶86, in *Majmū'a*, 1:111–12.

78. *SMM*, ¶185, in *SMj*, 1:452–53; see pp. 96–97 below.

79. Barnes, *Philosophers*, 102–3.

80. Diogenes Laertius, 8.4–5; *Iliad* 16:806–17:60; Pausanias 2.17.3, who says that the shield is on the right-hand wall of the front chamber of the temple of Hera outside Mycenae.

81. *HI*, ¶¶248, 273; *QDS*, 556. It is the view of the Ancients, including Pythagoras; *ShS*, 551–52; *QDS*, 511–12.

82. Ed. M. de Goeje (Leiden: E. J. Brill, 1894; repr. Beirut: Khayyat, 1965), 161.

83. *ITP*, 104.

84. *HI*, ¶4; *QDS*, 20; cf. *HI*, ¶247, which lists the four worlds as those of intellect, soul, body, and suspended images, i.e., the World of Image.

85. *ShNA*, 1:17–23; *ShNR*, 99.

CHAPTER 7. THE DIVINE PLATO

1. *KAA*, 72; cited in *ShNA*, 1:25; *ShNR*, 100–101.

2. There is no full study of Plato in Islamic sources. A useful summary is R. Walzer, *EI2*, s.v. "Aflāṭūn." *Aflāṭūn fi 'l-Islām*, ed. 'Abd al-Raḥmān Badawī (Wisdom of Persia 13; Tehran: McGill University Institute of Islamic Studies, 1974) contains a variety of texts, including Fārābī's "Philosophy of Plato" and "Epitome of the Laws," Galen's "Epitome of the *Timaeus*," quotations from the *Republic*, *Laws*, *Phaedo*, and *Crito*, and a collection of apocryphal texts ranging from wise sayings to alchemy. See also Paul Walker, "Platonisms in Islamic Philosophy," *Studia Islamica* 79 (1994): 5–25.

3. Cf. *SMN*, 2:88: *"Huwa ākhar al-mutaqaddimīn al-awā'il al-asāṭīn."* The usual terms used in Arabic to render 'Ancients' are *awā'il*, *mutaqaddimūn*, *qudamā'*, and *aqdamūn*, all of which are used by Suhrawardī and his commentators. Τις τῶν ἀρχαίων, 'one of the Ancients' is used to refer to Plato in Philo, *Quis*

Rerum Divinarum Heres Sit 181. For Aristotle οἱ ἀρχαῖοι were the Presocratics (*Meta.* 2.1, 2, *Gen. corr.* 1.1, 2; 1.8, 3. Aristotle refers to "the more recent Ancients" οἱ ὕστεροι τῶν ἀρχαίων, *al-muta'akhkhirūn min al-qudamā' (Phys.* 1.2, 185b26), referring among others to Lycophron, a student of Gorgias, and to those who posed the arguments rejected by Plato in *Philebus* 14D and *Sophist* 251A. Nicomachus refers to οἱ παλαιοὶ καὶ πρῶτοι "the Ancients and the first," rendered in Arabic as *al-qudamā' al-awwalīn*, by which he meant the philosophical tradition beginning with Pythagoras *(Introduction to Arithmetic,* 1.1.1) This usage was carried over into Arabic through the translations. Ibn Juljul, *Ṭabaqāt al-Aṭibbā' wa'l-Ḥukamā'*, ed. Fu'ād Sayyid (Textes et Traduction d'Auteurs Orientaux 10; Cairo: Institut Français d'Archéologie Orientale, 1955), 34, uses *mutaqaddimūn* to refer to the philosophers who came before Alexander, thus including Aristotle. Pseudo-Ammonius seems to use *awwalūn* (9.2, 24.24, 26.4) and *aqdamūn* (1.1) to refer to the older Presocratics.

Shahrazūrī uses "Ancients" to refer to the philosophers up through Plato: "Among the divine and learned sages were some of the Ancients *(qudamā')* who came some time before Aristotle, like Agathadaemon, Hermes, Empedocles, Pythagoras, Socrates, Plato and other ancient *(al-aqdamīn)* learned men whose learning is attested by the various nations" *(ShS,* 4). He contrasts a view of Aristotle with that "of his teacher, the divine Plato, and the rest of the ancient sages" *(al-ḥukamā' al-aqdamīn; ShS,* 529–30). Mullā Ṣadrā uses *aqdamīn* to refer to the Stoics, among others, *(al-Ḥikma al-Muta'āliya li'l-Asfār al-Arba'a* [Qom, al-'Ilmīya, n.d.], 1:299, 436), but this usage reflects his notion that the Stoics were Platonists; see chapter 11 below. I have capitalized 'Ancients' when it refers to the pre-Aristotelian sages but not when referring to the Greeks and Romans generally.

Suhrawardī and his commentators use 'modern', *muta'akhkhir*, of those who come after the "Ancients." It always includes the Islamic Peripatetics, especially Avicenna. In some cases, it is not clear whether Aristotle is to be included, or only his followers, as in *Talwīḥāt,* ¶45, 47, 89, in *SMj,* 1:58, 60, 118. Sometimes it clearly refers only to the Islamic Peripatetics, as in *al-Muqāwamāt,* ¶¶25, 27, 36, in *SMj,* 1:149, 153, 166; and *SMM,* ¶¶5, 135, in *SMj,* 1:206, 389. Often the referent can only be determined by recognizing the proponent of the views under discussion, as in *SMM,* ¶¶27, 35, in *SMj,* 1:238, 250.

Aristotle thus seems to occupy an intermediate position, neither one of the true Ancients nor clearly among the moderns: an Ancient by virtue of being ancient and a modern by virtue of being the master of the Peripatetics. I suspect that the exclusion of Aristotle from the "Ancients" represents Neoplatonic usage, but I cannot prove it.

4. *ShNR,* 269; *ShNA,* 1:168, which gives the name as "Asqalīnus." Ibn Abī Uṣaybi'a, ed. Müller, 1:50, citing Ibn al-Fātik, 126, gives the name as "Asqalībūs." Richard Walzer, *EI2,* s.v. "Aflāṭūn," attributes the supposed descent from Asclepius to a misunderstanding of an epitaph of Plato in Diogenes Laertius 3.45, "As the god's son Asclepius is a healer of the body, so is Plato of the immortal soul." There may be some additional confusion caused by the fact that Asclepius was the

first of the Eight Physicians referred to in Muslim sources, "Plato the Physician" (not our Plato; see p. 86 below) was the fifth, and Asclepius the second was the sixth.

5. *ShNA*, 1:168; *ShNR*, 270; Diogenes Laertius 3.6.

6. *ShNR*, 270; *ShNA*, 1:169.

7. Ibn Abī Uṣaybi'a, ed. Müller, 80.

8. *ShNR*, 272; *ShNA*, 1:170.

9. *ShNR*, 272; *ShNA*, 1:171, citing Ibn Fātik, 128. Descriptions are given of the physical appearance of a number of the Greek philosophers.

10. *ShNR*, 272; *ShNA*, 1:170.

11. *Fihrist*, 502, 515.

12. On Theon of Alexandria see al-Qifṭī, ed. Lippert, 108; *Fihrist*, 541–42; Julius Lippert, "Theon in der orientalischen Litteratur," *Studien auf dem Gebiete der griechisch-arabischen Übersetzunglitteratur* (Braunschweig, 1894), 39–44; *GAS*, 6:101–2.

13. Theon of Smyrna, *Philosophi Platonici: Expositio Rerum Mathematicarum ad Legendum Platonem Utilium. [Περὶ τῶν κατὰ τὸ μαθηματικὸν χρησίμων εἰς τὴν Πλάτωνος ἀναγνωσιν]*, ed. Eduardus Hiller (Leipzig: B. G. Teubner, 1878), 3.16, 146.4. There are French and English translations: *Theon de Smyrne, philosophe platonicien. Exposition des connaissances mathematiques utiles pour la lecture de Platon*, trans. J. Dupuis (Paris, Hachette, 1892); *Mathematics Useful for Understanding Plato*, trans. Robert and Deborah Lawlor (San Diego: Wizards Bookshelf, 1979).

14. *Fihrist*, 503, "*Kitāb Marātib Qirā'at Kutub Aflāṭūn wa-Asmā' mā Ṣannafahu.*" On Theon in general, see G. L. Huxley, *Dictionary of Scientific Biography*, s.v. "Theon of Smyrna"; Pauly-Wissova, 2nd ser., 10 (1934), cols. 2067–75; T. L. Heath, *A History of Greek Mathematics* (Oxford, 1921), 2:238–44; Lippert, "Theon," *Studien auf dem Gebiete der griechisch-arabischen Übersetzunglitteratur* (Braunschweig, 1894), 44–50.

15. *Fihrist*, 503.

16. Proclus, *In Platonis Timaeum Commentarii*, ed. E. Diehl (Leipzig: Teubner, 1903–6), 82:15–20; al-Qifṭī, ed. Lippert, 18.

17. Proclus, *In Tim.* 8.6–11.4; Proclus, *Commentaire sur la République*, trans. A. J. Festugière (Bibliothèque des Textes Philosophiques; Paris: Librairie Philosophique J. Vrin, 1970), 1:24–27.

18. Ibn Abī Uṣaybi'a, ed. Müller, 41–42; *Fihrist*, 586; *GAS*, 3:49.

19. *Sirr al-Khalīqa*, published as Ursula Weisser, ed., *Buch über das Geheimniss der Schöpfung und die Darstellung der Natur (Buch der Ursachen)* (Sources and Studies in the History of Arabic-Islamic Science, Natural Sciences Series 1; Aleppo: Institute for the Study of Arabic Science, 1979), 28, 32, 34; abridged translation, Ursula Weisser, *Das "Buch über das Geheimnis der Schöpfung" von Pseudo-Apollonios von Tyana* (Ars Medica, Texte und Untersuchungen zur Quellenkunde der Alten Medizin III. Arabische Medizin 2; Berlin: Walter de Gruyter, 1980), 77–78, 162–63.

20. *GAS*, 3:49, 126; Galen, *On the Doctrines of Hippocrates and Plato: De*

Placitis Hippocratis et Platonis, ed. Phillip De Lacy (Corpus Medicorum Graecorum 5.4.1–2; Berlin : Akademie-Verlag, 1978–84).

21. al-Qifṭī, ed. Lippert, 19.

22. *GAS*, 5:78–79. It is apparently lost.

23. *GAS*, 4:99; 5:78–79.

24. *GAS*, 7:59–60.

25. *Fihrist*, 692.

26. Punjab University Library MS Ar.h.III,128, f. 1a. *GAS*, 4:96–100. The *Kitāb al-Rawābī'* is published in 'Abd al-Raḥmān Badawī, ed., *al-Aflāṭūnīya al-Muḥdatha 'inda 'l-'Arab* (2nd ed.; Kuwayt: Wikālat al-Maṭbū'āt, 1977), 117–239, with the commentary of one Aḥmad b. al-Ḥusayn b. Jahār Bakhtār, as commissioned by Thābit b. Qurra.

27. *Fihrist*, 502–4. Some information on the Arabic Plato and more on medieval Latin versions of Plato is found in Raymond Klibansky, *The Continuity of the Platonic Tradition during the Middle Ages: Outlines of a* Corpus Platonicum Medii Aevi (London: The Warburg Institute, 1939). On Arabic translations see Felix Klein-Franke, "Zur Überliefergun der platonischen Schriften im Islam," *Israel Oriental Studies* 3 (1973): 120–39. On issues of transmission, see F. E. Peters, "The Origins of Islamic Platonism: The School Tradition," in Parviz Morewedge, ed., *Islamic Philosophical Theology* (Studies in Islamic Philosophy and Science; Albany: State Unversity of New York Press, 1979), 14–45.

28. Dodge, following Flügel, suggests that this is the *Cratylus*.

29. Dodge may be right in rendering the Greek name as "the Cretan," but 'Iqrīṭun' is the form used by Fārābī for the *Crito*, which also deals with laws.

30. *GAS*, 5:77–79.

31. *Fihrist*, 503. The evidence of translations of Plato, including information on manuscripts, is summarized in 'Abdurraḥmān Badawi, *La transmission de la philosophie grecque au monde arabe* (Études de philosophie médiévale 55; Paris: Librairie Philosophique J. Vrin, 1968), 35–45. Badawī includes more detail than I do on the pseudepigraphic works on the occult sciences and discusses the gnomological literature, which I do not deal with at all here.

32. Ilai Alon, *Socrates in Mediaeval Arabic Literature* (Islamic Philosophy, Theology, and Science, Texts and Studies 10; Leiden: E. J. Brill, 1991), 75–87. J.-Ch. Bürgel, "A New Arabic Quotation from Plato's *Phaido* and Its Relation to a Persian Version of the *Phaido*," *Actos do IV Congresso de Estudos Arabes e Islamicos* (Lisbon: 1968 [1971]), 281–90.

33. Joshua Parens, *Metaphysics as Rhetoric: Alfarabi's Summary of Plato's "Laws"* (SUNY Series in Middle Eastern Studies; Albany: SUNY Press, 1995), xxviii–xxxi.

34. *Fihrist*, 503.

35. al-Qifṭī, ed. Lippert, 17.

36. *ShNA*, 1:170; *ShNR*, 266.

37. *SMN*, 2:88. For "Eleatic" Shahrastānī reads *al-Nāṭis*, a misreading of *ilyāṭī* or some such form.

38. al-Qifṭī, ed. Lippert, 20.

39. *ShNA*, 1:170; *ShNR*, 269; al-Qifṭī, 17.

40. *ShNA*, 1:170–71; *ShNR*, 272.

41. Although tastes may be changing in our time as well. Leo Strauss championed the *Laws* in *The Argument and Action of Plato's Laws* (Chicago: University of Chicago Press, 1975), and in a study of Fārābī's epitome, "How Fārābī Read Plato's *Laws*," in idem, "*What Is Political Philosophy?*" *and Other Studies* (Glencoe, Ill.: The Free Press, 1959), 134–54.

As for the *Timaeus* there seems to be some new interest in it as a work of philosophy and science. In their *Inventer l'universe* (Paris, 1991); rev. trans. *Inventing the Universe: Plato's* Timaeus, *the Big Bang, and the Problem of Scientific Knowledge* (SUNY Series in Ancient Greek Philosophy; Albany: SUNY Press, 1995), Luc Brisson and F. Walter Meyerstein attempt to take the *Timaeus* seriously as science.

42. *ShS*, 21; cf. *QDS*, 16. This is probably a citation of *Theology of Aristotle* 1.40–41, in *Aflūṭīn 'inda 'l-'Arab*, ed. 'Abd al-Raḥmān Badawī (2nd ed.; Dirāsāt Islāmīya 20; Cairo: Dār al-Nahḍa, 1966), 24, trans. Geoffrey Lewis in *Plotini Opera*, ed. Paul Henry and Hans-Rudolf Schwyzer (Museum Lessianum series philosophica 34; Paris: Descläe de Brouwer, 1959), which cites the *Phaedo* (a misreading of the less familiar "Phaedrus") and the *Timaeus* in an account of the fall and redemption of the soul. The original source is Plotinus, *Enneads* 4.8.1.

43. *ShNA*, 1:169; *ShNR*, 269; Ṣā'id al-Andalusī, *Ṭabaqāt al-Umam*, ed. Ḥayāt al-'Īd Bū-'Alwān (Beirut, Dār al-Ṭalī'a, 1985), 76; trans. as *Science in the Medieval World: Book of the Categories of Nations*, trans. Sema'an I. Salem and A. Kumar (History of Science Series 5; Austin: University of Texas Press, 1991), 23. The translation is full of mistakes.

44. Plato, *Aflāṭūn*, 130n. Quotations from Galen's "Medical Timaeus" found in Bīrūnī's *India* are on 130–32. The Greek fragments of this work are collected in Carlos J. Larrain, *Galens Kommentar zu Platons Timaios* (Beiträge zur Altertumskunde 29; Stuttgart: B. G. Teubner, 1992). If the fragments are any guide, the "Medical Timaeus" summarized the portion of the "works of reason" dealing with the human soul and body (42E–46C) and the portion of the "works of necessity" dealing with pleasure and pain (64A–65A). The Arabic fragments of this work, as collected by Larrain, indicate that the "Medical Commentary" also dealt with the section on disease (81E ff.), as would be expected.

45. In the present work, I cite the translation of Francis Cornford, *Plato's Cosmology: The* Timaeus *of Plato Translated with a Running Commentary* (London: Routledge & Kegan Paul, 1937), and the Greek text of the Loeb edition.

46. The general question of the origin of Pseudo-Timaeus and other pseudo-Pythagorica is discussed in Holger Thesleff, *An Introduction to the Pythagorean Writings of the Hellenistic Period* (Acta Academiae Aboensis, ser. A: Humaniora: 24/3; Åbo: Åbo Akademi, 1961), 23, 59–65, and passim. For the text of Pseudo-Timaeus, see Holger Thesleff, ed., *The Pythagorean Texts of the Hellenistic Period* (Acta Academiae Aboensis, ser. A: Humaniora: 30/1; Åbo: Åbo Akademi, 1965), 202–25. A translation is "On the World and the Soul," in *PSL*, 287–96. *Timaeus*, trans. Cornford, viii–xii.

47. A. E. Taylor, *A Commentary on Plato's Timaeus* (Oxford: Oxford University Press, 1928), 11.

48. Plato, *Aflāṭūn*, 87.

49. Plato, *Aflāṭūn*, 87–88.

50. Plato, *Aflāṭūn*, 119.

51. "The Philosophy of Plato," in *APPA*, 65–66; Arabic text in Plato, *Aflāṭūn*, 24. On this work, see below, pp. 94–95.

52. *Taḥṣil al-Sa'āda* (The Attainment of Happiness), in *APPA*, 45; Arabic text, ed. Ja'far Āl-Yāsīn (2nd ed.; Beirut: Dār al-Andalus, 1983), 91.

53. *Durrat*, 1:5:85. The passage is discussed in *SML*, 120–22.

54. *Fihrist*, 520, 526–27. I render "Arshījānus" as "Aeschines" following Dodge. The virtue of this rendering is that Aeschines does appear in the *Phaedo*, and it seems to be the dialogues on the death of Socrates that Kindī is writing about. On the other hand, the Arabic rendering does not fit the Greek very well, and Aeschines plays no important part in the *Phaedo*. Another possibility might be Archedemus, who was an intermediary between Plato and the tyrant Dionysius. A third possiblity is that this is a deformed rendering of "Archytas," a more conspicuous associate of Plato.

55. *Risāla fī 'l-Qawl fī 'l-Nafs al-Mukhtaṣar min Kitāb Aristū wa-Falāṭūn wa-Sā'ir al-Falāsifa,"* in al-Kindī, *Rasā'il al-Kindī al-Falsafiya*, ed. Muḥammad 'Abd al-Hādī Abā Rayda (Cairo: Dār al-Fikr al-'Arabī, 1950), 272–80.

56. On Theon, see p. 85 above.

57. Rudolph, the editor of Pseudo-Ammonius, summarizes his conclusions in *DPA*, s.v. "'Ammonius' (Pseudo-Ammonius)." On Hippolytus see Jaap Mansfield, *Heresiography in Context: Hippolytus'* Elenchos *as a Source for Greek Philosophy* (Philosophia Antiqua 56; Leiden: E. J. Brill, 1992). For the text see Hippolytus, *Refutatio Omnium Haeresium*, ed. Miroslav Marcovich (Patristische Texte und Studies 25; Berlin: Walter de Gruyter, 1986); trans. Alexander Roberts and James Donaldson, eds., *The Ante-Nicene Fathers* (reprint; Grand Rapids: Eerdman's, 1981), 5:9–153.

58. *DPsA*, 10.1–8.

59. *DPsA*, 24.8–28; cf. 7.1–2, where Plato's opposition to Anaxagoras on creation is mentioned again.

60. 2:88–95.

61. Taylor and Cornford; see note 46 above.

62. This is stressed by the Tübingen school of Plato interpretation, which holds that the key to understanding the dialogues is the the "unwritten teaching"; see, for example, J. N. Findlay, *Plato: The Written and Unwritten Doctrines* (International Library of Philosophy and Scientific Method; London: Routledge & Kegan Paul, 1974), a work that has much useful to say to the student of Suhrawardī and of Neoplatonism generally, and Hans Joachim Kraemer, *Plato and the Foundations of Metaphysics: A Work on the Theory of the Principles and Unwritten Doctrines of Plato*, ed. and trans. John. R. Catan (Albany: State University of New York Press, 1990).

63. Porphyry, *In Aristotelis Categorias Expositio per Interrogationem et*

Responsionem (Commentaria in Aristotelem Graeca 4.1), trans. by Steven K. Strange as *Porphyry on Aristotle's Categories* (Ancient Commentators on Aristotle; Ithaca, N.Y.: Cornell University Press, 1992).

64. David Marsh, *The Quattrocento Dialogue: Classical Tradition and Humanist Innovation* (Harvard Studies in Comparative Literature 35; Cambridge: Harvard University Press, 1980), discusses the influence of Cicero on the Italian Renaissance dialogues of the humanists, which are patterned on Cicero's dialogues.

65. The debate is recorded in Abū Ḥayyān al-Tawḥīdī, *al-Imtāʿ wa'l-Mu'ānasa*, ed. Aḥmad Amīn and Aḥmad al-Zayn (Cairo: Lajnat al-Ta'līf, 1939–44), 1:108–28; trans. D. S. Margoliouth, "The Merits of Logic and Grammar," *Journal of the Royal Asiatic Society* (1905): 111–29. A French translation, along with analysis and translations of related texts, is in A. Elemrani-Jamal, *Logique aristotélicienne et grammaire arabe: Études et documents* (Études Musulmanes 26; Paris: Librairie Philosophique J. Vrin, 1983), 149–63.

66. Ibn ʿArabī, *al-Futūḥāt al-Makkīya* (Cairo, 1293/1876; repr. Beirut: Dār al-Ṣādir), 1:153–54; ed. ʿUthmān Yaḥyā and Ibrāhīm Madkūr (al-Maktaba al-ʿArabīya 127; Cairo: al-Hay'a al-Miṣrīya al-ʿĀmma li'l-Kitāb, 1972), 2:372–73; trans. in Claude Addas, *Quest for the Red Sulphur: The Life of Ibn ʿArabī*, trans. Peter Kingsley (Golden Palm Series; Cambridge, Eng.: Islamic Texts Society, 1993), 34, 37, and in Henry Corbin, *Creative Imagination in the Sufism of Ibn ʿArabī* (Princeton: Bollingen, 1969), 41–43. Muḥammad Ibn al-Munawwar, *Asrār al-Tawḥīd*, ed. Dhabīḥ Allāh Ṣafā (Tehran: Muḥammad-ʿAlī ʿIlmī, 1953), 209–11; trans. John O'Kane, *The Secrets of God's Mystical Oneness* (Persian Heritage Series 38; Costa Mesa, Calif.: Mazda, 1992), 300–302.

67. On the myths in general, see J. A. Stewart, *The Myths of Plato* (1st ed., 1905; red. G. R. Levy; Fontwell, Sussex: Centaur Press, 1970, and Paul Friedländer, *Plato*, 1: *An Introduction* (Bollingen Series 59; 2nd ed.; Princeton: Princeton University Press, 1973), 171–210. Socrates condemns rationalizing euhemeristic interpretation of myth in *Phaedrus* 229C–230A but goes on to give a brilliant allegorical interpretation of the myth—a quite different thing—of the chariot of the soul. Platonists ever since have been fond of allegorical interpretations of sacred texts.

68. There are many editions and translations of the *Tabula*. I have used John T. Fitzgerald and L. Michael White, *The Tabula of Cebes* (Society of Biblical Literature Texts and Translations 24, Graeco-Roman Religion Series 7; Chico, Calif.: Scholars Press, 1983). On the state of Cebes scholarship, see the introduction to Fitzgerald and White and Luc Brisson, Jean-Marie Flamand, and Dimitri Gutas in *DPA*, s.v. "Cebes."

69. *Tabula* 1.2–3, trans. Fitzgerald and White. Not surprisingly, the *Tabula* has inspired a good deal of art, mostly very cluttered book illustrations, collected in Reinhart Schleier, *Tabula Cebetis; oder Spiegel des meschlichen Lebens* (Berlin: Gebr. Mann Verlag, 1974). None of his examples are Islamic.

70. *Tabula* 4.2–5.2, trans. Fitzgerald and White.

71. Fitzgerald and White, 12.

72. Miskawayh, *Ḥikma*, 229–62.

73. "Min al-ḥukamā' al-mutaqaddimīn," that is, he was after Plato.

74. That is, the tablet portrays the world: "maqām al-nās fi 'l-dunyā"; Miskawayh, *Ḥikma*, 234; cf. Rosenthal, "Symbolism," 277, 280.

75. *ShNA*, 1:306; *ShNR*, 319. Aḥmed's manuscripts give his name as Fānis and Fāyis, which differ only by dots from the correct Qābis.

76. Miskawayh, *Ḥikma*, 229 with notes.

77. *RMP*, 34; Bürgel, "Quotation."

78. Rosenthal, "Symbolism," 273–83, which contains an introduction, the Arabic text, and an English translation. Ibn al-Ṭayyib uses the same Arabic translation as Miskawayh. It is preserved in the same manuscript as the *Golden Verses* commentary, Escorial Ms. 888. To add to the confusion, Ibn al-Ṭayyib gives Cebes' name as Qābūs, a familiar pre-Islamic Persian name.

79. Sufi epic poetry in Persian and other eastern Islamic languages is always allegorical. Examples easily accessible to English readers are 'Aṭṭār's *Conference of the Birds [Manṭiq al-Ṭayr]*, trans. Afkham Darbandi and Dick Davis (Penguin Classics; Harmondsworth, Eng.: Penguin, 1984), and Rūmī's *Mathnawī*, ed. and trans. R. A. Nicholson (8 vols.; E. J. W. Gibb Memorial Series, n.s. 4; Leiden: E. J. Brill, 1925–40). When later Persian Sufi authors assimilated more philosophical forms of Sufism, partly under Suhrawardī's influence, their allegories became more philosophical. An example is *Salāmān and Absāl* by the fifteenth-century poet and Sufi philosopher Jāmī. The morbidly curious English reader can find it in a singular translation by Edward Fitzgerald, better known for his translation of 'Umar Khayyām, in A. J. Arberry, *Fitzgerald's Salaman and Absal* (Cambridge: Cambridge University Press, 1956). Fitzgerald's experiment in imitating the meter of Longfellow's *Hiawatha* was particularly unfortunate; an anonymous reviewer of the first edition quotes with horror the line: "Nightingaling thus a noodle . . ." Arberry has included Fitzgerald's first and second versions and a literal translation of his own for comparison.

80. Avicenna, *Kitāb al-Ishārāt wa'l-Tanbīhāt ma'a Sharḥ Naṣīr al-Dīn al-Ṭūsī*, ed. Sulaymān Dunyā (Dhakhā'ir al-'Arab 22; Cairo: Dār al-Ma'ārif, n.d.), 3–4:790–93.

81. Henry Corbin, *Avicenna and the Visionary Recital*, trans. Willard R. Trask (Bollingen Series 66; New York: Pantheon Books, 1966; reprinted Irving, Texas: Spring Publications, 1980), 204.

82. In Avicenna, *Ishārāt*, 3–4:791.

83. Shlomo Pines, "The Origin of the Tale of Salāmān and Absāl—A Possible Indian Influence," in Shlomo Pines, *Studies in the History of Arabic Philosophy* (Jerusalem: Magnes Press, 1996), 343–53.

84. Pines, "Origin," 349–50, thinks that the story reflects Neoplatonic doctrines, although his interpretation is less fevered and more plausible than Corbin's. Both Corbin and Pines point out that the expression *al-anwār al-qāhira*, "triumphal lights," an important technical term in *The Philosophy of Illumination*, is used in the tale to refer to the realm between the Forms and the terrestrial world.

85. In Avicenna, *Ishārāt*, 3–4:796–99. Fedwa Malti-Douglas gives a "gender

reading" of several allegories, including both versions of *Salāmān and Absāl*, Ibn Ṭufayl's *Ḥayy b. Yaqẓān*, and Suhrawardī's *Occidental Exile;* see her *Woman's Body, Women's Words: Gender and Discourse in Arabo-Islamic Writing* (Princeton: Princeton University Press, 1991), 67–100, which should be read in the light of the review by Julie Scott Meisami, "An Anatomy of Misogyny?" *Edebiyât*, n.s. 6.2 (1995): 303–15. The results of this "gender reading" are unfortunate, as when the translation by Ḥunayn b. Isḥāq (a ninth-century Christian) of the Hellenistic narrative *Salāmān and Absāl* is taken as a reflection of "Muslim unconscious" (101) or in a Freudian interpretation of Suhrawardī's *Occidental Exile* in which the dungeon in which the pilgrims are imprisoned is taken to symbolize the vagina (108). Meisami is critical of Malti-Douglas' insensitivity to genre, especially in the case of allegory: "Allegorical narratives are in general so totally divorced from the real, or even the 'ideal,' world, and so limited in circulation, as to provide unreliable guides to social attitudes" (312).

86. In *Qiṣṣat al-Ghurba al-Gharbīya*, in *SMj*, 2:275; trans. *MVT*, 100. The other allegories are edited in *SMj*, 3, and translated in *MVT*. For Corbin's French translation of the allegories and some other short texts of Suhrawardī, see *SAe*. Hermann Landolt, "Suhrawardī's 'Tales of Initiation'," *JAOS* 107.3 (1987): 475–86, compares Thackston's translation with Corbin's and criticizes Thackston for a number of philosophical and historical errors. Like Corbin, Landolt generally privileges the mythical over the philosophical aspects of Suhrawardī's thought, the opposite of what I am doing in the present work. Nonetheless, his specific criticisms of Thackston's translation are to be taken seriously. Amin Razavi, *Suhrawardi*, 17–24, discusses six of the allegories as Sufi texts.

87. *Rūzī bā Jamā'at-i Ṣūfiyān*, in *SMj*, 3:242–50; translation in *MVT*, 44–50, and *SAe*, 361–81; cf. Landolt, 478. On the theme of the spiritual master, see Kazem Tehrani, "The Role of the Sage in the Works of Suhrawardī," in Parviz Morewedge, ed., *Islamic Philosophy and Mysticism* (Studies in Islamic Philosophy and Science; Delmar, N.Y.: Caravan Books, 1981), 191–205.

88. *Āwāz-i Par-i Jibrā'īl*, in *SMj*, 3:208–23; translation in *MVT*, 26–34; *SAe*, 221–64; and with an anonymous medieval commentary in Amin Razavi, *Suhrawardi*, 150–63; cf. Anthony K. Tuft, "Symbolism and Speculation in Suhrawardī's *The Song of Gabriel's Wing*," in Morewedge, ed., *Islamic Philosophy*, 207–21.

89. A Sufi master (d. 402/1011), the successor of Abu'l-Qāsim Gurgānī and an influence on Ghazālī.

90. *Risālat al-Ṭayr*, in *SMj*, 3:198–205; trans. *MVT*, 21–25. An analysis and translation of Avicenna's original version is in Corbin, *Recital*, 178–203.

91. *'Aql-i Surkh*, in *SMj*, 3:226–39; trans. *MVT*, 35–43, and *SAe*, 193–220.

92. *Fī Ḥālat al-Ṭufūlīya*, in *SMj*, 3:252–66; trans. *MVT*, 51–61, and *SAe*, 383–412.

93. *Fī Ḥaqīqat al-'Ishq, yā Mu'nis al-'Ushshāq*, in *SMj*, 3:267–91; trans. *MVT*, 62–75, and *SAe*, 289–337.

94. *Lughat-i-Mūrān*, in *SMj*, 3:294–311; trans. *MVT*, 76–87, and *SAe*, 413–39.

95. *Qiṣṣat al-Ghurba al-Gharbīya*, in *SMj*, 2:294–97; trans. *MVT*, 100–108, and *SAe*, 265–87.

96. The same can be said of Pseudo-Aristotle, *The Book of the Apple;* see chapter 8 below.

97. *QDS*, 15. Quṭb al-Dīn does not mention his source. For once, it is not Shahrazūrī.

98. In *SMj*, 3:405; Henry Corbin, in the French introduction, 118. It is not clear who he was, although his titles indicate that he was a government person, perhaps a vizier or local governor.

99. Mehdi Aminrazavi, "The Significance of Suhrawardī's Persian Sufi Writings in the Philosophy of Illumination," in Leonard Lewisohn, ed., *Classical Persian Sufism: From its Origins to Rumi* (London: Khaniqahi Nimatullahi Publications, 1993), 259–83, and idem, *Suhrawardi*, xvii–xx and passim, argues that the allegories are of central significance for understanding Suhrawardī's position since they reveal the practical mystical side of his work. This is true to a point, since practical mysticism is central to his philosophical enterprise. They do not, however, contain advanced doctrines. Rather they contain elementary cosmology and Sufi commonplaces. Of course, these commonplaces are commonplace because they are fundamental—but unlike the Illuminationist philosophical doctrines, they are not novel.

100. In *SMj*, 2:262–73. A manuscript collophon also gives the title as *'Aqā'id al-Ḥukamā'*. *ShNA*, 2:128; *ShNR*, 608, mentions it in a list of Suhrawardī's works, so it is presumably genuine. It is translated in *SAe*, 11–30. None of the manuscripts date the work.

101. *SMj*, 2:262.

102. *SAe*, 12–13.

103. *ShNA*, 1:29; *ShNR*, 104–5; *ShS*, 22.

104. *QDS*, 17–18.

105. *Quomodo Substantiae*, in *Theological Tractates*, trans. E. K. Rand and H. F. Stewart, rev. S. J. Tester (Loeb Classical Library 74; Cambridge: Harvard University Press, 1973), 38–39.

106. Henry Chadwick, *Early Christian Thought and the Classical Tradition: Studies in Justin, Clement, and Origen* (New York: Oxford University Press, 1966), 77–79.

107. *Alfarabi's Utterances Employed in Logic: Kitāb al-Alfāẓ al-Musta'mala fi'l-Manṭiq*, ed. Muhsin Mahdi (Beirut: Dar El-Machreq, 1968), ¶46.

108. *Platonic Theology* 1.4–5; cf. *OPR*, 198–99 on these passages.

109. Iamblichus, *In Timaeus*, frag. 5, in Iamblichi Chalcidensis, *In Platonis Dialogos Commentariorum Fragmenta*, ed. and trans. John Dillon (Philosophia Antiqua 23; Leiden: E. J. Brill, 1973), 108–11; and cited in *OPR*, 97. On the relationship between the written and unwritten teachings in the Platonic tradition, see n. 62 above.

110. In *APPA*, ¶¶3–4. There are two editions of the Arabic text: *De Platonis Philosophia*, ed. Franz Rosenthal and Richard Walzer (Corpus Platonicum Medii Ævi; London: Institutum Warburgianum, 1943), and in Plato, *Aflāṭūn*, 5–27.

111. See p. 85 above.

112. *JRH*. Charles Butterworth has prepared a new edition and translation for the Islamic Philosophy Translation Series; Provo, Utah: Brigham Young Univer-

sity Press. On this work see Majid Fakhry, "Al-Farabi and the Reconciliation of Plato and Aristotle," *Journal of the History of Ideas* 6 (1968): 469–78; reprinted in Majid Fakhry, *Philosophy, Dogma, and the Impact of Greek Thought in Islam* (London: Variorum, 1994), §v.

113. Richard Sorabji, "The Ancient Commentators on Aristotle," in Richard Sorabji, ed., *Aristotle Transformed: The Ancient Commentators and Their Influence* (Ithaca, N.Y.: Cornell University Press, 1990), 2–5.

114. On this work see J. Bidez, *Vie de Porphyre, le philosophe Néo-Platonicien* (Leipzig: Teubner, 1913; reprinted Hildesheim: Georg Olms, 1964), App., 68*; Rudolph Beutler, "Porphyrios," in Pauly-Wissova, 43, col. 282, 285; and Sten Ebbesen, "Porphyry's Legacy to Logic: A Reconstruction," in Sorabji, *Aristotle Transformed*, 145. Sorabji, "Ancient Commentators," 2, says that quotations from this work are preserved in al-'Āmirī, *al-Sa'āda wa'l-Is'ād fī 'l-Sīra al-Insānīya*, ed. Mujtabā Mīnuwī (Intishārāt-i Dānishgāh-i Ṭihrān 435, Hadīya-yi Duktur Yaḥyā Mahdawī bi-Dānishgāh 5; Tehran: Tehran University, 1336/1957–58). I could not find them, although Porphyry is quoted there at least four times, always in conjunction with quotations from Plato and/or Aristotle. No such work of Porphyry is mentioned in the *Fihrist*, although a commentary on the *Ethics* is; *Fihrist*, 512, where the name is given as "Gregorius," but cf. ed. Flügel, 252, which gives the name "Porphyry," and F. E. Peters, *Aristoteles Arabus: The Oriental Translations and Commentaries on the Aristotelian* Corpus (New York University Department of Classics Monographs on Mediterranean Antiquity; Leiden: E. J. Brill, 1968), 52, which follows Flügel.

115. Sorabji, "Ancient Commentators," 5.

116. *JRH*, 79.

117. I owe these insights to Muhsin Mahdi, from whom I learned to read Fārābī suspiciously, and ultimately to Leo Strauss.

118. *JRH*, 80.

119. *Metaphysics* Γ.1. Fārābī's wording does not agree with the text in Averroes, *Tafsīr*, which uses the early translation of Eustathius for book four.

120. *HI*, ¶¶3–4.

121. Alcinous, *Introductio in Platonem* 152.2–5; Alcinous, *The Handbook of Platonism*, trans. John Dillon (Oxford: Clarendon Press, 1993), 3; *Enseignement des doctrines de Platon*, ed. John Whittaker, trans. Pierre Louis (Budé; Paris: Les Belles Lettres, 1990), 1; cf. Jeremiah Reedy, trans., *The Platonic Doctrines of Albinus* (Grand Rapids, Mich.: Phanes Press, 1991), 21. There is a longstanding debate about whether "Alcinous" is a textual corruption for "Albinus," a well-known Platonist; John Whittaker, *DPA*, s.v. "Albinos," and Simone Follet, *DPA*, s.v. "Alcinoos."

122. *Kitāb al-Ta'rīfāt*, ed. G. Flügel (Leipzig, 1845; reprinted Beirut, Librairie du Liban, 1969), 176.

123. *HI*, ¶4.

124. *HI*, ¶¶52–106.

125. This is Rāzī the physician. He is to be distinguished from several other Rāzīs (of Rayy, near the modern Tehran) with philosophical connections. Abū Ḥātim al-Rāzī was a tenth century Isma'ili theologian/philosopher. Fakhr al-Dīn al-Rāzī (d. 1209) was a very important theologian and philosopher—and appar-

ently a classmate of Suhrawardī. He is mentioned above as the author of an influential commentary on Avicenna's *Ishārāt*. Quṭb al-Dīn al-Rāzī al-Taḥtānī (d. 1364) is said, probably wrongly, to have been a student of Suhrawardī's commentator Quṭb al-Dīn Shīrāzī. He wrote an influential supercommentary on the commentaries of Fakhr al-Dīn al-Rāzī and Naṣīr al-Dīn al-Ṭūsī on the *Ishārāt* and several other texts important in the development of the later school tradition of Islamic logic. His curious surname arose from the fact that there were two Quṭb al-Dīns in the same *madrasa* in Damascus, and he was the one who lived downstairs.

For the fragments of Rāzī's philosophical works, see Abū Bakr al-Rāzī, *Rasā'il Falsafīya* [ed. Paul Kraus], (2nd ed.; Beirut: Dār al-Āfāq al-Jadīda, 1977). For a bio-bibliographical study, see Mehdi Mohaghegh, *Faylasūf-i Rayy: Muḥammad b. Zakarīyā Rāzī* (Silsila-yi Intishārāt-i Anjuman-i Āthār-i Millī 73; Tehran: Tehran University, 1970). See also Lenn Goodman, "Muḥammad ibn Zakariyyā' al-Rāzī," in Seyyed Hossein Nasr and Oliver Leaman, eds., *History of Islamic Philosophy* (Routledge History of World Philosophies 1; London: Routledge, 1996), 1:198–215.

126. *ShNA*, 2:7; *ShNR*, 498.

127. Rāzī, *Rasā'il*, 196, cited from Ibn Taymīya, *Kitāb Minhāj al-Sunna al-Nabawīya* (4 vols. in 2; Cairo: al-Maṭba'ah al-Kubrā al-Amīrīya, 1903–4), 1:97. On Democritus, *GAS*, 4:49–50; *KAP*, 326–28. On Democritus' links with the *Timaeus*, see Majid Fakhry, "A Tenth-Century Arabic Interpretation of Plato's Cosmology," *Journal of the History of Philosophy* 6 (1968): 15–22; reprinted in Fakhry, *Philosophy, Dogma*, §vi.

128. *Fihrist*, 602: "Commentary on Plutarch's Commentary on the *Timaeus*." On Rāzī's views on the fall of the soul, see Lenn E. Goodman, "Rāzī's Myth of the Fall of the Soul: Its Function in His Philosophy," in George F. Hourani, ed., *Essays on Islamic Philosophy and Science* (Albany: State University of New York Press, 1975), 25–40.

129. *HI*, ¶4.

130. On Rāzī, Platonism, and the general question of non-Aristotelian philosophy and its sources in early Islam, see F. E. Peters, "Hermes and Harran: The Roots of Arab-Islamic Occultism," in Michel M. Mazzaoui and Vera B. Moreen, eds., *Intellectual Studies on Islam: Essays Written in Honor of Martin B. Dickson* (Salt Lake City: University of Utah Press, 1990), 185–215.

131. Franz Rosenthal, "On the Knowledge of Plato's Philosophy in the Islamic World," *Islamic Culture* 14.4 (Oct. 1940); 393; reprinted with addenda in Rosenthal, *Greek Philosophy*, sect. 2.

132. William E. Gohlman, *The Life of Ibn Sina* (Studies in Islamic Philosophy and Science; Albany: State University of New York Press, 1974), 32–35.

CHAPTER 8. ARISTOTLE AND THE PERIPATETICS

1. All of the major biographical and bibliographical sources have sections on Aristotle's life and works, often with collections of wise sayings *(ḥikam)* of the

usual dubious provenance. The main published sources are *Fihrist*, 504–12; Ibn Abī Uṣaybiʻa, ed. Müller, 1:54–69; Ibn Juljul, 25–30; Ibn Fātik, 178–84; al-Qifṭī, ed. Lippert, 27–53; Ṣāʻid, 76–82, trans. 23–25; *ShNA*, 1:22, 197–205; *ShNR*, 98, 289–309; Abū Sulaymān al-Sijistānī, *Muntakhab Ṣiwān al-Ḥikma*, ed. ʻAbd al-Raḥmān Badawī (Tehran: Bunyād-i Farhang-i Īrān, 1974), 81, 135–61; Muḥammad al-Daylamī, *Maḥbūb al-Qulūb*, ed. ʻAbd al-Karīm al-Shīrāzī (n.p., 1899), 97–107. In addition, a Greek account of Aristotle and his works, known only in Arabic, is attributed to one "Ptolemy al-Gharīb." It exists independently in a late, not very good manuscript and is cited by most of the Islamic biographers. Recent summaries of scholarship on the Arabic lives and bibliographies of Aristotle are in Maroun Aouad, *DPA*, s.v. "Aristote de Stagire: La version arabe"; Dimitri Gutas, "The Spurious and the Authentic in the Arabic Lives of Aristotle," in Jill Kraye, W. F. Ryan, and C. B. Schmitt, eds., *Pseudo-Aristotle in the Middle Ages* (Warburg Institute Surveys and Texts 11; London: The Warburg Institute, 1986), 15–35; Peters, *Aristoteles Arabus;* R. Walzer, *EI2*, s.v. "Arisṭūṭālīs."

2. Peters, *Aristotle Arabus*, 55–75; Maroun Aouad, *DPA*, s.v. "Aristote de Stagire. *De Pomo, Théologie d'Aristote*."

3. *KAA*, 74; cf. pp. 34, 59 above.

4. Qur'ān 18:84–99; W. Montgomery Watt, *EI2*, s.v. "Iskandar"; *EIr*, s.v. "Eskandar," forthcoming; A. Abel, *EI2*, s.v. "Iskandar Nāma." The Alexander romance had its greatest Islamic influence in Persian epic poetry. The best known versions are those of Niẓāmī *(Iskandar-Nāma, Iqbāl-Nāma)* and *Iskandarnamah: A Persian Medieval Alexander-Romance*, trans. Minoo S. Southgate (Persian Heritage Series 31; New York: Columbia University Press, 1978). A number of philosophers appear in the *Iqbāl-Nāma*, where they give advice to Alexander. A Shiʻite compilation on the lives of the prophets, Sayyid Niʻmat Allāh al-Jazāʼirī (d. 1112/1700), *Qiṣaṣ al-Anbiyā'*, ed. al-Ḥājj Muḥsin ʻAqīl (2nd ed.; Beirut: Dār al-Balāgha, 1413/1993), 174–93, contains mostly traditions in which Dhu'l-Qarnayn is not identified with Alexander. Its favored version says that "his name was "Īyāshī, and he was the first king after Noah, the king of East and West," 174. Ibn Taymīya, *al-Radd ʻalā 'l-Manṭiqīyīn*, ed. ʻAbd al-Ṣamad Sharaf al-Dīn al-Kutubī (Bombay: Qayyimah Press, 1368/1949), 182–84, attacks the traditions identifying Alexander with Dhu'l-Qarynayn.

5. *ShS*, 529–30.

6. *al-Talwīḥāt*, ¶60; in *SMj*, 1:85. For a modern view of Aristotle not so different from Suhrawardī's, see Christos C. Evangeliou, "Aristotle and Western Rationality," in Evangeliou, *Hellenic Philosophy*, 47–94.

7. *ShNA*, 1:195; *ShNR*, 296–97 writes: "The works of [Aristotle] that we have seen and are presently in circulation amount to some twenty books. There are eight books of logic, eight books on physics, the *Ethics*, the *Politics [al-Siyāsa al-Madanīya*, probably meaning the *Sirr al-Asrār]*, a large book on metaphysics known as the *Theology*, which means, "the divine discourse" *[al-qawl al-ilāhī]*." Unfortunately, it is not clear whether this is a reference to the *Theology* or to the *Metaphysics*. Most probably it is the latter, since the *Theology* is not a "large book." The passage actually is copied from Ibn Fātik, 183–84, so it does not tell

us what books Shahrazūrī had access to. The *Theology* is cited separately from the *Metaphysics* in the *Fihrist*, 512: "*The Book of Theology*, which Kindī commented on."

8. Gutas, "Arabic Lives," 31, 36 n. 61, points out that *The Book of the Apple* is obviously closely connected with the *Phaedo* and that two of the five known Arabic MSS replace Aristotle's name with that of Socrates. On this basis he infers that the Socrates version must have been the original. "Had the text first entered (rather than been composed in?) Arabic under the name of Aristotle, it would be difficult, if not impossible, to maintain that it was subsequently also attributed to Socrates." This seems implausible to me since the early independent witnesses—the *Rasā'il Ikhwān al-Ṣafā* and Nāṣir-i Khusraw—both associate the book with Aristotle, and the former also cites the *Phaedo* as a different work that gives an account of Socrates' death. Moreover, no one would write an account of the death of Socrates in which the great man succumbs to a fatal illness rather than execution. It seems more likely to me that Aristotle in a deathbed scene is a sort of *lectio difficilior* and that the replacement of Aristotle's name with that of Socrates is a natural, if erroneous correction.

9. In Pseudo-Aristotle, "*The Book of the Apple* Ascribed to Aristotle Edited in Persian and English," ed. D. S. Margoliouth, *JRAS* n.s. 24 (1892): 190.

10. *RIS*, 4:271.

11. *Kitāb Jāmi' al-Ḥikmatayn*, ed. Henry Corbin and Muḥammad Mu'īn (Bibliothèque Iranienne 3; Tehran: l'Institut Franco-Iranien, 1953), 99.

12. The history of the text and related bibliography is summarized in the introduction to Mary F. Rousseau, trans., *The Apple, or Aristotle's Death (De Pomo sive De Morte Aristotilis)* (Mediaeval Philosophical Texts in Translation 18; Milwaukee: Marquette University Press, 1968), and more recently in Aouad, "Aristote." The Arabic recension has so far been published in a very imperfect transcription of a MS belonging to the Greek Orthodox Partriarchate of Antioch in Damascus and in the form of the seventeenth-century Persian translation and an English translation made from it; see Pseudo-Aristotle, "Kitāb al-Tuffāḥa," ed. A. Ẓ. Khayr Allāh, *al-Muktataf* 55 (1919): 475–85, 56 (1920): 18–22, 105–10, 217–21, 295, and idem, "*Apple*," ed. Margoliouth, 187–252. Rousseau's translation is of the Latin version, but she reprints Margoliouth's translation as an appendix; see Rousseau, 60–76. Two translations of the Hebrew also exist: Hermann Gallancz, trans., *The Targum to "The Song of Songs"*; The Book of the Apple; *The Ten Jewish Martyrs; A Dialogue on Games of Chance* (London: Luzac and Co., 1908); and Isidor Kalisch, *Ha-Tapuach: The Apple: A Treatise on the Immortality of the Soul by Aristotle the Stagyrite* (New York: The American Hebrew, 1885). See also Jörg Kraemer, "Das arabische Original des pseudo-Aristotelischen *Liber de Pomo*," in *Studi orientalistici in onore di Giorgio Levi Della Vida* (Pubblicazioni dell'Instituto per l'Oriente 52; Rome: Instituto per l'Oriente, 1956), 484–95.

13. Ed. Margoliouth, 212; Rousseau, 66.

14. "Man bar ghā'ib hamān ḥukm kunam kih bar ḥāḍir," ed. Margoliouth, 215–16; Rousseau, 68. Fārābī discusses this form of reasoning; see Joep Lameer, *Al-Fārābī and Aristotelian Syllogistics: Greek Theory and Islamic Practice*

(Islamic Philosophy, Theology, and Science: Texts and Studies 20; Leiden: E. J. Brill, 1994), 204–32; Suhrawardī, *HI*, ¶31.

15. Ed. Margoliouth, 229; Rousseau, 76.

16. Trans. Margoliouth, in Rousseau, 75; ed. Margoliouth, 228

17. The translation, unless otherwise noted, is that of Lewis, in *Plotini Opera*, passim. This translation was made as part of the critical apparatus of an edition of the *Enneads* and thus is scattered through the text depending on where the excerpted passages are found. An index on 489–501 shows where the passages appear. The translation also includes the "Epistle on Divine Science" and the sayings of the "Greek Sage," that is, Plotinus. The translation is based on Plotinus, *Aflūṭīn*, 3–164. I have tacitly modified Lewis' transliteration to conform with my own.

18. "The Origins of the So-Called *Theology of Aristotle*," in Kraye et al., eds., *Pseudo-Aristotle*, 110–240, which also contains a very thorough survey of the literature to that date. On the longer version of the *Theology*, see also Paul B. Fenton, "The Arabic and Hebrew Versions of the *Theology of Aristotle*," in ibid, 241–264.

19. See p. 135 below and note 22.

20. *Theology*, 1.21–26, an expansion of *Enneads*, 4.8.1. I have omitted the italics marking quotations from Plotinus.

21. *HI*, ¶171. The passage is alluded to in ¶165 and again quoted in summary form in the *Talwīḥāt*, ¶86, 112.

22. Zimmermann, "Origins," 143–49, esp. 147.

23. *Theology*, 1.17–18, my translation.

24. See p. 129 above.

25. *Theology*, 1.27.

26. *ShNA*, 1:169. The passage is missing from *ShNR*, but is in Ibn Fātik, 127, and Ibn Abī Uṣaybi'a, ed. Müller, 1:50.

27. *ShNA*, 1:169; *ShNR*, 269.

28. ¶86, in *SMj*, 1:112–13. A complication is that Shahrazūrī mentions "the book of *mīmars*, which Empedocles wrote"; *ShS*, 21. This would surely be *The Theology of Aristotle*, whose chapters have the peculiar name *mīmar*. Shahrazūrī, however, does not attribute this book to Empedocles in the *Nuzhat*, nor does Quṭb al-Dīn repeat the attribution in the corresponding passage of his commentary; *QDS*, 17.

29. A convenient summary of the content of the *Theology* is in Majid Fakhry, *A History of Islamic Philosophy* (Studies in Oriental Culture 5; 2nd ed.; New York: Columbia University Press, 1983), 21–27.

30. Diogenes Laertius 5.2; Simplicius, *In Cat.* 3.30–4.9; Ṣā'id, 92–94, trans. 29; *ShNA*, 1:191; *ShNR*, 293.

31. The general question of the Illuminationist understanding of the relationship among the philosophical schools after Aristotle will be discussed in the context of the Stoics in chapter 11 below.

32. *HI*, ¶3, 6.

33. *ShS*, 4–5.

34. *ShNA*, 2, p. 106; *ShNR*, 589–90. On his death due to overindulgence in sex and his insistence on treating its ill effects himself, see Gohlman, *Ibn Sina*, 80–89; *ShNA*, 2:117–18; *ShNR*, 596. Another possible target of such accusations was Abū Bakr al-Rāzī, who defended himself against charges of worldliness in his essay *Kitāb al-Sīra al-Falsafīya [On the Philosophic Life]*; see Charles E. Butterworth, "The Book of the Philosophic Life," *Interpretation* 20.3 (Spring 1993): 227–36, and idem, "The Origins of al-Rāzī's Political Philosophy," *Interpretation* 20.3 (Spring 1993): 237–57.

35. *HI*, ¶14.

36. Corbin, *Recital;* see also Nasr, *Sages*, 43–45.

37. *HI*, ¶3.

38. L. G. Westerink, "Ein astrologisches Kolleg aus dem Jahre 564," *Byzantinische Forschungen* 64 (1971): 6–21, cited in Lloyd, *Anatomy*, 6.

39. *SMM*, ¶185, in *SMj*, 1:452.

40. *Al-Ghazali's Tahafut al-Falasifa [Incoherence of the Philosophers]*, trans. Sabih Ahmad Kamali (Pakistan Philosophical Congress Publication no. 3; Lahore: Pakistan Philosophical Congress, 1963), 8; al-Ghazālī, *Tahāfut al-Falāsifa*, ed. Sulaymān Dunyā (Dhakhā'ir al-'Arab 15; Cairo: Dar al-Ma'ārif, n.d.), 68.

CHAPTER 9. PLATO VERSUS ARISTOTLE (i): THE CRITIQUE OF PERIPATETIC LOGIC

1. *HI*, ¶6.

2. The only major study of Illuminationist logic is *ZKI*, particularly chs. 2–3.

3. *Sophistical Refutations*, 34, 183b15–19, 33–35; translated from the Arabic translation of 'Īsā b. Zur'a, in 'Abd al-Raḥmān Badawī, ed., *Manṭiq Arisṭū* (Dirāsāt Islāmīya 7; Cairo: Dār al-Kutub al-Miṣrīya, 1948), 1010–11.

4. Ṣā'id, 91; cf. trans. 24–25.

5. *al-Risāla al-Shamsīya*, my translation, from A. Sprenger, ed. and trans., *The Logic of the Arabians* (Bibliotheca Indica 88; Calcutta: Asiatic Society of Bengal, 1854), 1, in al-Tahānawī, *Kashshāf Iṣṭilāḥāt al-Funūn: The Dictionary of the Technical Terms Used in the Sciences of the Mussalmans*, ed. A. Sprenger (Bibliotheca Indica 88, app. 1; Calcutta, F. Carbery, Bengal Military Orphan Press, 1862).

6. My account of Aristotle's logic is somewhat simplified and is tainted by the Islamic logicians' understanding of Aristotelian logic. However, many puzzles emerge when attempts are made to give an interpretation of Aristotle's logic in terms of modern logic. An introduction to the difficulties and varying interpretations is found in Robin Smith, "Logic," in *The Cambridge Companion to Aristotle* (Cambridge: Cambridge University Press, 1995), 27–65.

7. *HI*, ¶14.

8. *HI*, ¶70.

9. Lloyd, *Anatomy*, 15–16.

10. On the Mattā/Sīrāfī debate see ch. 7, n. 65. Ghazālī summarizes his views

on logic in his *al-Munqidh min al-Ḍalāl* (The Deliverer from Error), ed. 'Abd al-Ḥalīm Maḥmūd (3rd ed.; Silsila fi 'l-Dirāsāt al-Falsafīya wa'l-Akhlāqīya; Cairo: Maktabat al-Anjlū al-Miṣrīya, 1962), 150–51; W. Montgomery Watt, trans., *The Faith and Practice of al-Ghazālī* (London: George Allen and Unwin, 1953), 35–36; Richard Joseph McCarthy, trans., *Freedom and Fulfillment: An Annotated Translation of Al-Ghazālī's* al-Munqidh min al-Ḍalāl *and Other Relevant Works of al-Ghazālī* (Library of Classical Arabic Literature 4; Boston: Twayne Publishers, 1980), 74–75.

Three works of Ibn Taymīya on logic have been published. The first is *al-Radd 'alā 'l-Manṭiqīyīn* (The Refutation of the Logicians), a large work of almost 550 pages. *Naṣīḥat Ahl al-Īmān fī 'l-Radd 'alā Manṭiq al-Yūnān* (Advice to the People of Faith as to the Refutation of the Logic of Greece), ed. 'Alī Sāmī al-Nashshār (Cairo: Maṭba'at al-Sa'āda, n.d.), and ed. Su'ād 'Abd al-Rāziq and 'Alī Sāmī al-Nashshār (Cairo: Dār al-Naṣr, 1970), is more or less an abridgment of the *Radd* and is published as abridged by al-Suyūṭī under the title *Jahd al-Qarīḥa fī Tajrīd al-Naṣīḥa* (The Effort of Common Sense in Abridging the *Advice*). The *Jahd* has been translated by Wael B. Hallaq, *Ibn Taymiyya against the Greek Logicians* (Oxford: Clarendon Press, 1993). *Naqḍ al-Manṭiq* (Critique of Logic), ed. Muḥammad b. 'Abd al-Razzāq Ḥamza (Cairo: Maṭba'at al-Sunna al-Muḥammadīya, 1370/1951), is an independent work, having no relation except subject to the other two. It is full of all sorts of things having little relation to logic but of theological or philosophical interest. References to logic are also scattered elsewhere in Ibn Taymīya's voluminous works.

11. *al-Radd*, 3–4.

12. *JRH*, 87.

13. The translation 'analysis' is also used.

14. *Phaedrus* 265e.

15. *JRH*, 87–88. The stairs are my example, not Fārābī's.

16. *ZKI*, 77–128.

17. My example, not Suhrawardī's.

18. *HI*, ¶15. *ZKI*, 115, incorrectly translates *ijtimā'* as "the thing's total whole."

19. *HI*, ¶¶21, 25, 27–29.

20. *HI*, ¶¶50–51; cf. Lloyd, *Anatomy*, 21–25, 29, on debates among the commentators on Aristotle concerning the priority, or lack thereof, of the first figure, with the Neoplatonists generally arguing against its priority.

21. On modal logic and its metaphysical implications and problems, see Graeme Forbes, *The Metaphysics of Modality* (Clarendon Library of Logic and Philosophy; Oxford: Clarendon Press, 1985).

22. *HI*, ¶¶19–20.

23. For a summary of the issue in medieval European philosophy, see Simo Knuuttila, "Modal Logic," in Norman Kretzmann, Anthony Kenny, and Jan Pinborg, eds., *The Cambridge History of Later Medieval Philosophy: From the Rediscovery of Aristotle to the Disintigration of Scholasticism, 1100–1600* (Cambridge: Cambridge University Press, 1982), 342–57 and 344, for the principle of plenitude,

and in more detail his *Modalities in Medieval Philosophy* (Topics in Medieval Philosophy; New York: Routledge, 1993), esp. 1–18. His work is based on that of J. Hintikka, which can be traced through Knuuttila's notes. Other recent work on modal logic in Aristotle is Richard Patterson, *Aristotle's Modal Logic: Essence and Entailment in the* Organon (Cambridge: Cambridge University Press, 1995), and Paul Thom, *The Logic of Essentialism: An Interpretation of Aristotle's Modal Syllogistic* (The New Synthese Historical Library 43; Dordrecht: Kluwer Academic Publishers, 1996).

24. Nicholas Rescher and Arnold vander Nat, "The Arabic Theory of Temporal Modal Syllogistic," in Hourani, ed., *Essays*, 189–21; Nicholas Rescher, "The Theory of Temporal Modalities in Arabic Logic and Philosophy," in Nicholas Rescher, *Studies in Arabic Philosophy* (Pittsburgh: University of Pittsburgh Press, 1966), 81–110; idem, "Ibn al-'Aṣṣāl's Discourse on Logic," in ibid., 11–36; idem, *Temporal Modalities in Arabic Logic* (Foundations of Language, Supp. Series 2; Dordrecht: D. Reidel, 1967).

25. A. C. Lloyd, *The Anatomy of Neoplatonism* (Oxford: Clarendon Press, 1990), p. 21, who attributes this move to a failure to distinguish rules of inference from major premises. Galen, *Institutio Logica*, trans. John Spangler Kieffer (Baltimore: Johns Hopkins University Press, 1964), text, §§iii–vii; comm., 66ff. On propositional logic in Aristotle, the early Peripatetics, and the Stoics, see Anton Dumitriu, *History of Logic* (New Delhi: Heritage Publishers, 1991), 1:182–83, 210–13, 242–52. Ibn Sīnā, *al-Shifā': al-Qiyās*, ed. S. Zayed (Cairo: al-Mu'assasa al-Miṣrīya al-'Āmma, 1964), 229–425. Nabil Shehaby, *The Propositional Logic of Avicenna: A Translation from* al-Shifā': al-Qiyās *with Introduction, Commentary, and Glossary* (Synthese Historical Library; Dordrecht: D. Reidel, 1973), covering books 5–9.

26. Cf. Galen, *Institutio*, 7.4.

27. *HI*, ¶16.

28. *In Parm.* 107, in Lloyd, *Anatomy*, 13. Lloyd, at least, is not convinced.

29. *HI*, ¶64.

30. *al-Munqidh*, trans. McCarthy, 75; ed. Maḥmūd, 151.

31. *HI*, ¶6. Olympiodorus, cited in Lloyd, *Anatomy*, 29.

CHAPTER 10. PLATO VERSUS ARISTOTLE (ii): PLATONIC EPISTEMOLOGY

1. Mehdi Hai'iri Yazdi, *The Principles of Epistemology in Islamic Philosophy: Knowledge by Presence* (SUNY Series in Islam; Albany: State University of New York Press, 1992).

2. *SML*, 105–8. A similar mixing of optics and epistemology occured in later medieval philosophy; see Katherine H. Tachau, *Vision and Certitude in the Age of Ockham: Optics, Epistemology and the Foundations of Semantics* (Studien und Texte zur Geistesgeschichte des Mittelalters 22; Leiden: E. J. Brill, 1988).

3. The history of the theory of vision in antiquity and the Middle Ages is con-

veniently summarized in David C. Lindberg, *Theories of Vision from al-Kindi to Kepler* (University of Chicago History of Science and Medicine; Chicago: University of Chicago Press, 1976), especially chapter 1. On Empedocles, see *HGP*, 2:234–35, 237, though the details of Empedocles' theory are obscure. On Plato, see *Timaeus* 45B–46C.

4. *JRH*, 91.

5. *JRH*, 92. The translation is a bit loose but faithful to the spirit of the original.

6. *JRH*, 92–94.

7. *JRH*, 94.

8. *HI*, ¶215.

9. *HI*, ¶145.

10. His critique is in *HI*, ¶¶101–3.

11. *QDS*, 264, 267, 268.

12. Lindberg, *Theories*, 6–9, 43–52.

13. Cf. Aristotle, *De Anima* 2.7 418b21–27, where he rejects a theory that he attributes to Empedocles according to which light travels from the lighted thing across the intervening distance to the eye.

14. *HI*, ¶100.

15. Aristotle, *De Anima* 2.12 424a18–23.

16. *HI*, ¶¶102–3.

17. *HI*, ¶105.

18. *HI*, ¶258. See also p. 70 above.

19. Some such theory is rejected by Aristotle, *De Sensu* 6 446b10–13.

20. 'Abd al-Raḥmān Badawī, ed., *Commentaires sur Aristote perdus en Grec et autres épitres* (Recherches de l'Institut de Lettres Orientales de Beyrouth, N.S. A. Langue Arabe et Pensée Islamique 1; Beirut: Dar El-Machreq, 1971), 26–30. On the reception of Alexander's works, see Silvia Fazzo and Hillary Wiesner, "Alexander of Aphrodisius in the Kindī-Circle and in al-Kindī's Cosmology," *Arabic Sciences and Philosophy* 3 (1993): 119–53.

21. *Fihrist*, 514, no. 12; Ibn Abī Uṣaybi'a, ed. Riḍā, 106–7. Each gives the title as *Maqāla fī anna al-ibṣār lā yakūn bi-shu'ā'āt tanbathth* (or *tabuthth*) *min al-'ayn.*" See also 'Abd al-Raḥmān Badawī, "New Philosophical Texts Lost in Greek and Preserved in Arabic Translations," in Morewedge, ed., *Islamic Philosophical Theology*, 3–13.

22. Ṣā'id, 82–83; trans. 25.

23. *ShNA*, 1:308; *ShNR*, 325.

24. *ShNR*, 325–26. This and the following passage are not found in *ShNA*.

25. Badawī, ed., *Commentaires*, 30.

26. *HI*, ¶226.

27. F. Th. Stcherbatsky, *Buddhist Logic* (New York: Dover, 1962), 1:163, 2:29–30.

28. *QDS*, 38.

29. *QDS*, 38.

30. Avicenna, *Kitāb al-Najāt*, ed. Majid Fakhry (Beirut: Dār al-Āfāq al-

Jadīda, 1985), pp. 210–13; F. Rahman, trans., *Avicenna's Psychology* (London: Oxford University Press, 1952), 41–44.

31. Ghazālī, *Munqidh*, ed. Maḥmūd, 152–58; trans. Watt, 37–38; trans. McCarthy, 76–77; *Tahāfut al-Falāsifa*, ed. Dunyā, 192–203, 268–92; trans. Kamali, 153–62, 229–48.

32. *SMj*, 1:70–74. On its order in the Illuminationist corpus, see *ZKI*, 10. One of the allegories, *In the State of Childhood*, takes knowledge as its theme, but it does not deal with knowledge by presence but rather with the more general question of mystical knowledge and its rejection by those who do not understand it.

33. *SMj*, 1:68–69; for a translation see appendix II below.

34. On the Neoplatonic views of singular terms as predicates and definite descriptions, see Lloyd, *Anatomy*, 43–47.

35. *HI*, ¶¶114–16.

36. *HI*, ¶¶104, 225–29, 244–48, 258–59.

37. *SML*, 45–46, 86, where I translate the term as 'intellectual fictions'.

38. *HI*, ¶¶56–69.

39. Marilyn McCord Adams, *William Ockham* (Publications in Medieval Studies, the Medieval Institute, University of Notre Dame, 26; South Bend, Indiana: University of Notre Dame Press, 1989), 18–22 and elsewhere. A substantial number of errors were corrected in the 1989 paperback edition, which should therefore be used in preference to the 1987 hardcover edition.

40. *Talwīḥāt*, ¶55, in *SMj*, 1:73–74.

41. Mas'ūdī, *Murūj al-Dhahab*, ed. C. Barbier de Meynard (Paris, 1861–1917), 4:64–65.

42. Proclus, *In Platonis Alcibiadem*, 1.4–5; ed. and trans. A. Ph. Segonds, *Proclus sur le premier Alcibiade de Platon* (Budé; Paris: Les Belles Lettres, 1985), 1:1; cf. *Phaedrus*, 230a, where Socrates identifies the knowledge of his self as his central philosophical interest.

43. Lloyd, *Anatomy*, chs.1–3; idem, "Neoplatonic Logic and Aristotelian Logic," *Phronesis* 1.1 (Nov. 1955): 59–72, 1.2 (May 1956): 146–60.

44. *Phaedrus* 247, *Symposium* 211, *Republic* 514–17. On the arguments for and against—mainly against—interpreting Plato as offering a theory of knowledge as perception, see J. C. B. Gosling, *Plato* (The Arguments of the Philosophers; London: Routledge & Kegan Paul, 1973), 120–39.

45. See pp. 178–79 below.

46. See pp. 134–36 above.

47. *QDS*, 465.

48. "Lahu rasā'il mawjūda," *Fihrist*, 503. See also *JRH*, 84, which refers to Plato's *aqāwīl* and *rasā'il* on politics, literally "sayings" and "letters," which would seem to refer to dialogues and epistles respectively. See also ibid., 85, which seems to contain a reference to a condemnation of writing philosophy, a theme of the *Seventh Epistle*.

49. 341C–D; trans. Glenn R. Morrow, *Plato's Epistles* (Indianapolis: Library of the Liberal Arts, 1962), 237.

50. 344B, trans. Morrow.

51. 342A–B, trans. Morrow. This passage is cited twice in Syrianus' commentary on *Metaphysics* M.4 and N.3 (*Commentaria in Aristotelem Graeca*, 6.1:115.23, 180.2), but these books are not attested in Arabic bibliographies, although his commentary on *Metaphysics* B is. The presence of translations of large Neoplatonic commentaries on Aristotle in Arabic, though almost all are now lost, is sufficient to explain all manner of Platonisms in Islamic thought.

52. 342B–343D.

53. 344A–B, trans. Morrow.

54. The main discussion of εἴδωλον in Plato is *Sophist* 266D.

55. On intuition in Avicenna, see Dimitri Gutas, *Avicenna and the Aristotelian Tradition: Introduction to Reading Avicenna's Philosophical Works* (Islamic Philosophy and Theology 4; Leiden: E. J. Brill, 1988), 159–76.

56. *HI*, ¶2; *ShS*, 16–17.

57. *QDS*, 14, regards the *wāhib al-'ilm* as the active intellect.

58. Qur'ān 71:23.

59. *HI*, ¶4.

60. See p. 206 below.

61. On philosophical elitism in Plato, see ch. 7, nn. 62, 109.

62. In his *Faṣl al-Maqāl fīmā bayn al-Ḥikma wa'l-Sharī'a min al-Ittiṣāl*, ed. Muḥammad 'Imāra (3rd ed.; Beirut: al-Mu'assasa al-'Arabīya, 1986); *Averroes on the Harmony of Religion and Philosophy*, trans. George F. Hourani (E. J. W. Gibb Memorial Series, n.s., 21: London: Luzac, 1961), reprinted in Ralph Lerner and Muhsin Mahdi, eds., *Medieval Political Philosophy* (Ithaca, N.Y.: Cornell University Press, 1972), 163–85, and Arthur Hyman and James J. Walsh, eds., *Philosophy in the Middle Ages* (2nd ed.; Indianapolis: Hackett, 1983), 297–316. On the larger question of this sort of esoteric philosophical writing, see Leo Strauss, *Persecution and the Art of Writing* (Glencoe, Ill.: The Free Press, 1952), 7–37.

63. Léon Gauthier, ed. and trans., *Hayy ben Yaqdhān, Roman philosophique d'Ibn Thofaïl* (2nd ed.; Beirut: Imprimerie Catholique, 1936); Aḥmad Amīn, ed., *Ḥayy b. Yaqẓān l' Ibn Sīnā wa-Ibn Ṭufayl wa'l-Suhrawardī* (Cairo: Dār al-Ma'ārif, 1952); L. E. Goodman, trans., *Ibn Ṭufayl's Ḥayy Ibn Yaqẓān, a Philosophical Tale* (New York: Twayne Publishers, 1972). This work was translated into Latin and then twice into English in the seventeenth century as part of the debates concerning the relation of reason, revelation, and religious authority.

64. Something should be said in explanation and defense of these renderings of *baḥth* and *ta'alluh*. 'Discursive philosophy' is not too much of a problem, since *baḥth* literarally means "investigation." It should not be confused with 'theoretical philosophy' (*al-ḥikma al-naẓarī*, i.e., θεωρία). Both the discursive and intuitive philosopher deal with theoretical philosophy, and the Illuminationists include ethics in theoretical philosophy; *ShS*, 3. *Ta'alluh* is much more of a problem, and Hossein Ziai and I experimented with a number of renderings when we translated *The Philosophy of Illumination*. The justification for 'intuitive philosophy' is that it accurately expresses the distinctive method of this philosopher, who uses intellectual/mystical intuitition along with or instead of demonstration and dialectic. Of course, literally the word has nothing to do with intuition, meaning rather "deification." 'Divinity' might have worked, used in the same sense it

appears in the title 'Doctor of Divinity', but it seemed to us to conjure up unfortunate images of Anglican clergymen of the Trollopean sort. 'Theosophy' has its own problems. 'Theurgy' is tempting, but it properly applies to the magical application of philosophy.

65. Ibn al-Munawwar, *Secrets*, trans. O'Kane, 30, slightly modified for clarity; ed. Ṣafā, 210.

66. 342B, trans. Morrow.

67. 344B, trans. Morrow.

68. *HI*, ¶5.

69. *Averroes on Plato's* Republic, trans. Ralph Lerner (Agora Paperback Editions; Ithaca, N.Y.: Cornell University Press, 1974), 22. Page references here are to the Hebrew edition of E. I. J. Rosenthal.

70. *Averroes on Plato's* Republic, 74.

71. Ibn Bājja, *Rasā'il Ibn Bājja al-Ilāhīya*, ed. Mājid Fakhrī (al-Dirāsāt wa'l-Nuṣūṣ al-Falsafīya 1; Beirut: Dār al-Nahār, 1968), 71 (*Tadbīr al-Mutawaḥḥid*, on incest), 125 (*Risālat al-Widā'*, on sensation), 168 (*Ittiṣāl al-'Aql bi'l-Insān*, on the cave).

72. Ibn Ṭufayl, *Ḥayy b. Yaqẓān*, ed. Amīn, 57–58; cf. trans. George N. Atiyeh, in Lerner and Mahdi, *Medieval Political Philosophy*, 135–36.

73. Ibn Ṭufayl, 59; cf. trans. Atiyeh, 136.

74. Ibn Ṭufayl, 60–61; trans. Atiyeh, 137–38.

75. *QDS*, 16.

76. *HI*, ¶165.

77. See my *SML*, 31–39, where I discuss this theme from the point of view of the logic of science.

78. *The Great Dialogues of Plato* (Mentor Classics; New York: New American Library, 1956).

79. Glenn R. Morrow and John M. Dillon, trans., *Proclus' Commentary on Plato's* Parmenides (Princeton: Princeton University Press, 1987), xiv.

80. See, for example, Findlay, *Plato*, and especially his brilliant account of the Platonic tradition in his final chapter in which he defends the validity of the Neoplatonic interpretation of Plato against interpretation based only on surface readings of the dialogues.

CHAPTER 11. THE STOICS

1. Mullā Ṣadrā, *Kitāb al-Mashā'ir*, ed. Henry Corbin (Dānishkada-yi Adabīyāt-i Iṣfahān 4; Tehran: Shahryār, 1961), ¶89.

2. Mullā Ṣadrā, *The Wisdom of the Throne: An Introduction to the Philosophy of Mullā Ṣadrā*, trans. James Winston Morris (Princeton Library of Asian Translations; Princeton: Princeton University Press, 1981), 106–7. Idem, *al-Asfār*, 1:5, 139–40; 2:224; 6:181. Doubtless there are other references that I missed, given the dismal state of the indexes of this book.

3. 'Alī-Akbar Dihkhudā, *Lughat-Nāma* (Tehran: Dānishgāh-i Tihrān, 1946–79), s.v. *Riwāqīyān*, quoting two nineteenth-century Persian dictionaries *Ghiyāth al-Lughāt* (1826) and *Ānandarāj* (1888).

4. On Stoicism in Islam see Fehmi Jadaane, *L'influence du stoïcism sur la pensée musulmane* (Beirut, Dar El-Machreq, 1968). Its limitation from the point of view of the present work is that it is concerned with actual influences of Stoic ideas on various areas of Islamic thought. Since such influences reached the Muslims by means of late classical texts more or less influenced by the Stoics, most of these ideas were not labelled as Stoic and consequently were not recognized as such by the Muslims. Jadaane also stops at the thirteenth century.

5. *al-Mashā'ir*, ¶89.

6. *al-Asfār*, 1:139–40.

7. *Wisdom*, 106–7; *al-Asfār*, 6:180–81.

8. See pp. 164–69 above.

9. *al-Asfār*, 2:224.

10. *al-Asfār*, 5:66–67.

11. *al-Asfār*, 1:5.

12. *al-Asfār*, 2:53, 59–60.

13. *al-Asfār*, 3:291.

14. *al-Asfār*, 5:94–98.

15. Daylamī, *Maḥbūb*, 21–22. On the author see Āqā Buzurg al-Ṭihrānī, *al-Dharī'a ilā Taṣānīf al-Shī'a* (2nd ed.; Beirut: Dār al-Aḍwā', n.d.), 20:141–42. It is also found in Ṣā'id, 92–94, trans. 29, and Qifṭī, ed. Lippert, 25–26. The ultimate source is probably Greek since similar lists are found in sources like Diogenes Laertius 1.17; Simplicius, *In Cat.* 3.30–4.9, trans. Hoffmann, 10; and Ammonius, *In Cat.* 1.14–3.19, trans. S. Marc Cohen and Gareth B. Matthews, *Ammonius: On Aristotle's Categories* (Ancient Commentators on Aristotle; Ithaca, N.Y.: Cornell University Press, 1991), 9.

16. Rosenthal, *Classical Heritage*, 144–45, citing Bahā' al-Dīn al-'Āmulī, *Kashkūl* (Cairo: 'Īsā al-Bābī al-Ḥalabī, 1961), 1:312.

17. Cited in Corbin, *History*, 9.

18. *SMN*, 2:60. Mullā Ṣadrā quotes this work in *al-Asfār*, 3:112.

19. *DPsA*, 60–65, 185–89. On this work see also Paul E. Walker, *Early Philosophical Shiism: The Ismaili Neoplatonism of Abū Ya'qūb al-Sijistānī* (Cambridge Studies in Islamic Civilization; Cambridge: Cambridge University Press, 1993), 39–42, and passim.

20. Mas'ūdī, *Tanbīh*, 8, 115.

21. Ibn Khaldūn, *The Muqaddimah: An Introduction to History*, trans. Franz Rosenthal (Bollingen Series 43; Princeton: Princeton University Press, 1958), 3:114–15; *Muqaddimat al-'Allāma Ibn Khaldūn* (4th ed.; Beirut: Dār al-Kitāb al-'Ilmīya, 1978), 480; cf. Ibn Juljul, 42–43, s.v. "Jālīnūs."

22. Ibn Khaldūn, *Kitāb al-'Ibar* (7 vols.; Beirut: Dār al-Kitāb al-Lubnānī, 1956–61; reprinted 1977), 2:382.

23. Al-Qifṭī, cited in 'Alī Sāmī al-Nashshār, *Nash'at al-Fikr al-Falsafī fī 'l-Islām* (3rd ed.; [Cairo]: Dār al-Ma'ārif, 1965), 1:148.

24. al-Qifṭī, ed. Lippert, 265.

25. Dimitri Gutas, "Pre-Plotinian Philosophy in Arabic (Other than Platonism and Aristotelianism): A Review of the Sources," in Wolfgang Haase and Hildegard

Temporini, eds., *Aufstieg und Niedergang der römischen Welt* (Berlin: Walter de Gruyter, 1994), II.36.7:4939–73.

26. *Ancient Alphabets and Hieroglyphic Characters* (London: 1806), 100.

27. Ṣadrā, *Wisdom*, 135; idem, *al-Asfār*, 1:5.

28. *SMN*, 2:101–2.

29. For the text and abridged translation of the passage in *Sirr al-Khalīqa*, see Weißer, ed., *Buch*, 67–68, and idem, trans., *"Buch,"* 82–83, respectively.

30. Ulrich Rudolph, *DPA*, s.v. "Cal(l)anus. Tradition arabe." On Calanus as an Indian sage, see Walbridge, *Wisdom*, forthcoming.

31. *al-Asfār*, 2:5960.

32. *al-Asfār*, 2:53, 59–60; 6:199.

33. In the version of this chapter earlier published in the *Journal of the History of Philosophy*, I included a list of possible parallels between authentic Stoic doctrines and Suhrawardī's philosophical views; pp. 524–30. On sober reflection this list seems to me to be unduly speculative. For some time I have been collecting material on Stoic materials available to the Muslims, so I hope eventually to return to this issue in a larger context and on the basis of a much more detailed understanding of the details of Stoics influences in Islam.

34. *KAA*, 70–75; *ShNA*, 1:24–28; *ShNR*, 99–103; Diogenes Laertius 1.13–15; Aetius 1.3.9.

35. *SMN*, 2:60, 101–2.

36. *HI*, ¶4.

37. On *usṭuwān*, see Jadaane, *L'influence*, 56–59.

CHAPTER 12. POLITICS AND THE FAILURE OF SUHRAWARDĪ'S POLITICAL AMBITIONS

1. Ibn Abī Uṣaybi'a, ed. Müller, 2:167; Ibn Khallikān, ed. 'Abbās, 6:272. 'Imād al-Dīn al-Iṣfahānī, a contemporary of Saladin, remarks in his *al-Busṭān al-Jāmi' li-Tawārīkh al-Zamān* that "in general, he lacked not knowledge but prudence (*'aql lā 'ilm)*"; cited from Claude Cahen, "Une chronique syrienne du VIe/XIIe siècle: Le *"Bustān al-Jāmi',"* *Bulletin d'études orientales* 7–8 (1937–38).

2. Slightly condensed from *ShNA*, 2, pp 125; *ShNR*, 605.

3. The political aspects of Suhrawardī's thought are discussed in Hossein Ziai, "The Source and Nature of Authority: A Study of al-Suhrawardī's Illuminationist Political Doctrine," in Charles Butterworth, ed., *The Political Aspects of Islamic Philosophy: Essays in Honor of Muhsin S. Mahdi* (Harvard Middle Eastern Monographs 27; Cambridge: Center for Middle Eastern Studies, Harvard University, 1992), 304–44, which treats the questions of Suhrawardī's political thought and the reason for his execution in more detail than I do here. I am in general agreement with Ziai's conclusions and indebted to this article. See also my "The Political Thought of Quṭb al-Dīn al-Shīrāzī," in idem, 345–78, where I argue that Quṭb al-Dīn in radically different political conditions largely abandoned the idealistic political thought of Suhrawardī.

4. David Morray, *An Ayyubid Notable and his World: Ibn al-'Adīm and Aleppo* (Islamic History and Civilization, Studies and Texts 5; Leiden: E. J. Brill, 1994), 41–42.

5. Ibn Abī Uṣaybi'a, ed. Müller, 2:168–69; the full passage is translated on pp. 52–53 above. A shorter version is in Yāqūt, *Irshād*, 7:269. Poverty, for obvious reasons, tended to undermine claims of proficiency in alchemy and the occult arts; see, for example, *Fihrist*, 712: one al-Khanshalīl "often claimed to me that he had mastered the Art [of alchemy], but I saw no signs of that and indeed never saw him except as an impoverished, ill-favored old man."

6. Ibn Shaddād, *Sīrat*, ed. Shayyāl, 10, and quoted by Ibn Khallikān.

7. Abū Rayyān, "Kayf Ubīḥ Dam al-Suhrawardī al-Ishrāqī," *al-Thaqāfa* 702 (16 Ramaḍān 1371/9 June 1952), 25–26.

8. The word is *ṭuruqī*, which a modern editor glosses as "the market wisdom circulating among the people in the streets"; *ShNR*, 602, n. 1. Dozy, *Supplément au dictionnaire arabe*, s.v. *ṭuruqī*, defines *ṭuruqī* as a "charlatan qui débite ses remédes en place publique," the basis of my translation.

9. Ed. and trans. Michael E. Marmura (Islamic Translation Series; Provo, Utah: Brigham Young University Press, 1997), 230.

10. *SMN*, 1:20, 44, 76, 86, 88, 90 (on the Jabrīya), 92, 193 (on the Isma'ilis). On the Isma'ili denial of the charge of *ta'ṭīl*, see Walker, *Philosophical Shiism*, 74, 78, 80, 98; al-Sijistānī, *Kashf al-Maḥjūb*, 14–15.

11. See pp. 61–62 above.

12. *HI*, ¶5.

13. Abū Rayyān, "Kayf Ubīḥ," 26.

14. *ShNA*, 2, p. 125; *ShNR*, 605.

15. Ibn Khallikān, ed. 'Abbās, 6:272.

16. Franz Rosenthal, "From Arabic Books and Manuscripts xiii: The Arabic Translation of a Pythagorean Letter," *Journal of the American Oriental Society* 95 (1975): 209–11.

17. The long introduction to Morrow's translation of the *Epistles* discusses the political aspects of Plato's adventures in Syracuse in detail.

18. *Epistle VII*, 328A–C, trans. Morrow.

19. *Munqidh*, ed. Maḥmūd, 171; trans. Watt, 53; trans. McCarthy, 89; Ṣā'id al-Andalusī, 73, trans. 21.

20. *Timaeus* 29D.

21. Morrow, *Epistles*, 148–55.

22. *In Carmen Aureum* 21–22, cited in *OPR*, 115.

23. *In Platonis Phaedrum scholia* 253.20–25, trans. *OPR*, 126.

24. *Epistle VII*, 324B–325A.

CHAPTER 13. THE PHILOSOPHICAL HERITAGE OF SUHRAWARDĪ

1. Ibn Khallikān, ed. 'Abbās, 6:273, citing the history of Sibṭ b. al-Jawzī.

2. *HI*, ¶280.

3. *HI*, ¶2–3, 260, 276, 278–80.

4. *ShNA*, 2: 121–22; *ShNR*, 601–2; *Sharḥ*, 6–7.

5. Ibn Abī Uṣaybi'a, ed. Müller, 2:204.

6. *Sharḥ*, 6–7; *ShNA*, 2:128–29; *ShNR*, 608–9.

7. The evidence for this account of the textual tradition of *The Philosophy of Illumination* will be found in the introduction to Ziai's and my edition. Since both Shahrazūrī and Quṭb al-Dīn refer to the manuscripts available to them, it is clear that the editions they used were already in existence when they wrote their commentaries, although Shahrazūrī probably did not have access to the "corrected edition."

8. *Rawḍat al-Ta'rīf bi'l-Ḥubb al-Sharīf*, ed. 'Abd al-Qādir Aḥmad 'Aṭā' (1st ed.; [n.p.]: Dār al-Fikr al-'Arabī, 1387/1967), 563–71. There is another edition by. Muḥammad al-Kattānī (Ribat: Dār al-Thaqāfa, 1978).

9. For a general account of the influence of Suhrawardī's philosophy in later centuries, see Amin Razavi, *Suhrawardi*, 121–45, and Ziai, "The Illuminationist Tradition," in Nasr and Oliver Leaman, eds., 465–96.

10. On the condemnations and the effect on natural philosophy, see Edward Grant, *The Foundations of Modern Science in the Middle Ages in Their Religious, Institutional, and Intellectual Contexts* (Cambridge: Cambridge University Press, 1996), 70–85. An earlier study by the same author is "The Condemnation of 1277, God's Absolute Power, and Physical Thought in the Late Middle Ages," *Viator* 10 (1979): 211–44, reprinted in Edward Grant, *Studies in Medieval Science and Natural Philosophy* (London: Variorum Reprints, 1981), §xiii. A commentary on the condemned propositions is found in Roland Hissette, *Enquête sur les 219 articles condamnés à Paris le 7 mars 1277* (Philosophes médiévaux 22; Louvain: Publications Universitaires, 1977). All or some of them are translated in various places including Hyman and Walsh, 582–91; Ralph Lerner and Muhin Mahdi, *Medieval Political Philosophy* (Ithaca, N.Y.: Cornell University Press, 1972), 335–54; and Edward Grant, *A Sourcebook of Medieval Science* (Cambridge: Harvard University Press, 1974), 45–50.

11. Quṭb al-Dīn, *Durrat.* On this work see my *SML*, 175–78.

12. A charming account of the teaching of logic in a modern Shi'ite seminary is Roy Mottahedah, *The Mantle of the Prophet: Religion and Politics in Iran* (New York: Simon & Schuster, 1985), 69–78.

13. Medieval Islamic science plays a significant role in the historiography of the Scientific Revolution. Historians of science are divided between those who see the Scientific Revolution as a discontinuity with the past and those who see medieval science as playing a critical role in preparing the ground for the rise of modern science, which thus represents a continuity with medieval science. For the latter Islamic science is an important test case, since there ought to be identifiable differences between Islam and Christendom explaining why Islam, with a head start and very similar materials did not have a Scientific Revolution. Most recent discussion has dealt with the supposed "marginalization" of science by religion in Islam and the presence of the autonomous institution of the university in Europe—that is, science failed in Islam due to some broad-based cultural deficiency, proba-

bly religious, in the Islamic world not shared by medieval and early modern Europe. Advocates of such a position include most recently Toby Huff, *The Rise of Early Modern Science: Islam, China, and the West* (Cambridge: Cambridge University Press, 1993), 47–90, 149–51, 202–4, and passim, and Edward Grant, *Foundations*, passim. Discussion to 1990 is summarized in H. Floris Cohen, *The Scientific Revolution: A Historiographical Inquiry* (Chicago: University of Chicago Press, 1994), 378–417. A vigorous rejection of the marginalization thesis is given by A. I. Sabra, "The Appropriation and Subsequent Naturalization of Greek Science in Medieval Islam: A Preliminary Statement," *History of Science* 25 (1987): 223–43, and "Situating Arabic Science: Locality versus Essence," *Isis* 87 (1996): 654–70; see also his "Science and Philosophy in Medieval Islamic Theology: The Evidence of the Fourteenth Century," *Zeitschrift für Geschichte der arabische-islamischen Wissenschaften* 9 (1994): 1–42. My own view, for whatever it is worth, is that the continuity thesis is correct in explaining the rise of science in Europe but that its advocates are wrong about Islamic science; see my "Islam and Science," *Islamic Studies* 37.3 (1998): 395–410.

14. *The Autobiography of Bertrand Russell* (Boston: Little, Brown, 1968), 2:30.

15. *al-Usus al-Manṭiqīya li'l-Istiqrā'* ("The Logical Bases of Induction"; 5th ed.; Beirut: Dār al-Ta'āruf, 1986). Al-Ṣadr, whose books on Islamic ideology and economics are read across the Islamic world, argues that theological propositions rest on the same logical bases and have the same level of certainty as scientific propositions. On his philosophy, see my "Muhammad Baqir al-Sadr: An Introduction to His Philosophy," in Linda Walbridge, *Most Learned*, forthcoming.

APPENDIX I. HENRY CORBIN AND SUHRAWARDĪ STUDIES

1. *EIr*, s.v. "Corbin," which contains detailed bibliography on Corbin's larger works and a summary of the major themes of Corbin's interpretive project. On his life and work see in particular C. Jambet, ed., *Henry Corbin* (Herne 39; Paris: Herne, 1981), containing a chronology of Corbin's life; a number of his short pieces; essays, appreciations, letters, etc., by associates; and a full bibliography of his works up to that time, and Shayegan, *Topographie*.

APPENDIX II. SUHRAWARDĪ'S DREAM OF ARISTOTLE

1. "Suhrawardī's *An Episode and a Trance*," in Morewedge, ed. *Islamic Philosophy*, 177–89; Amin Razavi, *Suhrawardi*, 59–60.

2. *HI*, ¶3. The dream is recounted in the metaphysics of the *Talwīḥāt*, in *SMj*, 1, ¶55, 70–74. It is cited by the nineteenth-century Sufi Ma'ṣūm 'Alī Shāh in his *Ṭarā'iq al-Ḥaqā'iq* (2 vols.; Tehran: Sanā'ī, 1970), 1:155, as evidence of the contrast between the speculative and mystical approaches to knowledge of the Afterlife.

3. I have systematically rendered *nafs* as "self" and *dhāt* as "essence." In ordinary Arabic, and to some extent here, both are 'self', components of what in

English would be reflexive pronouns like 'myself' and 'yourself'. In philosophical use both have stronger senses. *Nafs* is also "soul," rendering the Greek ψυχή or the stronger English senses of the word 'self'. *Dhāt* renders οὐσία and refers to the being of the thing. Suhrawardī is obviously aware of these ambiguities and is playing on them to make his argument work.

4. Probably *De Anima* 3.6 and *Posterior Anayltics* 2; cf. Ibn Sīnā, *al-Sifā': al-Ṭabī'īyāt 6: al-Nafs*, ed. Ibrāhīm Madkūr (Cairo: al-Hay'a al-'Āmma li'l-Kitāb, 1975), 151.

5. It is not clear whether Aristotle is speaking in the remainder of the paragraph or Suhrawardī is editorializing on Aristotle's earlier words. I have assumed the former in the translation.

6. Qur'ān 34:3.

7. Qur'ān 38:34, 39.

BIBLIOGRAPHY

Abū Rayyān, Muḥammad-ʻAlī. *Uṣūl al-Falsafa al-Ishrāqīya.* Beirut: Dār al-Ṭalaba al-ʻArab, 1969.

———. "Kayf Ubīḥ Dam al-Suhrawardī al-Ishrāqī." *al-Thaqāfa* 702 (16 Ramaḍān 1371/9 June 1952).

Aetius [Pseudo-Plutarch]. *Aetius Arabus: Die Vorsokratiker in arabischer Überlieferung.* Edited by Hans Daiber. Wiesbaden: Franz Steiner, 1980.

———. *De Placitis.* In H. Diels, ed. *Doxographi Graeci,* pp. 267–444.

———. *De Placitis.* Italian translation by L. Torraca. *I Dossografi Greci.* Padua: CEDAM, 1961, pp. 15–223

———. *De Placitis.* In Plutarch. *Plutarch's Morals.* Edited by William Goodwin. Boston: Little, Brown, and Co., 1878. Vol. 3. Pp. 104–93.

Afnan, Soheil. *A Philosophical Lexicon in Persian and Arabic.* Beirut: Dar El-Mashreq, [1968].

Alexander of Aphrodisius. *In Aristotelis Topicorum Libros Octo Commentaria.* In *Commentaria in Aristotelem Graeca.* Vol. 2, part 2.

Alon, Ilai. *Socrates in Mediaeval Arabic Literature.* Islamic Philosophy, Theology, and Science, Texts and Studies 10. Leiden: E. J. Brill, 1991.

Aminrazavi, Mehdi. "The Significance of Suhrawardī's Persian Sufi Writings in the Philosophy of Illumination." In Leonard Lewisohn, ed. *Classical Persian Sufism: From its Origins to Rumi.* London: Khaniqahi Nimatullahi Publications, 1993. Pp. 259–83.

———. *Suhrawardi and the School of Illumination.* Curzon Sufi Series. Richmond, Surrey: Curzon, 1996.

al-ʻĀmirī, Abu'l-Ḥasan. *Kitāb al-Amad ʻalā 'l-Abad.* In Rowson, *Philosopher.*

Ammonius, *In Aristotelis Categorias Commentrius.* In *Commentaria in Aristotelem Graeca.* Vol. 4, part 4.

Pseudo-Ammonius. *Die Doxographie des Pseudo-Ammonios: Ein Beitrag zur neuplatonischen Überlieferung im Islam.* Ed. and trans. Ulrich Rudolph. Deutsche morgenländische Gesellschaft, Abhandlungen für Kunde des Morgenlandes 49.1; Wiesbaden: Franz Steiner, 1989.

Pseudo-Apollonius of Tyana. *Buch über das Geheimniss der Schöpfung und die Darstellung der Natur (Buch der Ursachen) [Sirr al-Khalīqa].* Ed. Ursula Weisser. Sources and Studies in the History of Arabic-Islamic Science, Natural Sciences Series 1. Aleppo: Institute for the Study of Arabic Science, 1979.

———. *Das "Buch über das Geheimnis der Schöpfung" von Pseudo-Apollonios von Tyana.* Trans. Ursula Weisser. Ars Medica, Texte und Untersuchungen zur

Quellenkunde der Alten Medizin III. Arabische Medizin 2. Berlin: Walter de Gruyter, 1980. Abridged translation of *Sirr al-Khalīqa*.

Aristotle. *The Complete Works of Aristotle: The Revised Oxford Translation*. Bollingen Series 71.2. Princeton: Princeton University Press, 1984.

Pseudo-Aristotle. *The Apple, or Aristotle's Death (De Pomo sive De Morte Aristotilis)*. Trans. Mary F. Rousseau. Mediaeval Philosophical Texts in Translation 18. Milwaukee: Marquette University Press, 1968.

———. "*The Book of the Apple* Ascribed to Aristotle Edited in Persian and English." Ed. D. S. Margoliouth. *Journal of the Royal Asiatic Society* n.s. 24 (1892): 187–252.

———. *Theology*. See Plotinus.

Audi, Robert, ed. *The Cambridge Dictionary of Philosophy*. Cambridge: Cambridge University Press, 1995.

Averroes. *Averroes on Plato's* Republic. Trans. Ralph Lerner. Agora Paperback Editions. Ithaca, N.Y.: Cornell University Press, 1974.

———. *Tafsīr Mā Ba'd al-Ṭabī'a*. Edited by Maurice Bouyges. Bibliotheca Arabica Scholasticorum, Série Arabe vi; 2nd ed.; Beirut: Dar El-Machreq, 1967.

Avicenna. *Kitāb al-Ishārāt wa'l-Tanbīhāt ma'a Sharḥ Naṣīr al-Dīn al-Ṭūsī*. Ed. Sulaymān Dunyā. 4 vols. in 3. Dhakhā'ir al-'Arab 22. Cairo: Dār al-Ma'ārif, n.d.

Badawī, 'Abd al-Raḥmān, ed. *al-Aflāṭūnīya al-Muḥdatha 'inda 'l-'Arab*. 2nd ed.; Kuwait: Wikālat al-Maṭbū'āt, 1977.

———, ed., *Commentaires sur Aristote perdus en Grec et autres épitres*. Recherches de l'Institut de Lettres Orientales de Beyrouth, N.S. A. Langue Arabe et Pensée Islamique 1. Beirut: Dar El-Machreq, 1971.

———. "New Philosophical Texts Lost in Greek and Preserved in Arabic Translations." In Morewedge, ed. *Islamic Philosophical Theology*, pp. 3–13.

Baffioni, Carmela. "Una «Storia della Filosofia Greca» nell'Islam del XII Secolo. *Elenchos* (Naples) 2 (1981): 355–74; 3 (1982): 93–107; 4 (1985): 93–132, 261–345; 6 (1985): 409–52, 7 (1987): 381–429.

Barnes, Jonathan. *The Presocratic Philosophers*. The Arguments of the Philosophers. Revised edition; London: Routledge, 1982.

Bible. Revised Standard Version. *The New Oxford Annotated Bible*. Ed. Herbert G. May and Bruce C. Metzger. New York: Oxford University Press, 1977.

Bidez, Joseph, and Cumont, Franz. *Les mages hellénisés: Zoroastre, Ostanès et Hystaspe*. 2 vols. Paris: Société d'Éditions "Les Belles Lettres," 1938.

al-Bīrūnī. *Alberuni's India*. Trans. Edward C. Sachau. London: Trübner, 1888. Many reprints.

———. *Kitāb al-Bīrūnī fī Taḥqīq Mā li'l-Hind*. Dairatu'l-Ma'arifi'l-Osmania Publications 9. Hyderabad: Osmania Oriental Publications Bureau, 1958.

Blackburn, Simon. *The Oxford Dictionary of Philosophy*. Oxford: Oxford University Press, 1994.

Brisson, Luc, and Meyerstein, F. Walter. *Inventer l'universe*. Paris, 1991. Revised translation, *Inventing the Universe: Plato's* Timaeus, *the Big Bang, and the Problem of Scientific Knowledge*. SUNY Series in Ancient Greek Philosophy; Albany: SUNY Press, 1995.

Brockelmann, Carl. *Geschichte der Arabischen Literatur.* 5 vols. Leiden: E. J. Brill, 1937–49.

Bürgel, J.-Ch. "A New Arabic Quotation from Plato's *Phaido* and Its Relation to a Persian Version of the *Phaido.*" *Actos do IV Congresso de Estudos Arabes e Islamicos* (Lisbon: 1968 [1971]), pp. 281–90.

Cahen, Claude. "Une chronique syrienne du VIe/XIIe siècle: Le *"Bustān al-Jāmi'."* *Bulletins d'études orientales* 7–8 (1937–38): 113–58.

Cebes. *The Tabula of Cebes.* Edited and translated by John T. Fitzgerald and L. Michael White. Society of Biblical Literature Texts and Translations 24, Graeco-Roman Religion Series 7; Chico, Calif.: Scholars Press, 1983.

Claghorn, George S. *Aristotle's Criticism of Plato's 'Timaeus'.* The Hague: Martinus Najhoff, 1954.

Commentaria in Aristotelem Graeca. Academiae Litterarum Regiae Borussicae. Berlin: Georgii Reimeri, 1882–1909.

Corbin, Henry. *Avicenna and the Visionary Recital.* Translated by Willard R. Trask. Bollingen Series 66; New York: Pantheon Books, 1966. Reprinted Irving, Texas: Spring Publications, 1980.

———. *En Islam iranien.* 4 vols. Vol. 2, *Sohravardī et les Platoniciens de Perse.* Paris: Gallimard, 1971–72.

———. *History of Islamic Philosophy.* Trans. Liadain Sherrard. London: Kegan Paul International, 1993.

———. *Les Motifs zoroastriens dans la philosophie de Sohravardî.* Publications de la Société d'Iranologie 3. Tehran: du Courrier, 1946.

———. *Spiritual Body and Celestial Earth.* Translated by Nancy Pearson. Bollingen Series no. 91:2. Princeton: Princeton University Press, 1977.

———. *Suhrawardī d'Alep: fondateur de la doctrine illuminative.* Paris: G. P. Maisonneuve, 1939.

Dabashi, Hamid. *Theology of Discontent: The Ideological Foundation of the Islamic Revolution in Iran.* New York: New York University Press, 1993.

Dānā-Saresht, Akbar. *Kholāse-ye Afkār-e Sohravardī va Mollā Ṣadrā.* Tehran, 1934.

Dancy, Jonathan, and Sosa, Ernest, eds. *A Companion to Epistemology.* Blackwell Companions to Philosophy 3. Cambridge, Mass.: Blackwell, 1992.

al-Daylamī, Muḥammad. *Maḥbūb al-Qulūb.* Ed. 'Abd al-Karīm al-Shīrāzī. N.p., 1899.

al-Dhahabī. *al-'Ibar fī Khabar Man Ghabar.* Ed. Ṣalāḥ al-Dīn al-Munajjid. al-Turāth al-'Arabī 10. Kuwait: Wizārat al-Irshād wa'l-Anbā', 1963.

Dictionary of Scientific Biography. Ed. Charles Coulston Gillispie. New York, Scribner, 1970– .

Dictionnaire des philosophes antiques. Ed. Richard Goulet. Paris: CNRS Éditions, 1989– .

Diels, H. *Doxographi Graeci.* Berlin: G. Reimeri, 1879.

Diels, H., and Kranz, W. *Die Fragmente der Vorsokratiker.* 10th ed. Berlin: Weidmann, 1961.

Dihkhudā, 'Alī-Akbar. *Lughat-Nāma.* Tehran: Dānishgāh-i Tihrān, 1946–79.

Diogenes Laertius. *Lives of the Eminent Philosophers.* Trans. R. D. Hicks. 2 vols. Loeb Classical Library. Cambridge: Harvard University Press, 1925.

Empedocles. *The Poem of Empedocles: A Text and Translation with an Introduction.* Ed. and trans. Brad Inwood. Phoenix Presocratics 3. Toronto: University of Toronto Press, 1992.

Encyclopædia Iranica. Ed. Ehsan Yarshater. London: Routledge and Kegan Paul, 1982– .

Encyclopaedia of Islam. 1st ed. Leiden, E. J. Brill, 1913–34.

Encyclopaedia of Islam. 2nd ed. Leiden, E. J. Brill, 1954– .

Encyclopedia of Philosophy. 8 vols. New York: Macmillan, 1967.

Endress, Gerhard, and Gutas, Dimitri. *A Greek and Arabic Lexicon: Materials for a Dictionary of the Medieval Translations from Greek into Arabic.* Handbuch der Orientalistik Abt. 1: Der Nahe und Mittlere Osten 11. Leiden: E. J. Brill, 1992– .

Evangeliou, Christos C. *The Hellenic Philosophy: Between Europe, Asia and Africa.* Studies on Ancient Greek and Islamic Philosophy. Binghamton, N.Y.: Institute of Global Cultural Studies, 1997.

Fakhry, Majid. *A History of Islamic Philosophy.* Studies in Oriental Culture 5. 2nd ed. New York: Columbia University Press, 1983.

———. *Philosophy, Dogma, and the Impact of Greek Thought in Islam.* London: Variorum, 1994.

———. "Al-Suhrawardī's Critique of the Muslim Peripatetics *(al-Mashshā'ūn).*" In Parviz Morewedge, ed. *Philosophies of Existence, Ancient and Modern.* New York: Fordham University Press, 1982. Reprinted in Fakhry, *Philosophy, Dogma,* sect. xvii.

al-Fārābī. *Alfarabi's Philosophy of Plato and Aristotle [Taḥṣīl al-Sa'āda, Falsafat Aflāṭūn, Falsafat Arisṭū].* Translated by Muhsin Mahdi. Agora Paperback Editions; rev. ed. Ithaca, N.Y.: Cornell University Press, 1969.

———. *Kitāb al-Jam' bayna Ra'yay al-Ḥakīmayn.* Ed. Albayr Naṣrī Nādir. 4th ed.; Beirut: Dār al-Mashriq, 1968. Ed. and trans. Charles Butterworth. Islamic Philosophy Translation Series. Provo, Utah: Brigham Young University Press, forthcoming.

Findlay, J. N. *Plato: The Written and Unwritten Doctrines.* International Library of Philosophy and the Scientific Method. London: Routledge & Kegan Paul, 1974.

Fowden, Garth. *The Egyptian Hermes: A Historical Approach to the Late Pagan Mind.* Cambridge: Cambridge University Press, 1986. Corrected printing: Princeton: Princeton University Press, 1993.

al-Ghazālī. *The Faith and Practice of al-Ghazālī [al-Munqidh min al-Ḍalāl].* Ed. W. Montgomery Watt. London: George Allen and Unwin, 1953.

———. *Freedom and Fulfillment: An Annotated Translation of Al-Ghazālī's* al-Munqidh min al-Ḍalāl *and Other Relevant Works of al-Ghazālī.* Trans. Richard Joseph McCarthy. Library of Classical Arabic Literature 4. Boston: Twayne Publishers, 1980.

Gohlman, William E. *The Life of Ibn Sina.* Studies in Islamic Philosophy and Science. Albany: State University of New York Press, 1974.

Goichon, Amélie-Marie. *Lexique de la langue philosophique d'Ibn Sīnā*. Paris: Descläe de Brouwer, 1938.

Grant, Edward. *Studies in Medieval Science and Natural Philosophy*. London: Variorum Reprints, 1981.

Gutas, Dimitri. "The Spurious and the Authentic in the Arabic Lives of Aristotle." In Kraye et al., eds. *Pseudo-Aristotle*, pp. 15–35.

Guthrie, Kenneth Sylvan, ed. *The Pythagorean Sourcebook and Library*. Grand Rapids, Mich.: Phanes Press, 1988.

Guthrie, W. K. C. *A History of Greek Philosophy*. Vol. 1: *The Earlier Presocratics and the Pythagoreans*. Vol. 2: *The Presocratic Tradition from Parmenides to Democritus*. Vol. 5: *The Later Plato and the Academy*. Cambridge: Cambridge University Press, 1962– .

Guttenplan, Samuel, ed. *A Companion to the Philosophy of Mind*. Blackwell Companions to Philosophy 5. Cambridge, Mass.: Blackwell, 1994.

Hadas, Moses, and Smith, Morton, *Heroes and Gods: Spiritual Biographies in Antiquity*. New York: Harper & Row, 1965.

Hermias. *In Platonis Phaedrum Scholi*. Ed. P. Couvreur. Bibliothèque de l'École des Hautes Études: Sciences Historiques et Philologiques 133. Paris: Librairie Émile Bouillon, 1901.

Hippolytus. *The Refutation of All Heresies*. In Alexander Roberts and James Donaldson, eds. *The Ante-Nicene Fathers*. Reprint; Grand Rapids, Mich.: Eerdman's, 1981. Vol. 5, pp. 9–153.

Hirawī, Muḥammad-Sharīf b. Niẓām al-Dīn b. *Anwārīya: Tarjuma wa-Sharḥ-i* Ḥikmat al-Ishrāq-i *Suhrawardī*. Ed. Hossein Ziai. (Markaz-i Īrānī-yi Muṭāla'a-yi Farhanghā, Majmū'a-yi Muṭāla'āt-i Islāmī 3. Tehran: Amīr Kabīr, 1358/1980.

Hodgson, Marshall G. S. *The Venture of Islam: Conscience and History in a World Civilization*. Vol. 1: *The Classical Age of Islam*. Chicago: University of Chicago Press, 1974.

Honderich, Ted, ed. *The Oxford Companion to Philosophy*. Oxford: Oxford University Press, 1995.

Horten, M. *Die Philosophie der Erleuchtung nach Suhrawardi (1191)*. Abhanlungen zur Philosophie und ihrer Geschichte 38. Halle: Strauss and Cramer, 1912. Reprinted Hildesheim: Georg Olms, 1981.

Hourani, George F., ed. *Essays on Islamic Philosophy and Science*. Albany: State University of New York Press, 1975.

Iamblichus. *Neuplatonische Pythagorica in arabischem Gewande: Der Kommentar des Iamblichus zu den* Carmina aurea: *Ein verlorener griechischer Text in arabischer Überlieferung*. Ed. Hans Daiber. Koninklijke Nederlandse Akademies van Wetenschappen Verhandelingen, Afdeling Letterkunde, Nieuwe Reeks, Deel 161; Amsterdam: 1995.

Ibn Abī Uṣaybi'a. *'Uyūn al-Anbā' fī Ṭabaqāt al-Aṭibbā'*. Ed. A Müller. Königsberg, 1884.

Ibn al-Nadīm. *al-Fihrist*. Ed. Sha'bān Khalīfa and Walīd Muḥammad al-'Awza. Vol. 1. Cairo: al-'Arabī, 1991.

Ibn al-Ṭayyib. *Proclus' Commentary on the Pythagorean Golden Verses: Arabic Text and Translation.* Edited and translated by Neil Linley. Arethusa Monographs 10. N.p., n.d.

Ibn Fātik, al-Mubashshir. *Los bocados de oro [Mukhtār al-Ḥikam wa-Maḥāsin al-Kalim].* Edited by 'Abd al-Raḥmān. Badawī. Madrid, 1377/1958.

Ibn Juljul. *Ṭabaqāt al-Aṭibbā' wa'l-Ḥukamā'*. Ed. Fu'ād Sayyid. Textes et Traduction d'Auteurs Orientaux 10. Cairo: Institut Français d'Archéologie Orientale, 1955.

Ibn Khaldūn. *The Muqaddimah: An Introduction to History.* Trans. Franz Rosenthal. Bollingen Series 43. Princeton: Princeton University Press, 1958.

Ibn Khallikān. *Wafāyāt al-A'yān wa-Anbā' Abnā' al-Zamān.* Ed. Iḥsān 'Abbās. Beirut: Dār al-Thaqāfa, 1968.

———. trans. *Ibn Khallikan's Biographical Dictionary.* Trans. W. M. de Slane. Oriental Translation Fund 59. 4 vols. Paris, 1843–71. Reprinted Beirut, Librairie du Liban, 1970.

Ibn Rushd. See Averroes.

Ibn Shaddād, Bahā al-Dīn. *Sīrat Ṣalāḥ al-Dīn: al-Sīrat al-Yūsufīya.* Ed. Jamāl al-Dīn al-Shayyāl. 1st ed. Cairo: al-Khānjī, 1962.

Ibn Sīnā. See Avicenna.

Ibrāhīmī Dīnānī, Ghulām-Ḥusayn. *Shu'ā'-i Andīsha wa-Shuhūd dar Falsafa-yi Suhrawardī.* [Tehran]: Ḥikmat, 1985.

Ikhwān al-Ṣafā'. *Rasā'il.* Beirut: Dār Ṣādir, 1376/1957.

Izutsu, Toshihiko. *The Concept and Reality of Existence.* Studies in the Humanities and Social Relations. Tokyo: Keio Institute of Cultural and Linguistic Studies, 1971.

al-Jazā'irī, Sayyid Ni'mat Allāh . *Qiṣaṣ al-Anbiyā'*. Ed. al-Ḥājj Muḥsin 'Aqīl. 2nd ed. Beirut: Dār al-Balāgha, 1993.

al-Jurjānī, al-Sharīf. *Kitāb al-Ta'rīfāt.* Ed. G. Flügel. Leipzig, 1845; reprinted Beirut, Librairie du Liban, 1969.

Kim, Jaegwon, and Sosa, Ernest, eds. *A Companion to Metaphysics.* Blackwell Companions to Philosophy 6. Cambridge, Mass.: Blackwell, 1995.

Kingsley, Peter. *Ancient Philosophy, Mystery, and Magic: Empedocles and Pythagorean Tradition.* Oxford: Clarendon Press, 1995.

Kraye, Jill; Ryan, W. F.; and Schmitt, C. B., eds. *Pseudo-Aristotle in the Middle Ages.* Warburg Institute Surveys and Texts 11. London: The Warburg Institute, 1986.

Kuşpinar, Bilal. *Ismā'īl Anḳaravī on the Illuminative Philosophy.* Kuala Lumpur: International Institute of Islamic Thought and Civilization, 1996.

Lewisohn, Leonard, ed., *Classical Persian Sufism: From Its Origins to Rumi.* London: Khaniqahi Nimatullahi Publications, 1993.

Lindberg, David C. *Theories of Vision from al-Kindi to Kepler.* University of Chicago History of Science and Medicine. Chicago: University of Chicago Press, 1976.

Long, A. A., and Sedley, D. N. *The Hellenistic Philosophers.* 2 vols. Cambridge: Cambridge University Press, 1987.

Lloyd, A. C. *The Anatomy of Neoplatonism.* Oxford: Clarendon Press, 1990.

———. "Neoplatonic Logic and Aristotelian Logic." *Phronesis* 1.1 (Nov. 1955): 59–72; 1.2 (May 1956): 146–60.

Macuch, Rudolf. "Greek and Oriental Sources of Avicenna's and Sohrawardi's Theosophies." *Graeco-Arabica* 2 (1983): 9–22.

Pseudo-Majrīṭī. *Picatrix: Das Ziel des Weisen von Pseudo-Mağrīṭī.* Trans. Hellmutt Ritter and Martin Plessner. Studies of the Warburg Institute 27. London: Warburg Institute, 1962.

———. *Das Ziel des Weisen [Ghāyat al-Ḥakīm].* Ed. Hellmut Ritter. Studien der Bibliothek Warburg 12.1. Berlin: B. G. Teubner, 1933.

al-Mas'ūdī. *Kitāb al-Tanbīh wa'l-Ishrāf.* Ed. M. de Goeje. Leiden: E. J. Brill, 1894; repr. Beirut: Khayyat, 1965.

Miskawayh, Abū 'Alī Aḥmad b. Muḥammad. *Al-Ḥikma al-Khālida: Jāwīdān Khirad.* Edited by 'Abd al-Raḥmān Badawī. Dirāsāt Islāmīya 13; Cairo: al-Nahḍa al-Miṣrīya, 1952.

Momigliano, Arnaldo. *Alien Wisdom: The Limits of Hellenization.* Cambridge: Cambridge University Press, 1975.

Morewedge, Parviz, ed., *Islamic Philosophical Theology.* Studies in Islamic Philosophy and Science. Albany: State Unversity of New York Press, 1979.

———. *Islamic Philosophy and Mysticism.* Studies in Islamic Philosophy and Science. Delmar, N.Y.: Caravan Books, 1981.

al-Muthul al-'Aqlīya al-Aflāṭūnīya. Ed. 'Abd al-Raḥmān Badawī. Institut Français d'Archéologie Orientale du Caire, Textes et Traductions d'Auteurs Orientaux 12. Cairo: Dār al-Kutub al-Miṣrīya, 1947.

Nasr, Seyyed Hossein. *Three Muslim Sages.* Cambridge: Harvard University Press, 1964.

———. "Suhrawardī" In *A History of Muslim Philosophy,* ed. M.M. Sharif. 1:372–98.

Nasr, Seyyed Hossein, and Leaman, Oliver, eds. *History of Islamic Philosophy.* Routledge History of World Philosophies 1.1. London: Routledge, 1996.

Netton, Ian Richard. *Allāh Transcendent: Studies in the Structure and Semiotics of Islamic Philosophy, Theology, and Cosmology.* Exeter Arabic and Islamic Series 5. New York: Routledge, 1989.

O'Meara, Dominic J. *Pythagoras Revived: Mathematics and Philosophy in Late Antiquity.* Oxford: Clarendon Press, 1989).

Paulys Real-Encyclopädie der classischen Altertumswissenschaft. Ed. G. Wissowa, W. Kroll, and K. Mittelhaus. Stuttgart: J. B. Metzler, 1894–1970; Munich: A. Druckenmuller, 1973–74.

Peters, F. E. *Aristoteles Arabus: The Oriental Translations and Commentaries on the Aristotelian* Corpus. New York University Department of Classics Monographs on Mediterranean Antiquity. Leiden: E. J. Brill, 1968. Review by H. Daiber, *Gnomon* 42 (1970): 538–47.

———. "Hermes and Harran: The Roots of Arab-Islamic Occultism." In Michel M. Mazzaoui and Vera B. Moreen, eds., *Intellectual Studies on Islam: Essays Written in Honor of Martin B. Dickson.* Salt Lake City: University of Utah Press, 1990, pp. 185–215.

———. "The Origins of Islamic Platonism: The School Tradition." In Morewedge, ed., *Islamic Philosophical Theology*, pp. 14–45.

Plato. *Aflāṭūn fi 'l-Islām*. Edited by 'Abd al-Raḥmān Badawī. Wisdom of Persia 13; Tehran: McGill University Institute of Islamic Studies, 1974.

———. *Plato's Cosmology: The* Timaeus *of Plato*. Trans. Francis Cornford. London: Routledge & Kegan Paul, 1937.

Pseudo-Plutarch. See Aetius.

Proclus. *In Platonis Timaeum Commentarii*. Ed. E. Diehl. Leipzig: Teubner, 1903–6.

Quṭb al-Dīn al-Shīrāzī. *Durrat al-Tāj li-Ghurrat al-Dibāj*. 8 vols. in 3. Vol. 1. Ed. Muḥammad Mishkāt. Vol. 2. Ed. Ḥasan Mishkān Ṭabasī. Tehran: Majlis, 1939–46. [Vol. 3]: *Bakhsh-i Ḥikmat-i 'Amalī wa-Sayr wa-Sulūk*. Ed. Māhdukht Humāyī. 1st ed. Shirkat-i Intishārāt-i 'Ilmī wa-Farhangī 247. [Tehran]: Wizārat-i Farhangī wa-Āmūzish-i 'Ālī, 1990.

———. *Sharḥ Ḥikmat al-Ishrāq*. Edited by Asad Allāh Harātī. [Tehran]: 1895–97.

al-Rāzī, Abū Bakr. *Rasā'il Falsafīya*. [Ed. Paul Kraus]. 2nd ed.; Beirut: Dār al-Āfāq al-Jadīda, 1977.

Rosenthal, Franz. *The Classical Heritage in Islam*. Trans. Emile and Jenny Marmorstein. Berkeley: University of California Press, 1975.

———. *Science and Medicine in Islam*. Aldershot, Hampshire: Variorum, 1990.

———. "The Symbolism of the *Tabula Cebitis* according to Abû l-Faraj Ibn al-Ṭayyib." In *Recherches d'islamologie: Recueil d'articles offert à G. Anawati et L. Gardet par leurs collègues et amis*. Louvain, 1977, pp. 273–83.

Rowson, Everett K. *A Muslim Philosopher on the Soul and Its Fate*. American Oriental Series 70. New Haven: American Oriental Society, 1988.

Ṣadrā, Mullā (Ṣadr al-Dīn al-Shīrāzī). *al-Ḥikma al-Muta'āliya fi'l-Asfār al-Arba'a*. 9 vols. Qom, al-'Ilmīya, n.d.

———. *The Wisdom of the Throne: An Introduction to the Philosophy of Mullā Ṣadrā*. Trans. James Winstron Morris. (Princeton Library of Asian Translations; Princeton: Princeton University Press, 1981

Ṣā'id al-Andalusī. *Science in the Medieval World: Book of the Categories of Nations*. Trans. Sema'an I. Salem and A. Kumar. History of Science Series 5. Austin: University of Texas Press, 1991.

———. *Ṭabaqāt al-Umam*. Ed. Ḥayāt al-'Īd Bū-'Alwān. Beirut, Dār al-Ṭalī'a, 1985.

Sambursky, Shmuel. *The Concept of Place in Late Neoplatonism: Texts with Translation, Introduction, and Notes*. Jerusalem: Israel Academy of Sciences and Humanities, 1982.

Sezgin, Fuat. *Geschichte des arabischen Schriftums*. Leiden: E. J. Brill, 1970– .

al-Shahrazūrī, Shams al-Dīn Muḥammad. *Nuzhat al-Arwāḥ wa-Rawḍat al-Afrāḥ fī Tārīkh al-Ḥukamā' wa'l-Falāsifa*. Ed. S. Khurshid Aḥmed. 2 vols.; Heydarabad, 1976.

———. Ed. Muḥammad-'Alī Abū Rayyān. 1st ed. Alexandria: Dār al-Ma'rifa al-Jāmi'a, 1414/1993.

———. *Sharḥ Ḥikmat al-Ishrāq*. Ed. Hossein Ziai. Tehran: Institute for Cultural Studies and Research, 1993.

Shahrastānī. *al-Milal wa'l-Niḥal*. Edited by Muḥammad Sayyid Kīlānī. 1st ed.; Cairo, Muṣṭafā al-Bābī al-Ḥalabī, 1381/1961; 2nd ed. [actually reprint]; Beirut, Dār al-Ma'rifa, 1975.

Sharaf, Muḥammad Jalāl Abū'l-Futūḥ. *Al-Madhhab al-Ishrāqī bayn al-Falsafa wa'l-Dīn fī'l-Fikr al-Islāmī*. al-Maktaba al-Falsafīya. Cairo: Dār al-Ma'ārif, 1972.

Sharif, M. M. *A History of Muslim Philosophy*. 2 vols. Wiesbaden: Otto Harrossowitz, 1963–66.

al-Sijistānī, Abū Ya'qūb. *Kashf al-Maḥjūb*. Ed. Henry Corbin. Bibliothèque Iranienne A.1. Tehran: Institut Franco-Iranien, 1949.

Simplicius. *Commentaire sur les Catégories*. Translated by Ph. Hoffman. Philosophia Antiqua 50.1. Leiden: E. J. Brill, 1990.

———. *In Aristotelis Categorias Commentarium*. Ed. C. Kalbfleisch. *Commentaria in Aristotelem Graeca*. Vol. 8.

Sorabji, Richard. "The Ancient Commentators on Aristotle." In Sorabji, ed., *Aristotle Transformed*.

———, ed. *Aristotle Transformed: The Ancient Commentators and Their Influence*. Ithaca, N.Y.: Cornell University Press, 1990.

Stace, W. T. *Mysticism and Philosophy*. Philadelphia: J. B. Lippincott, 1960.

Stern, S. M. *EI2*, s.v. "Anbaduḳlīs."

———. "Ibn Masarra, Follower of Pseudo-Empedocles—An Illusion." In *Actas, 4 Congresso de Estudos Arabes e Islâmicos, Coimbra—Lisboa 1968*. Leiden: E. J. Brill, 1971, pp. 325–37. Reprinted in S. M. Stern, *Medieval Arabic and Hebrew Thought*, chap. v.

Stoicorum Veterum Fragmenta. Ed. H. van Arnim. 4 vols. Leipzig: Teubner, 1903.

Strauss, Leo, and Cropsey, Joseph, eds. *History of Political Philosophy*. 2nd ed.; Chicago: University of Chicago Press, 1981.

Suhrawardī, Shihāb al-Dīn Yaḥyā. *al-Alwāḥ al-'Imādīya*. In Suhrawardī. *Three Treatises*, pp. 1–78.

———. *Alwāḥ-i 'Imādī*. In *Majmū'a*, vol. 3, pp. 105–95.

———. *L'Archange empourpré: Quinze traités et récits mystiques traduits du persan et de l'arabe*. Paris: Fayard, 1976.

———. *The Book of Radiance: Partaw-Nāma*. Trans. Hossein Ziai. Costa Mesa, Calif.: Mazda Publishers, 1998.

———. *Hayākil al-Nūr*. Ed. Muḥammad Abū Rayyān. Cairo: al-Maktaba al-Tijārīya al-Kubrā, 1957.

———. *Hayākil al-Nūr*. Trans. in Kuşpinar, *Ismā'īl Anḳaravī*.

———. *Ḥikmat al-Ishrāq*, in *Majmū'a* 2:9–260; Suhrawardī, *Philosophy;* and Suhrawardī, *Sagesse*.

———. *Kalimāt al-Taṣawwuf*. In Suhrawardī, *Three Treatises*.

———. *Le Livre de la Sagesse Orientale: Kitāb Ḥikmat al-Ishrāq*. Ed. Christian Jambet. Paris: Verdier, 1986.

———. *al-Mashāri' wa'l-Muṭāraḥāt*, in *Majmū'a* 1:194–506.

———. *Majmū'a-yi Muṣannafāt-i Shaykh-i Ishrāq: Œuvres philosophiques et mystiques*. 3 vols. Edited by Henry Corbin. Bibliothäque Iranienne, n.s. Tehran: Academie Imperiale Iranienne de Philosophie, 1976–77. First published: vol. 1: Istanbul: Maarif Matbaasi, 1945; vols. 2–3: Tehran: Institut Franco-Iranien, 1954–70.

———. *Manṭiq al-Talwīḥāt*. Ed. 'Alī-Akbar Fayyāḍ. Intishārāt-i Dānishgāh-i Tihrān 270. Tehran, 1334/1955.

———. *al-Muqāwamāt*, in *Majmū'a* 1:123–92.

———. *The Mystical and Visionary Treatises of Shihabuddin Yahya Suhrawardi*. Translated by Wheeler M. Thackston Jr. London: Octagon Press, 1982. Review by Hermann Landolt. "Suhrawardī's 'Tales of Initiation'." *Journal of the American Oriental Society* 107.3 (1987): 475–86.

———. *The Philosophy of Illumination*. Ed. and trans. John Walbridge and Hossein Ziai. Islamic Philosophy Translation Series; Provo, Utah: Brigham Young University Press, forthcoming.

———. *Qiṣṣat al-Ghurba al-Gharbīya*, in *Majmū'a* 2:273–97.

———. *Kitāb al-Talwīḥāt al-Lawḥīya wa'l-'Arshīya*. In *Majmū'a* 1:1–121.

———. *Three Treatises*. Ed. Najaf-Gholī Ḥabībī. Lahore: Iran Pakistan Institute of Persian Studies, 1977.

al-Tahānawī. *Kashshāf Iṣṭilāḥāt al-Funūn: The Dictionary of the Technical Terms Used in the Sciences of the Mussalmans*. Ed. A. Sprenger. Bibliotheca Indica 88. Calcutta: F. Carbery, Bengal Military Orphan Press, 1862.

Thackston, Wheeler M., Jr. See Suhrawardī. *Mystical and Visionary Treatises*.

Urmson, J. O. *The Greek Philosophical Vocabulary*. London: Duckworth, 1990.

Walbridge, John. "Muhammad Baqir al-Sadr: An Introduction to His Philosophy." In Linda Walbridge, *Most Learned*.

———. "A Persian Gulf in the Sea of Lights: The Chapter on Nau-Rūz in the *Biḥār al-Anwār*," *Iran* 35 (1997): 83–92.

———. "The Political Thought of Quṭb al-Dīn al-Shīrāzī," in Butterworth, *Political Aspects*, pp. 345–78.

———. *The Science of Mystic Lights: Qutb al-Din Shirazi and the Illuminationist Tradition in Islamic Philosophy*. Harvard Middle Eastern Monographs 26. Cambridge: Harvard Center for Middle Eastern Studies, 1992.

———. "Suhrawardī, a Twelfth Century Muslim Neo-Stoic?" *Journal of the History of Philosophy* 34.4 (Oct. 1996): 515–33.

———. *The Wisdom of the Mystic East: Suhrawardī and Platonic Orientalism*. SUNY Series in Islam. Albany: State University of New York Press, forthcoming.

Walbridge, Linda, ed., *The Most Learned of the Shi'ah*. Forthcoming.

Walzer, R. *EI2*, s.v. "Aflāṭūn."

———. *EI2*, s.v. "Arisṭūṭālīs."

———. "Al-Biruni and Idolatry." In *Commémoration Cyrus: Hommage universel*. Acta Iranica, ser. 1. Leiden: E. J. Brill, 1974, vol. 3, pp. 317–23.

Watt, W. Montgomery. *EI2*, s.v. "Iskandar."

Werblowsky, R. J. Zwi. "Transmigration." In *Encyclopedia of Religion*. New York: Macmillan, 1987.

West, M. L. *Early Greek Philosophy and the Orient*. Oxford: Clarendon Press, 1971.

Westerink, L. G. "Proclus commentateur des *Vers d'or*?" In G. Boss and G. Seel, eds. *Proclus et son influence*. Zurich: GMB Editions du Grand Midi, 1989. Pp. 61–78.

Yāqūt al-Ḥamawī. *Kitāb Irshād al-Arīb ilā Ma'rifat al-Adīb al-Ma'rūf bi-Mu'jam al-Udabā' aw Ṭabaqāt al-Udabā'*. 1st ed. Cairo: Maṭba'a Hindīya, 1925.

———. *Mu'jam al-Buldān*. Ed. F. Wüstenfeld. Leipzig: F. A. Brockhaus, 1866–73.

Yarshater, Ehsan., ed. *Biruni Symposium*. Persian Studies Series 7. New York: Columbia University, Iran Center, 1976.

Yates, Frances A. *Giordano Bruno and the Hermetic Tradition*. Chicago: University of Chicago Press, 1964.

Ziai, Hossein. "Beyond Illumination: Suhrawardī's Illuminationist Path to Wisdom." In Frank E. Reynolds and David Tracy, eds. *Myth and Philosophy*. Albany: State University of New York Press, 1990.

———. "Explaining the Philosophical Meaning of Ṣadr al-Dīn Shīrāzī's 'Metaphysical Philosophy,' *Ḥikmat-e Mota'āliyeh*." *Iranshenasi* 5.2 (Summer 1993): 354–64.

———. *Encyclopaedia Iranica*, s.v. "Ebn Sahlān al-Sāvī."

———. "The Illuminationist Tradition." In *History of Islamic Philosophy*, ed. Seyyed Hossein Nasr and Oliver Leaman. Pp. 465–96.

———. *Knowledge and Illumination: A Study of Suhrawardī's "Ḥikmat al-Ishrāq."* Brown University Judaic Studies Series 97. Atlanta: Scholars Press, 1990.

———. "The Manuscript of *al-Shajara al-Ilāhīya*." *Iranshenasi* 2.1 (Spring 1990): 89–108.

———. Mullā Ṣadrā: His Life and Works." In *History of Islamic Philosophy*, ed. Seyyed Hossein Nasr and Oliver Leaman. Pp. 643–62.

———. "Shihāb al-Dīn Suhrawardī." In *History of Islamic Philosophy*, ed. Seyyed Hossein Nasr and Oliver Leaman, pp. 434–64.

———. "The Source and Nature of Authority: A Study of al-Suhrawardī's Illuminationist Political Doctrine." In Butterworth, ed., *The Political Aspects*, pp. 304–44.

Zimmermann, F. W. "The Origins of the So-Called *Theology of Aristotle*." In Kraye et al., eds. *Pseudo-Aristotle*, pp. 110–240.

INDEX

GREEK TERMS

43467331R00194

Made in the USA
Middletown, DE
10 May 2017